Fanon:
A Critical Reader

BLACKWELL CRITICAL READERS

Blackwell's *Critical Readers* series presents a collection of linked perspectives on continental philosophers, social and cultural theorists. Edited and introduced by acknowledged experts and written by representatives of different schools and positions, the series embodies debate, dissent and a committed heterodoxy. From Foucault to Derrida, from Heidegger to Nietzsche, *Blackwell Critical Readers* address figures whose work requires elucidation by a variety of perspectives. Volumes in the series include both primary and secondary bibliographies.

David Wood: *Derrida: A Critical Reader*

Hubert Dreyfus and Harrison Hall: *Heidegger: A Critical Reader*

Gregory Elliot: *Althusser: A Critical Reader*

Douglas Kellner: *Baudrillard: A Critical Reader*

Peter Sedgwick: *Nietzsche: A Critical Reader*

Lewis R. Gordon, T. Denean Sharpley-Whiting, and Renée T. White:
  Fanon: A Critical Reader

Fanon:
A Critical Reader

Edited, with an Introduction and Translations

by
Lewis R. Gordon
T. Denean Sharpley-Whiting
Renée T. White

BLACKWELL *Publishers*

Copyright © Blackwell Publishers, 1996

First published 1996

2 4 6 8 10 9 7 5 3 1

Blackwell Publishers Ltd
108 Cowley Road
Oxford OX4 1JF
UK

Blackwell Publishers Inc.
238 Main Street
Cambridge, Massachusetts 02142
USA

Library of Congress Cataloging-in-Publication Data
Fanon: a critical reader/edited, with an introduction, and translations by
  Lewis R. Gordon, T. Denean Sharpley-Whiting, Renée T. White.
    p. cm. – (Blackwell critical readers)
  Based on the eleventh annual Symposium on African-American Culture
and Philosophy, held at Purdue University on March 23–24, 1995.
  Includes bibliographical references and index.
  ISBN 1-557-86895-6 (alk. paper). – ISBN 1-557-86896-4 (pbk.: alk. paper)
  1. Fanon, Frantz, 1925–1961 – Contributions in social sciences –
Congresses. I. Gordon, Lewis R. (Lewis Ricardo), 1962–. II. Sharpley-
Whiting, T. Denean. III. White, Renée T. IV. Symposium on African-
American Culture and Philosophy (11th: 1995: Purdue University)
V. Series.
H59.F28F36   1996
300 – dc20

British Library Cataloging in Publication Data

A CIP catalogue record for this book is available from the British Library.

Typeset in Plantin on 10/12pt
by Best-set Typesetter Ltd., Hong Kong
Printed in Great Britain by TJ Press Ltd, Padstow, Cornwall.

This book is printed on acid-free paper

In memory of Frantz Fanon (1925–61) and Walter Rodney (1942–80),
and for Lisa, Mathieu, and Jenny, with love

LRG

In loving memory of Sterling Christopher Williams (1975–94),
Linda Diann (1950–89), and for my supportive family.
Gilman W. Whiting – *beaucoup de bises*

TDSW

For Clara Johnson-White, Richard White, and Alina Dovin

RTW

Contents

Contributors

Robert Bernasconi is Moss Professor of Excellence in Philosophy at the University of Memphis. He is author of numerous articles in philosophy and has written two books, *Heidegger's History of Being and the Question of Language* (Humanities) and *Heidegger in Question* (Humanities), and co-edited *Rereading Levinas* (Northwestern) and *Derrida and Différance* (Northwestern). He is currently researching on Sartre's, Fanon's, and Richard Wright's analyses of racism.

Nada Elia teaches English at Western Illinois University, Macomb. She has published articles and book chapters on resistance narratives, particularly by women, in a number of national and international journals. She is currently editing a collection of personal narratives by first-generation immigrants to the USA, entitled, *Bring Me Your Poor, Your Weary*.

Stanley O. Gaines, Jr. teaches psychology at Pomona College and Black Studies in the Montclair Graduate School. He is author of numerous articles on psychology and the mental life of African Americans.

Nigel Gibson has taught political science at Columbia University, where he received his doctorate in political science. He is editor of the forthcoming *Rethinking Fanon: A Critical Anthology on Aspects of Frantz Fanon's Thought*.

David Theo Goldberg is Director of the School of Justice Studies at Arizona State University and Professor of Justice Studies with joint appointments to the Ph.D. committee on law and social science, the Ph.D. program in communication studies, and an affiliate appointment in philosophy. He is the author of *Racist Culture* (Blackwell) and editor of *Anatomy of Racism* (Minnesota) and *Multicultural: A Critical Reader* (Blackwell), and coeditor of *Social Identities: A Journal for the Study of Race, Nation and Culture*. He is currently working on books on the racial state and on the politics of preferences.

Lewis R. Gordon teaches philosophy and African-American studies at Purdue University. He has written articles on philosophy of human science and racism, and he is the author of *Bad Faith and Antiblack Racism* (Humanities), *Fanon and the Crisis of European Man: An Essay on Philosophy and the Human Sciences* (Routledge), and *Her Majesty's Other Children: Philosophical Sketches from a Neocolonial Age* (forthcoming). He is editor of *Existence in Black: An Anthology of Black Existential Philosophy* (Routledge), and coeditor of *Black Texts and Black Textuality* (forthcoming).

Leonard Harris is Director of African-American Studies and Professor of Philosophy at Purdue University. He is well known for his articles on Alain Locke and critical race theory and he is editor of several books which include *Philosophy Born of Struggle* (Kendall/Hunt), *Children in Chaos* (Kendall/Hunt), *The Philosophy of Alain Locke* (Temple), *The Concept of Race* (Humanities), and he is currently working on *Ambiguity, Convergence, and Transgression in Black*.

Floyd W. Hayes, III teaches political science and African-American studies at Purdue University. He is author of numerous articles on public policy and political theory. He has published in numerous journals of politics and African-American studies, and he is editor of the anthology, *A Turbulent Voyage: Readings in African-American Studies* (College). He is currently working on a book, tentatively titled *African-American Cynicism: Cultural Crosscurrents in a Postindustrial-Managerial Polity*.

Paget Henry is Director of African-American Studies and Professor of Sociology at Brown University. He is also a member of Brown's Center for the Study of Race and Ethnicity and former president of the C. L. R. James Society. He has published numerous articles on the political economy of the Caribbean and African and Afro-Caribbean philosophy, and he is the author of *Peripheral Capitalism and Underdevelopment in Antigua* (Transactions) and coeditor of *C. L. R. James' Caribbean* (Duke).

Joy Ann James teaches feminist theory and critical race theory in women's studies at the University of Massachusetts at Amherst and in ethnic studies at the University of Colorado at Boulder. She is coeditor of *Spirit, Space, and Survival: African American Women in (White) Aca-*

deme (Routledge) and author of *Resisting State Violence in US Culture: Antiracism and Feminism in Coalition* (Minnesota) and *Transcending the Talented Tenth: Race Leaders and American Intellectualism* (Routledge).

Carolyn Johnson is Acting Director and Senior Researcher at the African-American Studies and Research Center at Purdue University. She is well known as an international consultant with specialties in global education, international development finance, and peace and justice concerns. She is President of United Methodist Women. She is the author of numerous articles in her fields of study and currently working on *Ambiguity, Convergence, and Transgression in Black*.

Ronald A. T. Judy teaches English and cultural studies at the University of Pittsburgh. He is author of a number of articles in cultural studies journals. He is currently completing a book on nihilism and the question of black subjectivity.

Sonia Kruks is Robert S. Danforth Professor of Politics at Oberlin College, where she teaches political philosophy and feminist theory. She is the author of *The Political Philosophy of Merleau-Ponty* (Humanities Press; reprinted by Gregg Revivals) and *Situation and Human Existence: Freedom, Subjectivity and Society* (Routledge). She is also coeditor of *Promissory Notes: Women in the Transition to Socialism* (Monthly Review Press). Her current research focuses on the intersections of phenomenology and feminist theory.

Gail Presbey teaches philosophy at Marist College. She is a specialist in political philosophy and African philosophy and is coeditor of *The Philosophical Quest: A Cross-Cultural Reader* (McGraw Hill).

Richard Schmitt teaches philosophy at Brown University. He is coeditor of *Alienation* (Humanities) and author of *Beyond Separateness* (Westview).

Tsenay Serequeberhan is Acting Chair of Philosophy at Simmons College. He is author of *The Hermeneutics of African Philosophy* (Routledge) and editor of *African Philosophy: The Essential Writings* (Paragon).

T. Denean Sharpley-Whiting teaches French and African-American studies at Purdue University. She is coeditor of *Spoils of War: Women, Cultures, Revolutions* (forthcoming) and author of two forthcoming books, *Black Female Bodies, White Male Imaginations: Nineteenth-century French Narratives on Black Femininity* and *Fanon and Feminist Theory*.

Eddy Souffrant teaches philosophy at Marquette University. His current research focuses on international political theory.

Maurice Stevens is a doctoral candidate in the History of Consciousness Program at Santa Cruz. His dissertation is an exploration of the ways in which mediated nationalist images work in the service of mobilizing various understandings of the black/African/American racialized subject position.

Olufemi Taiwo teaches philosophy at Loyola University of Chicago. A specialist in Marxism, jurisprudence, and African philosophy, he is author of a recent volume on Marxist jurisprudence and natural law (Cornell).

Lou Turner is a well known activist in Chicago, Illinois. He has published numerous articles on Marxist humanism and black liberation struggles. He is co-author of *Frantz Fanon, Soweto, and American Black Thought* (News & Letters).

Françoise Vergès is a doctoral candidate in political science at the University of California at Berkeley. Her work focuses on the history of psychiatry and colonialism, the birth of the clinic in the colony, and postcolonial psychiatry.

Renée T. White teaches sociology and African-American studies at Purdue University. She is coeditor of *Black Texts and Black Textuality* and *Spoils of War*. She is also completing *New Sexual Identities: Black Teenage Women and Sex in the Era of AIDS*.

Foreword

Leonard Harris and
Carolyn Johnson

Fanon's life was cut off early in his productive years, yet his work was developed so intensely by a life fully lived. What theoretical features of Fanon's life work are perennial, continual, and constantly engaging? Appreciating Fanon's works requires a complex reading and, as the editors correctly point out, not *theoretical decadence*, that is, a reading "reduced to one discipline over another." What is it about Fanon's life that can enrich existing modes of struggle? Is it possible to speak of Fanon when national liberation struggles, theories of oppression, and critiques of capitalism seem like historical discourses used to mask culturalist, nationalist, sexist, and ethnocentric forms of domination? Is it possible for Fanon to speak to us about the relationship of oppression, resentment, and rebellion? Is it reasonable to investigate the subtle similarities and differences between the views of W. E. B Du Bois and Fanon about Pan-Africanism in a world that seems bedeviled by nihilism and a lack of motivation?

The African-American Studies and Research Center's Eleventh Annual Symposium on African-American Culture and Philosophy sponsored "Fanon today: Rereadings, confrontations, engagements," March 23 and 24, 1995, at Purdue University. Lewis R. Gordon, T. Denean Sharpley-Whiting, and Renée T. White were the guiding voices for the symposium. Gordon was the chairperson of the conference committee and Carolyn Johnson the chief coordinator. The conference served as a contributing factor and resource for this volume. The symposium was a continuing feature of the basic intellectual orientation of the African-American Studies and Research Center established in January of 1991: identity and community. The insightful arguments presented at the symposium addressed, answered, and interrogated an array of challenging issues. Furthermore, those arguments and issues have been developed in an expanded discourse by the editors and new participants in the dialogue, a dialogue that now forms *Fanon: A Critical Reader*. In addition, this volume liberates Fanon's works from translations that were mainly concerned with making his works palatable to an English-speaking audience, by returning to the original texts and translating previously ignored subtleties. The questions we raised above, and the ones we raise below, are addressed in this volume.

In Fanon's explication of the world's reality, what experiences, actions, and events of the human odyssey are acutely portrayed, questioned, revalued? What form of the human sciences do we see differently by reading Fanon? Can there be a postcolonial psychology, for example, that allows for the import of history? Are there unspoken common features and practices of nonviolent direct action and violent revolutionary struggle?

Why is it possible now to speak of Fanonism just when it seems that organizations dedicated to liberation of the working class have been dissipated; when neither socialist nor capitalist African or Caribbean nation-states have rescinded the borders bequeathed to them by their colonial masters and formed new unions? Why is it possible to speak of Fanonism when anti-black racism is nowhere on the wane? What then are some parameters of a decolonizing psychology and sociological dimensions of Fanon's approach to the human sciences?

It is arguable that Fanonism is like an apparition, a specter in our memories analogous to Jacques Derrida's understanding of Marxism in *Specters of Marx*: a haunting in memory, empowered to shape our identity but empty as a theoretical source describing who or what we are, the why of our predicament, or the what of our particular theater. Derrida appeals to Paul Valery's imagery in *The Crisis of Spirit* of the European Hamlet that "looks at thousands of specters. . . . His ghosts are all the objects of our controversies . . . This one was *Lionardo* . . . and this other skull is that of *Leibniz* who dreamed of universal peace. And this one was *Kant qui genuit Hegel, qui genuit Marx, qui genuit* . . . Hamlet does not know what to do with all these skulls. But if he abandons them! . . . Will he cease to be himself?" (p. 993). The specters are not ghosts, in the sense of invisible disembodied spirits, but visible apparitions, re-apparitions, the sort that appears before major events in Shakespeare's *Hamlet. Ein Gespenst geht um in Europa – des Gespenst des Kommunismus.* ("A specter is haunting Europe – the specter of communism.") "Specter" is, as Derrida points out, the first noun in Marx and Engels's *Manifesto of the Communist Party*; it is singular. It is a thing, an ontological being, a static presence. Specter: haunting, hunting, impurity, and expunging the figure of the ghost are definitive themes in the *Manifesto*, and, *mutatis mutandis*, integral to what Marx means, to what we are/ mean. For Derrida, "they are always *there*, specters, even if they do not exist, even if they are no longer, even if they are not yet. They give us [*sic*] to rethink the 'there' as soon as we open our mouths . . ." (p. 176).

If Derrida is insightful about Marx, we may well ask: Whose identity and what dialectic of recognition are at stake? What, analogously, does it mean to speak of Fanonism when descriptions of alienation, anomie, self-deprecation, damnation, and wretchedness do not elicit responses of horror – responses of horror from whom? Can we speak of an antiracist feminist practice that employs Fanon, a Fanonian feminism?

Derrida interrogates Marxism as a haunting historical specter, a possible approach because for Derrida Marxism is no longer a discourse that requires political commitment, presumably driven by the authority and facticity of Marxism. Marxism for Derrida is available to us as enriching theory already embedded in our historical memory; it is a spirit, a *Geist*; no longer a dogma or a text expected to provide certain direction for action, a mirror of what the world will be like, and a script for why it is the way it is. Is Fanonism, like Derrida's Marxism, a quaint collection of interesting theory, a historical memory, available as enriching discourse without a further presumption of its direct applicability, explanatory power, or predictive efficacy? Is Fanonism a feature of our haunting past, an apparition, a skull?

There are, for certain, competing interpretations of Fanon just as there are competing interpretations of Marx. The competing, and in some instances mutually informing, interpretations of Fanon include the libertarian approach to Fanon by Henry L. Gates, Jr., Gayatri Spivak, Homi K. Bhabha; the Marxist approach by Cedric Robinson; the cultural studies approaches of Benita Perry, Abdul JanMohamed, and Edward Said; and the existential phenomenological approach by Lewis Gordon. Most certainly works by Hussein Adam, Emmanuel Hansen, Renate Zahar, and Hussein Bulhan, to mention only a few, enrich and situate Fanon scholarship.

Given competing interpretations it is not to, or from, a specter that this volume speaks: it is not engaged in a dialogue with itself, mediated through a simulacrum, an apparition solely reflecting what we project/ reflect. The reality of Fanonism, the reality of colonialism, the legacy of foreign domination and the pervasiveness of anti-black racism are realities of today – unmediated pain and suffering. "If Sartre's studies of the existence of others remain exact (to the extent, let us recall, *Being and Nothingness* describes an alienated consciousness) their application to *nègre* consciousness reveals itself to be fallacious. That is because the White is not only the Other, but the master, whether real or imaginary" (*Pn* 112 n. 22 / *BS* 138 n. 24). It is no ghost, no specter, no apparition, that Bigger Thomas in Richard Wright's *Native Son* kills; it was no phantom gun that Algerian, Vietnamese, Zimbabwean, and Cuban women used against their colonizers. It is not a specter that objectifies, denigrates, and excludes the black; the men and women who treat the black as abject other are not spirits moving through space. Possibly, it is simply that the use of literary analogies to account for social, psychological, and material realities does not sufficiently admit to seeing the terror of racism, its mode of making the other defective. Hamlet, for example, as a literary analog for Europeans, may well be seen as living through, and acting on, specters, but Bigger Thomas must kill the white to have the luxury of living through ghosts, the luxury of having historical figures – skulls – praised as philosophers, dreamers, rationalist, and dialecticians.

When we rethink the "there" of our identity and community, the historical and contemporary figures that we embody, we may ask, Who sings the praises of those valiant warriors that fought against the colonizers? Who laments the mothers raped, trapped, and left to die in the decadent slums of cities barely on the realm of modernity when they are no longer fit to be servants in the households of the colonizers – or servants in the households of the newly enriched postcolonial post-avant garde? Where are the mourners for those who suffer from the rotten foods sold to the postcolonials, enriching world metropolitan centers, now romanticized as postmodern? Who cares for the amputees from foreign-made land-mines, now abandoned by those who planted them?

The warriors, the mothers, the servants, the truck drivers, the children – these are not ghosts, they are not specters, they are not images in our heads. These are bodies, black bodies; bodies of black men seen as inherently criminal; bodies of black women unseen, commodities of exchange, objects, things, toys, subjectless receptacles; children seen as already damned and irredeemable.

The analyses, interrogations, explications, and voicing in *Fanon: A Critical Reader*, as the editors demonstrate, are a part of a continuing discourse, praxis, and reading of Fanon. The articles offer fresh words, spoken through Fanon, beckoned by his works; a living Fanon for our lives, future lives, and a better world. What, then, was it on March 23 and 24, at the "Fanon today: Rereadings, confrontations, engagements" symposium, to speak of Fanonism "in a nation of lynchers," as Fanon describes America when faced with the prospects of dying in America rather than on the battlefield? It is, arguably, to carry on, march on, stand with, and uplift our beloved.

Acknowledgments

A project like this one could not have been completed without the collective effort of a number of people. We would first like to thank our families for their understanding and support during the many hours of effort devoted to completing this work. David Theo Goldberg, who is also a contributor to this volume, deserves special thanks for encouraging our putting such a volume together. We would like to thank the members of the Fanon Group for their participation and valuable suggestions – especially Professor Emeritus William R. Jones, whose encouragement and advice at the early stages of this project cannot be measured. We would also like to thank Ms Christina Boyd, Ms Pamela Connelly, Ms Elizabeth Smith, and Ms Beth Turner for valuable clerical assistance. And we would like to thank our editor, Steven Smith, for contacting us at an early stage of the project and providing us with encouragement throughout.

Individuals who also participated in the early discussion stage of this project are Carl Briscoe, Jr., Thomas Broden, III, Victoria Coleman, Ralph Crowder, Adriela Fernandez, Anthony Keine, John Lew, Peter Okeafor, William McBride, Jacqueline Martinez, Naomi Pabst, Aparajita Sagar, and Harry Targ. These individuals participated in "Fanon today: Re-readings, confrontations, engagements," which was the Eleventh Annual Symposium on African-American Culture and Philosophy, held at Purdue University on 23 and 24 March, 1995. Two-thirds of the papers in this volume were presented in rough form at that historic conference. We would like to thank the African-American Research Center at Purdue for sponsoring that program, as well as the support of Purdue University's English and Philosophy doctoral program, the philosophy, foreign languages and literatures, and political science departments.

Finally, we would like to thank Routledge for permission to reprint an excerpt from chapter 4 of Lewis R. Gordon's *Fanon and the Crisis of European Man*.

Note on the Text

The translations from Fanon's French, where no translator has been given, are by the editors. In other cases the translators are indicated. The references will be firstly to the most recent French edition, and secondly to the English translation. The following are the abbreviations for Fanon's writings, and the editions quoted.

Pn   *Peau noire, masques blancs*. 1952, Éditions de Seuil.
BS   *Black Skin, White Masks*. 1967, Grove Press.

Sr   *Sociologie d'une révolution (L'An V de la révolution algérienne)*. 1968, Maspero.
ADC   *A Dying Colonialism*. 1965, Monthly Review and Grove Press.

Pra   *Pour la révolution africaine: Écrits politiques*. 1979, Maspero.
TAR   *Toward the African Revolution*. 1967, Monthly Review and Grove Press.

Dt   *Les Damnés de la terre*. 1991, Gallimard.
WE   *The Wretched of the Earth*. 1963, Grove Press.

In addition, *The Wretched of the Earth* will be referred to as *Les Damnés de la terre*. As the essays in this volume will attest, it is unlikely that Fanon intended his title to refer *only* to class interests on the one hand and, for readers who are familiar only with the English title, pity and lowliness on the other. Fanon's intentions, marked not only by the Catholic context of France and the role of the Communist Party there, but also the literary influence of Dante's *Inferno*, were most probably to articulate what it means to live in hell on earth without recourse to a benevolent god – in a word, to be *damned*. Thus, in this volume, the work will be referred to by its French title, although the page numbers in the English translations will be identified.

Finally, full references for all of the citations appear in the bibliography at the end of the volume. In cases where the author has one bibliographical entry, the date will not necessarily accompany her or his name in parenthetical citations.

Introduction: Five Stages of Fanon Studies

Lewis R. Gordon, T. Denean Sharpley-Whiting, and Renée T. White

[D]eath is always with us and . . . what matters is not to know whether we can escape it but whether we have achieved the maximum for the ideas we have made our own.

Frantz Fanon

Frantz Fanon is a towering figure in Africana philosophy and twentieth-century revolutionary thought. Psychiatrist, philosopher, social scientist, revolutionary, he posed a number of pressing questions that spanned many political milieux and academic disciplines. As the author of *Peau noire, masques blancs* (*Black Skin, White Masks*), *L'An V de la révolution algérienne* (*A Dying Colonialism* or *Year Five of the Algerian Revolution*), *Pour la révolution africaine* (*Toward the African Revolution*), and *Les Damnés de la terre* (*The Wretched of the Earth*), the latter of which was popularly characterized as "the handbook of the [people of color] revolution," he made a permanent stamp on twentieth-century intellectual and political history.

Fanon was born on June 20, 1925 (one month after Malcolm X) on the island of Martinique. He was the fifth of eight children and the youngest of four sons. He proved to be a precocious child with an unusual ability to exercise great self-control in stressful and exigent situations (see Bulhan 1985: 20). The Fanon family lived on a modest but dependable income from the labors of Madame and Monsieur Fanon, an income which enabled them to send their children to the *lycée* (a circumstance available only to approximately 4 percent of the black population of Martinique at that time). It was during his studies at the *lycée* that Fanon made the acquaintance and friendship of Aimé Césaire, author of *Discours sur le colonialisme* and *Cahier d'un retour au pays natal*, and for whom Fanon also developed long-term admiration. Césaire was the chief architect of negritude, the attitude and defense of a black, revolutionary consciousness.

In Fanon's seventeenth year, Martinique was under occupation by the Nazis, a situation whose transformative impact on the black Antillean population he later discussed in an essay, "Antillais et Africains." Fanon's response to the occupation was to escape from the island by rowing his way to the island of Dominica, where he trained for six months before being able to join the Allied forces against Germany in North Africa and then in Europe. In North Africa, he experienced a number of indignities both at the hands and voices of the white French settlers and the Arabic populations, but he was undeterred and, in Europe, fought with bravery on the battlefield, earning himself honors as a war hero. Yet, as Bulhan relates,

> The racism and humiliation Fanon and his friends experienced in the French Army was [*sic*] only exceeded by the abuses that the French populace they came to free poured upon them. When, for instance, these black soldiers disembarked in the port city of Toulon, in central France, they found the residents extremely hostile and racist . . . Even in victory, during mass dances or dinners held to welcome French troops, Fanon realized that the blood of black soldiers had been shed in vain. The very Europeans for whose liberation blacks risked their lives now avoided them. Public dances and victory celebrations only added insult to injury. European women found it easier to dance and mingle with Italian war prisoners. When Fanon returned to Martinique, decorated and a war veteran of almost two years, he brought with him not only memories regarding the horrors of war, but also serious doubts about his identity as a Frenchman. He immediately worked in the election campaign of Césaire, the Communist candidate. (p. 28)

After the elections, he decided to take advantage of the scholarships available for French veterans and to study at first to be a dentist, but he changed his mind and opted for psychiatry. This decision took him to Lyon, where he wrote a dissertation in 1951 entitled, "Troubles mentaux et syndromes psychiatriques dans Hérédo-Dégénération-Spino-Cérébelleuse: Un cas de Maladie de Friedreich avec délire de possession." Fanon's period of study in Lyon was full of turmoil. The community was a hotbed of radical politics in the midst of heated racial tension. During this period, Fanon edited *Tam Tam*, a student-run paper, and wrote three plays: "Les mains parallèles"; "L'oeil se noye"; and "La conspiration." At his request, those plays have never been published. His stay in Lyon is also marked by the birth of his first child, whose mother he did not marry. He subsequently married Marie-Josèphe ("Josie") Dublé in October 1952, a French woman whom he had known throughout his period of study at Lyon.

In 1953, Fanon accepted a post as head of Blida-Joinville Hospital in Algiers. He had written a letter to Léopold Senghor in hopes of obtaining a post in Senegal, but Senghor never answered, so Fanon accepted the only opportunity available to him to practice his profession in Africa. In Algeria, he worked with a number of colleagues on the development of humanistic techniques in psychiatric medicine. His fervor is also marked by six papers that he co-wrote and presented at a medical conference during the summer of 1953 on research during this period (see bibliography).

This period was also marked, however, by great turmoil in Algeria as the liberation forces (FLN) gained increasing support among the native Algerian population. Fanon supported the revolutionaries by utilizing hospital resources to train them in emergency medicine and psychological techniques for resisting torture, as well as fighting techniques that he learned as a soldier in the Second European World War. This period came to an end with Fanon's famous "Lettre au Ministre-Résident" in 1956, in which he declared,

> If psychiatry is the medical technique that proposes to enable the human being no longer to be a stranger to his environment, I owe it to myself to affirm that the Arab, permanently alienated in his native land, lives in a state of absolute depersonalization. The status of Algeria? A systematized de-humanization . . . My decision is not to assure responsibility at all cost under the fallacious pretext that there is nothing else to be done. (*Pra* 51–3 / *TAR*: 53–4)

From that point onward, Fanon served as one of the chief theoreticians of the Algerian struggle. In that capacity, he also became one of the most hated figures in France. That circumstance was exacerbated by the publication of *L'An V de la révolution algérienne*, a text which provided not only a provocative critique of French propaganda against the Algerian people and the assumptions of a "benevolent colonialism," but also a theory of values-forming revolutionary praxis. The book was immediately banned in France, but not before the first edition was in the hands of the general public.

Fanon lived throughout this period as a marked man. There were numerous assassination attempts – the most serious of which were the bombing of an automobile, in which he was both the sole survivor and suffered serious spinal injury, and the machine gunning of a hospital room in which he was reported to have been staying – but these attempts were not sufficient to dissuade him from his commitments. He served as Algeria's ambassador to Ghana, and he participated in numerous organizing activities in Tunis. He also managed to present papers at black writers' conferences and worked vigorously toward the construction of a Pan-African revolutionary agenda. As the Algerian war began to take turns that pointed toward victory, Fanon began to issue requests to be relocated as an Algerian representative to the island of Cuba. His efforts at this point dispel a myth that was cultivated by Henry Louis Gates, Jr. (1991), the noted literary scholar, a myth that may be well worth addressing here. Gates lambasted Fanon for not returning to Martinique, but as we can see, Fanon was only engaged in the Algerian liberation struggle for five years, and he had made an effort to return to the Caribbean. What was not discussed in Gates's essay, however, was the reason for Fanon's not making an effort to return to *Martinique* in particular. The fact of the matter is that had Fanon done so, he would have been dead within twenty-four hours of his arrival, since by that time Martinique, ironically under the executive control of Aimé Césaire, had affirmed its colonial status with France and thereby sealed its fate as a neocolonial state. As a consequence, the only place available for Fanon in the Caribbean was Cuba. Unfortunately, Fanon's plans did not come to fruition, since it was during this period that he discovered his fatal condition: leukemia.

It was at this time that he set about composing the work for which he is most known, *Les Damnés de la terre*. His health failing, he wrote at extraordinary speed, composing the work purportedly in ten weeks. He then decided, perhaps owing to his penchant for picking on the most influential Frenchmen but also certainly because of the revolutionary dimensions of the *Critique de la raison dialectique* and the publication by *Les Temps modernes* of "On violence" (the first chapter of the work), to invite Jean-Paul Sartre to write its preface. In their famous meeting in Rome, an account of which can be found in Simone de Beauvoir's *La Force des choses*, he and Sartre talked for nearly seventy-two hours. When de Beauvoir insisted that Sartre needed rest, Fanon replied, "I don't like men who hoard their resources."

Shortly thereafter, Fanon's health took a turn for the worse, and he was sent to the then Soviet Union for treatment. There, the physicians insisted that he seek medical attention in Maryland, in the United States, where there were supposedly the best facilities for him. Fanon was reluctant. He didn't want to die, in his words, "in a nation of lynchers" (Bulhan 1985: 34). To make matters worse, the agency that was to arrange the transportation was the Central Intelligence Agency (CIA). According to Peter Geismar and David Caute, Fanon's worst fears were realized. When he arrived in the United States, he was kept in a hotel room without treatment for ten days while he was grilled for information (Geismar 1971: 184). By the time he was under medical care, he had developed other ailments as a consequence of his leukemia and lack of medical attention. In his last days, he declared that he would have preferred to have been sent to die fighting on the battlefield instead of being left to rot away in a hospital room.

On December 6, 1961, it was over. Fanon died from pneumonia in Bethesda, Maryland. His body was shipped back to Algeria, where it was buried in a shallow grave on the Algerian battlefield. A letter, written a few days before his death, reveals a great deal about the man: "We are nothing on earth if we are not in the first place the slaves of a cause, the cause of the people, the cause of justice and liberty" (Geismar: 185).

Since the publication of *Les Damnés de la terre*, Fanon has been without question one of the most influential figures in Third World revolutionary thought – equaled in influence only, perhaps, by Karl Marx. Over the years, however, there has been an increasing appreciation of both the scope and the complexity of his thought. From the period of the last years of his life to the present day, a form of intellectual production has evolved which we shall refer to in this volume as "Fanon studies."

Fanon studies can be characterized by four stages. The first stage consisted of the various applications of and reactions to his work. This stage was represented by such revolutionary thinkers as Fidel Castro, Ché Guevera, Huey Newton, Paulo Freire, and many others on the one hand, and reactionary texts from such diverse figures as the liberals Hannah Arendt and Sidney Hook and the Marxist-Leninists Nguyen Nghe and Jack Woddis on the other hand.

The second stage was primarily biographical. This stage is best represented by the biographical writings of Irene Gendzier, Peter Geismar, and David Caute, among others. As should be evident, Fanon's life was far from boring. One outcome of this period, due primarily to some of the fictitious elements and license-taking by Gendzier in her biography, was the mythical pathological Fanon. Fanon's life was extraordinary. An unfortunate consequence was that some of his biographers felt that that warranted extraordinary explanations. Bulhan's study provides point-by-point dismissal of a number of extraordinary efforts to explain how Fanon "came into being," as it were.

The third stage was one of intensive research on Fanon's significance in political theory. The work of Hussein Adam, Emmanuel Hansen, and Renate Zahar stand out in this stage. The impact of their scholarship and of several determined political scientists is that the importance of

Fanon's writings has been recognized by political science departments and other political theorists.

The fourth stage, which is still under way, is linked to the ascent of postmodern cultural and postcolonial studies in the academy. This stage is represented by such scholars as Edward Said, Homi Bhabha, Abdul JanMohamed, Gayatri Spivak, Benita Parry, Henry Louis Gates, Jr., and, from a Marxist perspective, Cedric Robinson. Two striking features of postcolonial studies' treatment of Fanon are (1) the extent to which literature has become the lens through which Fanon is studied and (2) the extent to which, with the exception of Said, JanMohamed, and Parry, Fanon has been attacked under a number of fashionable political designations such as misogynous, homophobic, anti-black, anti-Caribbean, anti-Arab, and petit bourgeois. These attacks, particularly in their postmodern manifestation, have taken the form of familiar Lyotardian clichés that characterize denigrations of liberation theorists in this milieu. In a nutshell, liberation theorists, especially the 1950s and 1960s variety, are either structurally "modern" and hence passé, or prescriptively "totalizing" and hence terrorizing. A particularly popular turn has been to earmark their modernity and totalizing tendencies as exclusionary in practice and hence militating against marginalized groups – especially women. The editors' perusal of this scholarship has revealed, however, a tendency to *assert* more than *demonstrate* these characteristics in Fanon's thought. There are problems in studying Fanon because of the seriously flawed English translations available. In addition some of the arguments that are used (for example, about his failure to use gender-neutral language) are faulty not only in relation to 1950s writers, but also in relation to Fanon himself. Fanon devoted a number of pages to discussions of feminist theory and resistance that were in fact ahead of their time. For instance, Fanon was among the first theorists to point out the hypocrisy of critics who advocate gender emancipation through strengthening colonial stratification. Today we find that argument emerging from women of color who criticize poststructural feminism (see James 1996a). There is not enough space in an introduction for a detailed discussion of the complexities of these issues as they pertain to Fanon, but many of these concerns are taken up by some of the essays in this volume, especially those in Parts IV and V. The question of discipline-centrism is touched upon at the close of this introduction.

Postcolonial studies have fortunately not marked the final stage of Fanon studies, if it makes sense to speak of a "final" stage. Today, there is a fifth stage of Fanon scholarship. This stage consists of engagements with the thought of Fanon for the development of original work across the entire sphere of human studies. Its purpose is neither to glorify nor denigrate Fanon but instead to explore ways in which he is a useful thinker. The first major work of this period, in our view, is Hussein Bulhan's *Fanon and the Psychology of Oppression* (1985). That work examines Fanon's importance for the study of psychology. Bulhan's work, important though it may be, has not received the attention it deserves, perhaps because of its high published price. In addition, with the political and academic weight of the figures who dominate the postcolonial studies stage, there has not been much room for the cultivation of alternative research on Fanon, which thus has had less access to resources that could present it to wider audiences. As a consequence, it took some time until the fifth stage gathered some steam. The fifth stage can be said to be fully under way by 1995, however, by virtue of the publication of Tsenay Serequeberhan's *The Hermeneutics of African Philosophy*, which is greatly influenced by Fanon's work, and Lewis R. Gordon's *Fanon and the Crisis of European Man*, followed by Ato Sekyi-Otu's *Fanon's Dialectics of Experience*. A key feature of these works is that even in cases where Fanon's name is prominent in the title, the objectives are ultimately the disciplines themselves: Africana philosophy, philosophy of human sciences, and phenomenologies of experience. In addition, panels have been formed on Fanon studies at such scholarly associations as the Sartre Societies (in North America, the UK, and France), the Socialist Scholars Conferences, the American Political Science Association Meeting, and satellite groups at the American Philosophical Association, as well as meetings in Martinique, Canada, and Italy. Moreover, there have been meetings commemorating the significance of 1995 as the seventieth anniversary of Fanon's birth. A number of the essays in this volume were presented, for instance, in an historic meeting at Purdue University during the spring of 1995, where decisions were made to develop resources that will encourage ongoing critical dialogue in Fanon studies across a variety of disciplinary fields.

This volume is therefore squarely rooted in what we have been describing as the fifth stage of Fanon studies. It is the first collective effort of an interdisciplinary group of scholars and it is perhaps the most representative example of the fifth stage; for all of the contributors regard themselves as doing work *with* and *through* Fanon. The essays, in short, work within Fanon's own preference for independent thinking by using his work as a contribution to their authors' theoretical projects.

In closing, we would like to make two remarks. The first is to dispel one popular conclusion that may be drawn from our discussion thus far. The past ten years have sometimes been described as seeing a "resurgence" in Fanon's thought. As the reader can see, however, what each stage represents is an ongoing dialectical process. Fanon has never had to undergo a "resurgence" primarily because his ideas have never dropped from the stage of public discussion. They have, instead, taken on dimensions that suit the interests of each generation, with different insight, which is a testament to their fecundity in our view and, in the eyes of Fanon's critics, their flaws. This brings us to our second concern. It is our view that the tendency to read Fanon in terms of what we shall call "theoretical decadence," where Fanon's thought is expected to be reduced to one discipline rather than another, should be avoided in the interests of learning how to read him with imagination and clarity. It is fallacious to criticize a theorist for not being squarely situated in one's own field of inquiry. Fanon, as we have noted from the outset, was not only a psychiatrist or a philosopher or a revolutionary. He was a complex figure who utilized all of the disciplinary resources, whether "literary" or "scientific," at his disposal. He was therefore, in the truest sense, a *radical* thinker. He never pretended to be a man without flaws. It was Fanon who insisted in 1952, at the threshold of the upheaval that was his career, that his body should make of him, always, a man who questions.

So it has been.

Part I

Oppression

1

Fanon, Oppression, and Resentment: The Black Experience in the United States

Floyd W. Hayes, III

Aggrieved conceit, repressed envy – perhaps the conceit and envy of your fathers – erupt from you as a flame and as the frenzy of revenge.

Friedrich Nietzsche, Thus Spoke Zarathustra

Ressentiment must therefore be strongest in a society like ours, where approximately equal rights (political and otherwise) or formal social equality, publicly recognized, go hand in hand with wide factual differences in power, property, and education.

Max Scheler, Ressentiment

Racism . . . is only one element of a vaster whole: that of the systematized oppression of a people.

Frantz Fanon, Toward the African Revolution

The colonized is an envious man.

Frantz Fanon, Les Damnés de la terre

In early March 1995, some two hundred, mostly black marchers in Alabama re-enacted the Selma-to-Montgomery civil rights march of thirty years earlier. Among the participants was former Alabama Governor George Wallace. In 1965, he had ordered the Alabama state troopers to use violence – billy clubs and tear gas – to control, intimidate, and disperse the peaceful marchers on their way to Selma, Alabama. Wallace became the national symbol of white supremacy as he declared, "Segre-

I would like to thank my colleagues Lewis Gordon, Renée White, Tracy Sharpley-Whiting, Louis Beres, and Michael Weinstein for their valuable, constructive criticisms of earlier drafts of this chapter.

gation yesterday, segregation today, and segregation tomorrow."
Wallace went on to run for the presidency of the United States of
America, but during a campaign stop in Maryland in 1972, an assassin's
bullet crippled him permanently. In the years since he was shot, Wallace
has tried to repent, apologize, and beg for forgiveness. At 75 years old,
wheelchair-ridden, plagued by a multitude of illnesses, and in constant
pain, Wallace had an aide read his conciliatory speech to the 1995
marchers. Some black people, like the Reverend Joseph E. Lowery, the
national president of the Southern Christian Leadership Conference
and an organizer of the 1965 march, have forgiven Wallace. Many
others have not, however, forgiven him. Rufus Vanable, a black retired
construction worker who participated in the bloody 1965 march,
expressed an attitude of long-standing resentment when he said this
about Wallace:

> I ain't even interested in what he's saying. If you lived through it, you
> wouldn't be either. If he thinks this will ease his mind in some way, let him
> do it. I'm not interested in looking at his face. It brings back too many
> memories. Seeing him say that he's sorry ain't gonna do me no good at
> all . . . He's been about to die for the last 10 years, and he's still living.
> God's gonna make him pay. (Bragg 1995)

More than thirty years ago, Frantz Fanon declared that black people
are in every sense of the word oppressed by western, that is, white,
civilization. He characterized this civilization as a fundamentally anti-
black world where the structure of white superiority encouraged the
oppression, dehumanization, exploitation, degradation, and hatred of
black people. Because of Fanon's powerful analysis of European cultural
domination – racism, colonialism, and neocolonialism – people throughout the world have recognized him as one of the most profoundly
influential thinkers of the second half of the twentieth century. In the
1960s and in subsequent years, Fanon's works served not only as philosophical investigations into the dynamics of racist oppression and exploitation, but also as practical guidelines for people of color engaged in the
struggle for personal dignity, self-determination, and human rights.

It is precisely because Fanon spoke so timelessly on behalf of the
world's alienated, unwanted, and dispossessed masses of black and other
people of color, who were engaged in passionate battles for their liberation, that his ideas and analyses continue to have significance for us
today. As Fanon declared, the essentially tragic nature of modern human
existence is Europe's, and the United States of America's, ultimate gift
to people of color and to the world: imperialism, colonialism, and
racism. The modern historical moment also was a by-product of western

or white civilization, which has been overtaken by a cancer of the spirit. Nietzsche proclaimed the death of God; by killing Him, the West brought into existence the age of nihilism – a culture characterized by a hellish negation of all that is human (Heidegger 1977b; Kaufmann 1974; Nietzsche 1969b, 1974). Of this development, Lewis Gordon states:

> Humanity has died in Europe, the USA, and anywhere in the world in which Western Man – that is, White Man/White Culture – *is* Man and, therefore, Reason. In other words, humanity has suffered a global death. But Euro-man, ironically even in his "colored" manifestations, lives the fool precisely because he thinks he is morally and rationally alive. He has no pulse. But he walks. He seems to walk on air, since solid foundations no longer lay beneath him. (1995b: 8–9)

The broad purpose of this essay is to inquire into the character of resentment as an attitudinal response by black people to historical and present conditions of racial oppression. More specifically, the aim is to probe the meaning of a powerful, but often neglected, dimension of black consciousness brought into existence by the fact of institutional white supremacy. What does it mean to be the historical and contemporary marker of absolute negativity within a social order? What is the existential situation of the black subject in the context of racialized cultural domination, especially at the dawn of the twenty-first century when nihilism haunts the soul of American civilizations? How does Fanon assist us in understanding these questions? Focusing generally on the situation in the United States of America, it will be argued in what follows that African-American resentment is not simply consciousness of the absurdity of racist oppression, but also involves a sense of individual outrage and a visible demonstration or inescapable awareness of injustice.

Resentment and Injustice

For Nietzsche, resentment emerges in the context of nihilism, which is a symptom of a deep pathology in modern western culture and experience. His account of this condition traces a variety of interactions between political experience, culture, and subjectivity, and it turns out to be a story about how culture can refract oppression and perpetuate domination. Nietzsche's argument in *On the Genealogy of Morals* suggests that experiences of meaninglessness – with their correspondent bad conscience and resentment – can be explained as psychological remnants of political oppression. Nietzsche's genealogical narrative traces "slave morality" or resentment back to original slaves, the most politically dominated and culturally dispossessed classes of ancient civilizations. From this portrayal one can conclude that resentment will manifest itself wherever political oppression is coupled with cultural marginalization. In essence, resentment entails a consciousness not only of one's wretchedness, but also a personal outrage and an outward projection or overwhelming sense of justice denied (Solomon 1990, 1994).

According to Nietzsche, resentment is a corrosive and contemptible attitude that contaminates anyone who experiences it. In a world gone decadent and meaningless, resentment masks a self-imposed helplessness (in contrast to the real hopelessness of an actual slave) and an attendant submissiveness. Even the person consumed by resentment may condemn the world. Nietzsche conceives of resentment as a destructive attitude that disables the mighty (as "bad conscience") and also disables the weak. In Nietzsche's view, then, resentment is a basic dimension of human emotions in modern western culture.

Inherent in the experience of resentment is the question of power, domination, revenge, and repression (see Warren). Like Nietzsche, Max Scheler considers resentment to be a self-poisoning, but not self-pitying, mental attitude that begins with a consciousness of powerlessness. Therefore, resentment is reactive rather than proactive. It is long-lasting and caused by the systematic repression of certain emotions. For Scheler, resentment is characterized by an assortment of sentiments, including revenge, hatred, malice, envy, jealousy, and spite.

The hunger for revenge, Scheler states, is the fundamental cause of resentment. This hunger, which should be distinguished from active and aggressive impulses, is a response to a prior attack or injury. Yet, according to Scheler, the attitude of revenge is not quite the same as the impulse for retaliation or self-defense, even when this reaction is associated with anger, fury, or indignation. What marks revenge, anger, and rage as the key determinants of resentment is that these impulses are restrained or repressed. The consciousness that an immediate reaction would result in defeat postpones these impulses. Hence, a recognition of one's helplessness or weakness in the face of the powerful accompanies the attitude of resentment.

Scheler indicates that although revenge is resentment's main ingredient, there is a progression of attendant impulses: envy, malice, rancor. All of these impulses, he says, come close to resentment, but they are not its synonym. The desire for revenge, and its related impulses, vanishes for instance when one exacts vengeance, when the offender has been disciplined or has disciplined himself, or when one truly forgives the offender. Similarly, we cease being envious when the envied possession becomes ours. Resentment, on the other hand, is an attitude that is much more encompassing and long-lasting than revenge, envy, hatred, or rage. As Scheler observes: "Revenge tends to be transformed into *ressentiment* the more it is directed against lasting situations which are felt to be 'injurious' but beyond one's control – in other words, the more the injury is experienced as a destiny" (p. 33).

Ultimately, Nietzsche hoped for an age free of resentment, or at least an age in which some Overmen and resentment-free thinkers would emerge. To be sure, their time has not come. Rather, what seems to be occurring is a progressive expansion and intensification of resentment, subverting the hopefulness of western culture's enlightenment form of modernism. The emerging era appears increasingly to be distinguished not by a polite pessimism but by a cold-blooded cynicism and a new-found nihilism (Solomon 1990).

As historic bearers of racist oppression, black people have had to struggle with the long nightmare of living desperate lives as outsiders within the crucible of western civilization. In the particular case of the United States of America, the native African-American experience is unique, for its origins are characterized not by immigration but by chattel slavery. Moreover, no war of independence liberated African Americans, thereby creating their own sovereign nation-state. Rather, native African Americans have remained largely marginalized, ambiguously and simultaneously excluded from and included in the America political community.

In view of the above observations, it might be useful to point out that the argument here is not an appeal to transcendental or ideal resentment; rather, it is ordinary or general resentment that this paper explores. Resentment is not a necessary or universal response to racist oppression. Resentment is not essential to black identity. In his phenomenology of oppression, Fanon explores a complex of responses by black people to racism and colonialism.

Racism and Resentment

For African Americans, racial domination is both a historical and a contemporary phenomenon. One can trace its genealogy back to the period of the Atlantic slave trade and chattel slavery when slave traders and slave-owners sought to dehumanize captured Africans. Herein lies the original cause of the long nightmare of African-American resentment. Slave traders and slave-owners based the entire filthy enterprise of chattel slavery on the premise that black people were subhuman property, to be used, but not respected. As Orlando Patterson has written, enslavement constituted for captured Africans a form of "social death."

In his classic text, *The Peculiar Institution: Slavery in the Ante-Bellum South*, historian Kenneth Stampp recounts the psychological and physical violence slave-owners employed to create a good slave. Stampp collected material for this discussion primarily from the manuals and other documents slave-owners prepared on the system of managing and training slaves (see especially chapter 4, entitled "To make them stand in fear"). Stampp pointed out five recurring tactics of this dehumanizing system.

First, those who managed the slaves had to maintain strict discipline. One slave-owner said, "Unconditional submission is the only footing upon which slavery should be placed." Another said, "The slave must know that his master is to govern absolutely and he is to obey implicitly, that he is never, for a moment, to exercise either his will or judgment in opposition to a positive order" (p. 145). Second, slave-owners thought that they had to implant in the slave a consciousness of personal inferiority. They deliberately extended this sense of personal inferiority to the slave's past. Slave-owners believed that in order to control black people, the slaves "had to feel that African ancestry tainted them, that their color was a badge of degradation" (ibid.). The third step in the training process was to awe the slaves with a sense of the slave-owner's enormous power. It was essential, various slave-owners declared, "to make them stand in fear" (p. 146). The fourth aspect was the attempt to "persuade the bondsman to take an interest in the master's enterprise and to accept his standards of 'good conduct'" (p. 147). Thus the slave-owner sought to train slaves to accept unquestionably his criteria of what was good and true and beautiful. The final step, according to Stampp's documents, was "to impress Negroes with their helplessness: to create in them a habit of perfect dependence upon their masters" (ibid.).

Here, then, was the strategy employed to produce the perfect slave, a dehumanized person. Impose on the slave rigid discipline, demand from the slave unconditional submission, impress upon the slave a sense of innate inferiority, develop in the slave a paralyzing fear of white people, train the slave to adopt the slave-owner's code of "good" conduct, and instill in the slave a sense of complete dependence. The slave-owner's strategy of dehumanization, degradation, and depersonalization is similar to that which colonizers applied in order to construct the colonized African as the Other and to legitimize colonial domination and exploitation. In *Les Damnés de la terre*, Fanon describes the colonizer's tyrannous undertaking:

> As if to show the totalitarian character of colonial exploitation the colonist portrays the colonized as a sort of quintessence of evil. The colonized society is not only described as a society without values. It is not enough

for the colonist to affirm that those values have disappeared from or still better never existed in the colonial world. The natives are declared insensible to ethics; they represent not only the absence of values but also the negation of values. They are, let us dare to admit, the enemy of values and in this sense they are the absolute evil. They are the corrosive element, destroying all that comes near them; they are the deforming element, disfiguring all that has to do with beauty or morality; they are the depository of maleficent powers and the unconscious and irretrievable instrument of blind forces . . . The customs of the colonized people, their traditions, their myths – above all, their myths – are the very sign of that poverty of spirit and their constitutional depravity . . . At times this Manichaeism goes to its logical conclusion and dehumanizes the colonized, or to speak plainly it turns them into animals. (*Dt* 71–2 / *WE* 40–1)

The psychological roots of African-American resentment came out of the soil of chattel slavery and colonialism. Both systems of cultural domination are, to use Fanon's words, "divided into compartments."

Grounded in the economic imperative of capitalist profit-making, the system of chattel slavery in the Americas represented a new era of human degradation reinforced by the ideology and practice of white supremacy and black inferiority. Slave-owners came to define African slaves and their American descendants as subhuman. Yet chattel slavery produced slaves with a variety of personality types. According to historian John Blassingame, author of *The Slave Community*, the coercive power of the slave-owner largely dictated the personality development of the slave. A so-called kind or humane slave-owner might have good-natured, industrious, and trustworthy slaves. In contrast, the large majority of chattel slaves faced a daily existence of their owner's unrelenting viciousness: constant beatings, rape, cruelty, no formal education, family destabilization, overwork, insufficient food, indecent living conditions, and no health care. Therefore, the broad mass of chattel slaves – whether they became submissive, depressed, indifferent, or belligerent – despised and resented their slave-owners. As Blassingame reports: "Often the slaves had to mask their feelings in their relations with their masters because of their attitudes toward whites. Most slaves hated and were suspicious of all whites" (p. 209). In his speech, "Message to the grassroots," El-Hajiz Malik El-Shabazz (Malcolm X) made a similar observation about slaves' attitude toward their owners:

The field Negro was beaten from morning to night; he lived in a shack, in a hut; he wore old, cast-off clothes. He hated his master. I say he hated his master. He was intelligent. That house Negro loved his master, but that field Negro – remember, they [*sic*] were in the majority, and they hated the

master. When the house caught on fire, he didn't try to put it out; that field
Negro prayed for a wind, for a breeze. When the master got sick, the field
Negro prayed that he'd die. (1965a: 11)

In the context of the United States of America, the dehumanizing
system of chattel slavery and the vicious ideology of white supremacy
that buttressed it have become deeply embedded in the nation's cultural
and institutional beliefs and practices. After the Civil War, racial segregation supplanted chattel slavery. Significantly, a veritable culture of
racism distinguishes the American social order, notwithstanding the
overthrow of the system of legal apartheid (Goldberg 1993). Today,
large sectors of white America exhibit a particularly virulent form of
racism. They may acknowledge disenchantment with powerful images
of racism, like the Ku Klux Klan. However, much of white America
cynically refuses to see the systematic, historic, and *present* incidents of
more subtle forms of racist culture, for example, the refusal to rent or sell
houses to blacks in certain neighborhoods, persistent and often encouraged police brutality, the legal system's decadent economy of black
incarceration, the use of various kinds of racially charged language in
political and academic work, or the racial ceiling in matters of employment. As Lewis Gordon argues in his book, *Bad Faith and Antiblack
Racism* (1995a), a particularly virulent dimension of anti-black racism is
its denial as ordinary lived experience. Such a denial is an act of bad faith
or lying to oneself (see also Gordon 1995b and Sartre 1943/1956b). As
legal scholar Derrick Bell declares: "Racism lies at the center, not the
periphery; in the permanent, not in the fleeting; in the real lives of black
and white people, not in the sentimental caverns of the mind" (1992:
198).

America's culture of racism defines, delimits, and disfigures all
aspects of black social existence. The systematic practice of racist
oppression dramatizes the being of black people, constructing them
as representations of absolute negativity. For instance, white intellectual
and cultural elites frame black people as the criminal, ugly, lazy,
weak, useless, undesirable, or unwanted segments of civil society (see
Edelman 1988). The absurdity of racial oppression forces black people
to experience life as a series of negations; they are the depersonalized
markers of American society's problems: reverse racists, the underclass,
the poor, welfare queens, gang bangers, or teenage mothers (see Glazer
1975; Jewell 1993; Mead 1986 and 1992; Murray 1984; and Valentine
1968).

Yet, it so happens that black people internalize these negative social
and cultural constructions. This imposes a contradictory and ambiguous

consciousness upon black people's struggle to exist within the absurdity of America's anti-black culture. In this situation, the black individual often experiences a spiral of self-negation, self-hatred, and self-rejection. Significantly, writer Richard Wright effectively portrays the resultant tyranny of alienation, anxiety, and fear, in his novel *Native Son*. For the black individual, to survive in an anti-black world is often to experience a kind of ambiguity, bifurcation, or even a shattering of the self or the psyche. For example, W. E. B. Du Bois in his 1903 classic, *The Souls of Black Folk*, refers to this existential condition as double consciousness:

> After the Egyptian and Indian, the Greek and Roman, the Teuton and Mongolian, the Negro is a sort of seventh son, born with a veil, and gifted with second-sight in this American world – a world which yields no true self-consciousness, but only lets him see himself through the revelation of the other world. It is a peculiar sensation, this double consciousness, this sense of always looking at one's self through the eyes of others, of measuring one's soul by the tape of a world that looks on in amused contempt and pity. One ever feels his twoness, – an American, a Negro; two souls, two thoughts, two unreconciled strivings; two warring ideals in one dark body, whose dogged strength alone keeps it from being torn asunder. (1966: 3)

Importantly, Fanon corroborates Du Bois's observation with reference to the colonial situation:

> There is, in the *Weltanschauung* of a colonized people, an impurity, a defect that forbids any ontological explanation. Perhaps it will be objected that it is so with every individual, but that is to mask a fundamental problem. Ontology, when it is admitted once and for all that it leaves existence by the wayside, does not permit us to understand the being of the black. For the black no longer has to be black, but must be it in front of the white. Some critics will take it on themselves to remind us that this situation is reciprocal. We respond that this is false. The black has no ontological resistance to the eyes of the white. Overnight the Negroes have had two systems of reference with regard to which they felt the need to situate themselves. Their metaphysics, or, less pretentiously, their customs and the earnestness with which they are discharged, were abolished because they found themselves in contradiction with a civilization of which they were ignorant and which imposed itself on them. (*Pn* 88–9 / *BS* 109–10)

It is this psychologically fragmented black self that, as a result of the cultural imposition of white oppression, comes to be transformed when, on occasion, the spirit of revolt overtakes the attitude of resentment.

Resentment and Rebellion

In *The Will to Power*, Nietzsche refers to resentment as "the popular uprising, the revolt of the underprivileged" (p. 108). It often happens, therefore, that the long-standing and ever-present attitude of resentment gives way to rebellion. At times, the feelings of hatred, anger, and revenge are unleashed, transforming the individual experiencing resentment into a person who decides to embody a sense of freedom, as Fanon might say, by resisting the injustice of racist culture. Richard Wright's powerful and shocking novel, *Native Son*, is instructive on this subject in the portrayal of its anti-hero, Bigger Thomas. Thomas is a young black man caught in the corrosive clutches of urban poverty, despair, and alienation. Racism is an ever-present reality, circumscribing every aspect of his existence. He is profoundly resentful; he both fears and hates white people. Because of circumstances beyond his control, Thomas accidentally kills a white female. He later deliberately kills his black girlfriend. Although he attempts to escape, Thomas is caught and tried in court basically for raping and murdering the white woman. Ironically, he is not remorseful for his crimes; rather, he expresses hatred for the dead white woman and indifference toward the black girlfriend he murdered.[1]

Wright skillfully constructs this situation in such a fashion as to transform Thomas from a man of resentment to a man of rebellion. In a long defense statement, Thomas's attorney points out the issue of resentment and its nihilistic consequences:

> Kill him and swell the tide of pent-up lava that will someday break loose, not in a single, blundering, accidental, individual crime, but in a wild cataract of emotion that will brook no control. The all-important thing for this Court to remember in deciding this boy's fate is that, though his crime was accidental, the emotions that broke loose were *already* there; the thing to remember is that this boy's way of life was a way of guilt; that his crime existed long before the murder of Mary Dalton; that the accidental nature of his crime took the guise of a sudden and violent rent in the veil behind which he lived, a rent which allowed his feelings of resentment and estrangement to leap forth and find objective and concrete form. (pp. 330–1)

The lawyer suggests that Thomas's resentment emerges from and reflects the black individual's outrage about the lack of justice for black people in America. Attendant impulses, such as anger, rage, revenge, and spite emerge out of the contradiction between the theory and practice of freedom and justice. Cultural marginalization in a theoretically democratic society can transform resentment into intense cynicism and nihilism. The lawyer later states:

Every time he comes in contact with us, he kills! It is a physiological and psychological reaction, embedded in his being. Every thought he thinks is potential murder. Excluded from, and unassimilated in our society, yet longing to gratify impulses akin to our own but denied the objects and channels evolved through long centuries for their socialized expression, every sunrise and sunset make him guilty of subversive actions. Every movement of his body is an unconscious protest. Every desire, every dream, no matter how intimate or personal, is a plot or a conspiracy. Every hope is a plan for insurrection. Every glance of the eye is a threat. *His very existence is a crime against the state!* (pp. 335–6)

Much like Fanon's theory of the dialectic between violence and counter-violence, Thomas represents the dialectic between resentment and rebellion. Thomas's violence is as brutal as his perception of the marginalized, oppressive, and alienating character of his life. His predicament transforms him from passive victim to active rebel, very much like Fanon's colonized insurgent. In this regard, Fanon says: "At the level of individuals, violence is a cleansing force. It frees the colonized from their inferiority complex and from their despair and inaction; it makes them fearless and restores their self-respect" (*Dt* 127 / *WE* 73). In this instance, Thomas takes responsibility for his violent actions, which allows him to experience a sense of freedom. He says:

I don't know. Maybe this sounds crazy. Maybe they going to burn me in the electric chair for feeling this way. But I ain't worried none about them women I killed. For a little while I was free. I was doing something. It was wrong, but I was feeling all right. Maybe God'll get me for it. If He do, all right. But I ain't worried. I killed 'em 'cause I was scared and mad. But I been scared and mad all my life and after I killed that first woman, I wasn't scared no more for a little while. (p. 300)

Significantly, the spirit of rebellion can exist only in a society where a theoretical equality masks great factual inequalities. Wright's novel demonstrates why there is the ever-present possibility of revolt in American society. The Constitution and other sacred political texts, which set forth a theory of political freedom, are the very heart of the American social order. The failure to apply this political freedom can result in corresponding problems of resentment, discontent, and rebellion (see Camus 1991). When black and other oppressed people of color lash out in forms of hostile insurgency – as for example, the violent 1992 upheaval in Los Angeles following the exoneration of several white cops who brutally beat Rodney King – it evidences public outrage against structures of injustice. The practice of rebellion overtakes the attitude of resentment when justice is denied.

Conclusion

In the main, this essay has sought to probe the issue of black resentment. Fanon's powerful analysis served as a kind of beacon, shedding light on my attempt to understand the turbulent condition of racialized cultural domination and dehumanization. Constrained over time, the attitude of resentment is both consequence and cause of outrage about political injustice. Chattel slavery and segregation characterized America's past; a deeply rooted culture of racism distinguishes its present. A great melancholy of human existence is that the past cannot be changed. However, the future can be refashioned, but only if reconstituted communities of people so desire. Presently, prospects for societal renewal seem remote.

At the dawn of the twenty-first century, American society seems engulfed in a rising tide of cynicism and nihilism; it is a cancer of the spirit. Suspicion is increasing. Trust is declining. There is a mounting sense of despair about the modern culture of progress that America is supposed to embody. A growing proportion of Americans seem skeptical about whether the institutions of progress are viable and beneficial: political leadership, public bureaucracies, business corporations, public schools, universities, political parties, religious organizations, the legal system, the mass media, and even the family. Popular discontent is becoming more comprehensive, penetrating, and corrosive.

In the emerging managerial age of knowledge, science, and technology, America's political and managerial elites utilize their expertise and discursive power to define people of color and other less powerful classes as undesirables – for example, the poor, the aged, the young, the mentally ill – for the purpose of legitimizing their use in new forms of scientific experimentation and research (see Darity 1983, 1991; Darity *et al.* 1994). However, the mass public's growing cynical disillusionment regarding the legitimacy of society's governing elites poses a nihilistic threat to America's future. As the twenty-first century rapidly approaches, America will confront the alternatives of communal concern, social anarchy, or fascism. This society must find the will to provide historically excluded, oppressed, resentful Americans a sense of dignity, the formative modalities for social development, and genuine opportunities for democratic participation – a foundation for a people's society. Otherwise, a spiritually bankrupt America will continue to slide down the slippery slope of nihilism, chaos, and breakdown.

Note

1 Wright generally portrayed women unkindly. He was particularly unkind to black women, whom he represented as negative and devalued characters. Apparently, Wright experienced much frustration and conflict with the women in his life, beginning with his childhood. For an insightful exploration of this issue, consult Margaret Walker's *Richard Wright, Daemonic Genius: A Portrait of the Man, a Critical Look at His Work* (1988).

2

Perspectives of Du Bois and Fanon on the Psychology of Oppression

Stanley O. Gaines, Jr.

Perhaps the worst thing about the colonial system was the contradiction which arose and had to arise in Europe with regard to the whole situation. Extreme poverty in colonies was a main cause of wealth and luxury in Europe. The results of this poverty were disease, ignorance, and crime. Yet these had to be represented as natural characteristics of backward peoples. Education for colonial people must inevitably mean unrest and revolt; education, therefore, had to be limited and used to inculcate obedience and servility lest the whole colonial system be overthrown.

W. E. B. Du Bois

It is the white who creates the Negro. But it is the Negro who creates negritude . . . The colonized, in the face of the emphasis given by the colonialist to this or that aspect of their traditions, react in a very violent way. The interest placed on modifying this aspect, the opposing emotion the conqueror puts into his pedagogical work, his prayers, his threats, weave a whole universe of resistances around this particular element of the culture. Holding out against the occupier on this precise element means inflicting upon him a spectacular failure; it means more particularly maintaining "co-existence" as a form of conflict and latent warfare. It means keeping up the atmosphere of an armed truce.

Frantz Fanon[1]

It is ironic that mainstream social psychology, purportedly concerned with finding "universal" laws of human behavior, has never grasped a fundamental aspect of intergroup relations. Even the most brutal forms of exploitation, such as those emerging from the Atlantic slave trade, cannot obliterate the will of the oppressed to affirm themselves or to affirm the cultures to which they belong (Gaines and Reed 1994, 1995; White and Parham 1990). All too often, "modern" social psychology has cast Anglos in the role of Self (the subject) and persons of color in the role of Other (the object; see Howitt and Owusu-Bempah, 1994; van Dijk, 1993). Such contrived logic, taken to its extreme, implies that persons of African descent throughout the diaspora have come to view themselves as the less-than-human entities that persons of European descent historically have deemed them to be.

In contrast, the social-psychological perspectives of W. E. B. Du Bois and of Frantz Fanon maintain that persons of African descent have managed to survive in a white-dominated, individualistic world while retaining a commitment to communal beliefs that not only have been functional as tools against oppression but are consistent with beliefs that for centuries have characterized the *ethos* of Africa. In what follows, we shall examine some of the ways in which Du Bois and Fanon have articulated this oft-neglected psychology of the oppressed. Along the way, we shall explore the concept of pan-Africanism that links Du Bois's African-American viewpoint with Fanon's distinctly Afro-Caribbean viewpoint.[2]

Pan-Africanism, Colonialism, and Du Bois's "Two Souls"

It is fitting that W. E. B. Du Bois co-organized the first Pan-African Congress in Paris shortly after World War I. He had already gained prominence in the United States as the author of *The Souls of Black Folk*, as chief architect of the Niagara Movement, and as one of the founders of the National Association for the Advancement of Colored People (NAACP). Du Bois believed that black scholarship and activism should be fused together and pressed into service on behalf of black people in the United States and across the globe (Dunn 1993; Gaines and Reed 1994, 1995; King *et al.* 1983). Accordingly, the "two souls" described by Du Bois reflect the essence of Pan-Africanism as manifested in the intrapersonal and interpersonal lives of African-heritage persons throughout the diaspora. As Walters (1993) pointed out, African-heritage persons as individuals and *en masse* must continually assert themselves in the face of western cultural hegemony:

> [W]ith respect to the question of the role of African identity, African people in the Diaspora do not share the specificity of the African personality as it emerged from the colonial era into the nation state, seeking to establish its national and continental integrity. This is simply another way

of saying that Africans in the Diaspora are not a part of the daily particularities of African history and so cannot possess the identity which flows
from these experiences. However, they do share certain aspects of this
history, and the basis upon which they do so is (1) their affirmation of an
African heritage; (2) their participation in the Diasporic aspects of pan-
African political struggles; (3) their continuing concern with the status of
Africa and their efforts to improve it, and (4) their relationship to other
hyphenated Africans in the Diaspora. (p. 385)

In the Diaspora, the contradiction of possessing more than one identity
has never been resolved and will not be as long as the basic identity of
Africa continues to be the footstool of the world and African people . . . are
everywhere subordinated. The "twoness" is not yet one – if it ever will be;
the concepts are still at war, and in this war, many have chosen the "flag
of convenience," either the African identity or the American. Nevertheless,
no matter which is chosen, the other still continues fundamentally to color
the essence of life in a way that makes black culture uniquely different in
the world. (p. 387)

According to Du Bois, every African American struggles to balance
the oft-conflicting "two souls" of (1) Africanness (reflected in an orientation toward community) and (2) Americanness (reflected in an orientation toward self) in his or her own life (1903/1969). Although some
African-heritage persons assert that they never have experienced internal
turmoil regarding the "two souls" (for example, Asante 1993; Crouch
1993; Mitchell 1993), Du Bois argued that it is extremely difficult (if not
impossible) for any African American to avoid such turmoil. (In support
of his position, see Early 1993; Gaines and Reed 1994, 1995; Jones,
1987; McKnight 1993; Manning 1993; Walters 1993.) Moreover, Du
Bois did not propose an optimal or ideal balance between these two
aspects of black personality. Instead, he argued that no African American should be forced to choose between the "two souls" (King *et al.*
1983; McPherson 1993; Staples 1993).

In no way, however, was Du Bois naïve about the impact of European
colonialism on the psyches of African Americans or other African-
descent persons (Franklin 1993). Du Bois was well acquainted with the
history of European colonialism in Africa and documented that unsavory
history. According to Du Bois, the ransacking of African culture by
persons of European descent left many (if not most) Africans mentally as
well as physically impoverished:

With [European colonialism] went the fall and disruption of the family, the
deliberate attack upon the ancient African clan by missionaries. The
invading investors who wanted cheap labor at the gold mines, the diamond
mines, the copper and tin mines, the oil forests and cocoa fields, followed

the missionaries. The authority of the family was broken up; the authority and tradition of the clan disappeared; the power of the chief was transmuted into the rule of the white district commissioner. The old religion was held up to ridicule, the old culture and ethical standards were degraded or disappeared, and gradually all over Africa spread the inferiority complex, the fear of color, the worship of white skin, the imitation of white ways of doing and thinking, whether good, bad, or indifferent. By the end of the nineteenth century, the degradation of Africa was as complete as organized human means could make it. Chieftains, representing a thousand years of striving human culture, were decked out in second-hand London top-hats, while Europe snickered. (1965: 78)

Thus, Du Bois believed, European colonialism represented a formidable (and, quite often, unstoppable) enemy in the eyes of African-heritage persons throughout the diaspora. Although some authors have depicted African Americans as freed from the yoke of colonialism owing to their "immigrant" status in the United States (for example, Taft 1973), Du Bois stressed that most African-heritage persons prior to the Civil War did not come willingly to the United States and, hence, were victimized by colonialism (Gordon 1995a; Pollard 1993). Moreover, given that Anglos dispossessed Native Americans (and, later, Chicanos) of all of the land now constituting the United States (Ramirez 1983), it is hard to argue that *any* ethnic group (except, perhaps, "White ethnics"; Weed 1973) has truly escaped colonialism in America.

Fanon and the "Decolonization" of African-heritage Persons

Earlier, we noted in passing that the dean of the Afrocentric movement in the United States, Molefi Asante, once declared that he never had experienced the agonizing identity conflicts that Du Bois had viewed as part and parcel of the African-American experience. Perhaps it is no surprise, then, that Asante looked outside the borders of the United States for his primary intellectual inspiration. Rather than cast his lot with Du Bois, Asante chose to emulate Frantz Fanon and consciously emphasized his Africanness over his Americanness.

In what ways did Fanon differ from Du Bois regarding the dilemma of the "two souls"? In his classic, *Les Damnés de la terre*, Fanon stated unequivocally that no person of African heritage could serve two masters. In reality, Fanon surmised, African-descent persons fall into two categories, namely (1) those who are colonized and (2) those who are *de*-colonized (Fairchild 1994). Like Du Bois, Fanon believed that European colonialism constituted a grave threat to Africans' physical

and psychological well-being throughout the diaspora. Unlike Du
Bois, though, Fanon consistently concluded that the "me-" and "we-"
orientations never would coexist peacefully (Zack 1993). According
to Fanon, European colonialism was destined either to bowl over
Africans' psyches or to be bowled over by armed revolt from Africans
themselves:

> In the colonial countries where a real struggle has taken place, where the
> blood of the people has flowed and where the length of the period of armed
> warfare has favored the backward surge of intellectuals towards bases
> grounded in the people, we can observe a genuine eradication of the
> superstructure built by these intellectuals from the bourgeois colonialist
> environment. The colonialist bourgeoisie, in its narcissistic dialogue, ex-
> pounded by the members of its universities, had in fact deeply implanted
> in the minds of the colonised intellectual that the essential qualities remain
> eternal in spite of all the blunders men may make: the essential qualities of
> the West, of course. The native intellectual accepted the cogency of these
> ideas, and deep down in his brain you could always find a vigilant sentinel
> ready to defend the Greco-Latin pedestal. Now it so happens that during
> the struggle for liberation, at the moment that the native intellectual comes
> into touch again with his people, this artificial sentinel is turned into dust.
> All the Mediterranean values – the triumph of the human individual, of
> charity and of beauty – become lifeless, colourless knickknacks. All those
> speeches seem like collections of dead words; those values which seemed
> to uplift the soul are revealed as worthless simply because they have
> nothing to do with the concrete conflict in which the people is [sic]
> engaged. (*Dt* 77 / *WE* 46–7)

Even in his most avowedly socialist stance, Du Bois (1986) seldom
depicted the struggle between the "two souls" as all-out warfare (see
Pollard 1993). In contrast, Fanon seemed to relish the minutae of
planning and executing life-or-death battles over the "two souls." Although both Du Bois and Fanon breathed the rarefied air of black
intellectualism (Du Bois as a philosopher/sociologist, Fanon as a phi-
losopher/psychiatrist), Du Bois promoted the concept of the "talented
tenth," while Fanon repudiated black intellectualism (or at least the
form of black intellectualism that stymied the progress of the masses; see
Fairchild 1994).

Of course, we would be doing a gross injustice to Fanon if we were to
regard him solely as a counterpoint to Du Bois. Especially intriguing for
the purposes of our discussion is the manner in which Fanon (in *Peau
noire*) methodically laid out psychoanalytic theory as commonly applied
to the psychology of Africans, and then proceeded to deride psychoanalytic theory as a misrepresentation of black/African psychology. Accordingly, let us briefly consider psychoanalytic theory as applied (or, more

accurately, as *mis*applied) to the psychological experiences of African-heritage persons throughout the diaspora.

A central premise of psychoanalytic theory is that much (if not most) of what governs human behavior is located "within" the person (Schellenberg 1978). Despite the schism between Freudian and neo-Freudian camps over issues such as the importance attached to sexuality (a Freudian tenet) and the importance of society in shaping individuals' personalities and corresponding behavior (a neo-Freudian tenet), psychoanalytic theorists generally agree that individuals' earliest interactions with mothers and other caregivers largely determine individuals' psychological makeup for life. Not surprisingly, as Fanon observed (in *A Dying Colonialism*), psychoanalytic interpretations of black personality typically emphasize lifelong flaws in blacks' psychological states and personality traits (e.g. as suffering from Oedipus/Electra complexes or inferiority complexes; see also Gordon 1995a; Howitt and Owusu-Bempah 1994; Nobles 1986).

Mainstream social psychologists often have criticized psychoanalytic theory as accomplishing little more than the reification of psychoanalytic theorists' own biases (e.g. Nisbet and Ross 1980) or, even worse, as lending "scientific" credence to prevailing societal stereotypes (see Brown 1965). However, these psychologists have been almost uniformly silent on the issue of the applicability of psychoanalytic theory to persons of African descent. Fanon (in *Peau noire*) addressed that issue directly and concluded that psychoanalytic theory fails to account adequately for the influence of social, political, economic, and educational disparities upon the mental and physical well-being of African-heritage persons. Moreover, Fanon was far more optimistic regarding the potential of Africans to throw off their figurative and literal shackles in the face of oppressive colonialism than were even the most liberal psychoanalytic theorists (Robinson 1993).

Du Bois, Fanon, and the Resurgence of Africa

In the preceding section, we called attention to a number of differences between Du Bois's and Fanon's versions of the psychology of oppression. In fact, some authors (e.g. Manning 1993) have suggested that Du Bois unwittingly promoted precisely the type of psychic determinism (Schellenberg 1978) that Fanon criticized so roundly. Moreover, some authors (for example, Giovanni 1993) have gone so far as to characterize Du Bois as a "conservative," a label that surely no one would dare apply to Fanon (Fairchild 1994; Onwuanibe 1983; Perinbam 1982). It is also a label which overlooks a great deal of Du

Bois's later, "radical" period in which he became a member of the
Communist Party USA.

Lest we conclude prematurely that Du Bois and Fanon fundamentally
were at odds over the preferred course of action of African-heritage
persons throughout the diaspora, however, we must remember that both
Du Bois and Fanon died striving to ensure that all of the nations of
Africa would achieve and maintain sovereign rule. Du Bois died (and
was buried) in Ghana in 1963 at the age of 95, having served as an
adviser to Prime Minister Kwame Nkrumah after Ghana became the
first African nation to reclaim its sovereignty and thus achieve
"decolonization" (Du Bois 1965; see also Jackson 1970). Fanon died in
the United States at the age of 36 in 1961 but was buried in Algeria,
having taken up arms to win independence for the latter nation, which
was the last in North Africa to gain it. Both Du Bois and Fanon were
Pan-Africanists, and both epitomized the spirit of the true scholar-
activist (Asante 1988, 1993; Caute 1970; Dunn 1993; Fairchild 1994;
Gaines and Reed 1994, 1995; Hansen 1977; Lemelle 1993; McCulloch
1983; Onwuanibe 1983).

Although Du Bois and Fanon have not always been recognized for
their contributions to Afrocentrism, certain key passages from their
works attest to their abiding interest in unearthing the cultural treasures
of Africa (Estell 1994; Fairchild 1994; Moses 1993). In fact, both Du
Bois and Fanon saw the political and cultural affirmation of Africans
throughout the diaspora as necessarily linked (Walters 1993). The following passages illustrate Du Bois's and Fanon's belief in *communalism*
(Myers 1993) as an enduring cultural value orientation rooted in ancient
African civilizations:

> Pan-Africa, working together through its independent units, should seek to
> develop a new African economy and cultural center standing between
> Europe and Asia, taking from and contributing to both. It should stress
> peace and join no military alliance and refuse to fight for settling European
> quarrels. It should avoid subjugation to and ownership by foreign capital-
> ists who seek to get rich on African labor and raw material, and should try
> to build a socialism founded on old African communal life; rejecting on the
> one hand the exaggerated private initiative of the West, and seeking to ally
> itself with the social program of the progressive nations. (Du Bois 1965:
> 296)

> Self-criticism has been much talked about of late, but few people realize
> that it is an African institution. Whether in the *djemaas* of Northern Africa
> or in the meetings of Western Africa, tradition demands that the quarrels
> which occur in a village should be settled in public. It is communal self-
> criticism, of course, and with a note of humour, because everybody is
> relaxed, and because in the last resort we all want the same things. But the

more the intellectual imbibes the atmosphere of the people, the more completely he abandons the habits of calculation, of unwonted silence, of mental reservations, and shakes off the spirit of concealment. And it is true that already at that level, we can say that the community triumphs, and that it spreads its own light and its own reason. (*Dt* 78–9 / *WE* 47–8)

In turn, the message of African cultural and political unity throughout the diaspora – a message that was echoed repeatedly in the words and deeds of Du Bois and Fanon – helped shape the vision of Martin Luther King, Jr. (1964) within the Civil Rights Movement and of Malcolm X (1965b) within the Black Power Movement (see Esebe 1994; Jones 1987; Walters 1993). Just as obvious comparisons between Martin Luther King's nonviolent stance and Malcolm X's tacit approval of violence fail to capture their shared belief in the common fate of African-heritage persons across the globe, so too do distinctions between Du Bois's and Fanon's perspectives detract from our perception of their shared commitment to African unity.

This is not to imply that either Du Bois or Fanon (or, for that matter, Martin Luther King, Jr. or Malcolm X) were interested in glorifying Africa's past, present, or future. As Du Bois and Fanon pointed out, the mythology of African superiority is just as problematic as is the mythology of European superiority (Du Bois 1965 and 1969, and Fanon 1952 and 1961a). However, Du Bois and Fanon believed that those remnants of African culture that managed to survive the horrors of slavery and colonization were potential sources of pride that could serve as part of the basis for forging political as well as psychological bonds among African-heritage persons throughout the diaspora.

Post-Du Bois, Post-Fanon Reflections on the Psychology of Oppression

Having reviewed the contributions of Du Bois and Fanon to understanding the psychology of oppression, one might legitimately ask whether these two icons of progressive black intellectualism (and foes of European colonialism) are relevant to the social and psychological experiences of post-1960s Africans throughout the diaspora. After all, one might contend, an entire generation of African-heritage persons has been born (and, in fact, has begun to raise progeny of its own) during the decades that have passed since the deaths of Du Bois and Fanon (and also since the deaths of Martin Luther King, Jr. and Malcolm X). In what ways, if any, do Du Bois and Fanon speak to the plight of young African-descent persons across the globe gripped in the vise of nihilism (which West (1993c: 14) defines as "the lived experience of coping with a life of horrifying meaninglessness, hopelessness, and . . . lovelessness")?

In response to such potentially damning questions, I would argue that Du Bois and Fanon had more to say thirty years ago about today's nihilism in the African diaspora than do today's mainstream psychologists. As an example, a book entitled *Psychology and Nihilism* by F. Evans doesn't even include key concepts such as "culture," "ethnicity," and "race" in its index! In contrast, Du Bois (1965) and Fanon (*Les Damnés*) knew that European colonialism had created the very conditions of white power and black impoverishment throughout the diaspora that now leave millions of African-heritage persons grasping desperately for any way (whether legal or extralegal, nonviolent or violent) out of their current predicament (West 1993a and 1993b). As Cornel West observed, one cannot speak honestly about race without addressing the sense of purposelessness engulfing African-descent persons of today:

> Nihilism is not new in black America. The first African encounter with the New World was an encounter with a distinctive form of the Absurd. The initial black struggle against degradation and devaluation in the enslaved circumstances of the New World was, in part, a struggle against nihilism. In fact, the major enemy of black survival in America has been and is neither oppression nor exploitation but rather the nihilistic threat – that is, loss of hope and absence of meaning. For as long as hope remains and meaning is preserved, the possibility of overcoming oppression stays alive. The self-fulfilling prophecy of the nihilistic threat is that without hope there can be no future, that without meaning there can be no struggle. (1993b: 15)

If even middle-class blacks in America – ostensibly the embodiment of self-determination to "make it" in spite of the odds – continue to encounter institutional and interpersonal barriers blocking their way to socioeconomic and sociopolitical advancement (see Cose), then it is little wonder that less fortunate African-heritage youth in the United States or in Third World nations often feel that they never will be affirmed as fully human beings possessing inalienable rights. As long as selfhood is equated with whiteness, persons of African descent will be hard-pressed to escape the "double consciousness" of which Du Bois and Fanon wrote so eloquently. Ironically, even though both Du Bois and Fanon increasingly emphasized pan-Africanism and simultaneously de-emphasized the concept of the "two souls" in their later writings, they both seemed embittered toward the United States and other western powers for having forced them to deny those aspects of themselves that happened not to be African *per se* (see Franklin 1993 and Gendzier 1973).

Some authors (for example, Crouch 1993; Robinson 1993) have blamed Du Bois and Fanon for betraying personal identity conflicts when writing at length about the "two souls." Such a critique implies that even when they were among the living, Du Bois and Fanon were describing the effects of colonialism on themselves rather than on black Americans, black Algerians, or other African-heritage persons throughout the diaspora. However, the tremendous influence that Du Bois and Fanon have had upon social-scientific and philosophic theorizing on the psychology of oppression belies such a trivialization of either Du Bois or Fanon (Gordon 1995b; West 1993a and 1993b). When Du Bois and Fanon are allowed to speak for themselves (as surely they must), it is abundantly clear that their decades-old writings nonetheless capture the modern-day nihilism found so frequently in the African diaspora:

> In the Black World, the Preacher and Teacher embodied once the ideals of this people – the strife for another and a juster [*sic*] world, the vague dream of righteousness, the mystery of knowing; but to-day the danger is that these ideals, with their simple beauty and weird inspiration, will suddenly sink to a question of cash and a lust for gold . . . What if the Negro people be wooed from a strife for righteousness, from a love of knowing, to regard dollars as the be-all and end-all of life? (Du Bois 1969: 114)

> Intellectual alienation is a creation of bourgeois society. And I call bourgeois society any society that ossifies itself in determined form, forbidding any evolution, any advance, progress, any discovery. I call bourgeois a closed society where it is not good to be alive, where the air is rotten, where ideas and people are corrupt. And I think that a man who takes a stand against this death is in a sense a revolutionary. (*Pn* 182 / *BS* 224–5)

Conclusion

As we have seen in this chapter, W. E. B. Du Bois and Frantz Fanon have emerged as two of the major twentieth-century theorists on the psychology of oppression. Du Bois and Fanon appear not to have been aware of each other's presence (even though both could claim the friendship of influential pan-Africanists such as Ghanaian President Kwame Nkrumah; Drake 1993; McCulloch 1983), yet the two philosophers consistently articulated similar themes regarding the despair engendered by European colonialism, the hope engendered by pan-Africanism, and the dissociation between African-heritage persons' "two souls." Du Bois and Fanon are identified most often with the struggles of African-descent persons against European colonization in specific locales (Du Bois in the United States, Fanon in Algeria), but both intellectuals possessed an expansive vision of unity among persons of color that transcended racial and national boundaries (Masilela 1994). Furthermore, despite their difference in age (Du Bois was 93 years old in 1961, just two years before his own death, when Fanon died at age 36), both Du Bois and Fanon remain relevant to contemporary students of the psychology of oppression (Gordon 1995a, 1995b, and 1996c).

In closing, the relevance of Du Bois and Fanon for understanding the potential of individuals to transform the societies in which they live cannot be underestimated. Du Bois and Fanon argued that no matter how static a given social order might seem, revolutionary individuals born within that social order may eventually serve as the catalysts for social change (see Schellenberg 1978). Both Du Bois and Fanon offered their own lives as examples that the role of black scholar-activists working throughout the diaspora is essential if African-heritage persons ultimately are to break free of European colonialism and render the "psychology of oppression" null and void.

Notes

1   Epigraphs are from Du Bois (1965: 37), and Fanon (*Sr* 29 / *ADC* 47).
2   See Paget Henry's essay in this volume, below.

3

Racism and Objectification: Reflections on Themes from Fanon

Richard Schmitt

White people believe that they are better than anyone else on earth . . . The last thing they ever want to see is a black man stand, and think, and show that common humanity that is in us all. They would no longer have justification for having made us slaves and keeping us in the condition we are in.

Earnest J. Gaines, A Lesson before Dying

It is one of Fanon's many virtues that his questions about racism go to the very heart of the matter. He does not ask whether the concept of "race" is defensible, or whether racism is an affliction of the emotions – a kind of neurosis – or of the intellect – a form of irrationality. He asks, *What does racism do to people?* His answer is brief. Racism objectifies.

In this, as in other ways, Fanon follows Aimé Césaire who called colonialism "thingification" (1972: 21). Fanon writes:

The constantly affirmed concern with "respecting the culture of the native populations" . . . does not signify taking into account the values borne by the culture . . . Rather this behavior betrays a determination to objectify, to confine, to imprison, to harden. (*Pra* 36 / *TAR* 34)

He also stated that

All forms of exploitation are identical, for they are all applied against the same "object": man . . . [the] main problem . . . is to restore man to his place. (*Pn* 70 / *BS* 88)

This chapter owes a lot to the careful readings and comments by Lucy Candib, as well as to her relentless and thoughtful opposition to racism and sexism. I am also grateful to the editors of this volume for helpful comments.

The concept of objectification is not without difficulties, however. If by "objectification" we mean taking someone as a (quasi-)grammatical object, it needs to be argued that that is an injury to human beings. It is plausible that one is injured by being made the object of a "look," but not by being made the object of love, of a gift, of concentrated and thoughtful attention. It is not clear that those are injuries. If, on the other hand, "objectification" is taken to mean "making a person into a thing," it is not obvious that one can objectify another. Persons are *not* things as long as they are alive. One becomes an object – a dead body – when one dies. Hence it is not immediately clear what "objectification" could mean.

What follows is an attempt to clarify this concept of objectification. I shall argue that objectification is not best understood either as turning persons into things, or as depriving them of their freedom, but as a carefully orchestrated and systematic refusal of genuinely human relationships. Objectification turns out to be very common and pervasive, encouraged in our world by prevailing economic practices.

The Many Faces of Racism

At the outset, Fanon's claim looks like a vast and illegitimate generalization. Racism is very complex; it takes many different forms and finds expression in a large range of practices and institutions. It seems completely illegitimate to overlook all of these different practices and describe all forms of racism as objectification.[1] Fanon himself mentions a number of very different racist practices:

Infantilization. The members of a subject group are thought of and treated as children. This takes many different forms. The black French are often addressed in pidgin French. It is regularly assumed that a black French person would of course not have mastery of adult French. Members of subject groups are frequently patronized in many other ways. Well-meaning members of dominant groups assume that any subject group member needs help, is "disadvantaged." There is a tendency to assume that members of subject groups are "victims."[2]

Denigration. Related is the pervasive assumption that members of subject groups are defective. A gypsy is always assumed to be a thief, a Jew dishonest, and a black, incompetent. In the United States, African Americans must always prove their competence. Professionals must get accustomed to having their credentials checked and questioned by all. Students are initially presumed unqualified. If they have good records, that is attributed to "affirmative action" programs. If they have difficulties those are always taken as signs of lack of ability.

Without doubt Aimé Césaire was a great writer. The French intellectuals who praise him and who, for that reason, consider themselves particularly liberal, never fail to mention that Césaire was a *black* poet (*Pn* 31 / *BS* 39). If a member of a subject group is so phenomenally competent that no one can ignore or deny it, then that is assumed to be an exceptional case that deserves explicit notice. It is not surprising that there should be good white poets, but when a black person is exceptional it invites comment.

Distrust. Signs of competence, moreover, do not serve to dispel the automatic distrust: "just as a Jew who spends money without counting it is suspect, the black who quotes Montesquieu had better be watched" (*Pn* 27 / *BS* 35).

Should a Gypsy prove honest, a Jew uninterested in wealth, or a black display brilliance, that always requires special notice and caution. If most members of subject groups are not competent, their supposedly childlike nature does not have the innocence of children but is, instead, regarded as sinister. If there are members of that group who are talented to boot, they may well prove dangerous to the dominant groups. They therefore need to be watched carefully.

Ridicule. Like children, or incompetent adults, members of subject groups are thought to be amusing. Especially amusing are adults who act like children. Their supposed incompetence invites ridicule. Fanon mentions the standard black servant in Hollywood movies of the 1930s and 1940s, but there are many other examples of dark skin occasioning automatic amusement, similar to the ways in which children are automatically regarded as droll (see Pierterse 1992).

Exclusion. Racism excludes. That is not noteworthy. Private property rights exclude also, and so does the right to privacy. Institutions like marriage exclude, as does the institution of the family. I do not have private property rights in my children, but they are mine and not another man's. But racism excludes for reasons that are either imaginary – such as belonging to a fictitious group, the black race, or the Jewish "race," etc., or mendacious – such as the supposed incompetence or shiftlessness of members of subject groups. Racism excludes either without any reasons or, worse, for reasons that are thoroughly reprehensible.

Rendering invisible. The excluded become invisible. Their concerns are unknown, their lives of no interest to anyone but themselves. A whole world remains invisible behind the dark skin. The culture of white Europeans is still universal. It is simply "western culture" or even "culture" without qualification. It is, or ought to be, of concern to everyone. Not so with the cultures of persons of color; they are of interest only to members of those groups. Attempts to add some of those works to the canon of "great literature," etc. are perceived as coercive and "political" because there can be no intellectual or artistic justification for broadening the cultural canon beyond the works of whites who are mostly men.

Scapegoating. Their shadowy presence explains pervasive evils. The invisible network of Jews accounted for the disasters of the great depression. The decay of US inner cities is blamed on the African Americans who are forced to live in those crumbling hulks. They alone are to be blamed for their poverty, and the troubles of the dominant whites are also to be laid at their door. After invisibility and its shadowy presence comes scapegoating.

Violence. The invisible have no moral claims on us. Exploitation and overwork, torture, and death are the final manifestations of racism. The entire racist and colonialist enterprise is supported and kept viable by a steady stream of physical violence from soldiers, the police, and private vigilantes. Neocolonialism substitutes the violence of death-squads (often trained in the US) for the violence of colonial armies. The overseer from the days of slavery has been replaced by the urban police forces occupying the inner city. The names of the torturers are preserved in the heroic tales of the mother-country; the names of the victims were and remain unknown. Belonging to a designated lesser race, they never counted.

All of this is too familiar. I rehearse it here once more only to raise a question for Fanon: What is the connection between these and many other racist behaviors and objectification? It seems that if we say that each of these practices objectifies we impoverish our understanding of racism and the many different ways in which some groups oppress others. It is essential that we understand the complexity of oppression, that we see how racism seeps into the most varied relationships and actions. It does not seem useful to cover up the vast range of racist strategies under the common name of "objectification."

I am sure that Fanon would agree with that. But then we need to ask what the relation is between the particular forms of racism and objectification. If the observation that racism is objectification does not substitute for the observations that racism infantilizes, excludes, ridicules, scapegoats, and brutalizes, then we need to be clear how those different descriptions of racism are related. There are two kinds of answers we could give to that question. We can say that all the different forms of racism mentioned have the same structure, namely objectification. Each of these particular manifestations of racism thus are to be considered as instances of objectification. Or we can claim that all the particular forms are a *means* to the end of objectification. I will choose the second interpretation and try to develop it.[3] But that has the difficulties mentioned earlier, that human beings are by definition human and cannot be made into things as long as they are alive. This interpretation insists that in all the different ways in which racism manifests itself, it serves the purpose of objectification.

There are a number of reasons for insisting on that. To begin with, it is easy to focus on one particular form of racism and to pay attention only to that: for example, exclusion. Many people think that the evils of sexism and racism have been overcome now that everyone has free access to all opportunities. Here one particular racist strategy is regarded as the essence of racism. All else is ignored. That is clearly a serious error. It is important to see that there are very different ways of being racist, and that those different ways all work together. Not only are they all means to the general end of objectification but also, the more complex the interrelated strategies are, the more that end is likely to be reached and to be very pervasive. (I will return to that point below.)

Besides, we notice that racism uses a range of strategies: it calls people children and treats them as such, but it also sees them as utterly sinister and evil. It regards people as ridiculous, but it also sees in them the root cause of great evils. It would be easy to become confused by these tensions between racist strategies and begin to distinguish between different kinds of racism – some worse, some not so bad, etc. By insisting that racism centrally aims at objectification, the different forms it takes are shown to be nothing more than particular strategies for the purpose of objectification. Objectification is what racism is all about: exclusion, infantilization, ridicule, scapegoating, violence, exploitation are only so many means to the final goal or objectification.

In addition, objectification is, of course, an impossible project. Human beings are not things. The only way of turning a human being into a thing is by murdering him.[4] Once the person is no longer, there is only a corpse and it is, indeed, a thing. A fully objectified person is, literally, impossible. But that does not prevent some people from pretending that they have succeeded, or from forcing others into acting simple, unresponsive, and passive in the presence of the oppressor. Objectification is not turning people into things – that cannot be done – but *pretending* that they are things and, more importantly, forcing them to accept that pretense, at least in relations to the oppressor. But pretenses must be maintained. They are constantly in danger of being disrupted by reality. Hence the grand objectifications – male superiority, white superiority, Europeanism – are complex, continuing projects to maintain a certain pretense. This requires many different strategies, suitable for slightly different situations. But all of them are in the service of the same goal, of pretending that members of a certain group are not fully human at all. This is the basic insight of Fanon's claim that the great variety of racist behaviors are all strategies in the continuing project of falsification, of making people appear to be what they not only are not but cannot be.

The multiplicity of racist strategies and practices thus is not denied by saying that they are all means toward objectification. Instead Fanon points out to us that the different ways in which racism manifests itself all serve the same purpose of objectification.

Objectification Up Close

Objectification pretends to do what cannot, in fact, be done literally, namely to turn human beings into things. But we have not yet said, in detail, what it means to turn a person into a thing. It is tempting to say something like this: human beings are free; things are not. By pretending that persons are things, objectification denies the human freedom of subject groups and thereby pretends that these human beings are mere things.

But that approach to the concept of objectification soon proves to be useless. Consider this: one can take this idea that human beings are free in the ordinary sense in which all human beings are said to have certain rights from birth, one of which is the right to liberty. Persons who do not in fact enjoy that liberty are denied one of their rights. Objectification, on that view, comes to mean no more than "oppression," or "violation of human rights." To say that racism objectifies tells us no more than we knew all along. It is only a pretentious circumlocution. (We shall see later that objectification can be considered a restriction of freedom only if we extend the notion of rights far beyond its current meaning.)

Alternatively, one can regard human freedom as an essential human attribute. Here "freedom" takes on a different meaning. In the first sense it is applied to what actions people were allowed to perform in any given social setting. The freedom that is essential to our humanity we have, even when in chains. It is much more internal to the person. It is, as in Hobbes, the freedom to *choose* to resist. It is, as in other philosophers, more generally, the freedom to make choices, as well as the attendant responsibility for the choices one makes. We cannot deprive humans of that freedom to resist or to choose, except very temporarily. If objectification is understood as deprivation of the *essential* freedom, the analysis ends up racist, if it is thought that one can actually succeed in depriving people of some or all of these essential freedoms. For people lacking that freedom to choose or to resist are indeed less responsible, less in charge of their lives than the rest of us. If, on the other hand, one insists that no one can be deprived of his essential freedom because saying that it is "essential" just means that no one can take it from us, then objectification becomes impossible. Objectification becomes a pretense.

Now I think that it is clearly right that racism involves pretense. We have already seen different reasons for regarding objectification as a pretense. If we talk about racism as objectification, as denial of genuine humanity, then clearly racism is centrally a monumental pretense. But what is being pretended? On the present hypothesis that human beings are essentially free, because they can always choose to resist, objectification pretends that members of a subject group do not possess that freedom. It is difficult to square that description with the facts. The freedom supposedly being denied is the freedom to resist. I can think of no major example of racism where the dominant group is not constantly on the lookout for any signs of resistance and is not always ready to punish any such sign of resistance with considerable brutality.[5]

If, on the other hand, the freedom we are speaking of is some sort of Sartrian responsibility for who one is, we must admit that racists have never pretended that subject groups were not responsible for their actions. They have been only too glad to insist that the fate of subject groups was of their own making, and was no more than they deserved. In that sense of "freedom" – as far-going responsibility for what sort of person one is turning out to be – racists have never pretended that subject groups are not "free." So if objectification consisted of the pretense that certain groups were not free in that sense, one would have to deny that racism is objectification. The attempt to explicate objectification as the pretense that certain groups of people are not free does not promise us interesting results.

We need to approach the question about objectification from a different direction. I want to focus on the fact that human beings are intrinsically social. Relationships to other human beings are of the essence of being human. But these relationships can be of very different kinds. After all, the slavemaster and the slave have a relationship, and so does the executioner to the condemned prisoner. These, I want to argue, are instances of relationships that objectify. Other relationships do not. Racism, it turns out, is a particularly complex and powerful set of structures for imposing objectifying relationships.

Let us ask: What would the black French, like Fanon, want from his or her fellow French? Clearly the black French want what all other human beings want: they want to be seen and understood for who they are.[6] No one is *only* black or Jewish. One wants to be described in more complex terms. Fanon is a black psychiatrist, writer, revolutionary, and a fiery and passionate but also at times coldly rational person. Fanon does not want the full complexity of his person to be summed up in one word – *le nègre* – which means both "Negro" and "nigger." He wants to be understood in more intricate ways. But with each of these descriptive phrases the same difficulty crops up. Does he want to be known as an intellectual and thus thought to be otherworldly, impractical, and given to utopian flights of fancy, or does he want it to be known that he is, although an intellectual, like other human beings: he eats, sleeps, makes love, sweats in the heat or shivers when cold. In other words, he wants to be known not as an intellectual, in general, but as the particular intellectual he is. Now we cannot satisfy that perfectly reasonable demand on his part by simply adding more descriptive phrases to our characterization of Frantz Fanon, for each will, in its turn, demand more qualifications, more complex descriptions and modifications. It seems that Fanon's desire to be known as a man like all others cannot be satisfied because no one can have that. However one describes oneself or another, however much detail one adds, one always deals in generalities because language describes by using general terms. The uniqueness of each of us, what makes each of us just this person seems ineffable and thus not to be known. But that, it seems, is what Fanon, and everyone else, wants: to be seen and known for who they are, as just this person unlike any other.

To follow that line of thought would take us in the wrong direction, away from an understanding of racism and objectification. The issue is not that each person is descriptively unique. On that assumption we could easily involve ourselves in thorny philosophical issues for a very long time. The real issue is how we treat one another. When I approach a fellow human being, I will not judge her or him by outward appearances, but will interest myself in who this person is. What one is always looking for when getting to know another person is what differentiates this person from others. We want to discover who *this* person is; what makes her or him just this person. Whether there might be another one identical person is a question for tales of horror or science fiction. It does not matter in relationships to other persons. What we want from each other, what is central to genuinely human relationships, is this interest in, this openness to, this other person. It consists of a refusal to stop at the surface the Other presents to me, instead of finding out, step by step and very patiently who this other person is, in the relationship to me.

Racism makes such human relationships very difficult. The surface color stands in the way of seeing the person. So does what is often offered as the opposite of racism, namely "color blindness" – saying that we are "all the same" – for that too leads me to assuming that I already know you and hence do not have to make an effort to get to know you. What Fanon wants from his fellow French is that they should stop acting as if they already knew him. The problem is not that our specificity escapes language, but that language is used to keep others at arm's length. When Fanon meets whites who claim to believe, as George Mounin does, that "the blacks are like us" (*Pn* 161 / *BS* 199), he wants to be approached with an open mind, a curious mind, with a desire to know him, to engage with him, however briefly and superficially. He is asking for a certain kind of relationship, the sort of relationships one has to other human beings.

Objectification consists of the refusal to have that sort of relationship with the other. I already know all I need to know about him. Hence I need not to talk to him; if I do talk, I do not need to listen. If I listen, I do not need to hear what is being said to me.

Objectification: Refusing Genuinely Human Relationships

Genuinely human relationships have these characteristics:

1. As human beings we are not replaceable. My part in a relationship to another person cannot be taken by another person. It may be, of course, that my lover from many years ago now loves another. But the relation to that other is not the relationship that we had with one another. I have not been replaced. Our relationship came to an end. Now we have different relationships. That is true in relations central to a person's life. It is also true in ephemeral relationships. A new letter carrier may do the same job as the previous one. But this is not the same person. Our occasional, brief chats at the mailbox have a different rhythm and melody than my talks with the previous letter carrier.

The issue is here, once again, not a metaphysical one about the uniqueness of each person. The issue is how we approach each other. If I treat the letter carrier as "the letter carrier" or he or she treats me as a "postal patron" where all letter carriers are the same, more or less, and so are all postal patrons, we do not have a genuinely human relation to each other. But as soon as we talk to each other as the persons we each are, the relationship, however insignificant, is a human one. Such relationships require curiosity about the other, who that other is, what are his or her interests, thoughts or values. It also requires a certain openness, a willingness to let oneself be seen, not to be secretive and distrustful of strangers. Situations where prudence demands that one be distrustful preclude the possibility of genuinely human relationships.

2. This suggests a second aspect of such relationships: there must be a

certain kind of mutuality. If I cannot trust you, there is no point in being open, or in listening carefully to you. (Of course, I may have to listen carefully to you to try to figure out what's in store for me.) You are not prepared to reciprocate. A genuinely human relationship cannot get started.[7] This mutuality is not a matter of exchanges as much as of responsiveness to one another. What matters, for instance, in genuinely human teaching is not that teacher and student are equals, or that each provides for the other what they receive from that other. Teachers and students are not equal, and provide very different things for each other. But they do need to be responsive to each other. The good teacher notices a quizzical look on a student's face and stops to ask whether there is a question. Good teachers respond to expressions of distress, or boredom. (In that way the live teacher in the class room is superior to the video-tape of the "master teacher.") The teaching and learning in the classroom are at best understood by all to be a shared undertaking, where each contributes what she or he can and each gets what is appropriate for him or her to receive. Genuinely human relationships are mutual insofar as they are joint undertakings.[8]

Objectification refuses those sorts of relationships. It says, instead: I am "my own man" and you are yours. We are separate. We do not share with each other; at best we do things alongside each other. That is most obvious in the case of racism. The racist says to members of the subject groups: You and I have nothing in common. There are no joint efforts in which we both participate. There is not even a common humanity that binds us together into some all-embracing shared project. No common efforts tie us to one another.[9]

Here the notion of objectification as pretense is needed again. For the separateness that racists and sexists insist on is only a pretense. An example of that is the widespread talk among (mostly male) philosophers about how we are all autonomous men and each live according to a "life plan" chosen by us. Many of these autonomous men are fathers and husbands. In their eyes, their parenting and what we usually call "sharing one's life with an other" does not impair their exclusive ownership and control over their lives. That makes sense only if we understand what *appear* to be joint projects as undertakings where different roles are assigned to each person, and as long as each does his or her job, the undertaking prospers. But it is impossible to believe that there was never a time in this project when the two did not work out who did what jobs, and how the different jobs in the complex division of labor were to be coordinated. Nor is it credible that the assignment of jobs does not change and thus the basic outline of the marriage and family is a genuinely joint project, even if it were decided early along to suppress and conceal what the two share in order to enable the man to continue his pretense of separate autonomy. Thus the man can get his needs met, while all (even those who know better) feign that he is his own man, dependent on no one.[10]

The case of racism and colonialism seems, at first, to be different. As Fanon reminds us over and over, colonialism is brutally and openly violent. There is no pretense here. The settler regimes want to extract wealth from the colonies and are prepared to use their weapons, their soldiers, their police. They are prepared to manipulate local divisions and fan them into tribal warfare and to play the relatively westernized city folks off against the more traditional country dwellers (*Les Damnés*). It does not seem appropriate here to understand that openly violent colonialism, or openly violent slavery as a pretense of separation that hides a hidden joint project. But if we look more closely, we see that even here there is a minimal joint project. Violence provokes resistance, and the perpetrators of violence must constantly calculate whether the reaction to continued or increased resistance will provoke an even more vigorous resistance, and whether they are willing to risk that. The fact that the understanding between oppressed and oppressor – the invisible line in the sand that each knows to be there – is never openly discussed does not take away the fact that they have a part in formulating the understanding because the oppressors are the ones who draw the line, and all parties to colonial exploitation, or the exploitation of slaves, know where that line is. Secretly the oppressors keeps an anxious eye on the mood of the oppressed. But that secret watchfulness is hidden beneath the pretense that master and slave, settler and native have nothing that binds them together, that they do not belong to the same race.

Under neocolonialism the hidden understanding is more obvious. The investors from the major capitalist countries require "stability." Their governments are willing to go to great length in supporting oppression – by participating in it and by paying for it – but they know that there are limits to what they can impose on the indigenous population and thus regimes that become too brutal need to be deposed. The relations between the US and Haiti are an instance of this. In both colonialism and neocolonialism, the dominant groups pretend that they have it all their way. But the underlying reality is that oppressor and oppressed are in precarious balance: the limits of oppression and the conditions under which the current situation can continue, for the time being, are jointly understood and tacitly agreed upon. Separation is mere pretense. But the pretense does not primarily concern the nature of the oppressed – that they are less than human, happy children, or sinister conspirators – but about the needs and dependencies of the oppressors. The dependence of the oppressors on the services, hard work, and products of the oppressed is hidden behind a façade of white benevolence for African Americans or American beneficence for countries of the Third World.

To summarize our brief sketch: objectification is not best understood as denying the freedom of the objectified, but as denying and concealing the joint projects that underlie human relationships. Objectification consists of the pretense that the other does not participate in the human enterprise. But objectification is always a pretense until death, that one way or another, turns us into objects completely separate from other human beings.

This pretense restricts the options a person has. Suppose I come home tired from work and take my irritation and fatigue out on my child by picking a fight. What can my child do? He can try to explain himself, but I can shout, "I am not going to listen to you!" He cannot talk. I am still bigger than he, so he cannot respond by violence. Withdrawal seems the only possible choice. Most of the ways in which we are with each other in good times are not available at that moment. They are foreclosed by my refusal to encourage a genuinely human relation, by my objectification of him. Objectification of this relatively mild and limited kind is experienced by everyone: someone makes a slightly derogatory remark about my work; someone else is distracted and does not listen to me when I want to talk. These are mild cases of objectification and very limited in their scope; they occur in relation to one other person for a short period of time.

The objectifications of racism, by contrast, are more severe – such as a large pseudo-scientific literature claiming to prove the genetic inferiority of blacks to whites. Even more important, the objectifications of racism are pervasive. Targets of racism find that sort of objectification everywhere: at work, in schools, in public places, when they go to buy something or apply for a job or try to get the attention of a bureaucrat. It is hard to get a job if the person you apply to does not listen to you. It is difficult to stay out of trouble if the police already "know" who you are just by looking at you. It is difficult to get an education, if the teacher or school official does not take you seriously.[11] These objectifications injure because they are so relentless and inescapable. The saving grace for all but the inmates of total institutions is that, e.g., blacks or women (of all colors) have created free spaces for themselves in their own communities where genuinely human relations are not only possible but thriving (Gwaltney 1980; Raymond 1986).

Small insults, or even large ones, hurt our feelings, but we can escape the bully or forget the incident. The objectification of mild or limited assaults can be evaded. But if objectification is severe and pervasive, the injuries are not only that one *feels* constantly insulted or demeaned, but that one is also constricted in large areas of one's life – work, school, in the street and public places – where the possibility of genuinely human encounters is remote except within the limits of one's own community. One's life possibility, one's possibility to be an expansive, generous person everywhere and every day, is taken away from one – for long periods of time.

Some Final Questions and Clarifications

But I can have personal relationships with only a few persons. How does this analysis of objectification apply to all the others? Racism is directed against and impinges upon the persons I do not know as much as on the persons I do know. For instance, most Poles cannot know any Jews in a country where there are, at most, 5,000 surviving Jews. But anti-Semitism is said to be as virulent there as ever.

This is an important observation, but it does not weigh heavily against the interpretation of objectification offered here. Objectification occurs in relations to other persons. But it often occurs because persons are not willing to have any but objectifying relations to many others. Thus one objectifies others not only by refusing genuinely human relations with them, but also by deciding once and for all that one will never have such relations with certain groups of people, for example, Jews, if one lives in Poland. Objectification does not only apply to actual relationships but also affects one's readiness to have new relations.

But that still does not fully respond to the initial difficulty. Not only can I only have personal relations with very few persons, but I cannot even prepare myself to have such relations with everyone. In many situations I affect by my actions persons I know as well as persons I do not know, or some I barely know. As a teacher, I give grades, or comments to students I know and to some whose face is barely familiar. If I am always trying for personal, open relationships then I will deal very differently with the students I know from the way in which I will grade or comment on the work of those I do not know. That would clearly be unfair. There appear to be many situations where the same rules apply (or ought to apply) to all and one must deal with everyone – known or not – in the same way. Here objectification, as I have explicated it in this work, seem to be required. This is a difficult problem that has received some discussion in feminist theory, but the answers are still not clear.[12] It may be that justice sometimes requires us to objectify.

Fortunately, this difficulty need not detain us because the objectification practiced by racism is not in the service of justice. Instead it serves, as Fanon often points out, the purpose of exploitation. Racist objectification is needed to enable the settlers to expropriate the resources and the work of the natives.

If we have a genuinely human relationship and we participate in it jointly, there is mutuality, there is careful attention to the Other. We each make our contribution and value that of the Other. Then it is difficult to turn around and make the others work for subsistence wages, live in hovels, and blame them for their condition. It is harder if not impossible to make little children work twelve hours in the woolen mills, as the early capitalists did, or herd country women into electronics factories to make them work for a dollar a day, as contractors for American firms do today, if you have or are prepared to have a genuinely human relation to others. Objectification is a prerequisite for colonialism and for current economic practices. Racism is a particular form of objectification in a number of ways. It serves exploitation, not justice.[13] It is enormously complex and requires an intricate network of institutions and practices to be effective. Its ideational content is somewhat different, at least, in specifics from, say, sexism.

Racism is a complex phenomenon aiming at objectification by many different paths and using many different strategies. There are different systems of strategies for the purpose of objectification aimed at different target groups: women, working people, people of color are used to clear the way for exploitation.[14] One of the important implication of the analysis of objectification offered here is that what the racist visits upon his or her targets is not, in principle, different from what we do to each other, daily and hourly. Objectification is excessively familiar and perhaps in some settings necessary. Many instances of objectification can be found in current economic practices where persons are treated as commodities and thus replaceable, and which establish hierarchical rather than mutual relationships among persons. As more and more aspects of our lives are transformed into commodities, objectification spreads and genuinely human relationships become more and more rare. We have no hope of abolishing the systematic objectifications of racism as long as we are prepared to accept objectification in the economic sphere. Conversely, we will not be able to overcome the evils of capitalist objectification if we do not also put an end to objectification by race and gender.

Notes

1   Fanon is aware of the complexities of racist practices. He acknowledges that he, as a physician to Algerians, must suppress his tendency to talk pidgin-French to his patients (see *Black Skin*, ch. 1).

2   Throughout this work I use "subject" in "subject group" in the sense of

"someone subjected to the rule or authority of another." Subject groups are dominated by other groups.

3   The reasons for choosing this interpretation are briefly, as follows. Suppose one wanted to say that all the different specific actions of the racist – infantilization, etc. – are instances of objectification. Then we would have to face up to the question raised briefly in the introductory paragraph: Do we take "objectification" as "taking someone as a (quasi-)grammatical object" or as "making someone into a thing"? Now objectification cannot be used in the first sense, for infantilizing is no more or no less taking someone as a (quasi-)grammatical object than revering, loving, including, treating with respect, etc. So if infantilization, exclusion, etc. are to count as objectification, it must be "objectification" in the sense of "making into a thing." But that has the difficulties mentioned earlier, that human beings are by definition human and cannot be made into things as long as they are alive. I will return to this difficulty below.

4   This observation has important implications for the parallel between colonialism and the holocaust which Fanon draws repeatedly. It seems clear, however, that racist domination consists of the pretense that the members of the subject group are not (fully) human. Genocide, by contrast, does not dehumanize by pretending. It kills. The distinction between racist objectification and genocide is clear. Objectification and genocide are not to be confused because violence, including killing, is one of the strategies to bring about objectification. In the holocaust the camp inmates were objectified in order to be killed. Under racism, some people are killed, in order to objectify the rest. Keeping that distinction clear is compatible with the recognition that under some conditions the purposes of the ruling groups vacillate between objectification and genocide.

5   The reader in doubt may do well to read some of the novels of Earnest J. Gaines.

6   Marx clearly toyed with a similar idea. In more than one passage he seems to suggest that under communism we would be able to be individuals in our own right to an extent unknown under capitalism. See his *Early Writings* (1963) and *The German Ideology* (with Engels, 1947).

7   Fanon recognizes this point in his insistence that the violence of colonialism can only be overcome by violence. Being trusting towards those who go to great pains to objectify you is foolish and will bring you to a premature end. Objectification can only be met by objectification. Where the objectification is violent so must the response be (Fanon 1961a).

8   This understanding of human relationships emerges from very extensive work in feminist theory of the last 20 years. I have recently discussed those sorts of relationships in considerable detail in *Beyond Separateness* (1995).

9   This is less obvious, but no different in sexist relations between men and women. Yes, men and women have projects together, such as marriage and children. But often those are not fully joint projects, but rather projects that have several agents, each of whom has a role which is fulfilled alongside those of the others. Dad has his job and so does mom, and if each does what is required then there is a family, and children get raised. After they have been married for forty years, one of them leaves but the other never knew of

his or her partner's unhappiness.

10 I have developed this in detail in the first five chapters of *Beyond Separateness*.

11 The effects of objectification go far beyond any deprivation of freedom, in any ordinary sense, because our ordinary interactions with other persons are disturbed by objectification. We do not usually claim the right to be listened to, to be free to have our job applications taken seriously, to be valued as students. But perhaps we should.

12 Carol Gilligan's work beginning with *In a Different Voice* (1982) has spawned a wide-ranging discussion of those issues. See, e.g., an essay by Joan Tronto (1989).

13 This assumes that justice does indeed require objectification. But as many feminists, beginning with Carol Gilligan have argued, that is by no means self-evident.

14 Another complication is, of course, the fact that racism does not only affect the relations between exploiters and exploited: white workers objectify those who are black; male workers objectify women.

Part II

Questioning the Human Sciences

4

Fanon's Body of Black Experience

Ronald A. T. Judy

The title that Fanon gave to the fifth chapter of *Peau noire, masques blancs* was "L'expérience vécue du Noir," which Charles Lamm Markmann translated as "The fact of blackness."[1] The translation was undoubtedly prompted by the desire to preserve his characteristic "idiomatic" style, facilitating the accessibility of Fanon's thought for an American readership. Unfortunately the idiom is arrived at through paring away those philosophical formulations of Fanon's which might have reference for a relatively broad French-language readership but would require considerable elaboration for North American audiences. A result is that the focal movement of Fanon's thought is often obscured in the English-language translation of his book.

In the instance of Fanon's title for chapter 5, that movement is made inaccessible to the English-language readership by a paring that reshapes it nearly beyond recognition. What is cut away completely is the focal concern with experience. *L'expérience vécue* is conflated into "the fact," so that the adjective *vécue* becomes the substantive. Although *vécue* can be rendered in English as something like the "factual," it is the very nature of the referenced factuality that is vexing. Is the factual that which is in-itself, independent of consciousness, or is it that which is in-itself-for-consciousness? With *vécue*, we are thus brought to ponder experience. The equivocality of *vécue* and experience is already carried over into French common idiom with the formulation *l'expérience vécue*, which Robert traces to Merleau-Ponty's translation of the German *Erlebnis*, already a philosophically charged term that comes into English as "lived-experience." Even idiomatically *l'expérience vécue* is not the "the fact" but the "lived-experience"; it is not the objectively given or an event, but the process in which objects acquire their status as such for-consciousness. It is also in this sense that it is reality.

As for Markmann's handling of the rest of Fanon's title, the participle definite article construction *du* is easily recognized. When capitalized, as it is in Fanon's title, the French *Noir* is an analogue for the English "Black," referring to a conscious identity, and not a phenomenal event. Whether or not that identity is truly a state of being is the question which this chapter attempts to explore. So Markmann's unfortunate translation notwithstanding, "L'expérience vécue du Noir" is not about the "The fact of blackness" but "The lived-experience of the Black."

This translation of Fanon's title has the advantage over Markmann's translation in that it is more *descriptive* of the principal concern of the chapter: how can the existence of the black, *l'être du Noir* (*Pn* 88 / *BS* 109), be properly understood? The question recalls the chief presumption of *Peau noire, masques blancs* as stated in its introduction: "In effect, we think that only a psychoanalytic interpretation of the black problem [*du problème noir*] will reveal the anomalies of affect responsible for the complex edifice" (*Pn* 8 / *BS* 10). It is worthwhile to recall as well that this presumption is made in the service of Fanon's attempt at "a total lysis [*lyse totale*] of this morbid universe [*cet univers morbide*]" (ibid.), on the estimation "that an individual should assume the universalism inherent in the human condition" (ibid.). Yet psychoanalysis was not merely to capture from anthropology and ethnography the black as the subject-matter of objective study. Fanon struggled to get beyond the consideration of the black as an object to a consideration of the "authentic forces" at work in human existence. In revealing, through his analysis of the existence of the black, the anomalies of affect responsible for what Fanon comes to call *nègro-phobogénèsis* (*Pn* 123 / *BS* 151), he reveals a pathology that is coterminous with the very symbolic order of modernity, and not just colonialism.

The paramount task of *Peau noire, masques blancs* is to understand what the consciousness of and for the black is by understanding how it is, its process of becoming. It can be said that the entire book is arguably organized around the attempt to understand the forms of consciousness that occur in history. Whereas, since Freud, psychoanalysis had elaborated the forms of consciousness as the middle-term between subjectivity and objectivity, Fanon regarded them as the meeting-ground of subjectivity, objectivity, and the social. Fanon's claim is to have supplemented the ontogenetic perspective of Freud with the sociogenetic.[2] Or, in an even more crude formulation, the subject-matter of *Peau noire, masques blancs* is the forms of individual and social consciousness.

Fanon does not choose just any forms of consciousness but selects from those individual forms of experience deemed to be prevalent in the development of consciousness. So, for example, he follows Freud in regarding the family constellation as the primary psychic circumstance and engages Lacan's analysis of the mirror stage as the primordial form of the unity of consciousness to explain the aetiology of negrophobia. In his explanation of the aetiology of the Antillean's neurosis he analyses events of social encounter and confrontation, elaborating Mannoni's thesis that the encounter of difference characterizing the colonial situation produces collective neuroses and psychoses. To that extent, *Peau noire, masques blancs* appears to be comparable to a social psychology of racism. But Fanon also goes beyond such a social psychology, in that his consideration of the existence of the black in terms of lived-experience goes some way toward presenting the process in which true existence comes to be for-itself-and-for-others. This same process is what preoccupies him in *Les Damnés de la terre*, where it is reformulated as violence, which is how Fanon describes what he thinks of as consciousness in action (*en acte*). Although a detailed elaboration of the moments in Fanon's formulation of violence is more than I am prepared to do in this essay, it is worth noting that in that formulation the project of realizing black culture is disposed of as preempting authentic freedom.[3] What will be of importance to us a little later on, therefore, is how the existence of the black is a moment in the process of consciousness becoming in-itself and for-itself and for-others. Accordingly, the task here will be to adduce from Fanon's concern with affect the notion of the event of experience that concern presumes and to establish the relationship between that notion and his subsequent theory of violence. Affect has a definite epistemic status in Fanon's thought as the expression of an order of consciousness that is extra-representational. So, in a certain sense, what Fanon is striving for when claiming to attempt a total lysis of the morbid universe of colonialism is the recollection of the event of experience.

In order to understand the relationship between the event of experience and violence, we must first keep in mind that when Fanon is concerned with experience in *Peau noire, masques blancs*, it is always with regard to Hegel and hence to existence. That is to say, he is concerned with what Hegel called the experience of consciousness. But Fanon is quite emphatic about the inapplicability of Hegel's concept of experience to the colonial situation. For instance, in the opening page of "L'expérience vécue du Noir," he states:

> As long as the Black is with his own, he will not have occasion, with the exception of petty internal struggles, to experience his existence for others

[*son être pour autrui*]. There is undoubtedly the moment of existence-for-another (*Füranderesein*) [*l'être pour l'autre*] that Hegel speaks of, but all ontology is rendered unrealizable in a society [of] colonized and civilized . . . There is an impurity in the *Weltanschauung* of a colonized people, a defect [*taré*] that interdicts all ontological explication. Someone could perhaps object that this is so for every individual, but that obscures a fundamental problem. Ontology, when it has admitted setting aside existence once and for all, does not permit us to understand the existence of the Black. For the Black [*le Noir*] no longer has to be black [*noir*], but must be it in the perception of the White [*en face du Blanc*]. Some may take it in their heads to respond to us that the situation is reciprocal [*est à double sens*]. We respond that that is false. The Black has no ontological resistance in the eyes of the White. (*Pn* 88 / *BS* 109–10)

Fanon's formulation, "Car le Noir n'a plus à être noir" [For the Black no longer has to be black] is subtle and enigmatic. The subject of this sentence is the black; its action is the negation of being black. That negation is occurring "now," and as such is pointing to something that "has been." This is made more accessible if we ask the implied question: "What is the black now?" The answer given here is that the black *now* is not what he *was*: black. In other words, when we try to speak about what the black is now we can only point to what the black "has been." What has been *is* not, so it can be "now" only by virtue of the fact that its "having been" is negated by us. The black that Fanon is speaking of is, thus, the *negation of the negation* of the black that he meant now. This is a denegation (*Verneinung*), the point of which is not simply to establish that there is a paradox of sense certainty revealed by language when speaking of how "the black no longer has to be black," but that that play of language entails an attitude of perception, which is not the black's. Fanon writes in the subordinate clause "mais à l'être en face du Blanc" [but must be it in the perception of the White]. Being black opposite (as in *vis-à-vis*), or in front of (as in the presence of) the white is to be something black *for* the white that is not the black *in-itself* and *for-itself*. Denegation draws our attention to where Fanon wants it, on the process of becoming that is the consciousness of the black. But this consciousness has no ontological status in the perception of the white. Nor should it. Understanding how this works means dwelling a little more with the distinction Fanon wants to make between objects of sense certainty and those of perception.

What is the difference between the black and being black? Grammatically, the black is the subject, and being black is its predicate. Insofar as existence is the issue at hand, the distinction of subject and predicate warrants consideration. Assuming that only that which is subject to predication exists essentially, then the black is essentially, and being black, which we would now call blackness, is accidental. This makes a certain amount of sense in the immediate context of Fanon's asserting that the black no longer has to be black. It runs afoul, however, of his claiming that the black has no ontological resistance for the white, and that ontology does not permit understanding the existence of the black. The latter claim has as an appositive the claim that ontology has finally set aside existence, and so goes directly to the question of the inapplicability of Hegel's understanding of experience to the lived-experience of the black. Thus, we can go no further without giving some consideration to Hegel's understanding.

When writing about the "difficulties in the development of his bodily schema" that "the man of color encounters in the white world," Fanon states:

> All around the body there reigns an atmosphere of certain uncertainty. I know that if I want to smoke, I'll have to reach out my right arm and take the pack of cigarettes lying at the other end of the table. The matches, however, are in the drawer on the left, and I'll have to lean back slightly. All these movements are made not out of habit but out of implicit knowledge. A slow composition of my *self* as a body in the middle of a spatio-temporal world, such seems to be the schema. It does not impose itself on me, it is rather, a definitive structuring of the self and the world – definitive because it establishes an effective dialectic between my body and the world. (*Pn* 89 / *BS* 110–11)

In relation to the problem of the possibility of experience, Fanon refers to the totality of theoretical knowledge of existing beings. In this sense, experience designates the process by which determinate judgments are arrived at about things. Insofar as to be understood in a determinate way an object must be presupposed to exist in the phenomenal world, all determinate types of experience – say the experience of color, and smell – are reducible to the experience of existence. This sense of experience and existence is far more Kant's than it is Hegel's. It is Fanon's only with regard to the body, that is, with regard to the existence of biological entities with black skin-color. But this is precisely the being black that the black no longer has to be, except in the perception of the white. In his insistence on understanding the existence of black, he intends something else. To get to that something else we still need better to understand the Hegelian concept of experience he appears to be refuting.

Kantian experience entails the notion of demonstrating-intuition: the seeking recourse in the intuition of something as the means of its confirmation. If such a demonstrating-intuition is not restricted to the sensible, but understood to mean the procedure or manner of confirming a judgment, then it is plausible to talk of the intuition of essences (an example of such is logic, the intuition required in determining structural relations, such as that of a subject to a predicate in a proposition). Because this relation is extra-sensible, it needs to be demonstrated by "rendering its essence 'evident' as it *emerges out of the relationship itself*" (Heidegger 1988: 19–20). This, of course, is the sort of phenomenological experience Husserl strives for. Fanon appears to embrace this more contemporary notion of phenomenological experience, *pace* Merleau-Ponty, from whom he very likely got the concept *l'expérience vécue*. For, in determining the relation of the subject black and the predicate black in the proposition "the black no longer has to be black," he recognizes the essence of this relationship is consciousness, made evident as the distinction between the black and being black. The focus of his concern with the experience of existence is affectivity, then, and not the theoretical understanding of things. Such a reading supports the understanding of Fanon's project as being a sort of phenomenological existentialism. It would be dangerous, however, to conclude that he understands the existence of the black in this way without some further explanation of Hegel apropos of Fanon.

Admittedly, the Husserlian phenomenological experience is different from Hegel's concept of experience, whose emphasis is not on verifiability in terms of the confirmation of intuitions of any sort. Rather, it is on the process of undergoing experiences of something in the course of which the something itself will be confirmed. In Hegel's *Phenomenology*, these experiences are of consciousness, being "in reality, the detailed history of the education [*Bildung*] of consciousness itself."[4] In this regard, Fanon's denegation of the black is a determinate negation, it is taken as the result of that from which it emerges; thus, it is a new form that is a moment in the process of consciousness becoming in-itself and for-itself. This point will become crucial later, when we consider Fanon's refusal of negritude. What is important now is that in the process of coming to know itself, consciousness distinguishes itself from something, while at the same time relating itself to it. This something is said to exist *for* consciousness; and the determination of the being of something for consciousness is knowing (*PS* 52; *PG* 76). This being-for-another (*Füranderesein*), which Fanon acknowledges occurs even with the black, is distinguished from being-in-itself (*Ansichsein*). That which is related to knowledge (*Füranderesein*), but posited as exiting beyond this relationship (*Ansichsein*) is called truth.

To inquire into the truth of consciousness, then, is to ask what consciousness is in-itself. Yet, in this same inquiry consciousness is what is related to knowledge; it is for-consciousness. If knowledge is conceptual, in Hegel's terms, the Concept (*Begriff*), and the in-itself is the object that exists essentially, then the inquiry into consciousness is positivist. Verification consists of determining the correspondence of the Concept to the object (*PS* 53; *PG* 77). Yet that determination is of consciousness, that is, the object in-itself, seems to be only for consciousness in the way that consciousness knows it as such. What is taken to be something *in-itself* is only something in-itself for consciousness. To the extent that this is so, consciousness is of two moments: that in which "something is for it the in-itself; and knowledge, or the being of the object for consciousness" (*PS* 54; *PG* 77). These moments are related such that an alteration in the knowledge of the object changes the object, and change in the object gets an alteration of knowledge of it.

For Hegel, this dialectical movement "which consciousness exercises on it self" is what is called experience (*PS* 55; *PG* 78). Here is where Hegel seeks to get past the Kantian representation in which the senses present to consciousness a manifold that appears as something to perception. The in-itself of this appearance, its true essence, is unknowable. That is, it is *in-itself* beyond its being so *for* consciousness. With Hegel, however, what appears as the object in-itself for consciousness in being known as such, is changed for consciousness, becoming something that is the *in-itself* only *for consciousness* (*PS* 55; *PG* 79). This being-for-consciousness of this in-itself is the truth of consciousness; it is the essence or object of consciousness that "experience has made of it [*Gestalten des Bewusstseins*]; what appears to us as being-in-itself for-consciousness thus also appears as determinate moments as consciousness emerges in relation to them in the process of becoming. The examination of or inquiry into this process is what Hegel called the *Science of the Experience of Consciousness*, which, it will be recalled, is the original title of the *Phenomenology of Spirit*.

In leaving this exposition of Hegel's concept of experience, it warrants noting that the movement from the *Science of the Experience of Consciousness* to the *Phenomenology* results from understanding that in the experience of itself that consciousness goes through, it presses forward to its true existence. Consciousness will achieve the moment in which it no longer has the "semblance [*Schein*] of being burdened with something alien, with what is only for it, and some sort of alien 'other'" (*PS* 56; *PG* 81). At this point, appearance becomes identical with essence, and so the exposition [*Darstellung*] of essence will coincide with the "authentic Science of Spirit [*eigentlich Wissenschaft des Geistes*]" (*PS* 57; *PG* 81).

With these considerations in mind, returning to Fanon's assertion that the black no longer has to be black, the following can be stated. Fanon's critique of ontology notwithstanding, he remains engaged with the Hegelian concept of experience in his concern about the lived-experience of the black. The denegation of being black is the moment in the process of the black experience of consciousness in which it unburdens itself of the appearance of being something else. This entails the revelation of being itself, in perhaps the most absolute, and hence Hegelian, way (this is important because, as we will see later, Fanon's chief difficulty is in explaining the relationship between absolute being and blackness). Fanon's observation about the unrealizability of ontology in the bifurcated colonial society is not a call for the abandonment of ontology. On the contrary, it is insistence on the need to realize ontology by returning it to existence. The agenda is to correct the situation so that the black has ontological resistance in the eyes of the white. For Fanon, then, the fundamental problem that is obscured by ontology is the experience of consciousness of the black; that is, the process of consciousness becoming in-itself and for-itself and-for-another. Recall that even for the phenomenological experience in order for something to exist it must be presupposed as such, that is, it must be present as in-existence for some consciousness – it is intended. Thus, *what* something is in-itself, its true or essential existence, is *how* it is thought. Fanon's assertion is not that no one thinks of the black, but that there is no philosophical thought of the thought of the black. His critique of ontology is that in setting aside existence, it excludes whatever form of consciousness attends the black in the becoming of absolute spirit, because it has already been reduced and tied down to the moment of existence in-itself and for-another.

Returning to the opening page of "L'expérience vécue du Noir," Fanon embarks on his examination of the experience of consciousness here. What has gone before was an excursus of the field, the exposition of the capacity of psychoanalytic interpretation for discovering the quotidian psychopathology of negrophobia.[5] It is with "L'expérience vécue du Noir," however, that the examination of negrophobia truly begins. And it begins at a peculiar moment, that of presenting the experience of being recognized as a *nègre* in the actual world: " 'Sale nègre!' ou simplement 'Tiens, un nègre!' " [" 'Dirty nigger!' Or simply, 'Look, a negro!' "] (*Pn* 88 / *BS* 109).

Something needs to be born in mind before continuing. Being recognized as *nègre* is not the same thing as being perceived as *l'homme de couleur*, "the man of color," or *le Noir*, "the Black." Fanon employs these terms with relative consistency to designate that consciousness that is in-itself and for-itself, in contradistinction to the *nègre*. The sense of *nègre* is imprecise throughout *Peau noire, masques blancs* in a rather significant way. Although always referring to a specific order of representation in which *nègre* designates an aggregate identity, that identity is at times merely descriptive, and at other times highly charged with a negative value. In the first instance it is something like "Negro," and in the second something like "nigger." Whereas both the English-language "Negro" and "nigger" are cognates of the Latin *niger*, the former has a descriptive, and the latter a pejorative connotation.[6] The single French term *nègre*, also derived from the same Latin root, has both the descriptive and pejorative connotations.[7] This equivocality of *nègre* is crucial to the movement of Fanon's thought; it underscores the extent to which even the seemingly neutral descriptive terms presumes a dialectic in which *le nègre* is the antithesis of *l'homme*. Translating *nègre* varyingly as "Negro" and "nigger" means losing sight of this dialectic, so it will occur in the French throughout this essay. To become *nègre* is to die as a human. Although the implication is of the "social-death" of slavery – the historical enslavement of African in the New World – Fanon is concerned with expositing and analyzing the quotidian occurrences of the *nègre* as an anomaly of affect. The method of exposition in "L'expérience vécue du Noir" is that of autobiographical recollection, the presentation of specific lived moments in which there is a conscious awareness of what is becoming *nègre*. Inasmuch as these lived experiences of becoming the *nègre* are presented in the movement of the moments of recollection, in a very specific sense, "L'expérience vécue du Noir" is the presenting of the experience of consciousness. It recollects the process of the dialectic.

Bearing these things in mind, it can be said that "L'expérience vécue du Noir" does not commence its recollection from the first moment of consciousness – the moment when consciousness is aware of itself in-itself and for-itself has past, and now it sees itself for-another.

> I arrived in the world anxious to make sense of things, my spirit filled with desire to be at the origin of the world, and here I discovered myself an object amongst other objects.
>
> Imprisoned in this overwhelming objectivity, I implored others. Their liberating regard, running over my body that suddenly becomes smooth, returns to me a lightness that I believed lost, and, absenting me from the world, returns me to the world. But there, just at the opposite slope, I stumble, and the other, by gestures, attitudes, looks, fixed me, in the sense that one fixes a chemical preparation with a dye. I was furious, demanding an explication . . . Nothing happened. I exploded. Now the tiny pieces are collected by another self. (*Pn* 88 / *BS* 109)

We have already seen that the focus of Fanon's concern with this moment of existence-for-another (*Füranderesein*) is the problematic of the man of color's bodily schema in the white world. There are two moments in his formulation of this problematic. We have considered the first moment in which there emerges a definitive dialect between self, body, and world, a movement in and among objects, where otherness itself (*this* pack of cigarettes, *here* on *this* table) brings about self-posses-sion and self-sameness. At this moment the only property of conscious-ness known to it is as a universal unity an in-itself that is for-itself, and that is for-itself for-another. "A slow composition of my *self* as a body in the middle of a spatio-temporal world, such seems to be the schema" (*Pn* 89 / *BS* 111). The second moment brings about something else. Once again, we have the recollection of dialectic.

> Below the coporeal schema I had sketched a historico-racial schema. The elements that I used had been provided for me not by "residual sensations and perceptions primarily of a tactile, vestibular, kinesthetic, and visual character," but by the other, the white man, who had woven me out of a thousand details, anecdotes, stories. I thought that what I had in hand was to construct a physiological self, to balance space, to localize sensations, and here I was called on for more . . . "*Tiens, un nègre!*". (*Pn* 90 / *BS* 111–12)

The movement between these two moments is, arguably, an echo of the movement in Hegel's *Phenomenology* by which the experience of consciousness moves through perception and comes to the understand-ing of force. We are now at the beginning of Fanon's own understanding of forces, in which, unlike Hegel's, force as the thought of the dialectic (*Kraft*) is identified with the force of state (*Macht*), whose appearance is violence (*Gewalttätigkeit*). But the road back to and past Hegel is not a direct one, and the concern with force cannot be properly gained without following Fanon to where he is leading now.

The next recollection of being-for-another is that of being-for-self-as-another. This is not the sense of consciousness in-itself, nor even of consciousness in the body as an object, rather it is awareness of con-sciousness in-itself for-another: "Attacked from a plurality of points, the corporeal schema crumbles, ceding its place to an epidermal-racial schema" (p. 90). The discovery of the sublimation of the corporeal by the racial schema brings about a new form of consciousness: "I see in these white regards that it is not a new man who has entered, but a new type of man, a new genus. What, a *nègre!*" This new consciousness will be in-itself and for-itself, as well as for-another. It recognizes its negritude as a form of consciousness, the meeting-grounds on which the unity of the psychological to the historical consideration of black con-sciousness is determined.

The price of that determination is a creeping idealist monism where "negritude appears as the minor term of a dialectical progression: the theoretical and practical assertion of the supremacy of the white is its thesis; the position of negritude as an antithetical value is the moment of negativity" (Sartre 1948: xl). The capital outlay required to counter Sartre's assessment staggers Fanon. In the negritude of Césaire and Senghor, "the black consciousness is given as an absolute density, as filled with itself, a stage prior to any split, any abolition of self by desire." But such a procedure, as Fanon effectively reveals in his analysis of the pathology of Negro phobogenesis, is finally symptomatic of negrophobia. The only way through is in the examination of the experience of consciousness, whereby consciousness emerges *with* experience and is not a consciousness *of* experience. This, of course, is the science of the experience of consciousness that is Hegel's. What Sartre has done is to call it by its "proper" name; in so doing he "has destroyed the black enthusiasm" by appropriating negritude to the History of Consciousness (*Pn* 107, 111 / *BS* 132–3, 136–7). Protesting that he "*needed* not to know," Fanon is stymied by Sartre's naming.

> My Negro consciousness does not hold itself out as a lack. It *is* its own follower . . . What is certain is that, at the very moment when I was trying to grasp my own being, Sartre, who remained The Other . . . was reminding me that my *negritude* was only a minor term. In all truth, in all truth I tell you, my shoulders slipped out of the framework of the world, my feet could no longer feel the touch of the ground. Without a *nègre* past, without a *nègre* future, it was impossible for me to realize [*d'exister*] my *nègreness* [*nègrerie*]. Not yet white, no longer all the more so black, I was damned. Jean-Paul Sartre had forgotten that the *nègre* suffers in his body quite differently from the White. (*Pn* 111–12 / *BS* 137–8)

Since Gendzier, the conventional reading of this is as Fanon's acknowledging the validity of Sartre's analysis, but adhering to negritude nevertheless because of its elaboration on the question of personal identity, which is taken to be the preoccupation of *Peau noire, masques blancs*. Accordingly, as Fanon's concerns turn away from the psychobiographical towards the political he gradually relinquishes his sympathy, and by *Les Damnés de la terre* rejects negritude as politically limited. This view, admittedly, finds support in Fanon's footnote to the last sentence of the above passage:

> If Sartre's studies of the existence of others remain exact (to that extent, we reply, yes *Being and Nothingness* describes an alienated consciousness) their application to *nègre* consciousness reveals itself to be fallacious. That is because the White is not only the Other, but the master, whether real or imaginary.

Then again, as McCullogh has pointed out, taking some care with the text, Fanon's thinking on negritude is very complicated and caught up in the tension between the psychoanalysis of colonialism and his praxis of radical political action.[8] But we should be mindful that it was the dialectic that brought Fanon to Sartre, it was his need to understand the very process of becoming that seemed to make the *nègre* a necessity. Sartre's thought is a moment in the experience of the "dialectic that brings necessity into the foundation of my freedom and drives me out of myself. It shatters my unreflected position" (*Pn* 109 / *BS* 135). That is to say, the distinction between the subjective necessity and objective failings of negritude that McCullogh, correctly, discerns to be at work in Fanon's thinking is the process of the dialectic in which he recognizes negritude as a moment in the process of achieving absolute freedom, but not its force. Or, more exactly, he cannot give an account of how negritude either transforms or facilitates the transformation of the colonized masses into a polity, that is, into a willful collective consciousness. Negritude fails, to put things bluntly, to teach the people, to bring thought to action in the articulation of a new human subject.

The challenge facing Fanon is how to move from the psychological to the historical consideration of the *nègre* without losing all hope of gaining the event of experience. The claim of difference in the experience of the body between the *nègre* and the White, which Fanon makes in reaction to Sartre's appropriating negritude to the history of consciousness, poses significant problems. But what is the *nègre* who suffers his body? More precisely, what is the nature of the *nègre* consciousness that "suffers"?

These questions go straight to the conceptual difficulties raised by Fanon's analysis of the *nègre* and psychopathology, the focus of which is the Antillean. And as will be seen a little later on, the chief concern there is whether or not Fanon strives to think an extra-representational consciousness. If so, how does it unfold, that is, what is it unfolding for?

There is a temptation to read *Peau noire, masques blancs* in terms of Fanon's being burdened with Cartesian dualism. Proceeding from the premise of the homogenesis of consciousness – it is either wholly somatic or discursive in origin – Fanon presupposes a hierarchical relationship in which freedom is understood as consciousness in-itself against the body. To become truly free the black must gain this self-consciousness in spite of his body; he must no longer be a *nègre*. This reading confronts substantial difficulties, however, when it engages the text of chapter 6, "The *nègre* and psychopathology," where Fanon determines that the cause of the Antillean's psychosis has to do with the symbolization of the body.

The problem seems to stem from the difference between the *imago* of the "black" body, and its symbolization – between the representation of the body and the symbolic matrix the representation exemplifies. Fanon attempts to understand this difference within the framework of Lacan's theory of the mirror stage, which he engages in a lengthy (two-page) footnote (*Pn* 131 n. 25 / *BS* 161 n. 25). What is of importance to us here is that Fanon recognizes, according to his reading of Lacan's mirror stage, that the foundation for the Antillean knowing him- or herself subjectively as a conscious unity is in the infant's identification with the specular image of its own body. This unity of consciousness, this "I," is manifested in a primordial form, before its objectification in the dialectic of identification with the other, and before language restores it to its function as universal subject (Lacan: 90). It is the basis for the self that will function as the subject once it enters into the symbolic order, once it is taken up in language. Reiterating this fact later on in the Lacan note, Fanon states: "We shall see that this discovery is fundamental: every time the subject sees his image and recognizes it, it is always acclaimed in the same way as 'the mental oneness which is inherent in him'" (*Pn* 131n / *BS* 161 n. 25). And a little further on he stresses that for the Antillean the symbolic subject is not reducible to the *imago* of the body: "We affirm that for the Antilleans the mirror hallucination is always neutral. To those who have told us that they have experienced it, we regularly ask the same question: 'What color were you?' – 'I had no color'" (ibid.).

The representational construction of the *nègre* is recognized as belonging to a complex of historical praxis, whose organized collective expression is commonly called culture, and whose psychic expression is the collective unconscious. In other words, Fanon understands the symbolic matrix exemplified in the representational construction to be identical with the collective unconscious. What, then, does the *nègre* symbolize in this collective unconscious? We must take care to follow Fanon closely in addressing this question.

The first response we find to it is in chapter 6. We are told in the delineation of the pathology of negrophobia, that to suffer from this phobia is to be afraid of the biological. "The *nègre* symbolizes the biological" danger (*Pn* 134 / *BS* 166). This is reiterated in Fanon's reporting the results of his administering an association test on some 500 Europeans (French, German, Italian) in which he inserted the word *Negro*. By his assessment in almost 60 percent of the replies the word solicited associations with sexuality, physical prowess, animality, and evil. There is no doubt, "the *nègre* symbolizes the biological". Things get more complicated, however, with the assertion that "European culture poses an *imago* of the *nègre* that is responsible for all conflicts that may arise" (*Pn* 134–6 / *BS* 166–9). The complication has to do with what is merely implicit in this study: the relationship between the symbolic value of the word *nègre* and the biological entities so designated.

If, as Fanon's analysis has determined thus far, the *imago* is the unconscious prototype – the trace of primary (familial) intersubjective relationships – by which the subject represents the other to itself, then two problems present themselves. First, does this mean that each of the 300 subjects who associated *nègre* with the biological had an experience with another entity that is represented in its imaginary scheme as *nègre*? Second, how do such individual subjective representations of experience become or constitute a collective unconscious, as opposed to a numerical aggregate? Of course, it is clear that Fanon is not asserting this at all, but is analyzing the cumulative effect of particular manifestations of this *imago*, and inferring from these a common symbolic matrix exemplified in the *imago*. This procedure is made clear some pages later when it is determined that this symbolic matrix constitutes the collective unconscious of the European.

Contrary to Jung's locating the aetiology of the collective unconscious in physiological material – it is genetically encoded in the cerebral matter – for Fanon it is cultural, which in this instance means a transferable representational schema (*Pn* 152 / *BS* 188). We are brought, thus, to understand that the European collective unconscious is constitutive of European culture. And in European culture the *nègre* has one function: that of symbolizing the lower emotions, the baser inclination, the darker side of the soul. In the collective unconscious of *homo occidentalis*, "the *nègre* – or if one prefers, the color black – symbolizes evil, sin, wretchedness, death, war, and famine" (*Pn* 154 / *BS* 190–1).

Knowing what the *nègre* symbolizes in this collective unconscious does not bring us any closer to understanding the relationship between the symbolic value of the word *nègre* and the biological entities so designated. Knowing that the collective consciousness is a transferable representational schema (culture) does, however, help in understanding how those same entities identify with that symbolization. Although *Peau noire, masques blancs* contains no careful analysis of the socioeconomic structures of colonialism in the Antilles, focusing instead on the psychology of colonialism, those structures are implied in Fanon's notion of "unreflected cultural imposition" (*Pn* 154 / *BS* 191).[9] Because the Antillean has been subjected to the imposition of the European representational scheme, "there is no reason to be surprised when an Antillean exposed to waking-dream therapy relives the same fantasies as a European" (ibid.). It is noteworthy, however, that Fanon does not regard the Antillean as a European, but as an Antillean who "has the same collective unconscious as the European" (*Pn* 154 / *BS* 190). The distinction is crucial to understanding the relationship between the symbolism and designation of the *nègre*.

In his analysis, Fanon establishes negrophobia as a constitutive feature of the Antillean conscious. It is normal for the Antillean to be negrophobic, as long as his perception always occurs on the level of the imaginary where the ego identifies with the master discourse of Europe. It comes to psychopathology when the imaginary structures are short circuited, and "the Antillean has recognized himself as a *nègre*" (*Pn* 154–5 / *BS* 190–2). How this occurs was recollected in "L'expérience vécue de Noir." Fanon tells us here that what occurs is at around age 20, when the collective conscious in which the *nègre* symbolizes evil and the baser elements is repressed (ibid.), the subject becomes conscious that it is a *nègre*. There is no doubt here, Fanon means that the subject becomes aware of the fact that it is black, which is in conflict with its neutral body *imago*. The Antillean neurosis is due to the failure of the ego's proper identification with his body's *imago*. Or, more precisely, the ego's identification is with the order of representation in which his body symbolizes the no good, and that becomes the truth of what his body's *imago* has been. Or, more precisely, the ego's identification is with the order of representation in which the body symbolizes the no good, and that becomes the truth of what his body's *imago* has been. It could be stated that the event of experiencing the body will have been "properly experienced when the collective unconscious provides the ego with a conceptual framework. In which case, the *nègre* that is perceived by the conscious is not an event of experience at all, but a displacing of the event by the representation of the unconscious. Keep in mind, however, that the *imago*, even for Fanon, is representation, and not a perception. In terms of sensory material of the representation *nègre*, it is auditory; or visual in the case of its graphic representation.

Take for instance his example of the paranoid *nègre* who, having completed the baccalaureate, has gone to the Sorbonne to study to be a teacher of philosophy. The neurosis is accounted for as "the consequence of the institution in the consciousness of the slaves, in place of the repressed 'African' spirit, a representation of the Master's authority, an authority instituted in the innermost depths of the collective [consciousness] and in charge of surveillance there, like a garrison of the conquered city" (*Pn* 118 / *BS* 145). This citation of René Ménil quoting Michel Leiris carries a lot of significance. Not only does it indicate that there are different forms of consciousness, and the repression and substitution on one form by the other in a hierarchical order, but that the subjective identity, the self of the *nègre* results from this process. In the stages in the development of consciousness, the "African" is the primordial form.

This account recalls Fanon's elaboration of identification according to his reading of Lacan's mirror stage. In the case of the paranoid *nègre* at the Sorbonne, the primordial "I" gives way to the ego. According to Lacan, the ego as such really only takes on its specificity after the Oedipal passage. Fanon, however, was emphatic in asserting that "the Oedipus complex is far from coming into being among Negroes," and "that in the French Antilles 97 percent of the families cannot produce one Oedipal neurosis" (*Pn* 123–4 / *BS* 152). The objection is further supported by a bold assertion:

> With the exception of a few misfits within a closed environment, we can say that every neurosis, every abnormal manifestation, every affective erethism in the Antillean is the product of his cultural situation. In other words, there is a constellation of postulates, a series of propositions that slowly and subtly, with the help of books, newspapers, schools and their texts, advertisements, films, radio, penetrate an individual – constituting the world-view of the group to which one belongs. In the Antilles that world-view is white because no black voice exists. (*Pn* 124 / *BS* 152)

Fanon has disposed of the Oedipal complex as necessarily constitutive of neurosis, from the family constellation as the primary psychic circumstance to the cultural constellation. This does not mean, however, that he disposed of the tripartite topography of the psyche – ego, superego, id – with which Lacan conceives of the Oedipal complex in all its forms. To the contrary, he carries it over to what he calls here the cultural constellation, in such a way that culture and family are analogous constellations.

> In Europe and in every country characterized as civilized or civilizing, the family is a miniature of the nation. As the child emerges from the shadow of his parents, he finds himself once more among the same laws, the same principles, the same values. A normal child that has grown up in a normal family will be a normal man. (*Pn* 114–15 / *BS* 141–2)

I do not intend in this essay to explore in any detail the inconsistency with which Fanon refers to the collective historical and material circumstances that are beside individual psychic phenomena; he refers to them varyingly as "nation," "society," "culture," or "cultural constellation." It is enough for purposes here to note that with regard to the supra-familial origin of neurosis, these terms function as synonyms for that constellation that is other than the familial. Although it should also be noted that his use of "nation" is all the more confusing in that it seems to denote race, as well as the juridico-political constellation, i.e., the state. In any case, Fanon appears to understand the *nègre* as a particular type of historical consciousness, whose psychic structure can only be understood as emerging at the juncture of incommensurate symbolic matrices.

The Antillean's abnormality appears to stem, then, from the radical incompatibility of the two constellations. The result is the dissolution of the ego, the split, or double consciousness of the *nègre*: the same sort of disruption of the ego Freud discovered to be the consequence of different identifications seizing hold of consciousness in turn. Although Fanon traces the genesis of this ego-disruption to the incompatibility of the cultural and familial constellations – in opposition to Freud's and Lacan's finding it in aberrant outcomes of the Oedipal complex *within* the family constellation – he still presumes the constitution of the ego to be a function of what Freud called *nachtraglichkeit*, or deferred action. In temporal terms, the mirror event, the primordial "I," establishes what will have been the ego *after* the later event of the historico-racial schema. As Fanon observes in his lengthy footnote on Lacan's mirror stage, "there is on the part of the Antillean a negation [*méconnaissance*] of his *nègre* quality" (*Pn* 131n / *BS* 161n). This can be taken to mean that what appears in the corporeal schema in which the Antillean is primordially will only be recognized as having been the *nègre* after consciousness becomes the *nègre* of *homo occidentalis*. Very much like the Lacanian infant, the Antillean experiences an event (its body) and although having perception of it does not have the conceptual framework for understanding. Nonetheless, there is a "perceptual memory" that later, when the understanding of the European culture has been achieved, is recalled. But, because the Antillean's self identity is in terms of the white, what is now remembered is intolerable. So when the scene of corporeal schema get recalled by something in life – *Tiens un nègre!* – the self is constructed in such a way as to prevent the actual perception from coming to mind. Instead the self experiences the affect that it would have felt at the time of the original event if it had been the self it is now.

We could say that the original event at the time of its happening is what will have been the trauma of recognizing oneself as a *nègre*. It is in this sense that the *nègre* becomes from nothing – it is a *méconnaissance*. Care must be taken here. When considering the psychopathology of the *nègre*, Fanon's claim is that the Antillean has no remembrance of the event of cultural imposition, only the affective experience of the traumatic, which is why the memory is articulated in various neuroses. So the *nègre* is a symptom of a series of traumatic scenes: "The calamity of the man of color is he has been enslaved. The calamity and inhumanity of the White is he has killed man somewhere" (*Pn* 187 / *BS* 231).

This repression is a constitutive function of the colonial economy; it is the primary violence that makes the colonial scene determine its psychopathologies. Accordingly, the colonized's neuroses stem from unremembered reminiscences of the experience of events. These reminiscences do not erode with the passage of time; they retain their affective force, or such force retains them. But what is the nature of this force? In our preliminary reading of Fanon's attempt to examine the lived-experience of the black, the force appears to be that of self-consciousness, which begs the question since that force is already symbolic. The *nègre* is a symbolic repetition of the experience of the event; and it is only through its repetition that the event is recognized. It is recognized only symbolically. Revealing the symbolic necessity of this recognition in order to get beyond it to the true experience of the traumatic event is the principal objective of the analysis of *nègre* psychopathology. In seeing the phobic image of the *nègre* as a constitutive function of the modern psyche Fanon dwells on the problem with memory, relative to the trauma of colonialism.

Yet Fanon's understanding of the *nègre* as symptom of psychopathology yields an analysis that fails to explain the agency by which an event is transcribed as a sign: he cannot think of memory relative to consciousness without figuring out how the phenomenal character of the event of experience is perceived as affect, except that he rejects the very idea of consciousness as a function of energy cathexis. That is to say, in the experience of consciousness presented in the recollection of "L'expérience vécue du Noir," the body is lost as the cause of the structure of consciousness, and becomes its object (*Pn* 182 / *BS* 225). What is at stake in Sartre's presumptuous forgetting "that the *nègre* suffers in his body quite differently from the White" is exactly what Fanon *needed* not to know. There is no *nègre* body, only the *nègre imago*, and it is an object in-itself only for the consciousness that is human. True, the *nègre* is somehow imprisoned in his body, but only in the sense that it *is* in the dialectic of the corporeal and racial schemas. If it is this paradoxical moment in the becoming of the consciousness that must be overcome in order to gain freedom, then why does Fanon insist that what must be remembered is the fact of the *nègre* body? Precisely because the *nègre* is a symptom of the repression of the experience of the body. What Fanon calls "corporeal scheme" is arguably the expression (*Darstellung*) of the essence of consciousness *along with* "the residual sensations and perceptions primarily of a tactile, vestibular, kinesthetic, and visual character."

Granting that, if the event is of *Darstellung*, then how can this be subsumed to memory, which is by definition representative (that is, *Vorstellung*)? Fanon's deployment of this distinction between expression and representation falls closer to Kant's than it does Freud's, in that he fails to provide an account of the agency by which event *Darstellung* is transformed into *Vorstellung*, although the discussion of the connectedness of language and consciousness in the first chapter of *Peau noire, masques blancs* gives some indications. The critical issue here is that "memory" is a function of conceptual schemata, that is, the representational (metaphoric) condensation of time into valuable images. It is a genealogy of events. What concerned Fanon about *Darstellung* was its historicity, by which he intends the pure temporality of the event, enabling a correlation of event and consciousness. For Fanon, the pheno-menality of the event is valuable only as a thesis against which it becomes possible for consciousness to think itself as other than it – the other that is essential for the scene to occur at all. It would seem then that Fanon discovers expression (*Darstellung*) only to abandon it for the symbolic order of representation (*Vorstellung*), finding the conditions for possibil-ity to be exclusively representational. This, however, is not the case. Fanon discovered nothing else but that the conditions of possibility he sought occur with the correlation of event and consciousness. What this leaves us with is an understanding of consciousness as pure temporality (as only historical). This, in turn, means that we do not know how it is continued from event to event, or how it is constituted as a collective consciousness among aggregates of biological entities. Fanon's answer to these haunting problems was to read in the heterogeneity of event and consciousness the insignificance of *Darstellung* to the construction of human subjectivity; which is why he asserts that human freedom is the negation of the correlation of consciousness and thing, not the transfor-mation of event into representation or symbol. That is to say, we cannot think of memory except as the representation that forgets the event. Now it is true that Fanon understood this as repression, but it was the repression of memory of event, not the event, returning us to our initial critique: such repression presupposes ego.

To take that ego to be in the body is to be taken up in the pathology of negrophobia. To hold it to be a totality independent of the body, to be absolute Ego, is to preclude the possibility of understanding in any meaningful way historical difference in consciousness. Accordingly, the unrealizability of ontology signaled in the opening of "L'expérience vécue du Noir" stems from its leaving-off of the expression of conscious-ness attending the corporeal schema. What Fanon is trying to think about in his examination of how the psychopathology of colonialism yields a consciousness incapable of successfully alienating itself from the event of violence. This is the sort of consciousness possible with the event of experience. What would it be to think about such? Although uncertain in his approach to the first question, Fanon is convinced of the answer to the second: it will radically restructure the world.

Achieving the event of experience is to achieve authentic human liberty, to be (or exist) authentically. Genealogies of consciousness, which are highly dense structures of accumulated mnemic residues of experience – symbolic orders – function in the repression of the event of experience, and so preempt authentic freedom. For this reason, Fanon refuses negritude and recognizes it as a moment in the repressive process of colonialism/modernity. The *nègre* can only be (exist) in the process of consciousness becoming identified with modernity. This, however, presents him with a very challenging problem. It could very well be taken as a crisis in his thinking. Given such an apparently ahistorical event of experience, how can there be change? Is absolute Manichaeism the only way past the dialectic? Here is where Fanon is most insightful, revealing in the movement of his thought an interesting and important question: What is an event? There is a tortuous and careful thread through this question that turns us away from the questions of where is the human, and what is the human, to what do we do without the human. As is his want, Fanon leaves us with a perplexity to ponder.

"O mon corps, fais de moi toujours un homme qui interroge!"

Notes

1 The translations in this essay are my own, unless otherwise indicated as Markmann's.

2 Fanon's model for this is Octave Mannoni's *Psychologie de la colonisation* (1950). It was Mannoni who suggested to Fanon that the confrontation of two different peoples "brings about the *emergence* of a mass of illusions and misunderstandings that only psychological analysis can place and define" (Mannoni: 32, quoted in *Pn* 68); the italics are Fanon's. The key premises or central ideas, as Fanon puts it, of his and Mannoni's books are virtually identical, but not quite. Whereas Mannoni understands colonialism to be created by "a confrontation between civilized and primitive men," Fanon understands it to result from the juxtaposition of two different races. In Mannoni's case, the hierarchical distinction indicates a fundamental psychic difference, such that the Malagasy psychosis is not produced by colonialism; it was already a latent feature of the psyche that the colonial situation makes manifest. Fanon, on the other hand, understands any hierarchical difference to be wholly historical, a matter of technology and organization. Psychosis begins with colonialism.

3 "Imaginer que fera de la cuture noire, c'est oublier singulièrement que les nègres sont en train de disparaître, ceux qui les ont créés étant en train d'assister à la dissolution de leur suprématie économique et culturelle." [To imagine one will make Black culture is to singularly forget that *nègres* are disappearing just as those who created them are witnessing the dissolution of their [own] economic and cultural supremacy] Frantz Fanon, *Les Damnés de la terre* (1961a: 164).

4 G. W. F. Hegel, *Phenomenology of Spirit* (1977: 50), *Phänomenologie des Geistes* (1970: 73). Subsequent references to this text will occur in parenthesis, with *PS* referring to the Miller translation and *PG* to the Suhrkamp edition.

5 The introduction to *Peau noire, masques blancs* casts the thesis of negrophobia as a function of a social psychopathology that can be brought to lysis through

analysis. Chapter 1, "Le Noir et le langage," is an exposition of the complicated relationship of consciousness and language. Chapters 2 and 3, "La
femme de couleur et le Blanc" and "L'homme de couleur et la Blanche,"
employ the psychoanalytic interpretation of the novels of Mayotte Capécia,
Abdoulaye Sadji, and Réné Maran to delineate the pathology of negrophobia
in the Black. The critique of Mannoni's work in chapter 4 is indeed an
acknowledgment of Fanon's debt to that work, just as it is a going beyond it
that is all but dismissive. The particulars of that debt have already been
discussed. See note 2 above.

6 The *Oxford English Dictionary* gives the etymology of Negro as from the
Spanish or Portuguese *negro*, from the Latin *nigrum, niger*: black; it lists
"nigger" as a pejorative alteration of "neger," also a pejorative, whose etymology is given as either from the French *nègre* or the Dutch *neger*.

7 Roberts lists *nègre* as either a descriptive or pejorative reference to men and
women of the black race who are also designated as *mélano-africaine*, and
divided into five groups: "soudanais, guinéen, congolais, nilotique, sud-
africain ou zambézien."

8 Jock McCullogh, *Black Soul, White Artifact* (1983). Chapter 2 is of particular
interest.

9 It is worth pointing out at this juncture that, the invocation of Jung's concept
of collective unconsciousness, and the brief digression on the popular imaginary notwithstanding, Fanon's sociogenetic analysis of the black man's alienation bears a striking resemblance to Freud's *Das Unbehagen in der Kultur*
(*Civilization and its Discontents*). That is to say it interprets the sociogenesis of
psychopathology on the basis of ontogenetic analysis. It could be further
asserted that in *Peau noire, masques blancs*, Fanon neglects to provide any
analysis of the social construction of consciousness. Such an analysis would
have entailed, for example, further elaboration of the absence of Oedipal
neurosis in Martinique, focusing on the various familial constellations, from
the matrifocal to the patrifocal and the various intermediate combinations
between, relating these to the types of neurosis in evidence in the population.
On the contrary, however, Fanon's elaboration of negrophobia works from
the individual psyche outwards. Moreover, what is generally taken to be his
more careful analysis of collective repression and identification taken up in
Les Damnés de la terre and *L'An V de la révolution algérienne*, under scrutiny
proves to be extrapolation from case-studies whose methodology is almost
exclusively psychoanalytic, that is, ontogenetic. Now it can be rightly argued
that such a critique is unduly harsh, given the impossibility of extending
psychoanalysis to history without reverting to some sort of Idealistic monism.
Nonetheless, Fanon ceaselessly struggles with this issue. And, as I will argue
presently, it is in that struggle that other possibilities for understanding
emerge.

5

The Black and the Body Politic: Fanon's Existential Phenomenological Critique of Psychoanalysis

Lewis R. Gordon

His shadow, so to speak, has been more real to him than his personality.

Alain Locke

It is necessary to grow a new skin, to develop new thoughts, to set afoot a new man.

Frantz Fanon[1]

To speak of politics today, especially with regard to metaphors like the body politic and *body politics*, is to encounter an underlying feeling of wasting time. For as the chatter digresses, and as the common, perfunctory interplay of attempting to articulate "both sides" plays itself out, the impatient revolutionary call emerges with existential force: "So, my friends, what is to be done?"

Although V. I. Lenin had posed that question with considerable force in Eastern Europe, it was clear that for him the valuative body, on which stood the political body to whom his concerns were geared, was for the most part insular and hegemonic. It was, in other words, a European "in house" affair that was expected to affect "everyone."

When Frantz Fanon raises the question little over half a century later among fellow revolutionaries in *Les Damnés de la terre*, the circumstance is both similar and extraordinarily different. For Fanon's impatience, made particularly acute today by the values-stultifying dimension of neocolonial reversals, cannot lay claim to misguided universality. Fanon's revolutionary stands in relation to universal themes in ironic ways, for above all, the colored revolutionary is always earmarked in advance for particularity. There is never the point of value-neutrality, never the point of a sense of *presumed* grandeur, for after all, there is always the suprastructural context of the First World, the world in which "world" is constituted as a one-way mirror. In that world, only its reflection is seen. But in Fanon's world, the world of pervasive and invasive color, there is always the *de facto* "other side."

Fanon's political writings are well known. What is less known, or better yet, less articulated, is the existential phenomenological basis of Fanon's approach to what supports his revolutionary humanistic conclusions, particularly those premised upon constructing new values and a new humanity. What follows is an attempt to articulate some of those dimensions.

In 1952, when Fanon's *Peau noire, masques blancs* was published, western humanity had offered at least four hegemonic contenders for a science of the human being and as a consequence four hegemonic foundations of the body politic: (1) naturalism, best represented in its positivist form by Karl Popper and its pragmatic form by John Dewey, of whom we find such contemporary heirs as John Searle and, to some extent, Jürgen Habermas; (2) Hegel by way of Marx, best represented by Lukàcs and Gramsci on the one hand, and the Frankfurt School and the Sartre of the *Critique de la raison dialectique* on the other hand, from whom we have learnt the various ways of "rethinking" Marxism today; (3) Freudian psychoanalysis, best expanded yet represented in Fanon's time by Anna Freud, Gustav Jung, Erik Erikson, and Jacques Lacan, the last of whom has given rise to the variety of French poststructural feminists and English textual poststructuralists of today; and (4) phenomenology, best represented in its existential dimensions by Merleau-Ponty but most known through the work of Sartre and best represented in its sociological dimensions by Alfred Schutz. These various positions exemplify one of Rousseau's typically pithy remarks on the question of forging a rigorous human science:

> The most useful and the least advanced of all human knowledge seems to me to be that of man; and I dare say that the lone inscription on the Temple at Delphi contained a precept that was more important and more difficult than all the big books of the moralists . . . [Yet] it is by diligently studying man that we have placed ourselves outside of knowing him. (Rousseau 1971: 150)[2]

In Fanon, Rousseau's admonitions and failures, particularly his ruminations on *le primitif*, return with a vengeance. Fanon's challenge to all of these efforts was a deceptively simple demand. Explain "the black."

That the black is part of natural phenomena is true, which makes the naturalists' position valid but unfortunately in a trivial and naïve way,

since although sharing the natural world with the white, in the final
analysis the black does not live in an ordinary way and is not treated as
a natural phenomenon. That the black continues to be exploited is true,
which provides Marxism with its relevant force, but it is also a fact that
the black's exploitation is not treated as the basis of emancipation in the
same way that the abstract – that is, white – working-class is treated as a
locus of emancipation. That the black is conscious is similarly a valid
basis for a phenomenological treatment of blackness, but again in a
rather trivial way, since the root of intentionality is cleansed of blackness
in a way that fails to account for the phenomenon. To find the black,
then, it would seem that the symbolic world of psychoanalysis, governed
by repression and desire, the inner forces of darkness and instinct, can
offer a concrete instantiation of black reality and hence transcend the gap
between validity and reality. Fanon's early announcements in this regard
are, however, misleading. He writes,

> In effect, we agree that a psychoanalytical interpretation alone of the black
> problem can reveal the affective anomalies responsible for the structure of
> the complex. We shall attempt a total lysis of this morbid universe. It is our
> view that the individual should attempt to assume the universal inherent in
> the human condition. (*Pn* 7–8 / *BS* 10)

His announcement is misleading because his tactic is ultimately a
provocative literary device of demonstration by failure. He will show that
psychoanalysis cannot explain the black by attempting to explain the
black psychoanalytically. This failure will compel a re-evaluation of
the context of inquiry itself. And that context will demand what he
calls *sociogenic* explanations, explanations that are attuned to the social
origins of human problems. His reason is straightforward: "The black's
alienation is not an individual question" (*Pn* 8 / *BS* 11). In other words,
"The black must wage war on two levels": the subjective and the
intersubjective, lived-experience of social-historical reality.

In *Peau noire*, Fanon's argument is articulated through analyses of
alienated language, alienated love ("objects" of women and men of
color's desire), colonized apperception ("so-called dependency complex"), existential phenomenological lived-experience, psychopathology,
and existential Hegelian recognition. We can summarize his argument
thus: blacks have attempted to escape the historic reality of blackness
through the resources of language, which offer semiotic resources of self-
deluding performances of emancipation. If the black can speak the
European language well enough, perhaps there is the opportunity of
"being" a European. But by the time we arrive at the chapter on the
lived-experience of the black, we find that such resources are ultimately

irrelevant to the matter. In fact, the better the black is at that language, the more he becomes like, as Fanon observes, "Rodin's *The Thinker* with an erection" (*Pn* 134 / *BS* 165). The situation is moribund on the basis of the following "*évidence*": "Wherever he goes, the Negro remains a Negro" (140 / 173).

Fanon appeals to *évidence* ("obviousness," "clearness," "obvious fact") here in the same way that Husserl discusses evidence as a form of mental seeing at the heart of experience (1960: sec. 5, 12–14). The French verb *demeurer*, here translated as "remains," also means to dwell and to live. Although we have voiced some preliminary reservations about a phenomenological articulation of this problem early on, it should now be obvious that that does not entail the rejection of an *existential* phenomenological approach. We see here that the lived-experience of social reality *is* an aspect of the existential phenomenological turn that undergirds the Fanonian project, for how else can this two-leveled sociodiagnostic take place?

At the heart of the existential phenomenological approach is the question of human studies in general. It has been the modern project to do for human studies what Newton and his heirs have done for the natural sciences.[3] The effort to transform human studies into human sciences, however, has not been a particularly successful one. After many a gallant effort, it became increasingly clear that perhaps the source of failure was rooted in the conception of science at work in the inquiry. Perhaps the question of questioning should, that is, be more radically self-reflective. By the first half of the twentieth century, this question of radical reflectivity had, as at least one of its major proponents, Merleau-Ponty.[4]

Such is the philosophical context of developing a modern human science. The social-political context for Fanon is well known. It is a context of global racism and both colonial and neocolonial structuring of the dissemination of values and material resources.

The black is fundamentally conditioned in the modern world through the lens of racist re-presentation. The core of the problem faced by psychoanalysis, and consequently any theory of human science, is that of explaining the black in the context of anti-black racism. Our appeal to context supports a strength in the existential phenomenological approach, for that approach is premised upon a situational dimension, a dimension which Fanon refers to as *l'expérience vécue du Noir* ("lived-experience of the black"), that is, the lived-experience of racism. It is an experience of acidulously familiar instances of skewed racialized visibility: "Hey, a Negro!" and "Sho' good banana!"[5]

These instances of skewed visibility are in their purpose evasive. A stark evasion manifests itself in the face of the black body. The black body lives in what evinces itself as an anti-black world. In that world, it dwells as a form of absence of human presence. The denial of human presence is a form of bad faith (*mauvaise foi*).[6] Fanon here utilizes Sartre's description of this phenomenon's anti-Semitic manifestation, in *Anti-Semite and Jew*, as "overdetermination." Writes Fanon,

> I am overdetermined from outside. I am not the slave of the "idea" that others have of me but of my appearance. I move slowly in the world, accustomed to aspiring no longer to appear. I proceed by crawling. Already the white looks, the only true looks [*les seuls vrais*], are dissecting me. I am *fixed*. Having prepared their microtome, they slice away objectively pieces of my reality. I am disclosed. I feel, I see, in those white looks, that it is not a new man who enters, but a new type of man, a new genus. Why – a Negro! (*Pn* 93 / *BS* 116)

Overdetermination saturates consciousness in the flesh with the quality of being a thing, a form of being-in-itself. With such weight, the black body is confronted by the lived-experience of its absence. A binary world is imposed upon it which functions as a constant source of evasion. Like Dostoyevsky's Underground Man, who "lives in spite of logic," the black body finds itself existing in spite of Reason. "As the other said it, when I was there, it [Reason] was not; when it was there, I was no longer" (*Pn* 96 / *BS* 119–20).

This negative dialectical dimension of institutionalized racist rationality evinces a skewed logic. Rules that apply to white bodies change when applied to black bodies in a world conditioned by anti-black racism. In classic existential phenomenological technique, Fanon explores the lived-experience of the black's embodiment as

> An unusual clumsiness came upon me. The real world contested my place. In the white world the man of color encounters difficulties in the assimilation of his bodily schema. Consciousness of the body is a uniquely negating activity. It is a third-person consciousness . . . Then the bodily schema, attacked from several points, collapses and gives way to a racial epidermal schema. In the train, it is no longer a matter of knowledge of my body in the third person, but in a triple person. In the train, instead of one, I am left with two, three places . . . (*Pn* 89–90 / *BS* 110–12)

The black body in situation faces Du Boisian double-consciousness from *The Souls of Black Folk* on the one hand, where the black both learns about a white world and lives behind the veil of a black one, yet also more than the Du Boisian model, since Fanon, in effect, identifies three consciousnesses.[7]

Steeped within supposedly hidden realities, black bodies take on peculiar forms of what is known among phenomenologists of social science as *anonymity*. Alfred Schutz speaks of anonymity as the mundane ability to stand for another in the realm of understanding.[8] Anonymity both wipes away and preserves the very notion of a private language and epistemological privilege. In one sense, we are all like everyone else. But in another sense, there is no one like us. In this regard, anonymity is restricted to a form of universality of human presence, where the rules are expected to apply to all human beings. Yet this universality is simultaneously mundane and profound. The public dimension of the universal affords a dialectic between individual and social life that is so mundane that it ceases to function as the general concern of any one else. When concern emerges, it is in terms of recognizing an individual's uniqueness, not in the sense of a singular essence, but in the sense that although one can stand in another's place as a human being, as a member of the species, one cannot on the other hand stand in the place of that human being's life.

In a racist society, however, the logic of anonymity is perverted. If *a* black is overdetermined, then to see that black is to see every black. That black's individual life ceases to be regarded as a function of epistemological, aesthetic, or moral concern. For although an empathetic dimension of anonymity disappears, a racially-relative form of anonymity emerges. The black becomes an opportune, economic entity. One is led to believe that one can "have blacks" by virtue of having "this black," this anonymous black, as one can have chairs by virtue of having any chair. This is because a little bit of blackness is always too much blackness from an overdetermined reality. Blackness in an anti-black world is always superfluous.

Fanon has described this superfluous dimension of anti-black "perception" of blackness as "phobogenic," "anxiogenic" (*objet phobogène, anxiogène*, that is, a stimulus to anxiety (*Pn* 123 / *BS* 151)). What this means is that the black body does not live on the symbolic level in an anti-black world. It is locked in the serious, material values of the real. Thus, whereas the white body can live the symbolic alienation rich with neurotic content and thereby serve as a foundation for psychoanalysis, the black body, whether in dream content or awake intentions, always stands for "what it is" – *the black*. The black therefore does not symbolize crime and licentious sexuality in an anti-black world. The black *is* crime and licentious sexuality, bestiality, and all the arrays of embodied social pathologies. That is why, as Fanon says, it is on the biological level that both discourses on racism and the black begin. "The Negro," he contends, "represents the biological danger" (*Pn* 131, 134 / *BS* 161, 165).

In the chapter entitled, "Le Nègre et la psychopathologie," Fanon argues that what psychoanalysis could not achieve was an explanation of blacks in the world of dreams and even Jungian archetypical fantasy, for everywhere in the case of the former, the black has been structured as the material manifestation of evil or illicit desire, and everywhere in the case of the latter, the black or colored person has been negatively impacted by the growth of Europe. Psychoanalysis cannot therefore understand the black man and the black woman psychoanalytically (that is, in properly psychoanalytical terms) because both stand below the symbolic in the racist context of perverted anonymity: their alienation is not neurotic. It is the historical reality of a phobogenic complex. For psychoanalysis to be able to understand the black woman and the black man, the sexual molester in their dreams must be psychosexual displacements of histori- cal reality with an ultimate reference in family life – their father and mother. But racism and colonialism have left the matrices locked in a near historical-ontological schema. Black and whiteness in such a world are "real," and no amount of neurotic catharsis will in itself change the historical reality of their "place." The black woman and black man are therefore invisible beyond perverse anonymous objects, Fanon argues, in psychoanalysis, whether Freudian, Jungian, Lacanian, and we may add today, Irigarayan.[9]

The implications for our understanding of the body politic in our world, which is conditioned by the same racist apprehensions as Fanon's, are obvious. If psychoanalysis cannot articulate black reality in psychoanalytic terms without being fallacious, then the baggage of societal foundations associated with psychoanalysis – namely, sexuality, gender, and filial life – are also problematic bases of a body politic that militates against the presence of the black. Take, for instance, the family. The general view is that "A normal child that grows up in a normal family will be a normal person" (*Pn* 116 / *BS* 142). In these days of demagogic manipulation of family values, the problem becomes acute as we realize that normality in our society is wrought with definite prescrip- tions that may go against the political sensibilities of many of us. Fanon observes the opposite of the general view in the case of black child development. "A normal black child, having grown up with a normal family, will find himself abnormal [*s'anormalisera*] from the slightest contact with the white world" (117 / 143). We find, then, three levels of critique at work here.

First, there is the *radical* critique, where the socio-historical circum- stance blocks the emergence of the symbolic. Only the white, whether female or male, can be historically situated on the symbolic level. In his or her dream life, there is room for interpretation of dreams, since the dream-content is always "other" than what it appears to be. But both for coloreds and whites in an anti-black world, the black stands as the meaning-content of the dream – the phobogenic reality. This leads to the second point, which is *clinical* – that the context and content of psycho-analytical emergence are conditioned fundamentally by the lived-experience of the white. That is why clinical psychology emerged through the subjective life of white women and white men, with men of color emerging as an incarcerated reality. In his psychiatric practice in Algeria, for instance, Fanon studied the dream content of white French-men and women, but he found that men of color were usually committed to psychiatric institutions. In *Sociologie d'une révolution*, Fanon's explana-tion was that the political reality of the colonial regime, with its construc-tion of embodied Algeria as the Algerian woman and its Manichaeism of the masculine conqueror and the feminine conquered, laid the ground-work for constant structural conflict between the Algerian man and the colonizing nation.[10] The conflict itself was the constitution of madness. That is why his "therapy," if you will, was revolutionary praxis.

The third part is a direct critique of western psychoanalytical con-structions of woman. That the social-historical reality shatters the sym-bolic in the context of race means that the black woman is not even *understood* in such a world. Think, for example, of the development of heterosexual desire in terms of mothers and fathers.[11] The white woman can freely desire her father through purging rape in the material value of the black male. That she is a being conditioned by the social reality of rapeability, where her consent or lack thereof has occasioned and is the very meaning of the phenomenon in the corridors of a criminal justice system (that is, "political reality"), enables her dream content to be conditioned by the possibility of "rape," and therefore encounter with the black. She can be "taken" by the father, or "rescued" by him or the mother. What the black affords, however, is the "taken" dimension being freed of its incestual content. The one who rapes is the Other, and hence *not* the father. For the black woman, however, there is no such reality. The black father is the social reality of rape, which makes her dream content concrete, in spite of the concrete though invisible reality of white male license over black female bodies.[12] As a consequence, the psycho-analytical matrices are skewed when applied to a black.

Perhaps an illustration is in order. In a television program ironically entitled *The Real World*, in which a number of young people "live" together and are filmed documentary style, the following "situations" emerged, as described by one critic:

> In one of last year's installments, poet Kevin Powell, who was the only Black male in the show, was accused of attacking "southern belle" Becky. In a recent episode (with all new cast), David, an African American comedian, is portrayed as a sort of sex fiend. An ugly incident starts when Beth, one of the female characters, pulls a prank by taking the bed covers

off Dominick, an Irish free-lance writer. David retaliates by doing the same
to Tami, a Black social worker. At first, everybody laughs at the incident,
but Tami, although also laughing, screams "No!" In the end, Beth, who
started the whole thing, accuses David of rape. It may be juvenile to pull
covers off someone but it isn't rape. Despite this, the label sticks. The issue
of women's equality is pitted against African American equality. Later, the
female characters Tami, Beth, and Irene, are afraid to be in the same room
with David. David is stereotyped as violent, mindless, and savage.[13]

Now, the message in this scenario is clear, that women are safe in an
apartment, which is a microcosm for a world, without black men. The
lysis or disintegration of the disease sought here is the opposite of
Fanon's. Consider also the dynamics that emerge from the way in which
the black female character was approached. She was *aware* that she was
being "watched" by millions of predominately white viewers. Those
white viewers functioned as the normative framework of reality; they
were not the symbolic superego of classical psychoanalysis. They *were*
the superego or, in a word, "gods" – the prosthetic reality of value. In a
moment of double negation, then, the character David's shadow was
more real than he and he was consequently reduced to it: he became
rape.

The body politic of an anti-black world is therefore a social-
historically-situated *existential* reality. It is conditioned by what Fanon
describes as the "third term," an expression he borrows from Sartre's
L'Être et le néant,[14] which subjugates colored reality. This "governing
fiction [that is, the third] is not personal but social" (*Pn* 174 / *BS* 215).
It makes the white normative. It disintegrates the social world into a
fundamentally Manichaean reality.

Although today it is fashionable to reject binary analyses, what is often
missed in the dismissal is the distinction between identifying a phenomenon and identifying with or supporting a phenomenon. Rejecting the
binaries that separate humanity also involves recognizing that those
binaries exist as lived realities: "Facing the white, the black has a past to
make equal, a revenge to take; facing the black, the contemporary white
feels the need to recall anthropophagical times" (in a word, "man-
eating").[15]

By way of concluding, we can here derive at least three consequences.

First, it should be clear that political theories that separate society into
public political and private civil societies offer no resources for blacks,
for the terms are structured at the social-historical dimensions of the
society itself. As a consequence, societies that attempt to separate themselves from a symbiotic relationship between supposedly political and
civil societies ironically conceal injustices that sustain their force through
denying such a relationship – in a word, liberalism.[16]

Second, that change is demanded on both the civil and political levels leads to the demand for no less than revolutionary change.

And third, that the change focuses on the normative dimensions of society itself suggests that the sphere of everyday life must be addressed on the revolutionary level. This concern brings us back to the existential phenomenological thesis of anonymity, for, in effect, the Fanonian appeal is an effort to make visible the extraordinary dimensions of mundane racist life by showing that the black's ordinary life is in fact extraordinary. The black therefore calls for a transformed everyday that eliminates a suprastructural Third in the body politic. In Fanon's words, "Was my freedom not given to me then in order to build [*édifier*] the world of the *You?*" (*Pn* 188 / *BS* 232). Yes, it was. Fanon's choice of word is significant here, since *édifier* also means to edify and to inspire. In all of his writings, he has attempted to contribute to the building of a new world through inspiring his readers with literature *engagé*.

On the political level, however, the establishment of such a world remains to be seen.

Notes

1 The epigraphs are from Alain Locke's "The New Negro" (in Harris 1983: 242), and Fanon's is from *Dt* 376 / *WE* 316. All of the translations of French texts are mine.

2 See "Discourse on Inequality" in Rousseau (1986), p. 129.

3 The project (and sentiment) continues. See Stephen Hawking, "Is Everything Determined?" (1994: ch. 12).

4 See Merleau-Ponty's brilliant lecture, "Phenomenology and the sciences of man" (1964: ch. 3).

5 "'Tiens, un nègre!' . . . 'Y a bon banania'", *Pn* 90 / *BS* 112. The English edition states, "Sho' good eatin'!," but I've kept the French reference, since it refers both to the fruit and to the popular French breakfast food Banania made from banana flour, cocoa, and sugar. Fanon no doubt chose that product both because of its advertisement, which has a smiling Senegalese, whose face eventually became so caricatured by the late 1980s that it resembled a chimpanzee, and because of the associations of blacks with apes and apes with bananas. The associations are, in other words, African/the black → bananas → ape. For a discussion of this product and detailed analysis of black-face advertising and black mascots of white productions, see Jan Nederveen Pierterse (1992: especially 162–3).

6 See Jean-Paul Sartre's discussion of this phenomenon in *L'Être et le néant* (1943: part 1, ch. 2); *Being and Nothingness* (1956: part 1, ch. 2). I have provided a detailed, systematic discussion of this phenomenon and its significance for the understanding of anti-black racism in my book, *Bad Faith and Antiblack Racism* (1995a).

7 W. E. B. Du Bois's *The Souls of Black Folk* (esp. the Forethought and ch. 1).

8 See Schutz 1962, 1966, 1967, 1970, and Schutz and Luckmann 1973 and 1989. For recent discussions, see Natanson (1986) and Lewis R. Gordon (1995b: ch. 3).

9 For discussion of Luce Irigaray and race, see Patricia Huntington (forthcoming).

10 See ch. 1: "L'Algérie se dévoile" (Algeria unveiled).

11 I leave aside the question of lesbian and homosexual dimensions here since I have argued in more detail elsewhere why all sexual relationships are other than they appear to be in contexts governed by the social-historic weight of racism. See Gordon (1995b: ch. 17).

12 See Angela Y. Davis (1983) and Joy Ann James (1996a) for discussion.

13 Keith Mitchell, "MTV: Real Racist" (1993: 21). Epilogue: The black male is taken off the show, whereas one of the white males who remains eventually hosts a television dance-party that takes place in the inner-city and plays predominately black club music. This white male character sports all the style and clothing of black, inner-city youth.

14 See the third part, third chapter, third section (no coincidence on Sartre's part, I suspect). There, Sartre refers to alienated reciprocity, *le nous-sujet*, "the we-subject," as *le tiers*, "the third" (1943: 480–1; 1956b: 554–5). For French audiences, the connection is with *le tiers état*, the third estate, the people, and hence the bourgeois revolution that rendered the exploitation of working people invisible through claiming their universal membership in political society.

15 *Pn* 183 / *BS* 225. In the French: "En face du Blanc, le Noir a un passé à valoriser, une revanche à prendre; en face du Noir, le Blanc contemporain ressent la nécessité de rappeler la période anthropophagique." *Anthropophagique* means "man-eating."

16 The term "liberalism" is here meant in its philosophical sense, referring to the tradition identified by John Rawls (1971) and best exemplified in the Anglo contexts of the UK, North America, and Australia by the works of Thomas Hobbes, John Locke, David Hume, and John Stuart Mill, and in the French context by Jean-Jacques Rousseau. For a discussion of Fanon and liberalism, see Eddy Souffrant's "To Conquer the Veil" (in this volume, below).

6

To Cure and to Free:
The Fanonian Project of
"Decolonized Psychiatry"

Françoise Vergès

If psychiatry is the medical technique that aims to enable man no longer to be a stranger to his environment, I owe it to myself to affirm that the Arab, permanently an alien in his own country, lives in a state of absolute depersonalization.

Frantz Fanon[1]

The writings and practice of Frantz Fanon *as a psychiatrist* have rarely been assessed against the history of psychiatry in the colony and the general history of the clinic. Yet Fanon's salient questions about psychiatry are still with us: What kind of psychiatry is possible in the postcolony? What should be its goals? To discipline and to control? To facilitate reintegration into society? What should be the role of the psychiatrist? What is the relation between postcolonial psychiatry and psychoanalysis? What is the legacy of colonial psychiatry in today's psychiatry? The desire to see Fanon *as a psychoanalyst* (which he never was[2]) has often led postcolonial critics to ignore that, *as a psychiatrist,* he tried to redefine the goal and practice of psychiatry from within. Fanon's contribution as a psychiatrist in the colony was to insist on the importance of the cultural context in which symptoms appear, to demonstrate that therapeutic institutions need to maintain a concrete link and a structural similarity to the local culture of the patients. The condition for a successful therapy was that there existed, he said, a "common culture," shared by the patient and the practitioner. Fanon also opened the first day care (that is,

---

This chapter is part of a larger project about the history of psychiatry and colonialism, the birth of the clinic in the colony, and postcolonial psychiatry. All translations, unless otherwise stated, are my own.

"day hospital" (*hôpital du jour*)) psychiatric ward in the postcolonial world at the hospital Charles-Nicolle in Tunis. He was at first a reformist psychiatrist, a partisan of a psychiatry whose principles harked back to the great French psychiatrist Philippe Pinel, who practiced during the French Revolution: to reconcile the sick with the social world, to help them to find in themselves the strength to go back to the world and to use the resources of that world to become free of disease.[3]

European-trained psychiatrists, up to Fanon's time, were agents of French colonization. The discourse of colonial psychiatry, which chose to ignore the historical conditions of its formation, posited a fundamental difference between the psyches of Europeans and non-Europeans. This approach was applied to the Algerians by the military doctor Antione Porot, who founded the mental health service of colonial Algeria in 1913.[4] The Muslims, Porot claimed, were credulous, suggestible, and degenerate; they showed a weakness of moral and affective life, and an innate difficulty for introspection. Fanon strongly rejected this approach. He questioned the representation of the North Africans and, as early as 1952, proposed a new methodology to approach the mentally ill among North Africans (*Pra* 9–21 / *TAR* 3–16). Fanon wanted the psychiatrist "to help the patient to act in the direction of a change in the social structure" (*Pn* 80 / *BS* 100).

To retrieve Fanon's place in the history of psychiatry in the colony and to analyze his attempt to "decolonize psychiatry" would mean to retrace the history of colonial psychiatry and ask why and how, in the French colonial empire, the psychiatrist, like the missionary and the doctor, became an agent of colonization. How did colonial psychiatry define and describe the symptoms of the colonized? Who was sent to the colonial psychiatric institution? Who were the nurses? What was their training? Who were the patients? What was Fanon's practice as a *Chef de Service* (Director) in the largest psychiatric hospital in colonial Algeria in 1953?

Fanon was, with some of his colleagues in Algeria, among the first psychiatrists to apply "social therapy," or "institutional therapy," in the colony. This approach aimed to open the hospital, to humanize it, to make the patient a man among other men and to facilitate his re-socialization, as well as to organize workshops in which patients would exercise their skills and be paid for their work, create theater groups, a newspaper in which patients were the journalists, in brief, to make the hospital a social place.

Fanon was enthusiastic about institutional therapy, whose goals answered his vision of social transformation. When he was completing his psychiatric training in France in the early 1950s, he encountered the leaders of institutional therapy whose goal was to "restructure and transform the psychiatric hospital so that real psychotherapies could be practiced," and to "allow a therapeutic organization of social life in the hospital, based on group psychotherapy."[5] Influenced by the techniques of psychodrama,[6] determined to limit the role of the psychiatrist to that of "an actor among other actors" in the hospital, and to insist on the importance of the connection between the community of the patients and the larger community, these French psychiatrists tried to reformulate, in the late 1940s, the psychiatric institution's goals and function.[7] François Tosquelles, who deeply influenced Fanon, argued that the mental patient was first and foremost a man who had become an "alien to his social environment," and though the use of chemical drugs often remained a necessity, the "endeavor of re-structuration demanded the activist intervention of the social milieu."[8] To the psychiatrist, the "persistent and irreducible *sociality* of the patient" had to be the founding principle of his practice. The accent was put on the relation between psychiatrist and patient rather than on the symptom, and the asylum was conceived of as a micro-society, reproducing the activities and the social relations of society, in which prevention and post-cure follow-up were developed.

When he arrived at the hospital of Blida, Algeria, and was put in charge of one of the wards, Fanon energetically applied Tosquelles's principles.[9] He held meetings with the other psychiatrists and the nurses, whom he, like Tosquelles, believed were an essential part of the therapeutic project. He organized twice-weekly meetings of the patients, the staff, the newspaper, and initiated a holiday every two months. Committees were set up in charge of movies, records, and newspapers. At first sight, the conditions were like those in France at the time: patients abandoned to their own devices, overcrowded quarters, no place for the patients to meet or work, no psychotherapy.[10] But what was different, and it was a difference with many consequences, was that in Algeria these conditions were compounded by the colonial situation and shaped by the racist discourse of colonial psychiatry.

Colonial Psychiatry: Race, Gender, and Madness

Colonial psychiatry was the heir of the *psychologie des peuples*, which emerged, in the second half of the nineteenth century, as a discourse whose goal was to define a relation between race, culture, and the psyche. Its first subjects had been the French working class, the poor peasantry, and the vagabond, which were said to be prone to excesses and displayed a pathology of degeneration that ought to be studied in order to deploy preventive strategies.[11] Psychology and psychiatry were developed as sciences to study the "pathology of the dangerous classes" (see Perrot, as well as Pick). The transformation in industry, and therefore of the working class, the project of turning "peasants into Frenchmen,"[12] colonial expansion, the development of social sciences, but also of anti-Semitism, the Dreyfus affair, and the theories about nation and race, constituted the stage for the psychological theories of social behavior.[13] Race moved from being a "purely biological category to a purely psychological one" (Gilman 1993: 23).

Theories about the potential madness of the anarchist, the communard, the vagabond, were extended to the colonized. Gustave Le Bon, in *Les Lois psychologiques de l'évolution des peuples* (1894),[14] proposed the notion of "psychological race," which was in direct lineage with Gobineau's racist theory and influenced a generation of psychologists. Le Bon, who was a partisan of polygenesis, made a connection between gender and race, arguing that the "proof of female inferiority, and of similarities between women and Negroes, was provided by craniology" (as cited in Todorov 1993: 114). To him, race was imprinted on memory (Le Bon: 6, 13). Léopold de Saussure pursued Le Bon's approach in his *La Psychologie de la colonisation française dans ses rapports avec société indigènes* (1899). He wrote:

> The acquisition of shared mental characteristics creates veritable "psychological races." The psychological characteristics are as stable as the anatomic characteristics, upon which a classification of the species was made. Psychological characteristics are reproduced, with regularity and constancy, like anatomic ones, through heredity. (Saussure: 14)

As Antoine Bouillon has remarked, "the *psychologie des peuples* rested on the notion of the radical heterogeneity of beliefs of the racial groups, which it opposed to the philosophical idea of Reason, and to the dogma of the moral unity of humankind."[15] These theories paradoxically appeared through taking into account the diversity of cultures, through being more attentive to non-European peoples than to the colonial universalistic project. Yet their project was imperial as well since they ended up insisting on the hierarchy of cultures. Difference was the sign of inequality.

The advocates of a psychology of colonization argued that it was necessary to learn about the traditions, language, and culture of native societies, and defended a psychology which took its information from ethnological studies. They advocated the training, and the importance, of native mediators and informers for the dissemination of psychological knowledge. In 1912, Dr Reboul and Dr Régis spoke in favor of training colonial psychiatrists, of the elaboration of a legislation that would take into account local conditions, the construction of asylums, and a network of psychiatric assistance adapted to local needs.[16] Though colonial psychologists wanted to base their conclusions on clinical observations, their biases led them to conclusions that ultimately argued a constitutional inferiority of the colonized (see Aubin 1939; Lauriol 1938). The psychology of colonization competed with the other components of the colonial discourse, because it advocated a progressive assimilation through seduction, rather than a subjugation by force.

The *Revue de Psychologie des Peuples*, founded in 1946, offered a forum to the psychology of colonization.[17] In July 1947 Georges Hardy published in this review a very influential article entitled, "La psychologie des populations coloniales."[18] He criticized the ways in which "primitive populations" – whom he preferred to call *populations attardées* (backward populations) – had been studied: "Everything is judged in the light of one criterion of civilization, that has never been clearly defined, and which only expressed a naive egocentrism" (Hardy 1939: 26). Hardy called for a "new exploration of Africa, Asia, and Oceania" in order to investigate "the native souls". He argued that a "colonization without psychology would only be violence without a future." The first concept the colonial psychologist had to challenge was that of "universal man," proposed by "classic psychology." Hardy criticized the notion of "Negro soul" or "Muslim soul," because, he wrote, the differences between individuals were too great to justify such generalizations. Hardy, who opposed the notion of "race," preferring the notion of "ethnic family," advocated the union of psychology and politics in the colony (1947: 233–4). He claimed that such a union would enhance the understanding and cooperation between the peoples:

> We saw, in the ideas and practices different from our own, only barbarism, and we thought that it was sufficient to transform these shadowy parts by throwing a European light on them. We had to renounce this form of colonization, because the souls of the native populations, even when they appeared to submit, continued to move in their familiar atmosphere, and, by opposition, tended to adopt a different consciousness.
>
> Colonization has progressively abjured the forms of subjugation that, in its beginnings, made its enterprise a modern form of enslavement. Now, colonization does not rely solely on force. It has transformed domination into tutelage; it has proposed, as its ends, association, reciprocal trust, and now dreams of grafting European buds on these exotic roots. Colonization must know well the human groups on which it is working and psychology has become a preparatory school whose necessity is evident. (ibid.: 233–4)

Hardy's work exemplified the theoretical approach of the psychology of colonization, its positivism and its assimilation project. The site from which the text was produced, a Frenchman in the colony, its public, the metropolitan French, and the way it would be read as another proof of the hierarchical diversity of races, constructed a matrix from which colonization was to be justified. The scientific objectivity claimed by Hardy, his apparently sincere respect for other cultures, and the vocabulary of psychology gave to his project a legitimacy that the colonial discourse of conquest was not able to attain. The conquering soldier lent his place to the psychologist, militarist rhetoric to humanitarian rhetoric. The land had been conquered, the soul of the native was the new territory to map out and describe. Colonial psychology produced an idiom whose scientific terminology was easily adopted by the medical profession. The famous *École d'Algier de Psychiatrie* led the field of investigation in the "native soul." Its founder, Antoine Porot, laid out in his *Notes de psychiatrie musulmane* (1918), the basis of the school: clinical observations that show that the North African lack of symbolization was compounded by fatalism, credulity, suggestibility, and lack of curiosity (1918: 377).

The conclusions of the psychology of colonization rested on a series of observations and assumptions. On the one hand, it asked the vexed question about the relationship between culture and the psyche. Did culture determine the psyche, or were there universal human psychological mechanisms? On the other hand, it proposed a series of features characterizing the colonized: a poor language, and consequently an inability to conceptualize, a faith in magic, a belief in spirits, fatalism, credulity, and mimicry. Its objects of study were the natives, whose atavistic psychological features made them "natural" criminals, permanent children. Psychological theories developed in the United States opted for similar descriptions to argue the psychological inferiority of African Americans. About those, the psychiatrist John E. Lind wrote in 1916: "The precocity of children, the early onset of puberty, the *failure to grasp subjective ideas*, the strong sexual and herd instincts with the few inhibitions, the *simple dream life* . . . the low resistance to such toxins as syphilis and alcohol, the sway of superstitions, all these and many things betray the savage heart beneath the civilized exterior."[19]

The colonial relation was conceptualized as an unequal relation, in which the colonizer paternally led the colonized to adulthood and maturity. The rhetoric of paternal benevolence covered over a policy of death and dispossession. Colonial psychologists claimed to "describe" what they "saw." They were restoring in their exactitude, they said, the utterances and gestures of the colonized. Their scientific *regard* was a guarantee of neutrality and objectivity. Their language was "charged with a double function: with its value as precision, it establishe[d] a correlation between each sector of the visible and an expressible element that corresponde[d] to it as accurately as possible; but this expressible element operate[d], with its role as description a denominative function, which, by its articulation upon a constant, fixed vocabulary, authorize[d] comparison, generalization, and establishment within a totality" (Foucault 1973: 113–14).

Decolonizing Psychiatry

After World War II, starting with Octave Mannoni, a new approach was developed,[20] characterized by the belief that the colonial relation was one that "chained the colonizer *and* the colonized into an implacable dependence" (Memmi 1965: ix, emphasis mine). There was a shift in focus and the colonizer's motives were analyzed. Colonizers had not gone to the colonies with benevolent intent but because they were seeking a facile position of racial, economic, and political privilege. Their psychological complexes made them perfect colonizers; they arrived in a country which had been militarily conquered, and they found a social function, cheap labor, as well as sexual and economic privileges awaiting them. Being a colonizer brought invaluable narcissistic benefits. Fanon remarked that the "white colonial is motivated only by a desire to put an end to a feeling of dissatisfaction on the level of Adlerian overcompensation" (*Pn* 68 / *BS* 84). The colonizer–colonized relation was not as the popular psychology of colonization had construed it to be: an unselfish individual moved by the desire to uplift the backward and lazy native. The colonial relation was now understood dynamically. The portrait of the colonized as lazy, criminal, and dumb was a construction of the colonizers' projections and anxieties. There was no truth to it but instead a reflection of the need to rationalize racial and political subjugation. The colonizer's violence was not a hereditary trait but the result of the psychological and material violence of the colonial relation.[21] The new theories cast a suspicion on the long-held opinion that there was no road to "psychological development" which mirrored the "European psyche," and that there was a psychological solution to the political and economical situation produced by colonialism. Yet these new theories insisted on a psychological analysis of the colonial relation, for this relation had been translated into metaphors, tropes, iconographic material, whose content and consequences exceeded a strictly political analysis of conflictual forces. The colonial relation had been suffused with images of sexuality, bodies, and tropes of family relations.

As Fanon said, "The problem of colonialism includes not only the interrelation of objective historical conditions but also human attitudes toward these conditions" (*Pn* 68 / *BS* 84). How does one analyze these tropes without studying the motives of those who had produced them? These psychology theories allowed a radical critique of colonialism from within the concepts of psychology which had so well served colonialism. Psychology, it was said, could as well be a weapon against the colonialist project.

Mannoni and Fanon were both persuaded that economic explanation could not fully comprehend the dynamics of the colonial relation and that there was a partly conscious, partly unconscious set of symbols which shaped that relation.[22] Yet Fanon had a greater ambivalence than Mannoni toward psychoanalysis and its ability to explain racism and the colonial relation. Fanon wrote, "Indeed, I believe that only a psychoanalytical interpretation of the black problem can lay bare the affective anomalies responsible for the structure of the complex," yet he added that the "black's alienation is not an individual question. Beside phylogeny and ontogeny stands sociogeny." He also declared: "Psychoanalysis is a pessimistic view of man. The care of the person must be thought of as a deliberately optimistic choice against human reality."[23]

To Albert Memmi, a Tunisian Jew, the colonizer had constructed a "mythical and degrading portrait" of the colonized that the latter ended up accepting and living by to a certain extent (Memmi 1965: 87). The Mannonian notion of "dependency complex" had only a participle of truth, Memmi wrote. If there was an adherence of the colonized to colonization, this was the result of colonization and not its cause (ibid.: 88). The colonizer had no other choice than to enter into relation with the colonized because "It is this very alliance which enables him to lead the life which he decided to look for in the colonies; it is this relationship which is lucrative, which creates privilege" (ibid.: 8). Racism was a "consubstantial part of colonialism," the "highest expression of the colonial system and one of the most significant features of colonialism" (ibid.: 74). Memmi, like Fanon, thought that a social revolution was needed to accomplish decolonization. "Only the complete liquidation of colonization permits the colonized to be free," but this liquidation was "nothing but a prelude to complete liberation, to self-recovery" (ibid.: 151). Fanon and Memmi rejected the thesis that history could permanently determine identity. In Fanon's words, "Le densité de l'Histoire ne détermine aucun de mes actes. Je suis mon propre fondement" ("The density of history does not determine any of my actions. I am my rightful foundation") (*Pn* 187 / *BS* 231).

Social Therapy, Colonialism, and Culture

Fanon's decolonization of colonial psychiatry through the implantation of institutional therapy or social therapy ran into difficulties, however, when he tried to apply its methods in Algeria. He described these difficulties in an essay co-authored with the psychiatrist Jacques Azoulay.[24] In the Blida hospital, built with a capacity for 971 patients but housing more than 2,000 people, the majority of patients were men – poor Muslim men. In Fanon's division, there were 165 European women and 220 Muslim men, and they were segregated. Azoulay and Fanon noticed that if European female patients responded well to their propositions of activity, Muslim male patients resisted. They analyzed their failure in these terms: "A leap had to be made, a transmutation of values had to be carried out. Let us admit it; it was necessary to go from the biological to the institutional, from natural existence to *cultural existence*."[25] Since Arabic and Islamic culture defined social roles in different ways than Europe, therapeutic practices, they argued, elaborated to fit European social organizations could not be applied to Muslim society without provisions. Language and cultural barriers raised methodological difficulties; theater activities were irrelevant if they were seen as a "feminine activity"; a newspaper was worthless if patients were illiterate; the presence of an interpreter underlined the gap between the patients and the psychiatrists; group therapy was doomed to fail if speaking of one's feelings and emotions was not part of the "local culture." The solution was to train the psychiatrist in local culture, language, and customs. But, more important, the psychiatrist could not, in a colonial situation, exercise his technique. How could the psychiatrist perform his role, "to enable man no longer to be a stranger to his environment," when the colonized was condemned "permanently [to be] an alien in his own country" and psychiatric institutions could not in such situations properly fulfill their goal of "serving man's need." Since "madness was one of the means man has of losing his freedom" (*Pra* 51 / *TAR* 53) and colonialism was the systematic organization of the deprivation of freedom, therapy was impossible except if the psychiatrist entered the service of the struggle for decolonization.

It was in independent Tunisia, where Fanon went after being expelled from Algeria in 1947, that he was able to apply more freely his vision of a humanistic psychiatry at the hospital Charles Nicolle (see Fanon and Geronimi 1959d: 713–32). With the psychiatrist Charles Geronimi, Fanon explained why a day care center answered one of the goals of humanistic psychiatry. In this setting, the psychiatrist had to establish constant contact with other medical practioners so that he would "cease to represent a fantasmatic and mysterious character." He would become a doctor among other doctors, and this would affect his relation not only with the staff but with the patients as well. But it was the *medicalization of madness* that would carry greater therapeutic consequences. Fanon and Geronimi wrote, "The re-introduction of psychiatry within general medicine strongly corrects the prejudices which are generally rooted in public opinion and *transforms the mad person into a social person*" (p. 715, my emphasis). The hospital was transformed into a "society with its multiplicity of relations, duties, and possibilities so that patients can assume roles and fulfill functions." There was no gap between the social life in the hospital and social life outside of the hospital. The therapist would use the family, the "site of all medications," as a "normative value." Social therapy would take the "patient away from his phantasms and force him to confront reality on a new register"(p. 718). Fanon and Geronimi concluded that the addition of day care centers, "created and developed in highly industrialized countries could be transplanted in a so-called under-developed country without losing any of its value. Day care centers represent the form of psychiatric service most suitable to treat mental illness" (p. 715).

Through the relative failure of the Blida experience followed by the success of the Tunis experience, Fanon elaborated his psychiatric theory: a psychiatry grounded in the historical and cultural context of its practice, whose goal was to return the patient to his social environment. Fanon remained faithful to Tosquelles's teaching when he affirmed that the "veritable social-therapeutic milieu is, and remains, the society itself." Fanon's theoretical contribution to psychiatry was shaped by its clinical practice. He believed that psychiatry could become an emancipatory therapy, a means among other means of political and social emancipation, that its institutions could offer to disturbed persons a site in which to learn to be free again. Madness was exemplified by a loss of freedom, of agency, and psychiatric social therapy was the technique through which the psychiatrist would help the patient to shed his alienation. Fanon's position was that a successful cure meant freedom, freedom from symptoms that alienated, chained, the patient. The "very principle [of medicine] is to ease pain," he wrote (*Sr* 107–35 / *ADC* 121–46). Fanon criticized a medicine that remained deaf and blind to the suffering, values, mores, and culture of the people it treated, yet he believed in the possibility of its progressive project. His ambivalent position toward psychoanalysis could be partly explained by his desire to act decisively on the structure of the individual's personality, his profound aspiration to connect personal freedom with social and political freedom, and his rejection of psychoanalysis's approach that one's structure cannot be changed, that one can only learn to accommodate the world. Freud had said,

> Psychiatry can only say with a shrug: "Degeneracy, hereditary disposition, constitutional inferiority!" Psychoanalysis sets out to explain these uncanny disorders; it engages in careful and laborious investigations, devises hypotheses and scientific constructions, until at length it can speak thus to the ego: "Nothing has entered into you from without; a part of activity of your own mind has been withdrawn from your knowledge and from the command of your will.[26]

Freud, then Lacan, had posited a fundamental alienation of the subject (Lacan's notion of *méconnaissance*). But to Fanon, alienation was entirely the result of social, cultural, and political conditions. Social and cultural emancipation meant as well psychological emancipation. In the introduction to "Colonial war and mental disorder" (in *Les Damnés*), Fanon claimed a direct relation between colonization and madness. "There is *therefore* in this calm period of successful colonization, a regular and important mental pathology directly produced by oppression."[27] Yet the rich and fascinating cases that he presented all referred to symptoms produced by the colonial *war* in Algeria. Fanon's text produced a divided approach: one as a committed activist and another as a professional psychiatrist. The professional psychiatrist, confronted by the great suffering and deep mental troubles of some patients, could only admit, in some cases, his impotence to cure the patient.[28] The activist, in contrast, had difficulty admitting his failure.[29] The psychiatrist, in his daily practice, was confronted by the possibility of *failure* in the cure, of the impossibility of a return to what was considered "consciousness" and freedom. The activist, engaged in a struggle whose goal was freedom and which demanded a quick resolution in order to save lives, could experience only impatience with the resistance of the psyche, with the length of time that a cure demanded. This tension between two practices, whose goals seemed similar, resulted in Fanon's voluntaristic rhetoric, a form of rhetoric that was contradicted by his professional practice. Fanon showed in his psychiatric practice, as it was related in his professional articles and in *Les Damnés de la terre*, a deep concern for his patients. The tone of his psychiatric texts often differed from his political texts: less messianic, less moralistic, less populist.

Fanon's psychiatric project was inseparable from the history of psychiatry and of decolonization. In the 1950s, the discovery of new neuroleptic drugs offered a new opportunity for the "liberation" of mental patients. Those patients, whose symptoms could be controlled by the drugs, could be returned to the world, to their work, to their family.

This discovery was revolutionary. The problematic of the subject and of his or her alienation could be understood in terms of liberation. The parallel with the movement for national liberation, of subjects culturally and socially alienated, was made by many psychiatrists. Social therapy and new psychotropic drugs were among the tools of a psychiatry whose goal was to decolonize the subject, to dis-alienate the subject, along with the subject's social dis-alienation. This approach, full of revolutionary promise, was attractive. One could not resist the attraction of such promises. Yet, as the Algerian psychiatrist M. Boucebci has argued, "The prevalent socio-cultural articulation and the constant reference to the freedom of the subject confronts the psychiatrist, in his practice, with a major obstacle: the *politicization* of his approach, at the risk of politicization of psychiatry" (Boucebci: 952–61; emphasis in original).

Fanon's argument that medical practioners must know the historical and social conditions of formation of the society in which they exercise, as well as its cultural practices and beliefs, radically questioned a medical practice which wants to believe in its intrinsic neutrality. Such a practice would end up ignoring, denying the subjectivities of its patients. Yet, Fanon's desire to show that *politics* and *psychology* were inseparably linked limited the dimension of his argument. For if a political solution to social alienation could be pursued with determination, the same voluntarism in psychiatric practice would lead to the dismissal of problems whose solution escaped the immediate political resolution. In Algeria, problems related to identity, filiation, sexual life, and consanguinity, were not erased by independence. Though Fanon never made this proposition, many of his statements encouraged this connection. His call for "la libération totale qui concerne *tous* les secteures de la personalité" (the total liberation of all sectors of the personality) meant that "l'homme nouveau n'est pas une production a posteriori de cette nation mais coexiste avec elle, se développe avec elle, triomphe avec elle" (the new man is not a production *a posteriori* of this nation, but co-exists with it, develops with it, triumphs with it).[30]

However, mental pathology escapes such determinism. Thus, in contemporary Algeria, in the words of Boucebci, "the increasing frequency of problems of mental pathology" demonstrates a permanence of human alienation, which resists all projects of control and discipline. A part of the human condition, psychological alienation is not the loss of freedom. Fanon himself seems to recognize this when he said, "Le fait que je sois moi est hanté par l'existence de l'autre" (That I am I is haunted by the existence of the other) (1959–60).

Notes

1 "Letter to the Resident Minister" (*Pra* 50–3 / *TAR* 52–4), emphasis mine.
2 Fanon had no training in psychoanalysis and never entered analysis. However, he used the psychoanalytical technique with two patients in Tunisia.
3 On Philippe Pinel and "moral treatment," see Jean Garrabé, (1994), Joan Goldstein (1987), Jacques Postel and Claude Quetel (1994), and Gladys Swain (1977).
4 On Antoine Porot and the image of the Muslim in colonial psychiatry, see Robert Berthelier (1994).
5 See François Tosquelles (1984), in which the history of this movement is presented. Tosquelles was the Director of the Hospital of Saint-Alban, where most of the theory and practice of "institutional therapy" was developed.
6 The technique of psychodrama, developed in the United States in the late 1940s, was extremely well received in France. The psychiatrist Moreno's work on group psychotherapy deeply influenced Tosquelles's group.
7 Many among these psychiatrists who had been in the Resistance during the war were close to the Communist Party and generally sympathetic to radical social theories. Tosquelles, who was born in Catalonia, had reorganized the psychiatric services of the Spanish Republican Army. He started an analysis in 1933 with a Jewish analyst refugee in Barcelona. After the defeat of the Spanish Republic, Tosquelles escaped to France and worked as a psychiatrist in the camps of Spanish refugees. He was then named Director of the Hospital of Saint-Alban, which during the war became a refuge for intellectuals and scientists, such as Georges Canguihem.
8 Tosquelles (1984: 74). I have kept the term "man" because it was the term used by Fanon, Tosquelles, and other psychiatrists cited in this essay. Though it can be said that "man" was the generic term, its constant use nonetheless reveals an indifference toward sexual and gender difference among these writers. Regarding Tosquelles's influence on Fanon, Fanon trained with him at the hospital of Saint-Alban in 1952. Roger Gentis, another leading psychiatrist of institutional therapy, has described his encounter with Tosquelles's work in these terms: "I heard of Saint-Alban through Fanon, who was in the same year of medical school as I and who had been an intern there. Fanon introduced me to students in psychiatry who were connected with the Saint-Alban experience" (in Gentis 1995: 127–8). Fanon contributed with Tosquelles to three presentations at the Congrès des médecins aliénistes et neurologistes de France et des pays de langue française (see bibliography).
9 There were other wards at Blida each with their respective Chef de Service.
10 There are stories about Fanon delivering patients from their chains. Colleagues of Fanon at Blida have contested these stories, yet it is understandable that such a myth could have emerged. It presents a power-

ful and attractive image: along with the political struggle for decolonization, for liberation from the chains of the colonial power, other chains are broken.

11   One of the most influential essays was Benedict Augustin Morel's *Traité des dégénérescences physiques, intellectuelles et morales de l'espèce humaine* (1857). Morel's writings greatly influenced French psychology. He claimed to describe the "mode of production of degenerated beings, their classification, hygiene and treatment" (p. 7). His conclusions, which were made from his observations of the poor proletariat and of poor agricultural workers around the city of Rouen, drew him to advocate moral education and reform in order to slow down the process of "degeneration."

12   The expression is Eugene Weber's in *Peasants into Frenchmen* (1976).

13   The historian Robert Nye has shown how, toward the beginning of the twentieth century, the entire focus was no longer on "seeking to determine simply whether an individual deserved punishment for his crime or cure for his illness," but on determining the degree of danger or threat posed by an individual to society. The "criterion for incarceration or internment should no longer be responsibility but 'dangerousness'" (1984).

14   Le Bon's numerous books, written round the time of the Dreyfus affair, were translated into some ten languages and sold hundreds of thousands of copies.

15   Antoine Bouillon (p. 111). Bouillon's study is extremely valuable and his bibliography on "colonial psychology" is one of the most complete treatments one can find.

16   Mamadou M'Bodj (p. 14). Reboul and Régis's propositions were adopted in the French colonies. The colonial government of the Afrique Occidentale Française issued a decree in June 1938 that established the first Service d'Assistance Psychiatrique en AOF.

17   The review was published by the Institute of Sociology on the Economy and Psychology of Peoples, based at Le Havre, an important harbor and place of trade for the French colonial empire. The review advertised for shipping companies, companies that sold "exotic woods," and other businesses trading with the colonies. Essays in this review foreshadowed the work done by the proponents of "ethno-psychology." (The review was renamed *Ethno-Psychologie* in 1970).

18   Hardy, who was a prolific writer, a colonial administrator and a member of the *Académie des Sciences Coloniales*, pursued throughout his life his goal of defining a coherent and detailed psychology of the races. See Hardy (1925; 1929; 1934; 1936). In a 1948 article, "Psychologie et tutelle," Hardy argued that one of the reasons for colonial discontent was that "civil servants who are far from having the same conquering faith, the same fecund illusions [as] the colonial conquerors" were now making the decisions in the colonies. There was a solution, he thought: a training in psychology.

19   Thomas S. Szasz (1971a, 1971b: 469–71), emphasis mine. See also Alexander Thomas and Samuel Sillen (1972).

20   These writings were Octavio Mannoni's *Prospero and Caliban*, which gained

this title from its first English edition (the original was *Psychologie de la colonisation*); Fanon's *Peau noire, masques blancs*; Albert Memmi's *The Colonizer and the Colonized* (originally *Portrait du colonisé précédé du portrait du colonisateur*).

21 In France, psychology had constructed workers' violent rebellions as the result of atavistic traits, inborn criminality, and alcoholism.

22 On the economic conditions in the colony, Mannoni wrote, "Economic questions are certainly important; they may not absolutely determine the future of the colonial peoples, but that future will undoubtedly depend on them to a very great extent. I ought therefore to explain why they are given so little place in this book. It is because economic explanations are too general in their application to account very accurately for the facts of colonization: economic exploitation occurs wherever political and social conditions favor it, in the colonies as elsewhere. In the colonies, however, its character changes and it becomes colonial exploitation" (p. 202). And later, "There is, moreover, considerable danger in adhering too closely to the economic explanation, for it implies that colonization would have been a good thing if it had been economically honest, if lust for gains had not falsified the accounts, if the colonizers had been economically disinterested" (p. 204). For a detailed reading of Fanon's critique of Mannoni, see Jock McCullogh (213–21).

23 *L'Information Psychiatrique* 51 (December 1975): 10.

24 Frantz Fanon and Jacques Azoulay (1954). See also Azoulay's unpublished thesis (1954).

25 Fanon and Azoulay (1954: 355–6). I have adopted Irene Gendzier's translation (1973: 81). Emphasis mine.

26 Cited in Sander Gilman (1993: 162). Freud wrote these remarks in 1917. See Gilman's examination of Freud's reaction to the thesis of degeneration, which dominated science in his time (pp. 157–68).

27 *Les Damnés de la terre* (1995 Folio edition: 301). Emphasis mine.

28 See, for instance, the case of the young Algerian man whose mother had been killed by the French soldiers and had consequently killed a European woman. He is haunted at night by a murdered woman whose image is confused with his mother's. Fanon concludes, "aussi peu scientifique que cela puisse sembler, nous pensons que seul le temps pourra apporter quelque amélioration dans la personnalité disloquée du jeune homme."

29 About Fanon's role in the Algerian nationalist movement, the guest reference remains the Algerian historian Mohamed Harbi (1954 and 1980). Harbi has made a remarkable contribution to postcolonial scholarship on decolonization by going against the orthodoxy which set up a heroic, unified, unilingual Algerian people and giving back to Arabo-Islamism its place in the nationalist struggle.

30 Conclusion of the chapter "Guerre coloniale et troubles mentaux" (quoted earlier in English). Emphasis mine.

7

Revolutionary Theory: Sociological Dimensions of Fanon's *Sociologie d'une révolution*

Renée T. White

Revolutionary struggle and resistance always involve multileveled trans-formation. We can speak of the individual's role in changing his or her particular political commitments – in taking sides, if you will. We can also focus on the historical record of the resistance movement: key factions and splinter groups, strategies, political maneuvering and so on. Another perspective is ideological. As people are forced to resist the imposition of a "foreign leadership," they are also made to shift, trans-mute and transform how they see, what they see, and how they organize in response to what (and who) surrounds them.

Sociologie d'une révolution (*A Dying Colonialism*) is an account of all of these perspectives, and much more. In documenting the minutiae of occurrences, from the most seemingly mundane to the most revelatory, Fanon sets the scene for revolution: revolution both from within and without. Individual transformation and resistance is associated with shifts (both self-conscious and reflexive) in social groups, and ultimately, in an entire society. By asking a fundamental question, "What and how do people survive in resistance, and resist to survive?," Fanon develops a theoretical framework. This is a framework which can address the individual and psychosocial as easily as it addresses the systemic and structural. Fanon uses a conceptual model, one that L. Adele Jinadu calls "methodological individualism." By juxtaposing the individual within a societal context, the concern is directed on to the effect of social structures and institutions on the individual: what opportunities are provided and what constraints are imposed by structures and institutions in the way of individuals realizing their interests (see Jinadu: 126).

This is the task for a sociologist. More specifically, this is the accomplishment of a sociological thinker. Not only does Fanon accomplish this, but much more. Fanon was able to connect the psyche of Algerians with the colonial institutions they encountered, and he relayed how *complex* social networks can be, how revolutionary ideology can be borne of the mundane, and the way collective and individual identities can undergo complete transformation: "One of Fanon's greatest virtues as a writer is that he constantly relates the psychological predicament of the individual to his environment without losing sight of the individual" (Caute: 35).

Fanon has also provided both theoretical and applied lessons for the methodologist. Using at times what social anthropologist Clifford Geertz calls "thick description," Fanon guides readers through the innermost psychosocial workings of a people. With these snapshots, along with analyses of societal phenomena, one is given a comprehensive perspective and analysis of a country and a people in revolution. Geertz clearly argues for the importance of ethnography and historiography in mapping out the changes in a nation:

> This view of change, or process, stresses not so much the annalistic chronicle of what people did, but rather the formal, or structural, patterns of cumulative activity. The period approach distributes clusters of concrete events along a time continuum in which the major distinction is earlier or later; the developmental approach distributes forms of organization and patterns of culture along a time continuum in which the major distinction is prerequisite and outcome. Time is a crucial element in both. In the first it is the thread along which specific happenings are strung; in the second it is a medium through which certain abstract processes move. (Geertz: 5)

Throughout the brief period in which he wrote, Fanon illustrated a keen sociological eye; he is a powerful and persuasive sociological analyst; he echoes some of the foundational thinkers in social theory, and his analyses are present in the works of many who follow him.[1] Through the use of descriptive data, Fanon's work has reinforced the importance of linking macro and micro analysis – especially the importance of field work and ethnography in sociological research. He evokes images of symbolic representations of national identity, and uses symbolic interactionism and structural functionalism to show how social roles can be transformed through revolution and resistance struggles.

Collective Identities and Social Meanings

According to Fanon,

> There is not an occupation of the territory and independence of
> persons. It is the whole country, its history, its daily pulsation that are
> contested, disfigured, in the hope of a definitive annihilation [*définitif
> anéantissement*] . . . From this point on, the real values of the occupied
> quickly acquire the habit of existing clandestinely. (*Sr* 49 / *ADC* 65)

In order to occupy people, you occupy their land. At first, this merely
appears to be a "traditional" military strategy, but as Fanon indicates,
there are wide-ranging social outcomes. In the case of Algeria, social life
was destroyed by France's colonial presence. The social life of any
group or community is dependant on the entire system of beliefs and
expectations which enable citizens to interact in their daily lives. One's
social position and status is determined within this system of social
meaning. The institutionalization of colonial rule resulted in the rigid
definition of social status and position along racial-ethnic and class lines.
Even though the status of *colonized* was shameful to the citizenry of
Algeria, they found themselves assuming social roles associated with
this positioning because the constancy and predictability of social life
required that they do so.

The self-hood of Algerians, whether as individuals, or as members of
a nation with its own national identity, also depended on social life and
social organization. Being Algerian had particular social meaning which
was defined within the context of Algeria's self-determined national
identity. Once national identity was devalued and denied, Algerians
became strangers in their own land.

Nationhood provides citizens with a national identity and thus national consciousness. The collective experiences and traditions of a
nation provide it with the foundation for social living and sociality. In the
works of Emile Durkheim is an acknowledgment of the importance of
collectivity and identity in the existence of a community or social group
(see Durkheim *The Division of Labor in Society*).

Durkheim's account of the "glue" which holds a social group together
is closely tied to Fanon's description of the psychosocial effects of
colonialism and revolution. Any group of individuals which shares some
kind of socially defined label share in what Durkheim called "conscience
collective." This notion of collective conscience refers to the totality of
beliefs and sentiments common to a group of people. It is an independent, determinate, cultural system. Group membership is determined by
a sense of common values and norms, or collective representations,
which are *sui generis* unique and irreducible to the individual.

Thus there is an organic nature to the way collective identity is created and maintained: "[t]he rationality of human action is to be sought in the nature and goals of collective human life" (Jinadu: 127). If one is to oppress a nation through social control, this must obviously require destroying or demeaning anything unique to the collective identity of the people being oppressed. France's attempts to deny Algerians their right to citizenry (that is, independence and self-determination) was advanced on the basis of anything from paternal to purely racist grounds. However, the "doctrinal terms of colonialism in its attempt to justify the maintenance of its domination almost always force the colonized to some clear-cut, rigid, static counter-proposals" (*Sr* 47 / *ADC* 63). Algerians resisted ideological and identity-based attempts at infiltration.

In *Social Theory and Social Structure*, Robert Merton describes how disequilibrium in a social system occurs when components of the system no longer "fit," when people no longer willingly assume the social statuses and roles ascribed to them. The result of this lack of fit, or maladaptation, is anomie; individuals feel disconnected from the whole, their sense of normative structure is weakened, and they engage in deviant behavior.

As in any case of colonialism, there were numerous efforts to strip Algeria of its identity and replace it with a European one. This replacement process was not in the hopes that Algeria could become France, since it was believed that on the grounds of essential difference this was not possible, but in the hopes that Algeria could be a representation of France through mimicry.

Structural functionalist theory posits that for any social system to survive a social stress, components of the system have to shift and adapt. Colonial domination and the subsequent revolution were the stressors in Algerian society. The survival of Algerian society depended on the systemic rejection of this colonial domination. There was a gap between the value-orientation of Algerians and the cultural expectations of the French. This gap resulted in a culture conflict which could only be resolved through revolution.

The irony of colonial rule and domination, as Fanon notes, is that while the aim of oppression is to exploit humans in all of their capacities, what actually results is the following:

> While in many colonial countries it is the independence acquired by a party that progressively informs the diffuse national consciousness of the people, in Algeria it is the national consciousness, the collective sufferings and terrors that renders it ineluctable that the people take its destiny into its own hands. Algeria is virtually independent. The Algerians already consider themselves sovereign. (*Sr* 10 / *ADC* 28)

Coercive action became the tool with which Algerians reinforced their sense of national identity and thus facilitated the start of revolution – individual, cultural, social, and political.

In documenting the way social movements develop, theorists continue to reflect this paradoxical nature of oppression and colonialism. First, in any state of oppression, at least a small segment of this group of individuals will organize and strike back. Second, the very identity which was used to single them out and oppress them becomes the site of struggle. In the case of ethnicity, race, or culture, the very symbols of collectivity are used to oppress. These symbols, in dialectical fashion, are eventually redefined and then represent struggle, survival, strength, and liberation. Considering the effects of *internal* colonialism on black Americans, Kwame Ture and Charles V. Hamilton note:

> Black people must redefine themselves, and only they can do that. Throughout this country, vast segments of the black communities are beginning to recognize the need to assert their own definitions, to reclaim their history, their culture; to create their own sense of community and togetherness. (Ture and Hamilton: 37)

The violence visited upon men and women of the diaspora, when studied within specific historical contexts, will support this fact. The analyses of the Rodney King beating in *Reading Rodney King, Reading Urban Uprising* (Gooding-Williams) supports this fact. What oppression does is "merely" reinforce the very social identity the colonizer wishes to suppress.

Cultural Representation and Revolution

Revolution is about territory: political, economic, geographic, ideological and cultural. The key tool of oppression, outside of violence and physical assaults, is cultural terrorism. Those same cultural representations which distinguish a people from others are denied them. As Fanon observes, "The style of clothing, the traditions of dressing, of finery, constitutes the most marked forms of originality, that is to say that which is most immediately perceptible of a society . . . Yet the general look remains homogeneous, and great areas of civilization, immense cultural regions, are grouped together on the basis of original, specific styles of men's and women's wear" (*Sr* 16 / *ADC* 35).

In a very concrete and sociologically relevant way, clothes make the man and woman. Destabilization of national identity can occur by simply transforming the meaning of dress. In sociological and anthropological terminology, acculturation refers to the process of shifting from one cultural foundation to another. One assumes the cultural signifiers of the dominant group out of choice or necessity. In either case, acculturation leads to a shift in social status, or in many cases, insures basic survival. Cultural specificity, holding on to one's cultural heritage, makes one visible, and thus vulnerable. Cultural assimilation, what Fanon calls counter acculturation, requires the modification of one's most fundamental values and beliefs. They become less visible and thus less reprehensible to the eye of the oppressor.

Cultural traditions, and the elements that symbolize them, are laden with social meaning for both colonizer and colonized people. Both engage in using cultural artifacts to symbolize the very being of a community or society of people. They do so, however, to different effect. For an oppressor, whatever represents an oppressed group becomes both exoticized and vilified. The need to own and possess these symbols is challenged by the need to eradicate them through the process of acculturation. Those facing colonialism respond differently. For them, whatever basic signifiers are associated with identity will eventually become reified as tools of resistance. "In the face of the violence of the occupier, the colonized is led to define a position as a matter of principle with respect to a formerly inert element of the native cultural configuration" (*Sr* 29 / *ADC* 46). This is a way to deny the colonizer's ability to penetrate into the inner sanctum of collective self.

In the case of Algerian women, removing the veil was strongly encouraged by the French. Such a gesture had cultural and symbolic meaning. The Algerian women who supported this gesture were "Europeanized" and therefore made safe and accessible for the French. They represented the slow acceptance of colonialism and the rejection of Algerian national tradition. This is the "destructuring" of Algerian society at its foundations. The veil symbolizes the collective representations of a nation. Its rejection is the rejection of national values and thus the nation's identity:

> The occupying forces, in applying their maximum psychological attention to the Algerian women's veil, obviously had to harvest some results. Here and there it thus happened that a woman is "saved," is symbolically unveiled. These test-women, with bare faces and free bodies, henceforth circulated like sound currency in the European society of Algeria . . . With each success, the authorities were strengthened in their conviction that the Algerian women would support Western penetration into the native society. (*Sr* 24 / *ADC* 42)

In this way, the veil became another locus of struggle for Algerian men and women. An essential referent for their belief system was at risk.

The battle over the symbolic is a battle over consciousness, ideology, and knowledge. The self – not the individual, but one's membership in a collective national identity – is under siege. Social theorist Anthony Giddens argues that societal membership is elemental to individual survival because social membership shapes collective and individual identities:

> Societies, then, in sum, are social systems which "stand out" in bas-relief from a background of a range of other relationships in which they are embedded. [Other identifying features of a society] include: The prevalence, among members of the society, of feelings that they have some sort of common identity, however that might be expressed or revealed. Such feelings may be manifest in both practical and discursive consciousness and do not presume a value consciousness. (Giddens: 165)

In what Giddens would call a struggle over the symbolic, the transformation of the social meaning of the veil is an example of cultural warfare. Social symbols represent ideology. When the dominant controls and redefines these symbols they are actually attempting to tamper with a society's ideological underpinnings.

In this cultural war, maintaining the veil as a part of Algerian womanhood (whether according to spiritual, social, or ideological terms) is akin to revolutionary struggle. The everyday meaning of the veil is transformed to mean more than is seen on the surface. Such cultural inversion is latent warfare.

Contrary to some critics' claims, Fanon was clearly aware of the changing roles of Algerian women during the country's fight for independence. He observes that revolution cannot leave anyone unchanged, including what he calls feminine society; "In the course of the multiple episodes of the war, the people came to realize that if they wished to bring a new world to birth they would have to create a new Algerian society from top to bottom" (Sr 86 / ADC 101). Normative expectations for men and women, fathers and mothers, sons and daughters, were irrevocably altered, and "the tight, hermetic, and hierarchical structure of the Algerian family was now exploded" (Caute: 53). Arguably, women's social roles were most affected.

What Fanon observes is the link between the transformation of social institutions, group identity, and the individual. The shift in the perception of the Algerians' (regardless of gender) status from oppressed to agent resulted in a change in the role expectation associated with all Algerians. Both men and women were expected to act as revolutionaries within the resistance movement. As a result, the meaning of masculine and feminine gender identities were transformed. In the case of young women,

> The Algerian girl knows only two stages [of development] – childhood-puberty and marriage . . . All these restrictions were to be knocked over and called back into question by the national liberation struggle . . . The freedom of the Algerian people is thus identified with [the Algerian] woman's liberation, with her entry into history . . . This woman who writes the heroic pages of Algerian history explodes the narrow and irresponsible world in which she lives and conjointly collaborates in the destruction of colonialism and in the birth of a new woman. (*Sr* 92–3 / *ADC* 107)

In war and revolution, gender roles often change in order to increase the productivity of those under siege. By virtue of their feminine identities, Algerian women were effective couriers who could infiltrate "enemy zones." Their invisibility, as women and as Algerians, became tools of resistance; they often transported explosives undetected.

The resistance movement of Algeria rejects the French colonial model and is innovative in that it enables the citizens to create a new Algeria. Traditional roles are rejected on ideological bases and out of necessity. The continued existence of a people depends on this transformation of societal mechanisms and social roles. For example,

> Algerian society in the fight for liberation, in the sacrifices willingly made in order to liberate itself from colonialism, renews itself and effects new sexual relations from new values. Woman ceases to be a complement for man. *She literally wrenches out her place by her own efforts.* (*Sr* 94 / *ADC* 109)

In this scenario women became warriors out of necessity. Their rigid roles became more fluid in response to the need for lasting social change in Algeria.

Cultural Warfare through Technology

This cultural inversion also occurred through the transformed meaning and relevance of the radio in Algeria. Originally the radio symbolized the colonial. As a source of information and as an object possessed only by Europeans and assimilated Algerians, the radio's social and political position in Algeria became a different locus of struggle. As long as what it broadcast fell under colonial rule, the radio represented and reinforced the French presence. The radio is an example of the Gramscian notion of social hegemony. It is a mechanism by which the directions of the dominant group concerning Algerians' social behavior could be mass marketed and controlled.

Information breeds knowledge, which enables people to create more options from which to act. Radios in Algeria were not only visual representatives of oppression, they also became tools of ideological oppression by suppressing and shaping what constituted knowledge.

In a contemporary sense, warfare is the battle for knowledge and information. Control over information guarantees control over people. This is generally true; in the example of the Algerian revolution, control over access to information coupled with the ability to interpret information became the point of contention between the French and the Algerians. As one of the media, the radio mediates communication between members of the public. Cultural communication and transformation is possible without social contact. Universally valued and understood, information is filtered through the media.

In his account of technological change and ideological transformation, the sociologist Alvin Gouldner argues that normative forms of discourse, whether rational or grounded in false consciousness, can be communicated with and through technology (see Gouldner 1982). Considering that in the Algeria of 1954 the radio was defined as a new frontier in technology, much of Gouldner's assessment applies. Public forms of communication are verbalized consciousness (ideology). In many circumstances these ideologies can be focused on public kinds of politics that mobilize power. The radio became a mechanism for the redefinition of Algerian national (anti-colonial) identity; "[a] shared morality . . . can also create a mutuality of obligation that is so basic and vital to the creation and sustenance of viable structures" (Jinadu: 132). Here again, control over the mechanism of communication allows for shaping what is communicated.

The state, especially in repressive societies, use the symbolic and linguistic control wielded by controlling the media to replicate the dominant hegemony – one of false consciousness. In a period of revolution, any support for the transmission of anti-colonial information becomes another act of resistance. Those Algerians who boycotted local papers, or jammed radio programs in order to broadcast *The voice of fighting Algeria* were engaged in the struggle to control information. "Since 1956, in Algeria, the purchase of a radio has not been lived as adoption of a modern technique for getting information, but as the sole means of entering into communication with the Revolution, of living with it" (*Sr* 67 / *ADC* 83). Fanon later notes:

> With the creation of a *Voice of Fighting Algeria*, the Algerian finds him or herself virtually committed to listening to the message, to assimilating it and soon to accepting it. Buying a radio, getting down on one's knees with one's head against the speaker, is no longer wanting to get the news concerning the formidable experience in progress in the country, it is to *hear* the first words of the nation. (*Sr* 78 / *ADC* 93)

And so a new Algeria is born.

Fanon and the Sociological Imagination

Fanon's descriptive and analytical skill as a sociologist is unarguable. He utilizes ethnographic data plus political theory to document what he calls "a new humanity" (*Sr* 9 / *ADC* 27). The work of Fanon is present both explicitly and subtly in the political critiques of many contemporary theorists, particularly those engaged in the analysis of race, class, and ethnic struggle. Contrary to the claim that "It is also true that Fanon's treatment of the Algerian family and the Algerian woman lacks a sociological dimension [because] he does not distinguish between the *fellah* in the *bled* and the urban petty bourgeois,"[2] it is clear that there are many sociological nuances in his analysis which account for variations along ethnic, religious, class, and gender axes.

If the ultimate goal of a sociological analysis is the integration of a range of ideas concerning social life, then Fanon has greatly surpassed this task.

Notes

1   In preparation for this chapter I began with a relatively simple exercise. I started identifying the range of fields within the discipline that are represented in *Sociologie d'une révolution*. My tally is as follows: Sociology of knowledge, social psychology, sociology of culture, political sociology, medical sociology, and the sociology of religion.

2   Caute (1970: 53). See also Jack Woddis. Woddis claims that Fanon depends on a selective investigation of the peasantry's place in revolutionary struggle, and that parts of his Marxian analysis lack predictive strength. He criticizes Fanon for being too sweeping and imprecise, and for defining revolution in terms of armed resistance, when in fact, Fanon considers revolution in many social spaces including cultural and identity-based loci.

Part III

Identity and the Dialectics of Recognition

8

Casting the Slough: Fanon's New Humanism for a New Humanity

Robert Bernasconi

The closing lines of Fanon's *Les Damnés de la terre* read, in the Constance Farrington translation, "For Europe, for ourselves, and for humanity, comrades, we must turn over a new leaf, we must work out new concepts, and try to set afoot a new man" (*Dt* 376 / *WE* 316). The phrase translated as "we must turn over a new leaf" is "il faut faire peau neuve." It literally calls for a new skin, as when a snake casts its slough. That is a good measure of what "the new concepts" were supposed to produce. Fanon recognized that the disappearance of colonialism necessitated the disappearance not only of the colonizer, but also of the colonized. The process would be complete only with the disappearance of racism, if not as a shedding of skin, at least as a shedding of what skin color has come to mean in a world defined by colonialism. But what would this involve? In his 1959 statement to the Second Congress of Black Artists and Writers, Fanon explained how the liberation struggle itself would sketch new directions for culture:

> This new humanity cannot do otherwise than define a new humanism, both for itself and for others. It [this new humanism] is prefigured in the objectives and methods of the struggle. (*Dt* 294 / *WE* 246)

The present essay falls short of a full-blown defence of Fanon, although it does defend him against some current misunderstandings of what he meant by a new humanism. These misunderstandings have arisen not so much because Fanon had little to say about what this new humanism might be like, but more because the reason for that silence has not been properly appreciated.

It should be said straightaway that, with a few notable exceptions, one gets little help from the secondary literature as to how Fanon understood this new humanism.[1] Furthermore, Sartre's Preface to *Les Damnés* is positively misleading in this regard. Fanon combined his introduction of a new humanism with a critique of the old humanism. He wrote:

> The Western bourgeoisie, though fundamentally racist, most often manages to mask this racism by a multiplicity of nuances which allow it to preserve intact its proclamation of mankind's outstanding dignity. (*Dt* 205 / *WE* 163)

Sartre faithfully recorded the impact on Europeans of the critique of the old humanism:

> First, we must face that unexpected revelation, the strip tease of our humanism. There you can see it, quite naked and it's not a pretty sight. It was nothing but an ideology of lies, the exquisite justification for pillage, its honeyed words, its precocity were only alibis for our aggressions. (*Dt* 54–5 / WE 24–5)

Sartre acknowledged that racism was constitutive of Europe's self-understanding: "with us there is nothing more consistent than a racist humanism since the European has only been able to become a man through creating slaves and monsters" (*Dt* 56 / *WE* 26). By focusing on the critique of western humanism, Sartre had certainly identified an important strand of *Les Damnés*. Nevertheless, he emphasized that the critique of western humanism had already been accomplished by an earlier generation. Referring to "the yellow and black voices" who had spoken of "our humanism but only to reproach us with our inhumanity," Sartre declared:

> By and large, what they were saying was this: "You are making us into monstrosities; your humanism claims we are at one with the rest of humanity but your racist methods set us apart." (*Dt* 37–8 / *WE* 8)[2]

Sartre rehearsed the critique of the old humanism in his Preface to *Les Damnés*, even though he recognized that it was not novel. By contrast, he was silent about Fanon's new humanism, almost as if Fanon had blundered by reintroducing the term, so that it was more polite to pretend not to notice.

Fanon was in no doubt that the western bourgeoisie's "proclamation of mankind's outstanding dignity" was merely a mask for racism (*Dt* 205 / *WE* 163). If Sartre's Preface was faithful to Fanon in this regard, it was in part because Fanon's brief analysis was itself in full agreement with Sartre's own account in the *Critique of Dialectical Reason*: "Humanism is the counterpart of racism: it is a practice of exclusion."[3] This exclusion was forced, Fanon confirmed, by the classic gesture of imposing a western model on all humanity:

> Bourgeois ideology, however, which is the proclamation of an essential equality between men, manages to appear logical in its own eyes by inviting the sub-men to become human, and to take as their prototype western humanity as incarnated in the western bourgeoisie. (*Dt* 205 / *WE* 163)

Fanon recognized that this feature of bourgeois ideology was even adopted by the bourgeois caste in the new nation, which, as a result, became less a replica of Europe than its caricature (*Dt* 217 / *WE* 175). He undercut this line of development by declaring that if one wanted to turn Africa and America into a new Europe, it would be better to leave the destiny of those countries under the control of Europeans (375 / 315). The old humanism separated theory from practice. Its announced goals were less a call for action than fine phrases concealing the true nature of the system of exploitation it helped to sustain. The new humanism would already be different if it was a praxis.

That Fanon intended his new humanism to be radically different from the old western humanism is clear, but his success in realizing this difference has been challenged. In *White Mythologies*, for example, Robert Young issued this criticism:

> The question . . . becomes whether we should – and whether we can – differentiate between a humanism which harks back critically, or uncritically, to the mainstream of Enlightenment culture and Fanon's "new humanism" which attempts to reformulate it as a non-conflictual concept no longer defined against a subhuman other. For to some extent Europe fulfills this function in Fanon. (Young 1990: 125)

Robert Young did not examine Fanon's "new humanism" in his book, but his implication that Fanon simply reversed the terms in the humanist equation so that Africans were to be dignified by exposing Europeans as monsters does not square well with what Fanon actually said. This is especially clear from Fanon's Introduction to *A Dying Colonialism* from June 1959, which on the subject of humanism is less circumspect than the later text:

> The new relations are not the result of one barbarism replacing another barbarism, of one crushing of man replacing another crushing of man. What we Algerians want is to discover the man behind the colonizer; this man who is both the organizer and the victim of a system that has choked him and reduced him to silence. (*Sr* 15 / *ADC* 32)

That is why the physical removal of the colonizer was not the main issue. The colonial system would be destroyed only by the radical transformation of the colonized (*Sr* 172 / *ADC* 179). In answer to Robert Young one can say that whereas European humanism is differential and survives only so long as the non-European is defined as subhuman, the new humanism liberates both colonized and colonizer. This is the "new humanity" that Fanon evoked in the book's final sentence when he explained that the true revolution changes man (174 / 181). But have we not heard it all before? In place of Robert Young's question, therefore, we must still ask: can we secure a reading of Fanon's new humanism that does not eventually fall back into a variation of western humanism, even if only as the fulfillment of western humanism? That this is not what Fanon had in mind as the thrust of, for example, his insistence in the Conclusion of *Les Damnés* that the Third World be the start of "a new history of Man." "When I search for man in the technique and the style of Europe, I see only a succession of negations of man, and an avalanche of murders" (*Dt* 372–3 / *WE* 312). But it is easier to recognize that it was Fanon's intention to open the space for a humanism that was not western and to recognize how he sought to think this possibility or how we, his readers, might preserve that possibility without falling back into old habits of thought.

One can take certain passages from, for example, the essays collected under the title *Toward the African Revolution*, deprive them of their context and give the impression that Fanon believed that it was sufficient for decolonization to be accomplished thoroughly for the new humanism to prevail:

> It is essential that the oppressed peoples join up with the people who are already sovereign if a humanism that can be considered valid is to be built to the dimensions of the universe. (*Pra* 118 / *TAR* 114)

The formulation is at best unguarded and at worst irreconcilable with the more dialectical formulations of *Les Damnés*. The essay "Racism and culture" revealed the lacuna in his thought at this time all too clearly. After a profound analysis of the logic of racism and the stages it follows, Fanon announced that "the end of race prejudice begins with a sudden incomprehension" (*Pra* 44 / *TAR* 44). The claim is that a people struggling for its liberation refuses to legitimize race prejudice. This frustrates the recourse of the dominating nation to it. Once the oppressed are liberated the two cultures are in a position to enrich each other:

> In conclusion, universality resides in this decision to recognize and accept the reciprocal relativism of different cultures, once the colonial status is irreversibly excluded. (*Pra* 45 / *TAR* 44)

Of course, if colonialism is defined as "the exploitation of man by man" (*Pra* 147 / *TAR* 145), as Fanon sometimes did, then this bold thesis can be made to appear more plausible: the end of exploitation might indeed be accompanied by a new universality. The trouble with these formulations on their own is that the historical process they describe is less dialectical than magical. This is because, away from their context, they are deprived of any reference to the transformative power Fanon ascribes to violence. The new humanism does not arise only from the departure of the colonizers as a result of decolonization. It arises from the conflict (*Dt* 294 / *WE* 246). Fanon's account of violence may be unusual, but it is not wholly mysterious. Nor was it, as I shall show, mysterious to Sartre, whose refusal to acknowledge explicitly that the new humanism that pervades *Le Damnés* has another source.

It seems likely that the reason why in his Preface Sartre ignored Fanon's "new humanism" was precisely from fear of falling back into the old humanism. One can excuse Sartre a certain nervousness about the word humanism, as he was one of the initial targets of the suspicion of humanism that Heidegger helped to inaugurate in "Letter on humanism," his 1947 essay on, among other things, the relation of thinking and acting. Sartre in "Existentialism and humanism" had distinguished the humanism in which man as the end-in-itself is the supreme value from his own existentialist humanism according to which man is outside of him- or herself and thus is yet to be determined (Sartre 1968b: 54–5). Nevertheless, Heidegger considered both to be still within the orbit of metaphysics (Heidegger 1977a: 202). In 1948, in "Black Orpheus," Sartre's humanism showed another face, one that was concerned with universal history. Sartre's Preface to Senghor's *Anthologie de la nouvelle poésie nègre et malgache de langue française*, went much further than an account of negritude. Negritude was placed within "the evolution of Humanity." Sartre declares that

> Strange and decisive turn: *race* is transmuted into *historicity*, the black Present explodes and is temporalized, negritude – with its Past and its Future – is inserted into Universal History, it is no longer a *state*, nor even an existential attitude, it is a "Becoming." (1988: 325)

It was this which led Sartre to offer a dialectical account of negritude:

> It is when negritude renounces itself that it finds itself; it is when it accepts losing that it has won: the colored man – and he alone – can be asked to renounce the pride of his color. He is the one who is walking on this bridge between past particularism – which he has just climbed – and future universalism, which will be the twilight of his negritude; he is the one who looks to the end of particularism in order to find the dawn of the universal. (p. 329)

It was in this spirit that Sartre had issued the famous declaration that "antiracist racism is the only road that will lead to the abolition of racial differences" (p. 296).

Fanon's well-known response in *Black Skin, White Masks* to Sartre's analysis in "Black Orpheus" is far from simple,[4] but one of his strategies was to expose it as another variation of the old humanism. This is the true measure of Fanon's rejection of Sartre's dialectical presentation of negritude in "Black Orpheus," even though Fanon complained most loudly about its effects. "What is certain is that, at the very moment when I was trying to grasp my own being, Sartre, who remained the Other, gave me a name and thus shattered all illusion" (*Pn* 111 / *BS* 137). Fanon's objection was that he needed to lose himself in negritude and that Sartre had destroyed black zeal by presenting negritude as only a transitional stage in the process of historical becoming (*Pn* 109 / *BS* 135). Sartre had claimed that "negritude is *for* destroying itself" (Sartre 1988: 327). Fanon responded that he needed "the unforesee-able," he "*needed* not to know" (*Pn* 109 / *BS* 135), which is somewhat ironic, given that Sartre presented "Black Orpheus" as an attempt to tell whites what blacks "already know." Later, in *Les Damnés*, Fanon denied altogether that negritude still had a role as a vital moment in the dialectic,[5] but the decisive point was already made in *Black Skin* about the notion of the unforeseeable (*l'imprévisibilité*, *Pn* 109). Sartre had reduced the historical role of blacks to a transitional stage in a process whose goal was already given in advance, thereby denying them the possibility of playing a truly creative role within history. If Sartre robbed Fanon of his zeal, it was not just because Sartre was already looking beyond negritude to the next stage, but because Sartre wrote as if the end of the dialectic was already known to him in advance. This made it seem that the negritude movement had been reduced to a merely mechanical function.

Fanon's criticism of Sartre's "Black Orpheus" alerts us to the fact that what is at issue is a question of the difference between the settler's logic and the apparently similar logic of the colonized in which there is a "correspondence, term by term, between the two trains of reasoning" (*Dt* 126 / *WE* 93). On the one hand, there is the Aristotelian logic of the colonizer and, on the other hand, there is the dialectical logic that responds to it. It is through the dialectic that the new humanism avoids reduplicating the logic of the old humanism. Fanon did not identify all of the features of the dialectic. He made his point by concentrating on the "'It's them or us'" principle which the colonizer imposes on the colonized (116 / 84). He began with the transformation of the Manichaean world of colonialism:

The zone where the natives live is not complementary to the zone inhabited by the settlers. The two zones are opposed, but not in the service of a higher unity. Obedient to the rules of pure Aristotelian logic, they both follow the principle of reciprocal exclusivity. No conciliation is possible, for of the two terms, one is superfluous. (*Dt* 69 / *WE* 38–9)

Fanon envisaged that "the destruction of the colonial world" would take place through the abolition of one of these zones (*Dt* 71 / *WE* 41). There was to be a reversal, "a total, complete, and absolute substitution", whereby " 'the last shall be the first' " (*Dt* 65, 67 / *WE* 35, 37). In isolation these passages provide fuel for the kind of objection raised by Robert Young, but that is because they focus on only one aspect of the "creation of new men" with "a new language and a new humanity" (67 / 36). Fanon's decisive insight was borrowed explicitly from Sartre, who in the *Critique* had insisted that the temptation of the settler to want to massacre the natives was absurd, because it would only succeed in abolishing colonization.[6] This means that violence has a different result, depending upon who does it and who suffers it: it is only the violence of the colonized against the colonizer that is positive. The colonized's violence unifies the people and counteracts the separatism of colonialism (*Dt* 127 / *WE* 93–4). It is also the means of "reintroducing mankind into the world, the whole of mankind" (141 / 106), as it is only when the colonized no longer exist, that the colonizers are free to be human themselves. Whereas the colonizers are committed to keeping the oppositional relation intact, the violence of the colonized is dialectical, transforming both colonizer and colonized into a new humanity.

Sartre in his Preface to *Les damnés* may have avoided acknowledging both Fanon's new humanity and his new humanism, but he did recognize the "new violence which is raised up . . . by old, oft-repeated crimes" and he saw that this "irrepressible violence . . . is man recreating himself" (*Dt* 60, 51 / *WE* 31, 21). It might seem that it was in response to Fanon's criticism in *Black Skin* that Sartre in his Preface to *Les Damnés* explicitly located "the end [*le dernier moment*] of the dialectic" in a war that would divide, on the one hand, Europe and "that super-European monstrosity, North America" (55–6 / 26) and, on the other hand, Fanon's "brothers" [and sisters] in Africa, Asia, and Latin America (41 / 11). It might seem that Sartre only used the provocative phrase "last moment of the dialectic" because he did not want to be told a second time that he had jumped the gun, but it is clear from some of Sartre's other writings that he already understood the unifying aspect of violence. It is, for example, brilliantly portrayed by him in the *Critique of Dialectical Reason* in his discussion of the fraternity of the black rebels of

San Domingo, who found their reciprocal obligation in the color of their skin (1991a: 437–8). Furthermore, the connection of violence with humanism was set out by Sartre already in his 1952 discussion, "The May 28th demonstration." Because this discussion is not well known to all of Fanon's readers, it is worth recalling. Sartre there analyzed the situation of the French worker who is "simultaneously a man and a piece of machinery":

> The contradiction is not only *in* him: it is imposed on him; mass produc-
> tion requires that he be contradictory . . . Thus the original violence is not
> the oppression: the latter merges with justice and order; it's the *interiorized*
> *oppression*, the oppression *lived* as an internal conflict, as constraint exer-
> cised by one half of one's self on the other half. (1968c: 53)

This enabled Sartre to say that the violence that is supposedly born at the moment of a riot or a strike is in fact merely the exteriorization of violence, the point at which the docile worker, who rejects the human in himself, becomes the rebelling worker who rejects the inhuman. Sartre added, "This refusal is itself a humanism – it contains the urgent de-mand for a new justice" (p. 54).

> the worker is answerable to a historic right which doesn't yet exist and may
> never exist; from the point of view of a future society which will be born
> thanks to his efforts, his violence is a positive humanism; seen in our
> present society, it is in part a right (to strike) and in part a crime. In fact,
> humanism and violence are the two indissoluble aspects of his effort to go
> beyond the condition of an oppressed being. (1968c: 54–5)

The phrase "his violence is a positive humanism" is glossed by Sartre in a footnote which reads, "Not a means of achieving humanism. Not even a necessary condition. But the humanism itself, insofar as it asserts itself against 'reification'" (55n). In the same sense, the war between North and South described by Fanon could be understood as already a human-ism, the last moment of the dialectic.

If I have not set out the new humanism as a program, that was not only out of deference to Fanon's silence, but also out of loyalty to his logic which necessitates that it be left as an empty marker. The fact that Fanon had so little to say about the new humanism is not a lack that should be good. Fanon was at his most explicit and most precise when he translated the claim "the violence is a positive [new] humanism" into the claim that the new humanism is to be "prefigured in the objectives and methods of the struggle" (*Dt* 294 / *WE* 246). This does not mean that there is nothing beyond violence, still less that violence is the goal. Violence helps to mobilize the masses and introduces ideas of national destiny and of collective history, but Fanon also speaks, for example, of a second phase that is the building up of the nation to which these ideas, born of the struggle, contribute (126–7 / 93). To say that the new humanism is prefigured in the struggle allows for a restoration of the unforeseeable to its place within historical becoming and promises a refiguring of the relation between theory and practice. One could still set objectives, organize priorities and develop strategies locally, but one would no longer try to envisage the end of the dialectic. To do so would threaten the novelty of the new humanism and its claim to have put the old humanism behind it. Not that novelty of itself was the crucial issue for Fanon. What Fanon's account of the two logics suggested was that a new humanity could arise only through the creative praxis of the colonized. Theirs was a violence that would not only destroy the old order, but produce a new one. Theoreticians should avoid trying to disarm it ahead of time by presuming that they always know where it will lead.

Notes

1 Among those who discuss the new humanism, see especially Lou Turner (1989: 47–64).
2 The classic statement on this position is perhaps Aimé Césaire's 1950 text, *Discourse on Colonialism* (1972). Césaire was, of course, one of the founders of the negritude movement in the 1930s and it is worth noting that they did not as a group abandon the word "humanism." See, for example, L. S. Senghor, *Liberté I* (1964: 7–9).
3 Sartre (1991a: 752). It was after reading the *Critique* that Fanon asked François Maspero to approach Sartre and invite him to write the Preface to *Les Damnés de la terre*. See Annie Cohen-Solal (1987: 431–3).
4 For a slightly fuller discussion, see my "Sartre's gaze returned: The transforming of the phenomenology of racism" (1995: 201–21).
5 Fanon's main objection was that the idea of negritude disregarded the diversity of black culture. By contrast, when Sartre some ten years later, in 1971, questioned negritude, it was because it was "an internalization of the value judgments and the *Weltanschauung* of the enemy" (Sartre 1987: 175).
6 Sartre's *Critique* (p. 346), as quoted in *Les Damnés* (84–5n).

9

Fanon, Sartre, and Identity Politics

Sonia Kruks

Questions about "What is to be done" are frequently displaced on the Left today by questions about who "we" are: by questions of identity. The politics of identity, or "identity politics" as it is more often called, is based on a set of propositions that, although widely held, are for the most part only loosely formulated or even tacitly presupposed. There is not one author or text one can turn to for a systematic formulation of the tenets of identity politics, and indeed the very notion of identity is open to radically divergent interpretations, ranging from the biological to the discursive.

Even so, as much from observing identity politics in action as from written sources, I believe one can characterize its core propositions as follows: (1) that differences of race, class, ethnicity, gender, sexual orientation, and so on have for too long been obscured by a hegemonic white, male, upper-class and heterosexual elite which, under the guise of claiming that there exists a universal human condition, has constructed accounts of reality that serve its own ends; (2) that those groups whose identities were previously subjugated by this elite should now be privileged as sources of both epistemological and moral authority, since their oppression gives them a unique capacity and right to speak about and judge what is true and what is good; (3) that (implicit in the first two claims) access to truth and the authority to make moral and political judgements is not universal, but is always relative to who one is; (4) that to "unmask" or "deconstruct" privileged, universalist readings of reality and to make possible the expression by the previously silenced and subjugated of their own identity and truth are not only valid forms of political action, but *the* most important forms of political action today; (5) that such a politics of unmasking privilege and enabling the subjugated to come to voice needs also to be conducted internally, within groups and movements on the Left.

Identity politics is a comparatively recent and, I think, radically new version of what Charles Taylor aptly calls "the politics of recognition." Taylor argues that it was with the collapse of ascribed identities and social hierarchies, that is, with the transition from feudal codes of honor to modern, universalist claims about equal human dignity, that the politics of recognition was born (1991: 46ff). For with the collapse of the unproblematic, ascribed social identities of pre-modern society, it became necessary to discover, create, or negotiate social and personal identities.

It was, of course, Hegel who first powerfully formulated the demand of the modern self for recognition: to be fully human, to attain full consciousness of self, is possible only through the reciprocal struggle for recognition by the other. Although Hegel's "master–slave dialectic" was couched in the abstracted terms of a reciprocal struggle only between two consciousnesses, and although it constituted only an account of an ethico-existential struggle for selfhood, the demand for free recognition by the other which Hegel postulated has been fundamental to broad political struggles for at least two centuries. It has subtended not only demands for "the rights of man," for equality under the law and adult white male suffrage, but also the abolition of slavery, the demand for women's suffrage, visions of socialism and, more recently, the black civil rights movement.

What makes identity politics a significant departure from such earlier forms of the politics of recognition is its demand for recognition on the basis of the very grounds on which it has previously been denied: it is *qua* woman, *qua* black, *qua* lesbian or gay – and not *qua* incarnation of universal human qualities – that recognition is demanded and moral superiority sometimes asserted. The demand is not for inclusion within the fold of "universal humankind" on the basis of shared human attributes, nor even for respect in spite of one's difference. Rather, what is demanded is respect for oneself as fundamentally different.

This recasting of an earlier universalistic politics of recognition that today culminates in identify politics had, I believe, its classic philosophical formulation in the early works of Sartre and Fanon. Principle are Sartre's treatment of the "Jewish question," and Fanon's creative and critical reappropriation of that analysis in terms of black identity. Thus I turn first to Sartre and then to Fanon in the subsequent sections of this paper. In examining the pyscho-existential accounts of dialectics of recognition and non-recognition that Sartre and Fanon develop, I intend, first, to retrieve an important strand of the intellectual roots of identity politics; second, to show that there are ways in which identity politics can learn from these earlier thinkers; finally, to suggest that some of the inadequacies of present-day identity politics can be brought more sharply into focus by examining certain difficulties found in these originary texts.

I

Sartre's paradigmatic account of non-recognition as oppression, together with his strongest call for the oppressed authentically to affirm their identify, is found in his 1946 essay, *Anti-Semite and Jew* (cited as Sartre 1976a). Of course, the issue of recognition had already been extensively explored in *Being and Nothingness*, published three years earlier. There, Sartre argued that the Other is always a threat to my own experiences of self, having the power to objectify me and to cause me to flee into self-objectification. However, such dynamics are portrayed by Sartre in *Being and Nothingness* as reciprocal: each can equally objectify or be objectified (Sartre 1956b: esp. Part Three). Anti-Semitism, by contrast, is not simply "the expression of our fundamental relation to the Other." For in the operation the anti-Semite performs upon the Jew something further is involved, which precludes the mutuality or reversibility of the objectifying relationship: "The Jew has a personality like the rest of us, and on top of that he [*sic*] is Jewish. It amounts to a doubling of the fundamental relationship with the Other. The Jew is over-determined" (Sartre 1976a: 79). In short, there is not a reciprocal relation of objectification between the Jew and other people. For the Jew, in an anti-Semitic world, is never free not to be the Jew, the Other.

In a passage that I think all too well also captures the dynamic between white liberals and people of color in the USA today, Sartre writes: "The liberal, when he met a Jew, was free, completely free to shake his hand or spit in his face; he could decide . . . but the Jew was not free not to be a Jew" (p. 77). In explaining the dynamics of this "over-determination," Sartre in significant ways anticipates more recent anti-essentialist accounts of the construction of racial, ethnic, and gender identities. To be a Jew, he argues, is not to be born of a physical race, or even – since many Jews are non-practicing – into a religion. If one asks what it is that Jews have in common, it is no fixed essence but rather "the identity of their situations" (p. 145). Sartre describes being-in-a-situation as living in "an ensemble of limits and restrictions" that one does not freely choose, but which one can choose to invest with various meanings. The situation of the Jew in Sartre's account is one above all constituted by the anti-Semite – just as others will later argue that of women is constituted by the sexist and that of people of color by the racist. "The Jew is one whom other men consider a Jew . . . it is the anti-Semite who *makes* the Jew" (p. 69).

How then can the Jew (or member of another oppressed group) respond to this over-determination? Sartre suggests that the most common response is "flight," the attempt to avoid fully confronting the pain of the situation through a variety of self-evasive strategies that he describes as choices of "inauthenticity." For example, he explains the attraction to many Jews of rationalism as a form of flight, for in the abstract life of the mind it would appear that we are all "men" and particularity can be transcended (pp. 111ff).

In contrast to the Jew who flees, Sartre describes the authentic Jew: the one who demands recognition for what he is. Authenticity, as proponents of black pride, gay pride, and other forms of identity politics also insist, does not involve the mere admission that one is what the Other says one is. Rather it involves re-appropriating, as a positive value, the self that the Other has imposed on one. Thus, "The authentic Jew . . . ceases to run away from the obligation to live in a situation that is defined precisely by the fact that it is unlivable; he derives pride from his humiliation" (pp. 137–8).

Whether or not an individual chooses authenticity, to be a Jew is to live in a situation one has not chosen, yet which constitutes part of one's very being. One is not "just" a human being who happens, in addition, to be a Jew: one *is* one's situation. And although one can give to one's being-for-others various meanings, one can never slough it off. Thus, anticipating later critiques of universalism, Sartre argues that the old style abstract humanism of the liberal democrat is not merely inadequate, but itself oppressive. Liberal universal humanism puts Jews – and other minorities – in a double bind. For it seeks to suppress the particularities of concrete groups and individuals that are, for better or worse, integral to their existence. It also obscures the dynamics of oppression behind the assertion of a universal human essence that "we" all share.

It seems to be indubitably the case that what is today under attack from identity politics, including liberal ideology and the western humanist tradition, have frequently – though I would argue not necessarily – functioned as exclusionary discourses. However, this is not to say that all universalist values should – or indeed can – be simply thrown out. Indeed, I am troubled by the radically relativist and frequently subjectivist thrust of much of the critique. For, as Marnia Lazreg has observed: "The rejection of humanism and its universalistic character . . . deprives the proponents of difference of any basis for understanding the relationship between the varieties of modes of being different in the world" (Lazreg: 339). We can make sense of difference,

I think, only by also recognizing a certain commonality to the human condition; generality is the horizon against which particularity must be configured. The demand to be recognized in one's particularity or difference is itself an implicit call for wider human reciprocity and respect. For if recognition by the negating other was not needed for the integrity of the self, non-recognition *per se* would not present itself as a problem.

It is here that I find Sartre's position to be more coherent than that of much recent identity politics. While formulating a cogent critique of abstract humanism, he does not claim that difference irredeemably fractures knowledge, truth, and reality. Instead, Sartre asserts the need to hold together in tension both difference and a certain commonality of the human world. He thus further argues that oppression must also be resisted by those who are not directly its victims because lives are in fact demonstrably interconnected. The fate of the oppressed is also "ours" (1976a: 123), not because we share a common human "nature" but because we are embedded in one and the same historical world.

But here Sartre runs up against a disjunction between the realm of moral and existential experience (in which the demand for recognition takes place) and the world of concrete political transformation, a disjunction that I think also haunts identity politics. Having portrayed anti-Semitism as above all an existential relation of anti-Semite to Jew, in which the Jew cannot escape the objectifying portrait constructed by the anti-Semite but can choose to live it either authentically or inauthentically; and having urged authenticity – the active and prideful taking up of the identity – on the Jew, Sartre points out that, although authenticity might permit the affirmation of existential freedom in the face of oppression, it does not *in itself* address the social situation of the Jew. The individual Jew may resist the self-objectifying look of the anti-Semite, but authenticity provides no clear orientations toward the elimination of anti-Semitism. On the contrary, Sartre concludes that, "The choice of authenticity appears to be a *moral* decision, bringing certainty to the Jew on the ethical level but in no way serving as a solution on the social or political level" (p. 141).

The problem that Sartre leaves us with in *Anti-Semite and Jew* is this: how to bring the realm of moral and existential self-affirmation into a practical engagement with the actualities of a realm of politics that extends beyond personal experience – that is, the realm of institutions and enduring social structures? Power does not rest on objectification alone. Anti-Semitism is more than the sum of the actions of a collection of individual anti-Semites: it takes enduring historical and structural forms. Sartre is, of course, aware of this. But in *Anti-Semite and Jew* he can only acknowledge the hiatus and try schematically to bridge it with a hopelessly rationalistic appeal at the end of the book for a classless society as the end to all ills, including anti-Semitism (pp. 140–51). Sartre here becomes guilty of embracing a de-situated and schematic vision of history, which ignores his own valuable insights into the concrete particularities of oppression.

What is missing, both in Sartre's account and in much recent identity politics, is a sense of *mediation*, of the dynamics through which issues of interpersonal recognition and identity pass into (and from) the domain of concrete institutions. How, for example, do they pass into anti-Semitic legislation, into segmented labor markets that perpetuate low black and female wages, into pension plans that discriminate against gay couples, into mechanisms that grant differential access to health care or education by class and race?

II

For better and for worse, the influence of Sartre is pervasive in Fanon's earliest work, *Black Skin, White Masks*, to which I now turn. In Fanon's hands, Sartre's account of the dialectics of recognition and non-recognition deepens and brilliantly mutates as it is extended to issues of racial identity. Yet a similar abandonment of a careful phenomenology of situated experience and abrupt shift to rationalism also mar Fanon's work. However, what Fanon also brought to his topic was something that Sartre did not have: first-hand experience. While Sartre writes as a progressive, but as neither anti-Semite nor Jew, Fanon writes as a black man. There is both a concrete knowing and a depth of passion to this work that have rendered it a classic for later movements for black consciousness. Even though the book focuses on the experiences of black Antilleans in the 1940s and 1950s, it has resonated far beyond these boundaries of time and place.

Fanon's starting point in *Black Skin* is the problem of authenticity. Most colonized black men, he observes, are not capable of an "authentic upheaval" today (*Pn* 6 / *BS* 8). For they are the victims of a socially produced, but real, situation of inferiority which they have internalized. They thus suffer from a "psycho-existential complex" (9 / 12), that inhibits them from authentic self and social transformation. The black (*le Noir*) – the Negro (*le nègre*) – is, he suggests, characterized by a "situational neurosis . . . a constant effort to run away from his own individuality, to annihilate his own presence" (48 / 60). Fanon hopes to help "cure" this neurosis through his analysis.

The social origin of this neurosis lies with the attitudes of white, colonial society to blackness. "Negrophobia" is in many ways a similar phenomenon to anti-Semitism as Sartre had depicted it, but there are also profound differences. For the Jew can sometimes be anonymous, but the black is always visible as such. Creatively appropriating Sartre's notion of the overdetermined otherness of the Jew, Fanon writes: "I am overdetermined from outside. I am not the slave of the 'idea' that others have of me but of my appearance" (*Pn* 93 / *BS* 116). In the white unconscious, as well as in the white culture, Fanon argues, the Negro, even more than the Jew, denotes evil. "Is not whiteness in symbols always ascribed in French to Justice, Truth, Virginity? . . . The black is the symbol of Evil and Ugliness" (145 / 180). But the Negro does not stand for abstract evil so much as for the threat of uncontrolled carnality and sexuality. The Jew is an intellectual or economic threat, but the Negro "symbolizes the biological danger. To suffer from a phobia of Negroes is to be afraid of the biological. For the Negro is only biological. The Negroes are animals" (134 / 165). Thus, the experience of alienation in one's body, that self-doubling process in which one experiences oneself as a body-for-others, is more profound for Fanon's Negro than for Sartre's Jew. The project that Fanon undertakes in *Black Skin* is less to account for white negrophobia than to explore the lived-experience and moral possibilities open to a black living in a negrophobic world.

Like Sartre's Jew, Fanon's Negro most frequently engages in forms of flight. Indeed, it would seem almost impossible to do otherwise. For virtually all paths to an authentic self-affirmation seem to Fanon to be blocked or co-opted. From childhood onwards, exposure to the values of white culture induces an inauthentic identification with whiteness – particularly in the educated child, such as Fanon himself had been.

> The young black in the Antilles, who in school never ceases to repeat, "our forefathers, the Gauls," identifies his [or her] self with the explorer, the civilizer, the white who brings truth to the savages – an all-white truth. There is identification, that is to say that the young black subjectively adopts a white attitude. The hero, who is white, is invested with all aggression. (*Pn* 120 / *BS* 147)

Indeed, Fanon reports that this is so much the case that many Antilleans simply do not think of themselves as black: Antilleans are French; Negroes are black and primitive – and they live far off in Africa (see also *Pra* 22–31 / *TAR* 17–28).

But once a direct encounter forces on an Antillean knowledge of his own personal blackness – when, as Fanon did, he goes to metropolitan France and experiences white fear and hostility as he walks down the street – further forms of inauthenticity are elicited. Having internalized

white negrophobia and the belief in the superiority of white "civilization," the Antillean cannot accept the designation *black*. To speak
French well, to be educated, are after all signs of being French – that is,
white. But suddenly, there he is, irrevocably marked by his body as the
feared and despised other, the threat to "civilization." For many, Fanon
included, the response is to internalize the white negrophobe's gaze, to
engage in the kind of self-objectification that Sartre described in the
inauthentic Jew. "On that day," Fanon writes, "disoriented, incapable of
being abroad with the other, the white, who imprisoned me without
pity – I took myself far off from my own presence – making myself an
object" (*Pn* 91 / *BS* 112).[1] This self-objectification is the source of the
alleged black "inferiority complex," a complex that has nothing to do
with family dynamics or the Oedipus complex, but everything to do with
what Fanon so aptly calls the "epidermalization" of social inferiority
(8 / 11).

Another response – one that also enticed Fanon – is to attempt to
escape into a universal humanity through the appeal to reason. Just as
the Jew seeks to evade his particular situation through rationalism,
claiming that reason makes him a "man" like any other, so too there is
a temptation, especially for the black intellectual, to try to escape
from his racialized situation by an appeal to reason or other transcendental universals. But this attempt is always thrown back in his face by
racism:

> this Negro who is looking for the universal. He is looking for the universal!
> But in June 1950, the hotels in Paris refused to rent rooms to Negro
> pilgrims. Why? Purely and simply because their Anglo-Saxon customers
> (who are rich and who, as everyone knows, hate Negroes) threatened to
> move out. (*Pn* 150 / *BS* 186)

There is yet another strategy, which looks at first sight more promis-
ing: "I decided, since it was impossible for me to get away from an *inborn
complex*, to affirm myself as BLACK. Since the other hesitated to recognize me, there remained only one solution: to make myself known" (*Pn*
93 / *BS* 115). Here might appear to be the authentic response to racism.
This, surely, is what Sartre had advocated for the authentic Jew, even
though he noted that it would not resolve the Jew's social situation. Here
also is the move that distinguishes identity politics from earlier forms of
the politics of recognition: the demand to be recognized in one's difference. But Fanon is deeply ambivalent, for he sees this as a reactive
politics. Of course, the Negro "who is driven to discover the meaning of
black identity" (11 / 14) is an advance on the Negro who still seeks to be
white. But the search for black identity is itself fraught with problems.

For, he argues, "what is often called the black is a white construction" (ibid).

It is through an examination of *négritude* that Fanon explores the dilemmas of the affirmation of black identity. *Négritude* is at once untenable and yet necessary. Through extensive citation from the works of Senghor, Césaire and others, Fanon illustrates that much of its affirmation of black identity rests on a simple reversal, a re-appropriation of white stereotypes of black culture. What is celebrated as authentically "Negro" is rhythm, the magical, the irrational, the emotional, the intuitive – and all of these are saturated with the sexual (for example, *Pn* 99–104 / *BS* 122–8). Fanon explains the logic that leads to such a reversal:

> I had rationalized the world and the world had rejected me on the basis of color prejudice. Since no accord was possible on the level of reason, I threw myself back toward irrationality . . . I wade in the irrational. Up to the neck in the irrational. And how my voice vibrates! (*Pn* 99 / *BS* 123)

There is a distinctly ironic tone to Fanon's presentation of the mythic splendors arrayed by the poets of *négritude*. Yet, however reactive it might be, *négritude* is also necessary. For it does effect a shift in black–white relations. Not only does it offer the black sources of pride, but the white suddenly recognizes in the Negro qualities that he now experiences himself as lacking, such as closeness to nature, spontaneity, simplicity. Thus, for the first time, a certain *reciprocity* of recognition emerges. A friend told Fanon, "when the whites feel that they have become too mechanized, they turn to men of color and ask them for a little human sustenance." Comments Fanon, perhaps not wholly ironically: "At last I had been recognized. I was no longer a nothing" (*Pn* 104 / *BS* 129).

But the recognition, even if real, is ephemeral. For white culture still has at its disposal the overwhelming means of devaluing black experience. Although Negro simplicity is said to be delightful, "History" is still on the side of rationalism, technology, and industry – that is, Europe. Negro culture thus becomes appropriated as a diversion, as a realm for momentary relaxation. "I will be told," says Fanon, that "now and then when we are worn out by our lives in big buildings, we will turn to you as we do to our children – to the innocent, the ingenuous, the spontaneous" (*Pn* 106 / *BS* 132).

The unkindest cut comes from white progressives who also claim that history is on the side of European society – now in the form of the industrial proletariat as revolutionary class. Here, Sartre is Fanon's chief culprit. For just as Sartre had rationalistically adduced the classless society as the solution to the Jewish question, so he had argued in "Black Orpheus," his preface to Senghor's collection of black poetry, that *négritude* as a celebration of difference would, in time, dissolve itself in the world revolutionary movement that transcends both class and race. "In fact," Sartre had written, "negritude appears as the minor term of a dialectical progression . . . it is intended to prepare the synthesis or realization of the human in a society without races. Thus negritude is the root of its own destruction" (cited by Fanon, *Pn* 108 / *BS* 133).

Fanon's objection is not that Sartre is in error in asserting that *négritude* is a transitional movement. Sartre's mistake, in fact, is to have told the truth! But it is the short-circuiting, objectifying, disembodied, truth of a *pensée de survol*, which ruptures immediate, lived-experience. Using Sartre the phenomenologist to criticize Sartre the rationalist, Fanon points out that "a consciousness committed to experience *is* ignorant, *has to be ignorant*, of the essences and the determinations of its being" (*Pn* 108 / *BS* 134, emphasis added). In explaining the transitional social and historical function of *négritude*, Sartre has destroyed its vitality. By dissecting it in the cold light of reason, he "has destroyed black zeal" (109 / 135). And, Fanon adds, "I needed to lose myself completely in negritude . . . I *needed* not to know . . . at the very moment when I was trying to seize my own being, Sartre, who remained The Other, gave me a name and thus shattered all illusion" (109, 111 / 136, 137).

A question which comes to mind in considering Fanon's critique is whether Fanon is saying that it is because Sartre is white that he does not have the right to pass historical judgment on *négritude*. But this is not Fanon's point. Unlike later advocates of identity politics, he is not claiming that a person who has not suffered white racist oppression *cannot* understand the significance of *négritude*. Fanon's complaint is rather that Sartre, who could and should have understood, was guilty of an individual failure of judgment. Sartre made a "mistake," he says. He "had *forgotten* that the Negro suffers in his body quite differently from the white man" (*Pn* 112 / *BS* 134, emphasis added). He failed to consider the psycho-existential effects of his schematic rationalism. Yet once having given *négritude* its full existential weight, Fanon also seeks a way beyond its celebration of black difference.

In the final chapter of *Black Skin*, Fanon develops his own vision of a transition beyond *négritude*. Paradoxically, however, he ends up in as schematic a position as Sartre's, indeed, his position owes much to Sartre at his most rationalistic. "I do not want to be the victim of the *Ruse* of a black world," Fanon writes, "I am not a prisoner of history. I should not search there for the meaning of my destiny" (*Pn* 186 / *BS* 229). He thus criticizes as irrelevant *négritude*'s search for black identity through the retrieval of great African cultures of the past. He also argues that resentment over past injuries and demands for reparations is misguided, for it represents an orientation towards the past whereas freedom is always oriented toward the future (186–7 / 230–1).

Unfortunately, in making these arguments Fanon draws on the most radical transcendental conception of freedom that Sartre had developed in *Being and Nothingness*. He interprets the Sartrean claim that in authentic freedom "I am my own foundation," to mean that one can, after all, through sheer commitment, leap beyond the bounds of historical situation. At the level of authentic freedom he writes,

> The Negro is not. No more than the white. Both must turn their backs on the inhuman voices of their respective ancestors in order to give birth to authentic communication . . . Superiority? Inferiority? Why not simply attempt to touch the other, to feel the other, to reveal myself to the other? (*Pn* 187–8 / *BS* 231)

Why not, indeed? Earlier in the book Fanon has already given us cogent reasons why this is not possible. Like Sartre, he ends here by undermining his own argument. If *négritude*, that "white construction," that necessary "illusion," has a profound psycho-existential significance that Sartre should not have cut short in the name of the universal historical dialectic, then neither should Fanon have finally abandoned it in the name of an abstract, universal freedom beyond situation.

How should we assess the fact that Fanon and Sartre both leap so abruptly across the gulf that separates their nuanced accounts of concrete difference from the terrain of abstract universalism? The attempt both make to link the affirmation of difference to a movement beyond particularity is, I believe, laudable, even if their manner of doing so is overly schematic. For, as I have suggested, one of the difficulties of more recent identity politics is its tendency to wed itself so tightly to difference that an acute relativism and a politically debilitating fragmentation often ensue. Both reified notions of difference and postmodern claims that the search for common ground is implicitly "totalitarian" too frequently lead to a politics that eschews engagement (either analytical or practical) with the wider world of structures, institutions, and macro-historical processes in which the politics of recognition is embedded.

But, what both Sartre and Fanon lack, at least in these influential early works, is a middle level of investigation. Neither can analyze the dynamics that mediate between particular existential experiences and more general historical processes. It is this lack that perhaps accounts for their sudden leap from the most concrete treatment of difference to such abstract universalism. They offer no tools with which to theorize the interconnections between the realm of existential experience, in which the dynamics of non-recognition and self affirmation are played out, and the broader world of political and historical processes, in which the dynamics of oppression they describe are enmeshed.

By the late 1950s, both Fanon and Sartre came to address this lacuna in their earlier work. In the *Critique of Dialectical Reason*, Sartre situated dynamics of self and other in a broader world of social ensembles, structures, and historical forces, developing a complex account of social mediations. Meanwhile Fanon, having become deeply involved in the Algerian liberation struggle, argued increasingly strongly that freedom cannot be sought in the realm of interpersonal affirmation and recognition alone. In his later works, particularly his final book, *Les Damnés de la terre*, he does not abandon his earlier concern with the politics of recognition, as much as he attempts to formulate an argument that it can only be realized, at least in Africa, through engagement in national liberation struggle and the development of "national culture" (*Dt* 251–96 / *WE* 206–48). Fanon's specific prescriptions – including the need for armed struggle to bring about territorial liberation and an end to the colonial state – are of course time and place specific. But his warning, that the affirmation of identity can be liberating *only* in the context of a struggle also to transform wider material and institutional forms of oppression, is still relevant today. To affirm, express, or celebrate one's identity is, as Fanon insisted, psychologically empowering. It is also, as Sartre claimed, a vital moral affirmation. But to affirm one's identity is not, in itself, to change the world.

Note

1   Much of Fanon's semi-autobiographical account of the avenues of flight which tempt the black intellectual are set out in the fifth chapter of *Black Skin, White Masks*. This chapter is entitled in the English translation "The fact of blackness," in the original, "L'expérience vécue du Noir."

10

On the Difference between the Hegelian and Fanonian Dialectic of Lordship and Bondage

Lou Turner

I

She and Sartre had gone for vacation to Italy "without scruples" because Mussolini had cut railway prices 70 percent to attract tourists to the Fascist Exhibition, Simone de Beauvoir recalls prosaically in her memoir, *The Prime of Life*. Of this and Sartre's later sojourn as a scholar at the French Institute in Hitler's Germany, de Beauvoir gives a frank account of the suspended engagements of left intellectuals tarrying in the shadow of Fascism in the immediate pre-war years:

> We would not set our own shoulders to the wheel of history, but we wanted to believe that it was turning in the right direction; otherwise we would have had too many problems to rethink. (de Beauvoir 1992: 146)

No doubt the burden of escaping history once again encumbered Sartre one steamy summer evening in Rome, in 1961, when a terminally ill Frantz Fanon insisted on talking with him into the night about the turn "the wheel of history" had taken in the direction of what Marx called in the *Grundrisse*, "new epochs of social revolution." An intense and physically depleted Fanon told of having "watched men being created by revolutionary beginnings," of having to rethink (too) many problems, and of having made a beginning in shouldering the responsibility for the task history had assigned him in the form of a manuscript he had only just completed in "a ten-week eruption of intellectual energies" (Geismar 1971: 179). The work for which he had come to solicit Sartre's collaboration, by way of a preface, had begun as a series of three lectures he had given to the political and military cadre of the FLN (Front de Libération Nationale) at its military operations encampment at Ghardimaou, Tunisia. (The tape recordings of Fanon's lectures to the general staff of the FLN, to my knowledge, remain under guard in the vaults of the Political Commissariat in Algiers to this day.)

From the death of a hero we can infer the origin and course of his life history, Marx once observed. It is no less true of the *curriculum vitae* of the thought of Frantz Fanon, which had concentrated itself to such an absolute point of expression that summer's night in Rome in the company of an ailing Sartre and a strangely irritable de Beauvoir, that Sartre's biographers and commentators consider his Preface to Fanon's *Les Damnés de la terre*, his most revolutionary writing. There is no irony to be found in this ailing engagement between Sartre and Fanon, in part because of what we are able to infer from the curriculum vitae of a philosophy of revolution like Fanon's. He no longer despaired, as he had at the time of his resignation as chief resident of the psychiatric facility at Blida-Joinville outside Algiers, that hope had become, in the dark days of the 1956–7 Battle of Algiers, "but the illogical maintenance of a subjective attitude in organized contradiction with reality" (*Pra* 50 / *TAR* 53). Indeed, his letter of resignation signaled a rupture with Sartrean existentialism, reading, as it did, like a manifesto announcing his final plunge to freedom. Inferring the life history of the thought of Frantz Fanon from its most concentrated point of expression necessarily returns us to his youthful explorations into dialectical philosophy for which at many points Sartre had provided inspiration.

Interestingly, Fanon's now fetishized notion of a racialized or colonized society as a "Manichaean world" was initially posited as a menacing paradigm of his own Martinican society, and quite provocatively as a description of the occluded topography of gendered differentia that inscribe it. The Hegelian notion of subjective certainty made flesh by the Martinican "dream . . . of magically turning white" (*Pn* 35 / *BS* 44) represented a painful construction of that Manichaean world. That the truth of consciousness, certain of itself, emerges from an "inverted world" of errant, contradictory forces is itself a troubled reflection of the confused boundaries of identity held tenuously together in the subjective certainty of the colonized mind. This febrile identity is barely able to sublate the temporal rupture at the center of subjective certainty, inasmuch as its objective truth is only made present to itself in the ontic ruins of the colonial city.

Evidently, the "dialectic of being and having" (*Pn* 35 / *BS* 44) that Fanon refers to as the social ontology of the colonial city is a constructed epidermis that has always already existed, that is to say, it was *already*

there waiting for us. This most material "flesh" – "[a] house in Didier
[and] acceptance into that high society" that sets on "a hill that dominates the city" (*Pn* 35 / *BS* 44) – has *always* been there, and is *already*
there when the colonized subjectivity of the woman of color seeks the
certainty of herself or rather seeks to make the certainty of herself *flesh*.
The high society of Didier is there – is already, always there – as the
exteriorized womb of the mother country that makes her subjective
certainty flesh; flesh made flesh by Didier's houses and its high society.
It is a dream made flesh, however, only in an indeterminate future. So
between the flesh of the colonial world (the mansions of Didier), and the
dreams of the colonized mind that are only made flesh in some undis-
closed future, there emerges a subjective certainty whose truth is determined by a dialectic of being and having.

This topography of the colonial city is, as well, the bodily schema of
the colonized woman, on which are inscribed "a veritably Manichean
conception of the world" (*Pn* 36 / *BS* 44–5). The identification of the
body of the woman of color with the world is immediate and self-
possessing, as in the opening moves of Hegel's treatment of self-
conscious certainty in the *Phenomenology*. Fanon described her as "the
incarnation of a complete fusion with the world . . . an abandonment
of . . . ego in the heart of the cosmos" – a condition that "no white man,
no matter how intelligent he may be can ever understand" (36 / 45).

The dialectic of being and having constitutes an insularity of the black
mind, one in which the only way out is through the white world (*Pn* 41
/ *BS* 51). Even when "the black is among his own, he will have no
occasion . . . to experience his being through others," simply because
"every ontology is rendered unrealizable in a colonized and civilized
society" (88 / 109). There is here an anticipation of the *difference*
Fanon later posits between the dialectic of Hegel's concept of self-
consciousness and his reconstruction of it as a consequence of introduc-
ing a specifically black ontos into the dialectic.

Fanon contends that a so-called black ontology is at best an
amphibolous issue of civilization and custom, insofar as, historically, the
sources on which such an ontos rested "were wiped out because they
were in conflict with a civilization that he [the black] did not know and
that imposed itself on him". Again, as in the case of the woman of color,
"difficulties in the development of . . . bodily schema" (*Pn* 89 / *BS* 110)
arise. The whole enterprise of *Black Skin* is set within the parameters of
this dialectic of sensuousness-within-the-life-world. As we will see, this is
less a Heideggerian than a specifically Hegelian concern.

There remains little doubt that for Fanon this dialectic is infused with
historical content. Not satisfied to leave it at an abstract schematic level,
he explains that "Below the corporeal schema I had sketched a historico-
racial schema . . . I thought that what I had in hand was to construct a

physiological self, to balance space, to localize sensations, and here I was called on for more" (*Pn* 90 / *BS* 111). Homi Bhabha takes Fanon's engagements with the artifice of race and identity to be a consequence of the epidermality of the lived-experience of the black in white society, and the artifice of otherness that western culture inscribes on the black body. We're "called on for more." For it is no less apparent that Fanon overreaches Bhabha's aversion to Hegelian dialectic in his discovery of a syllogistic alterity, or what Hegel refers to as "the *other in its own self*, the *other of an other*" (Hegel 1989: 835): "It was no longer a question of being aware of my body in the third person but in a triple person . . . I was responsible for my body, for my race, for my ancestors" (*Pn* 90 / *BS* 112). Not only history but *historicity* evokes resistance to a racist biologism determinate of the deranged syllogism of body, race, and history. But whereas Fanon sought to strip the artifice of racism from human relations through revolutionary *praxis*, Bhabha and other postmodernist critics of Fanon find it sufficient merely to shift the "Manichaean boundaries" of identity and difference.

The Negro is a fixed *veritas* in the schemata of the life-world of western consciousness and its discontents, "a necessary surplus excluded from the closed-circuit of the social edifice" (Zizek: 235), in the sense in which Slavoj Zizek extrapolates the "metaracism" of western civilization from its universalizing *Zeitgeist*. Fanon knows full well that the ontos of the West's life-world is no mystery to Being or its modern displacements, but rather a "historicoracial schema . . . woven . . . out of a thousand details, anecdotes, stories" (*Pn* 90 / *BS* 111). Ontology is merely the repetitiveness of custom and habit that at some level gets hypostatized as the epochal recursiveness of "civilization." So Fanon has sufficient reason to locate the dialectic of the lived-experience of the black at the sensuous level where self-consciousness is counterposed to its life-world. This *naturalism* leads, however, to serious interpretive problems regarding Fanon's reading of Hegel's master–slave dialectic. Several preliminaries still need to be taken into account before we turn to Fanon's Hegelschrift.

II

From the metaphysicality of the Negro's sensuousness being "open to all the breaths of the world" (*Pn* 103 / *BS* 127), Fanon runs headlong into another kind of historicism, one possessed of a technological imperative. The world is not only a place found in a state of nature, but a place constructed and possessing the sublimity of reason. In that world, the Negro, according to Sartre, is "a minor term of a dialectical progression" (107 / 133) in which his negritude is transitive and self-eliding. Fanon, as we know, takes his leave of Sartre here, even as he retreats into the night of Hegel's Absolute.[1] Not only had that "born Hegelian" Sartre to be answered on the ground of the dialectic proper, but in virtually Spinozist terms, Fanon incorporates the abject state to which Sartre's Marxism had reduced him, declaring that "In opposition to rationalism, he [Sartre] summoned up the negative side, but he forgot that this negativity draws its worth from an almost substantive absoluteness" (*Pn* 108 / *BS* 134).

Fanon's response to Sartre enjoins two lines of argumentation. First, as I've already noted, Fanon must encounter the Hegelian dialectic proper. This necessity leads him, secondly, to an appropriation of the Marxian dialectic of revolution. If Sartre's attitude to negritude represented "a date in the intellectualization of the *experience* of being black" – and he has already taken critical stock of theories of experience as ignorant of the "determinations of its being" (*Pn* 108 / *BS* 134) – Fanon is nonetheless still committed to discovering meaning in this constructed world dominated by *techné*. Is there a meaning in the capitalist-imperialist world that is "pre-existing, waiting for me," Fanon wonders aloud. It is not the meaning of black misery and wretchedness out of which the torch is shaped "with which to burn down the world" (109 / 134). With an almost Heideggerian flourish, Fanon turns his philosophical glance to a Marxian level of meaning,[2] where he finds "the torch that was already there, waiting for that turn in history" (ibid). This pre-existing world of *techné*, unlike the colonial city of his native land, has made men who have already discovered its *meaning* and the *means* to burn it down. The role of this dialectic in making Fanon an originary of Third World revolution cannot be overestimated, as it has contributed to the contradictory appeal Fanon has exerted on Third World intellectuals as diverse as Iran's Ali Shariati and South Africa's Steve Biko.[3]

This juncture, where the revolutionary meaning of the "wretched of the earth" coincides with that of the "workers of the world," is "waiting for that turn in history" to become an actuality. Fanon's talk of losing himself in negritude, and in the depths of an unhappy consciousness, has already begun to spend itself at this point, disclosing that the need to complete the movement of negativity presupposes its own negation, a need that involves an absolute standpoint that "brings necessity into the foundation of my freedom." Fanon had become a partisan of the dialectic of revolution in the modern world, and has commenced the critical deduction of a new black ontology, one wherein "black consciousness is immanent in its own eyes" (*Pn* 109 / *BS* 135), even as black experience is diversified, "for there is not merely *one* Negro, there are *Negroes*" (110 / 136). His proposition that "I defined myself as an absolute intensity of beginning" is reinscribed a decade later within a new historic moment, one in which he had "watched men being created by revolutionary beginnings."

Let us, then, recapitulate the path taken by Fanon to his encounter with Hegel. Ontology appears as nothing more than a science of the appearances of the historical enormity of material forces that shaped the Negro. Out of this ontological crisis, Fanon discovers a naturalism capable of comprehending the schema of body, race, and history, one which made Fanon's encounter with Hegel irresistible. The abject historical content of tom-toms, cannibalism, intellectual inferiority, religious superstition, "racial deficiency, slave-ships, and above all else, above all: 'Sho' good banana!'" could not be elided by the mysteries of western ontology and civilization.[4] For Fanon, the result was a devastating retreat: "I took myself far off from my own presence, far indeed, and made myself an object" (*Pn* 90 / *BS* 112). Once that "bell curve" had tolled the end of the Negro as subject, a liberal humanitarianism commenced the salvaging and exhibition of an eviscerated black self. "Two centuries ago I was lost to humanity, I was a slave forever. And then came men who said that it all had gone too far too long" (97 / 120). The Negro does not so much save himself, as he *is saved* by the western missionary heart. Time flies, but suffices as the ontology of black being, and timing is everything. "Too late," writes Fanon. "Everything is anticipated, thought out, demonstrated, made the most of. My trembling hands take hold of nothing" (97 / 121). On Fanon's view, René Ménil's description of this black eviscerated self cannot be seen except "in Hegelian terms":

> the consequence of the replacement of the repressed [African] spirit in the consciousness of the slave by an authority symbol representing the Master, a symbol implanted in the subsoil of the collective group and charged with maintaining order in it as a garrison controls a conquered city. (*Pn* 118 / *BS* 145)

This eviscerated black self, this subjectivity starved for recognition as a subject, discovers to its abject surprise that it is "a phobogenic object, a stimulus to anxiety" (*Pn* 123 / *BS* 151). It is here, Fanon tells us, that the specter of Richard Wright's "native son" appears full-blown. In the real world, of course, where the visage of Hitler lives on in ethnic cleansings and in the daily savageries of western civilization, the dialectical substitutionism in which "we change worlds" is normative. While negrophobogenesis may be one of the forms in which biologism metastasizes itself in the western mind, for the Negro himself, "historical and economic realities come into the picture" (131 n. 25 / 161 n. 25). "To suffer from a phobia of Negroes is to be afraid of the biological. For

the Negro is only biological. The Negroes are animals" (134 / 165).
At the psychopathological level, the white man's negrophobia makes the
Negro the theme of his action, whereas when we come to Hegel the
process is reversed in the dialectic of recognition. The process of
negritude's disalienation thus runs up against an ontological inertia
formed by the conjunction of culture and history. And Fanon is at pains
to differentiate revolution from negritude's metaphysical retreat to a
sublime universalism.

When founder and editor of *Présence Africaine*, Alioune Diop, argues
in his introduction to Placide Tempels's *Bantu Philosophy*, that "Bantu
ontology knows nothing of the metaphysical misery of Europe" (*Pn* 149
/ *BS* 185), Fanon sounds a sharp caution that resounds even against the
metaphysicality of negritude's progeny today: Diop had drawn the "dangerous inference" that "The very idea of culture conceived as a revolutionary will is as contrary to our genius as the very idea of progress"
(149–50 / 185). "Be careful!" warns Fanon.

> It is not a matter of finding Being in Bantu thought, when Bantu existence
> subsists on the level of nonbeing . . . It is quite true that Bantu philosophy
> is not going to open itself to understanding through revolutionary will:
> But it is precisely in that degree in which Bantu society, being a closed
> society, does not contain that substitution of the exploiter for the ontologi-
> cal relations of Forces. Now we know that Bantu society no longer
> exists. And there is nothing ontological about segregation. (*Pn* 150 / *BS*
> 185–6)

III

> On some "fine morning," whose noon is not red with blood, the infection
> has penetrated to every organ of spiritual life. It is then the memory alone
> that still preserves the dead form of the spirit's previous state, as a vanished
> history, vanished men know not how. And the new serpent of wisdom,
> raised on high before bending worshippers, has in this manner painlessly
> sloughed merely a shriveled skin.
>
> *Hegel*, Phenomenology of Spirit

None of this represents anything so simplistic as Fanon allegedly turning
away from philosophy towards a Nietzschean irrationalism. And, to be
sure, the Diop polemic implicates some of the issues at stake in Fanon's
engagement with Hegel. While we must here pass over Fanon's account
of "The Negro and Adler," that is, section A of chapter 7 of *Black Skin*,
entitled "The Negro and recognition," it is not without importance that
whereas section B of this chapter, "The Negro and Hegel," is devoted to
the problem of reciprocity between black and white, the Adler section

examines the phenomenon of recognition amongst blacks in the colonial milieu of the Caribbean. The inference here is that black intraracial relations in the Caribbean find their original subsistence in Hegel's dialectic of lordship and bondage. Black intersubjectivity is thus mediated by the white other in the colonial milieu, even one in which the white other is absent.

Fanon's Hegelschrift is divisible into two parts, the first part comprising the first ten paragraphs of section B, "The Negro and Hegel." The five formulations Fanon quotes from the "Lordship and bondage" chapter of Hegel's *Phenomenology of Spirit* all appear within these ten paragraphs, and are all aimed at affirming Fanon's contention that "At the foundation of Hegelian dialectic there is an absolute reciprocity" (*Pn* 176 / *BS* 217). The dialectic of the second part of Fanon's treatment results in the evisceration of that view, insofar as race becomes the central intervening verity in the independence and dependence of self-consciousness. The logical consequence of the naturalism we encountered earlier now becomes transparent.

In taking the inherent nature (*an Sich*) of any supposed object to be "a way in which it is for an other," Hegel's first reference to the notion of *other* is derived from our *understanding* of things giving way to our *experiencing* them (Hegel 1931: 218). What western consciousness understood to be the "Negro," and what happened when it *experienced* the Negro, are more than the opening moves of an historicized epistemology. In contradistinction to Mannoni's existential speculations regarding the trauma (*Erlebnisse*) indigenous peoples are alleged to have experienced in their initial contact with Europeans, Fanon contends that the trauma Europeans experience to the psychic structure of their ego upon coming into contact with blacks is no less an instance of Hegel's claim. In large measure, Hegel's very notion of self-consciousness can be said to be an *Erlebnisse* in the structure of the ego brought on by the irruption of experiencing the bare being of natural existence, or, as Fanon observed earlier, the biological, in our understanding. The notional field that had formerly assumed so absolute a standpoint *vis-à-vis* the object "gives way" to a relative relation which becomes as *localized* by experience as the objects of experience. Science now comes under the hegemony of experience and the empirical, at first eviscerating reason, and only then masquerading as it. In mythology, the evisceration and consumption of the antagonist is sought in order to ingest his powers, and then to masquerade as him. This seems a fitting metaphor for the diremption of reason and experience.

The "first immediate idea" of the Negro is naïve and "is cancelled in the course of experience" (Hegel 1931: 218), only in the end to dispense a "truth" adequate to the claims of experience. The claims of experience become the site of a new mode of science, whose anthropocentrism makes it susceptible to the *Erlebnisse* of the ego that originally brought about the hegemony of experience. Hegel calls this "new form and type of knowledge, the knowledge of the self" (p. 219), before which the conceptual knowledge of the other has vanished, although its moments have subsisted in a new form. As its turns out, those moments by which consciousness formerly understood the other are inherently consciousness itself. That is to say, all of the moments of sensuous consciousness and reflective understanding are moments of self-consciousness, derived from the ontological status of the object of the consciousness. What has gotten lost is the ontological status of *what* exists for and independently of consciousness. It so happens that the ontological status of the "world of sense and perception" (ibid.) is a condition from which consciousness takes its point of departure in order to become self-conscious through a new authentication of its experience. Because it is in search of its own authentication, self-consciousness must experience its object as itself, and thereby bring it under the hegemony of its own experience. Hence, it is not the object *per se* but self-consciousness's authentication of itself through its subsumption of the object's authenticity that it takes for "experience."

There is no reciprocity engendered in this relation, for had there been, it would at least have implied some degree of cognitive distance between self-consciousness and its object. Instead, experience constitutes a relation *in vacuo* between the two, a suffocating identity which is indifferent to difference. Furthermore, there is sufficient reason to regard the self-reflective formalism of self-consciousness, Fichte's Ego = Ego or I = I, as no more than the reflexive impulse of a socio-historical condition; it is characteristic of the subjugation of authentic otherness and difference by a new authentication of experience that cannot be conceived except under the hegemony of identity, I = I. This "motionless tautology" (p. 219) has an epochal status which Fanon attributes to the moral "stasis of Europe," a "motionless movement where gradually dialectic is changing into the logic of equilibrium."

What some have referred to as Hegel's second beginning to the *Phenomenology*, that is, the introductory section to this treatment of self-consciousness, situates us in his dialectic of otherness. Otherness, like blackness, is a fact of European consciousness that does not exist as a distinct moment, except insofar as it exists under the hegemony of identity. The strange truth of this hegemony is that the estrangement of the truth of the world from its appearance engenders a desire in self-conscoiusness for unity. Desire emerges here as that impulse that wants to suspend anything that appears to be an independent life-form in contradistinction to its ego. "Convinced of the nothingness of the other," writes Hegel, "it definitely affirms this nothingness to be for itself the truth of the other, negates the independent object, and thereby acquires the certainty of its own self, as *true* certainty, a certainty which it has become aware of in objective form" (Hegel 1931: 225).

Fanon is quite sensitive to Hegel's critical attitude towards this mode of subjective certainty. That it convinces *itself* of the nothingness of the other, then "affirms this nothingness to be for itself the truth of this other," intimates the self-deception upon which consciousness establishes the "truth" of its self-certainty. In other words, this mode of subjective certainty is acquired by negating what it already takes to be nothingness. What Fanon profoundly sensed is that subjective certainty comes, as Hegel observed in another context, from nothing through nothing to nothing. There is an irony in consciousness satisfying its desire by experiencing the independence of the other through negating it. The logical consequence of this desire is a world without the other, which can nevertheless be satisfied only by the existence of the other. With an ironizing logic that Fanon himself rehearses on many occasions, Hegel writes that self-consciousness "is thus unable by its negative relation to the object to abolish it; because of that relation it rather produced it again, as well as the desire" (1931: 225).

The heuristic turn at paragraph eleven of Fanon's Hegelschrift, commencing the second part of his essay, is coextensive with Hegel's transition from "The truth of self-certainty" to "Lordship and bondage." Having exposed the self-deceptive grounds upon which self-consciousness posits the certainty of itself, or otherwise satisfies its desire through the sublation of the other, Hegel "deconstructs" satisfaction as a condition arising from the inherent deprivation of the object/other. Satisfaction is guaranteed only through the object/other effectively bringing about "negation within itself." In short, "The object must *per se* effect this negation of itself, for it is inherently (*an sich*) something negative, and must be for the other what it is" (1931: 226). It is this negativity of the object/other that is constitutive of its status as another self-consciousness. In Fanon's slave, "steeped in the inessentiality of servitude" (*Pn* 178 / *BS* 219), and summarily "set free" by the master, the deprivation of the object/other engenders an historical attachment that determines a very different fate than met with in Hegel's slave. What Fanon was most sensitive to is that the negativity inherent in the object/other, which is constitutive of its being an independent self-conscious subject, for that very reason makes it an other that is not easily subjugated. So while self-consciousness may "attain its satisfaction only in another self-consciousness" (Hegel 1931: 226), it is only that self-consciousness whose *historical experience* has been that of subjugation and relegation to objecthood who thereby possesses a negativity that is *absolute* in the Hegelian sense of being the affirmation of human possibilities.

Hegel is quite clear that the form of consciousness we have before us is one that "has an object which implicates its own otherness or affirms distinction as a void distinction" (p. 226). While Lacan appropriated this specific side of self-consciousness as the basis of the "mirror stage" of his developmental theory of psychological structuration, Fanon is adamant that "For the black . . . historical and economic realities come into play" (*Pn* 131 n. 25 / *BS* 161 n. 25). For Fanon, as for Hegel, there is a constant irruption of the historical in the synchronicity of cognitive phenomena at whatever stage of development. Indeed, it is the force of "history and its process" which is at once internal to the structures of cognition and impels Hegel's more explicitly historical treatment of self-consciousness as the sociogenic phenomenon of lordship and bondage, and as the philosophical tendencies of stoicism, skepticism, and the unhappy consciousness.

IV

The division of his Hegelschrift into two areas of exposition is symptomatic of Fanon's reinscription of Hegelian dialectic with the very terms of negritude that Sartre had syllogistically subordinated to a "minor term," and with the economic and historical realities that extend beyond Lacan's "mirror stage." In the first ten paragraphs of "The Negro and Hegel" there is only one reference – a key one it turns out – to a racialized relationship between master and slave. The one reference actually anticipates Fanon's argument in the second part of his Hegelschrift, creating a tension between itself and the surrounding text of Fanon's reading of Hegel. In contrast to the conflict engendered by the struggle for recognition found in Hegel's master–slave dialectic, Fanon interjects the theme of his later argument, that "There is not an open conflict between white and black. One day the White Master, *without conflict*, recognized the Negro slave" (*Pn* 176 / *BS* 217).

Fanon follows this with a statement which necessarily flows from and reflects the tension inherent in his new reading of Hegel: His formulation that "the former slave wants to *make himself recognized*" (*Pn* 176 / *BS* 217) returns him to the Hegelian dialectic proper, but responsive now to new depths of meaning the dialectic could disclose if reinscribed with the problematic of negritude. He is now concerned with how the "absolute reciprocity" he found at the foundation of the Hegelian dialectic nevertheless gets annulled. Although he has abruptly interjected race into the dialectic of class relations, Fanon finds that there is sufficient reason to believe that the development of the formal terms of the dialectic itself could account for the condition in which the slave, or former slave, is impelled beyond his natural existence toward action that would make him recognized. The suspension of reciprocity constitutes that condition, one which Fanon will later argue is determined by specific economic and historical realities.

The absolute reciprocity of Hegel's dialectic is an historical presupposition of the natural, no less than human, reality from which his concept of self-consciousness is deduced. The presumed racial homogeneity of differentiated class strata presupposed in the absolute reciprocity of Hegel's master–slave dialectic is occluded as a consequence of Fanon's interrogation of Hegel's contention that "Action from one side only would be useless, because what is to happen [if there is to be mutual recognition] can only be brought about by means of both" (*Pn* 176 / *BS* 217). The *raison d'être* of Fanon's understanding of this occluded dialectic arises from the question: What happens *when* action comes from one side only? The closure of the circuit of recognition and the suspension of reciprocity, while seemingly not the course taken by Hegel, nevertheless is a result that can still be recovered from his dialectic.

In the second part of his Hegelschrift, beginning with paragraph eleven, where the history of subalternity erupts in the master narrative, Fanon writes that, "Historically, the Negro steeped in the inessentiality of servitude was set free by his master. He did not fight for his freedom" (*Pn* 178 / *BS* 219). From this point onward, Fanon constructs a case for what he calls, near the end of the chapter, the "alterity of rupture" (180 / 222). This recapitulates the noted double consciousness thesis found in Du Bois's *The Souls of Black Folk*, and which so infused the writing of the negritude school.

Despite the difference Fanon detects between his master–slave dialectic and Hegel's, he persists in adhering to an Hegelian reading of the *crisis of liberation* he describes in the second part of his analysis. Nonetheless, it is still permissible to ask: on what grounds can Hegel still be relevant to Fanon's concerns? Moreover, what are the ramifications of the torque Fanon has introduced into the Hegelian dialectic?[5] Hegel has, in fact, become more indispensable to Fanon's concerns. Firstly, the significance of reciprocity and recognition has become not less but more a compulsion in the face of their utter subsumption during slavery and its emancipatory aftermath; black desire centers even more on the task of acquiring recognition. Secondly, the conditions that conspired to cheat the French Negro of conflict and a life-and-death struggle is commensurate with that exteriority of freedom posited by Sartre and de Beauvoir, which holds that the liberation of the dependent self is the burden of the independent other, namely, the western white male. Though Fanon assumed a similar point of departure, he nevertheless recognized that conferring freedom externally was not, as it was for Sartre and de

Beauvoir, the resolution of the contradiction. On the contrary, Fanon saw that "the dialectic that brings necessity into the foundation of my freedom drives me out of myself" (*Pn* 109 / *BS* 135), necessitating a real revolution. Finally, there are the ontological circumstances that condition the tragic values of black life and bring into being the unforeseen possibilities of revolution. Here the intimations of another dialectic at work in Fanon's Hegelschrift become apparent, beginning with the rupture between life and freedom.

It is not only that "the upheaval reached the Negro from without," it is that it "did not make a *difference* in the Negro" (*Pn* 178 / *BS* 220; emphasis mine). Without the upheaval having posited an inner differentiation in his being, the Negro simply "went from one way of life to another, but not from one life to another" (ibid.). The Negro became an *emancipated slave*, a condition that Marx describes, in his writings "On the Jewish question," as the true mode of social existence underlying western bourgeois democracy. With the failure to instill an inner differentiation in the emancipated Negro, there is no impulse to transcend the given. Hegel describes the ontic relapse that occurs when consciousness is unable to transcend the natural existence of life that encloses the master–slave dialectic: "life is the natural 'position' of consciousness, independence without absolute negativity . . . which thus remains without the requisite significance of actual recognition" (1931: 233).

Emancipation becomes a dilemma in which the stage of productive-life is so undeveloped that in barely rising above the level of natural existence, it merely becomes the basis of a new form of "social death," or slavery. And yet, Hegel's concept of life is where we are most likely to find the other dialectic at work in Fanon's analysis. One clue that this originates in "The truth of self-certainty" section of Hegel's treatment of self-consciousness is Fanon's formulation of the subject–object relation as an absolute or primal value that goes beyond life, so long as the possibility exists that subjective certainty is transformed into objective truth. On Fanon's view, this signifies that "risk means I go beyond life toward a supreme good that is the transformation of subjective certainty of my own worth into a universally valid objective truth" (*Pn* 177 / *BS* 215).

This dialectic of risk carries, in embryonic form, Fanon's future dialectic of revolution. Hegel posits this teleology of subjective certainty passing into objective truth in his transition from "The truth of self-certainty" to "Lordship and bondage" (Hegel 1931: 226). As this, however, is *not* what informs the crisis of liberation, we still need to come to terms with the dialectic of the natural existence of life that holds black emancipation enthralled.

V

The dialectic of life is one of invertedness. The naïve understanding and its scientific appendage take the Negro first and foremost to be an independent life form. Not identity but *difference* is the hegemon of this racialized attitude. The unity that this racial attitude gives itself is constructed on the "fluent continuity of differences, or universal dissolution" (Hegel 1931: 223). Whereupon the universalism, which had come to be the privilege of western understanding, takes its essential being from the inversion of natural difference into its own self-subsistent identity. This inversion is constitutive of its recognition of its own subsistence as an independent life form. Self-existence is acquired by virtue of a self-reflexive process that brings the *other* into the self, sunders its simplicity, and imparts an impulse to transcend the diremption.

The hegemony of difference leaves the Negro in an unfulfilled state of desire because in this form the self-subsistence of the white other allows it to withhold recognition. Where the invertedness of this self-subsistence would be constitutive of a *difference* driven to its absolute end by the power of the understanding, "invertedness in itself as such" (Hegel 1931: 233) is the fluid medium of the life process whose organic forms have their other imparted within them. Again, it is at the level of natural existence, where the productive forces of a "civilizing" West become the mechanical measure of humanity, that the Negro is posited as the other of capitalism's class other, the proletariat. The only "ancient rivalries" that matter here, and that cannot be resolved without an epochal transformation of the material structures of society, are class rivalries. Hence, at the level of natural existence, where the Negro is cast as an amphibolous other, that is, as labor and an alien life-form, the innermost desire of Fanon's slave is to acquire the condition of "pure self-referent existence" (Hegel 1931: 237) that it perceives in the master. Far from Fanon's slave being spared the total dissolution from which Hegel's slave is preserved through remaining engaged in the formative activity of labor, a condition which allows it to cancel it "attachment to natural existence" (p. 238), labor for Fanon's slave becomes a bestial condition.

Hegel *recapitulates* and again *repeats* the triad of moments that condition the subjugated existence of the slave as well as the means by which the slave sets himself up as the permanent negation of this negative, alien reality (p. 239). Hegel recapitulates the following moments of this dialectic of *absolute negativity* (Hegel's synonym for his concept of the "negation of the negation," or double negativity):

1   With the *master*, the slave feels that self-existence is something exter-
     nal and objective.
2   With *fear*, the slave comes to feel his or her own inner self-existence
     (that is, self-existence as an inner *presence*).
3   With *labor*, or the formative activity of fashioning things, the slave not
     only comes to *feel* his or her self-existence for-itself, but becomes
     conscious of his or her *right* to an independent existence.

This triad of moments constitutes the wretched path by which a
subjugated subject attains a "mind of his own" (p. 239). Hegel's *repetition* of these moments has the intended consequence of suggesting three
divergent courses of development a subjugated subject could follow
under changed conditions:

1   Without the discipline of service and obedience, fear remains formal
     and does not spread over the whole human reality of existence.
2   Without the formative activity [of labor] shaping the thing, fear
     remains inward and mute, and consciousness does not become ob-
     jective for itself.
3   Should consciousness shape and form the thing without the initial
     state of absolute fear, then it has a merely vain and futile "mind of its
     own." (pp. 239–40)

While it is tempting to situate Fanon's master–slave dialectic among
these deviant or relative forms, the attempt would fall short on two
counts. First, Fanon identifies the conditions of his slave with that of
Hegel's, and does not entertain any deviation from the conditions set
down by Hegel. And second, and seemingly in contradiction with the
first point, Fanon's slave recapitulates the same or similar outcomes as
Hegel's slave, without involving the same circumstantial causes. So why,
after being subjected to the discipline of service and obedience, after
enduring the absolute fear of subjugation to the master, and after attain-
ing subjective certainty of his or her own right to independent existence
through the dignity of labor, should Fanon's slave nevertheless end up
with, in Hegel's words, "a type of freedom which does not get beyond
the attitude of bondage" (p. 240)? Surprisingly, Hegel provides an
answer, one which does not conflict with the one for which I have
argued, but, in my view, complements it.

It seems that the *real* dialectic of lordship and bondage is not the one
that Hegel initially recapitulates as the ideal moments of his expositions,
but is rather the one articulated in his repetition of those moments as
deviant or relative forms *vis-à-vis* the aforementioned "pure form" (p.
240). It is with the repetition of the *relative forms* as deductions from the
pure form that Hegel intends to posit a new immediacy or beginning,
which is, or corresponds to, a real moment or event. The sufficient

reason underlying this turn towards realism is due to the pure form's inherent incapacity to realize its essential nature. The pure form requires an intermediate series of relative forms in order to realize (*qua* reveal) its own essential nature. It is by this process of (inter)mediation that the real immediacy of new beginnings is borne into existence. It seems, then, that Hegel is saying that his master–slave dialectic is a pure form which necessarily breaks down into real, historical, relative forms, but that the pure form is the way in which to comprehend the historical reality of the latter form.

Fanon's Hegelschrift has the merit of having comprehended this methodological realism at the core of the Hegelian dialectic. The dividing of his analysis into the two parts we have discussed is indicative of this comprehension. Taking Hegel's master–slave dialectic as the pure form from which to deduce real, historical, relative forms is what Hegel himself privileges. One such relative form, which is in-itself an absolute form, corresponds to what I have argued are the ontological implications of Fanon's master–slave dialectic: that the subjugating and subjugated others are prefigured, or inscribed in the onto-genesis of self-consciousness. On my reading, in other words, Fanon's master–slave dialectic indicates to what extent subjugation is implicated in the onto-genesis of self-consciousness at the level of life.

Fanon provides a description of the phenomenon whose implications are unmistakable: The satisfactions of Fanon's slave are evanescent, to the extent that he or she "lacks objectivity or subsistence" (Hegel 1931: 238) and makes the master and his independence the object of his or her desire. It is on this side of desire that the dissolution of Hegel's concept of agency commences. Defined in quite precise terms, Hegel's concept of "agency" is spelled out as a subject, specifically a subjugated subject, whose productive activity places him or her in a position of negative mediation *vis-à-vis* a negative, independent objectivity, a mediation that is equally the active striving after self-existence. The revolutionary potentiality of the slave elides itself when these terms of its agency succumb to the desire to substitute himself for the master, that is, when the subjugated opt for a "self-limiting revolution" in which they merely move "from one way of life to another, but not from one life to another" (*Pn* 178 / *BS* 220).

It was only with the experience of the African revolution that Fanon's slave discovered the *work* that had formerly been abandoned, that is, discovered the work (*praxis*) of dismantling colonialism. For national liberation is quite simply the "absolute substitution" of one "species" of human beings by another, without any period of transition (*Dt* 65 / *WE* 35). The irruption of black subjectivity on the world-historic stage is also a rupture in the thought of the world. Accordingly, in *Black Skin, White Masks*, Fanon was led to differentiate his notion of the black slave from

Hegel's bondsman by virtue of the former being so utterly determined by the lack of reciprocity that rather than lose "himself in the object and find in his work the source of liberation," he instead, "turns toward the master and abandons the object" (*Pn* 179 / *BS* 221). The material basis which was only presupposed in *Black Skin, White Masks* is explicated in full nearly a decade later in *Les Damnés de la terre*. Thus, it is not only how and under what circumstances "the wretched of the earth" enter and make history, but what the dialectic of liberation reveals when the material conditions appear to militate against the subjective impulses who, "without any period of transition," are impelled to embody history and make a new beginning.

Appendix

The torsion Fanon introduces into Hegel's master–slave dialectic is schematically illustrated in the helix formed by the contraposition of Fanon's and Hegel's categories:

Notes

1 Regarding Fanon's development of Hegel's Absolute as a dialectic of *praxis* in *Black Skin, White Masks* and *Les Damnés*, see Turner (1989: 47–63).
2 I have explored the Marxian dimension of Fanon's thought, especially the significance of Marx's *18th Brumaire* for Fanon's analysis of colonialism, in Turner (1991).
3 For an analysis of the impact of Fanon's thought on Biko and the black consciousness movement, see Lou Turner and John Alan (1986).
4 See the note 4 of chapter 5 of this volume for explanation of "Sho' good banana!"
5 See the schematic illustration depicting the contraposition of categories differentiating the master–slave dialectic of Fanon and Hegel in the Appendix of this chapter.

Part IV

Fanon and the Emancipation of Women of Color

11

Anti-black Femininity and Mixed-race Identity: Engaging Fanon to Reread Capécia

T. Denean Sharpley-Whiting

Fanon's thought has experienced a revival of sorts among postmodern academics, particularly with the movement of postcolonial studies coming to the fore in areas of literary and cultural criticism. Fanon is noted for his Sartrean-influenced existential bent, Marxist proclivities, psychiatric observations of colonial subjects, but added to this lengthy list of scholarly mentionables is a patriarchal and sexist tendency. It is within *Black Skin, White Masks* that these glitches have been located. Marginalization and invisibility sum up Fanon's representation of women: white women are neurotics, while black women are simply erased and disparaged. Some of the most deft criticism is leveled at Fanon's "castigation" of fellow female compatriot Mayotte Capécia and her Prix des Antilles-bestowed autobiographical novel, *Je suis martiniquaise*. In turn, Fanon scolds and chides Capécia:

> One day a woman named Mayotte Capécia, obeying a motivation whose elements are difficult to detect, sat down to write 202 pages – her life – in which the most ridiculous ideas proliferated at random . . . For me, all circumlocution is impossible: *Je suis Martiniquaise* is cut-rate merchandise, preaching unhealthy behavior. (*Pn* 34 / *BS* 54)[1]

After this harangue, Fanon, some 125 pages later, delivers, what some rereadings have interpreted as a contemptuously erasing blow toward women of color: "As for the woman of color, I know nothing about her" (*Pn* 145 / *BS* 179–80).

In an article in the *Publications of the Modern Language Association* (*PMLA*) entitled, "Who is that masked woman?: or, the role of gender in Fanon's *Black Skin, White Masks*," the author, Gwen Bergner, writes:

> If women function as commodities mediating social and symbolic relationships between men, then colonialism may be contested largely through the ability of black men and white men to control and exchange "their" women . . . Fanon's scathing condemnation of black women's desire in the second chapter of *Black Skin, White Masks*, "The Woman of Color and the White Man," [is] illustrative, in part, of his own desire to circumscribe black women's sexuality and economic autonomy in order to ensure the patriarchal authority of black men. (1995: 81)

Bergner's observations are not only flawed, but reductive. Reconciling colonialism and homosocial desire, Bergner positions black women's bodies as commodities of exchange, contestatory sutures, in the symbolic relations between white men and black men in the colonial situation. In sum, colonialism castrates black men, divests them of all powers and prowess. And Fanon, the classic "Super Macho," as the Bergner scenario would have it, wants to police black women's desires, wants to exercise some semblance of patriarchal control. But Bergner's assertions go even further, demonstrating a blindness in her crusade to uncover Fanon's sexist-patriarchal, "invisibilizing" penchants. "Fanon," she says in footnote 19, "does not mention the long standing abuse of black women by white men" (p. 87). In her haste to get to the heart of the matter, perhaps Bergner missed Fanon's discussion of the sexual abuse suffered by women of color (Malagasy, Algerian, and Martinican) at the hands of French colonizers in the very chapter she aims to analyze. Instead, Bergner credits Mary Anne Doane's essay "Dark continents: Epistemologies of racial and sexual difference in psychoanalysis and the cinema" in her book *Femmes Fatales: Feminism, Film Theory, Psychoanalysis* with recovering black female identity and their specific history of sexual abuse from Fanon's abyss of erasure. Yet Doane's essay, devoted to discussing the historic construction of blackness and femininity as "dark continents," and therefore indiscernible or invisible, in psychoanalytic theory, loses sight of her black female subject in the fray. She slips back into a primary discussion of white women, mediated through black female bodies, and black men.

And while certain of Fanon's observations may appear puzzling, even problematic, his "scathing condemnation" of *Je suis martiniquaise* was rooted initially in the novel's commercial success and appeal to French audiences, an appeal undeniably linked to Capécia's seemingly effortless adeptness at acting as a mirror for the French, reflecting back their idealized conceptions of themselves. To romanticize *Je suis martiniquaise* as simply a black feminist manifesto on gender and class that "sometimes lapses into valorizing whiteness" (p. 83), to pretend that this is not on a profound level "unhealthy behavior," is to decontextualize the colonialist framework out of which Capécia was writing, which has as its a priori function to inspire acute racial/sexual *malaise* in the psyche of colonial subjects. Capécia has, in the words of James Baldwin, "believed what white people said about [her]" (1993: 4).

Thoroughly imbibed with anti-black rhetoric, Capécia is blackphobic. Her sexploitive affair with the French officer, André, is partly, as Bergner argues, motivated by socioeconomic aspirations, but it is more a self-validating venture that can only succeed through white male love. Indeed, Capécia writes in *Je suis martiniquaise*, "I should have liked to marry, but to a white man" (p. 202). To be valued in the anti-black world that is colonialism means, as Lewis Gordon observes, "to receive value outside of blackness. It means to be valued by a white" (1995a: 100). And in a patriarchal, white supremacist culture, the white male stands for the black as the ultimate purveyor of value. Gordon further observes a hierarchy of values in which "to be least valued is to be valued by someone who is black and a woman." Capécia may receive a semblance of value in her relationship with the Frenchman, but it is merely fleeting, for her love offers him nothing but carnal pleasure, illicit sex: of absolutely no value. She is impregnated, quickly abandoned, and thus concludes her saga with the realization that "A woman of color is never altogether respectable/'valued' in a white man's eyes" (p. 202).

But rather than reread Capécia's much celebrated first novel, I have chosen to engage Fanon in a black feminist rereading of Capécia, specifically through her second, scarcely-read semi-autobiographical novella: *La Négresse blanche*. Although it was not an award-winning work, reviews of this novel in the French press were complimentary. As critic Robert Coiplet wrote,

> The style of Miss Mayotte Capécia is lively . . . her narrative is pleasant, free . . . *La négresse blanche* has this tone . . . it is the story of a mixed-race woman who tends bar . . . At twenty years of age, she has a three-year-old son whiter still than she. Her black blood taunts her. It also brings her some humiliations. She will leave the island for France. (1950: 7a)

Capécia's heroine suffers humiliation because of her strain of black blood; blackness, not colonial oppression and its psychological and material manifestations, is the fundamental source of *angst*. Her convoluted responses to this existential dilemma range from condescending pity to hatred toward the island blacks and desire to be recognized as anything but a negress by the whites. Hence, our rereading will focus particularly on Capécia's black woman phobia exhibited in her often-times contemptuous and stereotyped sexualized portraitures of black femininity, in which the heroine incessantly tries to situate herself as "different" from, or a step above, black women.

The Adlerian exaltation that Fanon ascribes to Capécia is no longer exclusively premised upon "white male love," but bound up with such a feeling of inferiority linked explicitly to black femininity that transcendance is necessarily articulated in terms of a mixed-race female identity. Given Capécia's conclusion regarding the respectability of the woman of color (to be read "black woman"),[2] the desire to transcend black femininity in *La négresse blanche* becomes ever pressing.

Written in 1950, *La Négresse blanche* recounts the story of the 25-year-old Isaure. The plot of *Je suis martiniquaise* frames that of *La Négresse blanche*. The heroine, Isaure, is a single, working mother, whose child, François (as in the first novel), is fathered by a white Creole who seduced and abandoned the trusting Martinican some years before. Isaure will marry a white, childhood friend, Pascal, who was equally ostracized among the white Creoles because of his family's poverty, but whose family nevertheless objects to his marrying a black woman. Pascal ironically declares a profound affinity for and understanding of the island's "Negroes," but nonetheless insists that his wife, Isaure, is not really black. He, Isaure, and François live on the sugar plantation where Pascal works as overseer of the black natives. In an upheaval over pay inequities and colonial injustices, Pascal dies horribly at the hands of the "savages" he so loves and (mis)understands, and Isaure will flee Martinique to France.

Fanon writes of Capécia's second work,

> She must have recognized her earlier mistakes, for in this book one sees an attempt to reevaluate the Negro. But Mayotte Capécia did not reckon with her own unconscious. As soon as the novelist allows her characters a little freedom, they use it to belittle the Negro. All the Negroes whom she describes are in one way or another either semi-criminal or "sho'-good" niggers. (*Pn* 42 n. 12 / *BS* 52 n. 12)

From the novel's opening scenes, blacks are described as sexually jealous savages and *sales nègres* ("dirty niggers"). When questioned about the sexual practices of black men by the white colonial officers who frequent her bar, she reassures them, "No, I have never made love to a black man. They disgust me, they make me scared" (1950: 12). Isaure even refuses to allow her black compatriots in her bar, calling one patron a *sale nègre*. She is, however, punished for this indiscretion in a court of law when the judge tells her that "One does not use 'black' and 'nigger' interchangeably, for Martinique is not a part of the United States" (13).

But one is struck straightaway by the novel's title, a reification of Capécia's *mal de couleur* presented initially in her autobiography. *La Négresse blanche* or *The White-Negro Woman* seemingly supports Fanon's assertion that Capécia's entrepreneurial endeavor as laundress in *Je suis martiniquaise* was indicative of a desire to whiten (*blanchir*) herself (*Pn* 56 / *BS* 45). Isaure struggles with her racial identity, eschewing both blackness and whiteness for the concept of *métissage*. She cannot claim to be a *mulâtresse*, but she will not accept the term *négresse*. But this refusal to situate herself racially is betrayed by a clear desire to flee blackness.

Capécia's project bears an uncanny resemblance to some postmodern critical race theorists with her heroine's rhapsodic waxings over the profound alienation of being "alone, neither black nor white," and her quasi-philosophical ponderances on the "unfairness" of the categories of race (pp. 86–7).[3] Race, it seems, is pure fiction; however, every one of Isaure's pronouncements on black women are undergirded by racist logic. Superficial distinction after distinction, reducible to color, between the heroine and black women are proffered as evidence of difference. Besides Isaure's color, a blend of fruits – banana, coconut, orange – and coffee, her difference manifests itself in the articulation of the notorious French *r*: "She had a soft voice, a bit melodic: the accent of Island girls that resembles English accents. It was not at all like that of the black girls who completely eat the *r*. Even Isaure's cheekbones "had the appearance of a white face" (p. 9). And to highlight this air, she would put a "touch of pink on her cheeks which she thought made her appear less black. . . . She did not exaggerate like those black women disgustingly made up, whom one encounters in the cafés at the port" (p. 92).

Capécia chronicles each and every minute detail of Isaure's difference – in gestures, accent, physiognomy – from the "black girls" towards whiteness via the unfixed racial identity of *femme métissée*. And personage after personage affirm Isaure's *métissage*. Yet in the chapter entitled, "The love of Lucia," Capécia provides another yardstick by which to measure Isaure's veritable difference.

Lucia is Isaure's buffoonish, "*r*-eating" maid servant. Capécia describes Lucia as

> not being able to wear real shoes. Like many other negresses, she had large heels. She was of the most pure African type. She had full lips, a flat nose, frizzy hair and brilliant black skin. She was beautiful in her way, distinguishing her from all the half-whites and half-blacks which form the

foundation of the population of Martinique. Since her distant ancestors imported by slave traders, from the time of Father Labbat, there must not have been any mixing in her ancestry. Not a drop of white blood . . . A sort of familiarity was established between the black woman and the mixed woman. (p. 36)

Indeed, Capécia's comparing and contrasting reads like a nineteenth-century text on natural history or Gobineau's *Essai sur l'inégalité des races humaines*, as Lucia's pure blackness is physiognomically, physiologically, and psychologically gleaned and syncretized. Her devotion and deference, a remanent of "her slave mentality" bequeathed by ancestors, to Isaure is so self-sacrificing, deprecating, that (Capécia tells the reader) Isaure could have been a white woman (p. 36). Isaure's attitude towards the negress is one of condescension, indulging Lucia's tales of her many wanton sexual escapades:

> The mistress was up-to-date on all her servant's adventures and which were numerous . . . She sought pleasure with such a frenzy, she was worse than a cat in heat. Isaure listened to her with a mysterious smile. Sometimes she was envious of the black woman who didn't have any more scruples than an animal. (pp. 36–7)

And while Isaure contemptuously envies Lucia's reckless abandonment, she, possessing "drops of white blood," is governed by an entirely different and higher sexual morality. Lucia is the embodiment of the lascivious negress stereotype. This black woman is reduced to her base corporeal, specifically sexual, function, copulating like an unscrupulous animal with the poor *békés* (whites) and the even poorer *sale nègres*. Love is a fleeting as an orgasm; and Lucia is forever on the look out for a quick fix. For Lucia, love is sex and sex is love. Thus her love story, or rather love stories, are ones driven by sheer need for satiation.

For Capécia, black femininity represents bestiality and immorality; black women are either hideously made-up prostitutes, like the negresses at the cafés, or possess prostitute proclivities like Lucia. They are aberrations for Isaure; her mirrors, rearing their loathsome black female heads in identification, dragging her down with their very presence and proximity. Yet one is left wondering why Isaure expresses such a profound alienation in Martinique where the population is, as she relates in the novella's first chapter, utterly mixed. Why does she at the novel's end seek to exile herself to a country where she is neither black, nor white, but dare one say it, "raceless"? And finally, how does this self-imposed exile and desire to flee blackness cloaked in the ambiguity of racelessness relate to her contempt for black women? For Fanon, the answer is simple. To situate oneself as a *négresse blanche* among hypersexual negresses is but a small feat, a too-easily drawn fine line. It is most essential, writes Fanon, "to avoid falling back into the pit of niggerhood" that black femininity represents (*Pn* 38 / *BS* 44).

And so, we conclude our engagement and rereading with a discussion of Fanon's relevance to an antiracist feminist praxis. To dismiss Fanon as anti-feminist because he does not fit poststructural feminist paradigms undermines intellectual and pragmatic integrity, leaving instead a postmodern mythology – Fanon as a misogynist. Nowhere is this "truism" more apparent than in Bergner's specious reading of gender inequity in Fanon's rigorous critique of Mayotte Capécia and his "sympathetic" reading of René Maran. This false equivalency, the conflation of Fanon's analyses of two very distinct psychoses of novelists, whose works are written in two extremely different authorial tones, represents a feminist literary/cultural critique strangely unfettered by racist and sexually-racist logic.[4]

To recuperate Capécia's story as an example of black feminism in practice, as "a rare, unapologetic, and invigorating representation of a black woman's effort to carve economic and sexual autonomy" (Bergner 1995: 87, n. 23), because she is a black woman, and because she was vigorously, but importantly taken to task by Fanon, is to say the least, a dangerous feminist politic. Indeed, as bell hooks writes in her "Feminist challenge: Must we call every woman sister?": "While it is crucial that women come to voice in a patriarchal society that socializes us to repress and contain, it is also crucial what we say, how we say it and, what *our* politics are" (1992: 80).

Attempts to shame Fanon out of the category of a liberation theorist whose ideas are relevant to the lives of black women are, at best, disingenuous. Fanon's honesty in *Black Skin, White Masks* may be brutal, but it is not brutalizing. In an anti-black world, black male and black female bodies are imagined as excess. Black males are constructed as more sexist, violent, and sexual. And black females, who have been historically vilified as sexually licentious, and consequently rendered more vulnerable to sexual victimization by black *and* white males, are often solely and more comfortably highlighted as victims of black males.[5] Given these constructions, it is not surprising that Mayotte Capécia would be immortalized as the lamb at Fanon's sacrificial altar rather than victim of the sexploitive, anti-black colonial condition.

But can we speak of such a concept, past and present, of Fanonian feminism, Fanon as a feminist, or a liberatory anti-racist feminist praxis that employs Fanon? Given the totality of Fanon's writings on Algerian women, the veil, feminist resistance to colonial exploitation, his usefulness in revealing Capécia's *blackfemmephobia* and racial *malaise* as an attendant response to the colonial enterprise, and his continued relevance for the colonized in the United States and contemporary black feminist literary and cultural studies,[6] one is compelled to deliver a resounding "yes."

Notes

1 All excerpts from *Black Skin, White Masks*. I have taken the liberty of translating the original French *malsain* as "unhealthy behavior." As I will argue and as Fanon rightly pointed out, Capécia's behavior is quite unhealthy. The translations of Mayotte Capécia, *La Négresse blanche* (1950) are all mine.

2 Woman of Color for Capécia is a woman who is perceptibly black. In her construction of the mixed-race female identity, her heroine is consistently rendered not necessarily white, but most importantly, not black. But whiteness is undoubtedly the heroine's goal.

3 See Naomi Zack's *Race and Mixed-Race* (1994). I must be clear here. My "castigation" of Zack and Capécia relates not to the articulation of a mixed-race identity, but to the desire for an identity that is somehow perceived as better than a culturally-degraded black one, while whiteness remains normative.

4 René, Maran's character, Jean Veneuse, does not at all invoke Capécia's nor Nini's blatant anti-black racism and feminism. Fanon's choice of Capécia's works for analysis was predicated upon their suspect popularity at the time in the *métropole*. While black women clearly experience oppression differently than black men, and one can even explain away Capécia's complicity in her sexploitation, one has to go a long way to ignore Capécia's re-inscription of sexually-racist stereotypes of Martinican women. Indeed, throughout *La Négresse blanche*, Isaure disdains her black female compatriots who are forced to prostitute themselves in the colonies. Moreover, Fanon's critique of Capécia is not related to her interracial relationship, but to the anti-black racist rhetoric she invokes in articulating her desire for white men. The articulation of authentic love without racial *malaise* or exoticism guides Fanon's critique.

5 Even Bergner relegates the discussion of white male sexploitation of black women to the margins – a footnote – when a great deal of Capécia's adult female troubles begin and end with André, her white male lover in *Je suis martiniquaise* and Daniel, Emmanuelle, and Pascal in *La Négresse blanche*.

6 For the US context in this volume, see chapters by Floyd Hayes and Richard Schmitt. Also see bell hooks's use of Fanon throughout her writings on decolonization and Gordon (1995a). For a contemporary antiracist feminist reading in French literature and culture using Fanon, see my *Black Female Bodies, White Male Imaginations* (forthcoming).

12

Violent Women: Surging into Forbidden Quarters

Nada Elia

We must invent and we must make discoveries.

Frantz Fanon

The master's tools will never dismantle the master's house.

Audre Lorde

In this essay, I seek to claim Fanon's discourse on liberation as a framework for women's emancipation. I hope to interact with the gaps left unfilled by Fanon's discourse on liberation, by seeking to transpose it back to an analysis of the emancipation of women not as members of a broader oppressed/colonized group, but as an oppressed class by themselves. Through this Fanonian lens, I also hope to explain certain actions undertaken in the name of liberation, which would be hard to describe as feminist – namely the adoption of physical or psychological violence by women. The subject of my discourse will be women of color, since I am most familiar with their circumstances, but also because I believe an analysis of their emancipation can be transferred to that of white women with much less difficulty than the other way round.

Decolonization as Mimesis

To show how Fanon's theory of liberation can be used as a framework for understanding the dialectics of violence and female emancipation, I will be referring to *Les Damnés*, focusing on the introductory and concluding chapters, where he articulates this theory.

In the first chapter of *Les Damnés*, Fanon writes that the colonial world is divided into two opposed yet mutually constitutive spheres, peopled by different "species": the colonizer and the colonized. He viewed these two "species" as a polarized binary, one end of which has been deemed good, the other evil. Thus:

> The colonial world is a world cut in two . . . The two zones are opposed, but not in the service of a higher unity. Obedient to the rules of pure Aristotelian logic, they both follow the principle of reciprocal exclusivity. (*Dt* 69 / *WE* 38–9)

Decolonization can only be achieved when this artificial and oppressive order is questioned:

> In decolonization, there is therefore the need of a complete calling in question of the colonial situation. If we wish to describe it precisely, we might find it in the well-known words: "The last shall be first." Decolonization is the putting into practice of this sentence. (*Dt* 67 / *WE* 37)

This "calling in question" is a necessary first step toward liberation, and must be followed by the reversal of that situation, producing a new situation that is the exact opposite of the former status quo. Fanon then goes on to make his famous claim that only violence can remedy this situation:

> The violence which has ruled over the ordering of the colonial world, which has ceaselessly drummed the rhythm for the destruction of native social forms and broken up without reserve the systems of reference of the economy, the customs of dress and external life, that same violence will be claimed and taken over by the colonized at the moment when, deciding to embody history, the colonized masses surge into forbidden quarters. (*Dt* 71 / *WE* 40)

As the formerly dominated become the dominant, equality is not achieved. Instead, the same separatism, discrimination, even oppression of the "other" is now indulged in by the insurgent, as they duplicate the abuse they have long endured.

Resorting to violence, however, is the second but not the last step towards liberation, and serves as empowerment, but not equilibrium. It cannot, and should not, last. This is because at that early stage in decolonization, the two "species" Fanon speaks of are two opposite poles of a valorized binary, one positive and the other negative, and decolonization functions not as the elimination of this binary, but as its reversal. Hence the first becoming the last. Fanon is fully aware of the valorized opposition that is the colonial situation: "The colonial world is a Manichaean world" (*Dt* 71 / *WE* 41), he writes, illustrating that simple yet powerful assertion with a plethora of images: natives and men, the quarry and the hunter, the oppressed and the persecutor. "This world divided into compartments, this world cut in two is inhabited by two different species," he writes, adding that

> When you examine at close quarters the colonial context, it is evident that what parcels out the world is to begin with the fact of belonging or not belonging to a given race, a given species. In the colonies the economic structure is also a superstructure. The cause is the consequence; one is rich because one is white, one is white because one is rich. That is why Marxist analysis should always be slightly stretched every time that we address the colonial problem. (*Dt* 70 / *WE* 39–40)

After this explosive opening, Fanon concludes *Les damnés* with a call for a genuine mental emancipation from the symbiotic relationship between the two poles of the binary. The colonized, Fanon writes,

> ought equally to pay attention to the liquidation of all untruths implanted in his being by oppression. Under a colonial regime such as existed in Algeria, the ideas put forward by colonialism not only influenced the European minority, but also the Algerians. Total liberation is that which concerns all sectors of the personality . . . Independence is not a word which can be used as an exorcism, but an indispensable condition for the existence of men and women who are truly liberated, in other words who are truly masters of all the material means which make possible the radical transformation of society. (*Dt* 367 / *WE* 309–10)

Following Fanon's suggestion and "slightly stretching" Marxist analysis, I suggest that women's emancipation also follows these three steps: the calling into question of the status quo, the reversal of the status quo in a mimetic moment essential for the creation of a dialectic tension that would ultimately, in the third stage, bring about the dissolution of the polarized binary.

And Ain't I a Woman?

The first stage, for women, is the questioning of the inevitability of a patriarchal system that posits female subordination. Such questioning

has happened throughout history, in all cultures, in the form of individual rebellion and resistance, and more recently in organized women's
movements. None of the major gains achieved by women have happened
"just so," a fortunate consequence of temporal change. They happened
because we questioned our exclusion from the evolution of our human
race, and demanded representation. When and where the right to vote,
the right to an education, the right to drive, the right to speak in public
– to name but a few – were obtained, it was through a serious questioning
of the system that deprived us of them.

In the US, I believe the questioning stage is epitomized by Sojourner
Truth in her address to the Ohio Women's Rights Convention in Akron,
Ohio, May 29, 1851, as she denounced the denial of her very humanity
by white men and women, the latter being, on the racial level, also her
oppressor:

> I think that 'twixt the Negroes of the North and the South and the women
> at the North, all talkin' 'bout rights, the white men will be in a fix pretty
> soon. But what's all this here talkin' bout?
>   That man over there say that women needs to be helped into carriages,
> and lifted over ditches, and to have the best place everywhere. Nobody
> ever helps me into carriages, or over mud-puddles, or give me any best
> place! And ain't I a woman? Look at me? Look at my arm! I have
> ploughed, and planted, and gathered into barns, and no man could head
> me! And ain't I a woman? I could work as much and eat as much as a man
> – when I could get it – and bear the lash as well! And ain't I a woman?
> (p. 186)

Truth's outrage is both powerful and justified, for it is a denunciation of
racism aggravated by sexism, the double yoke women of color have
endured in "the land of the free." Speaking one full century before
Fanon (101 years to be exact), her insistent questioning also illustrates
the incapacity of the binary to accommodate "other others," leading to
the silencing of their experience and existence.

The continuing relevance of questioning the political realities of female oppression is obvious in various parts of the Majority World as well
as the West, even as we approach the twenty-first century. The alienation
of female labor is a global reality, as illustrated in the growing
feminization of poverty with its corollary, women's economic dependence. Women are also excluded from medical research, because our
menstrual cycles are said to "muddy" the research data (Rothman and
Caschetta: 66). Medical experts are also reluctant to perform experimen-
tal treatment or procedures on women of childbearing age, because of
the potential risk to a potential fetus. Consequently, most medical rec-
ommendations made to the male and female populations are modeled

upon the responses of the Caucasian male body (ibid.). Because of cultural and scientific dependency on the West, these are then exported to various parts of the Majority World, resulting in, at best, inadequate health care. The fields of law, public policy, and religion are still primarily institutions of social control for women. The prohibition of women from driving in parts of the Arab world is but one example. In November 1990, forty-seven Saudi women decided to drive a few yards in their own country. When the police moved in, asking them what they thought they were doing, the women responded: "Driving. Why?"

Empowerment can indeed be summarized at times with this simple question, "why?" This example also demonstrates, however, that questioning alone is not sufficient – hence the need for further action. Fanon concluded his first book, *Black Skin, White Masks*, with what he called a "final prayer": "Oh my body, make of me always a man who questions." Always, we too must question.

Be All (the Monster) You Can Be

Like Fanon's rebellious colonized, eager to put themselves in the place of the settler, insurgent women also want to try their hands at all the symbols of power traditionally associated with masculinity. Examples of the second stage abound today, a phenomenon at once disturbing and hopeful: disturbing because it increases the oppressive system perpetrated by the masculine species, and hopeful because of its intricate function in the final dissolution of the Manichaean division. Now women of color are "surging into forbidden quarters" whose entry was for centuries banned to the female "species." It is in this light that we must view women's participation in military combat, the epitome of masculine aggression at its ugliest, or law enforcement, which is well known for its insensitivity to women of color, even as it secures them a monthly paycheck.[1]

Deserting the Master's House

Women in the Army do not feminize this institution. They become "All the Monster They Can Be." Having accessed the traditionally masculine space, we know that we too can be oppressors. Yet surely if we question exploitation, alienation, objectification, or discrimination, we cannot assume that the remedy is in another form of the same. Hence the third stage must be totally creative, fully independent of the former oppressor. In the conclusion to *Les Damnés*, Fanon writes:

> So, comrades, let us not pay tribute to Europe by creating states, institutions, and societies which are themselves inspired by Europe.
>
> Humanity is waiting for something from us other than such an imitation, which would be almost an obscene caricature . . .
>
> But if we want to bring humanity to advance a step further, if we want to bring it up to a different level than that which Europe has shown it, then we must invent and we must make discoveries. (*Dt* 275–6 / *WE* 315)

It is this creativity, this complete novelty that women must seek to achieve, since a duplication of masculinity cannot be liberating. Fanon had explained that the "native" is a creation of the settler, the "Negro" a creation of the European, and that to celebrate nativism or negritude is merely to perpetuate the inventions of a system that is collapsing. Similarly, a celebration of "femininity" cannot advance the cause of women, if femininity means submissiveness, subordination, meek acquiescence, and other such "lovely" and "delicate" attributes. "Femininity" cannot advance the cause of women if it continues the Manichaean binary division into two species "not in the service of a higher unity," but one subservient to the other, whichever the subservient pole is. "Femininity" is one of the untruths taught us by patriarchy, just as nativism is an untruth taught by colonialism. A celebration of womanhood, on the other hand, would constitute genuine change. To cite Audre Lorde: "for *the master's tools will never dismantle the master's house*. They may allow us temporarily to beat him at his own game, but they will never enable us to bring about genuine change" (p. 11). Thus if we are genuinely seeking to move away from the oppressive effects of racism, sexism, homophobia and other divisive systems of exploitation and silencing, we must not allow ourselves to duplicate these systems, just as we refuse to be, and sometimes cannot be, defined through them.

Notes

1   Although American women of color enlist in the military in fairly large numbers, it should be borne in mind that the impetus for their participation is the same as for men of color: their economic opportunities are limited, which makes the military the *only* employment opportunity for many.

Fanon's argument about the structural dimension of racism replicating itself in all facets of a racist society holds as well for the distinction between the experience of women of color in the American and European militaries and their white female counterparts. Advancement in the military is, after all, related to educational status, which is, between women of color and white women, structurally unequal.

13

To Conquer the Veil: Woman as Critique of Liberalism

Eddy Souffrant

Fanon's account of the French presence in Algeria is in essence the account of the colonial power's attempt to unveil the Algerian woman. The French administration in Algeria thought the woman to be the last *pièce de resistance* in the struggle for the country. The struggle, identified as one between Algerian and western culture, was waged around the woman. Her resistance, best expressed in her unwillingness to acquiesce to the western habits, was symbolized in her veil. So the French seeking to gain Algeria thought that the unveiling of the Algerian woman would complete the secularization of the people. The unveiling of the woman would also constitute an assertion of the universality of liberal democratic ideals. What follows is an exploration of Fanon's critique of that liberal ideal as it manifests itself in the conflict over the emancipation of the Algerian woman.

Contemporary Liberalism

We begin by formulating our interpretation of the classical liberal ideal. The liberal ideal is best represented by arguably its most enduring formulation and defense in the work of John Stuart Mill. Mill believed that a thriving civilized society is one where individuality is nurtured (see *On Liberty*). His conception of individuality was connected to his conception of liberty, where he regarded liberty as freedom from interference. At first look it would be clear that this conception of liberty does not determine what the agent is free to do but rather emphasizes the concept of non-interference and asserts the limits of the individual's expressions and actions. And that limit is that the individual cannot harm any of his fellow human beings. This ideal of negative liberty has influenced contemporary political theories. Ronald Dworkin formulates his political theory of liberalism from Mill's principle. According to Dworkin's version of liberalism, government is required to treat "all those in its charge *as equals*, that is, as entitled to its equal concern and respect" (p. 62).

Dworkin thinks that according to liberalism, government's concern is with providing the basic fundamental resources for individuals to make their own decisions about what is in their eyes good for them. He suggests that the liberal political theorist who wants to maintain a productive conception of individuality, to maintain the free expression of individuality, will introduce the concept of procedural rights and as such would wish to protect individuals who are adversely affected by the forces of the market. In effect, for Dworkin, the liberal theorist and practitioner will protect those who are disadvantaged by ability or inheritance. He thinks that

> the liberal, drawn to the economic market and to political democracy for distinctly egalitarian reasons, finds that these institutions will produce inegalitarian results unless he adds to his scheme different sorts of individual rights. These rights will function as trump cards held by individuals; they will enable individuals to resist particular decisions in spite of the fact that these decisions are or would be reached through the normal workings of general institutions that are not themselves challenged. The ultimate justification for these rights is that they are necessary to protect equal concern and respect. (p. 71)

His justification for the position is:

> The liberal . . . finds the market defective principally because it allows morally irrelevant differences, like differences in talent, to affect distribution, and he therefore considers that those who have less talent, as the market judges talent, have a right to some form of redistribution in the name of justice. (p. 73)

The contemporary liberal might be said to emphasize the economic interpretation of individuality and wishes to make the socioeconomic environment more fair, more just. Liberalism, as far as Dworkin is concerned, is

> anxious to protect individuals whose needs are special or whose ambitions are eccentric from the fact that more popular preferences are institutionally and socially reinforced, for that is the effect and justification of the liberal's scheme of economic and political rights. (p. 78)

Dworkin's suggestion is, in the end, similar to that offered by Mill against tyranny (see Mill, ch. 1). They both think that we ought to guard against it. Dworkin's suggestion, however, is more explicit than that of Mill in that he offers that we establish in the institutions of society some protective devices. Rights for him are such safeties against the possible tyrannies of others. In this sense, non-interference with individuality is as important to the contemporary liberal as it is to the traditional liberal.

Traditional Liberalism, Fanon and Applied Philosophy

The resurgence of Islam in the contemporary political history of Algeria is not a surprise. Islam is a countering force today in that country because the secular leadership has not heeded the warnings of Frantz Fanon. Fanon did not consider traditional liberalism to be applicable to Algerian affairs. In *L'An V de la révolution algérienne*, Fanon's position is in direct opposition to the classical liberal model of Mill. Although both Mill's and Fanon's work attempt to show how sociopolitical and ethical theories ought be extended to some issues of international affairs, they part company on the significance of the prospects of colonial articulation of those theories. For Mill, colonization was an activity engaged in by the "European family of Nations" (p. 68), and it was both beneficial to Great Britain and a means by which to emancipate individuality ironically on a global scale. Individuality, he thought, is best expressed in and protected by a liberal democratic government. Mill's approach was thus based on the belief that Utilitarianism (upholding the greatest happiness principle), individuality, and representative government would contribute to a thriving international environment, an environment where individuality is nurtured.

Fanon is intuitively aware of Mill's perspective and in effect attempts to determine which individuality is to be nurtured, a western (that is, economic) individuality or a more indigenous individuality. For Fanon, the secular individualism advocated by the French would not, and could not, fit Algerian society and culture. The French adopted a conception of the individual consistent with the nineteenth-century tradition and sought to implement that conception in the Algeria of Islam.

For the French, the individual is to be free to express her or his individuality unencumbered. They saw that, in Algeria, women were not accorded this privilege. And they believed that women were oppressed by Algerian men. Governmental or administrative interference against the oppressor would be justified, and justified indeed, by the liberal principle.

In Fanon's assessment, however, the French misinterpreted Algerian culture and that misunderstanding contributed to the former's own demise in Algeria. The French plan of attack was to unveil the Algerian woman, and to wrest her away from her "oppressive" Algerian menfolk. The French liberation policy was also consistent with their goal of conquering all of Algeria. So to conquer the veil would be doubly advantageous. It would "free" the Algerian woman and would hasten Algeria's transition to a French district. Fanon argued that the French underestimated the value and the hold of Algerian Muslim tradition in that country.

The Veil and its Symbolism

Islam, according to Fanon, presented a challenge to traditional liberal democracies. That challenge was best expressed in the woman's wearing of a veil, an ostensible symbol of her allegiance to the Islamic culture in the face of French colonialism. So it is not surprising at all that a facile application of western political theories, an application that would over-look the hold of Muslim culture on the members of the society, would indeed clash with Algerian society. But presuming that the French had in fact underestimated the hold of Islam in that country, why was the veil so significant? Why would it hold such a significance both to the outsider and the Algerian? Fanon's answer is:

> The fact of belonging to a given cultural group is usually revealed by clothing traditions. In the Arab world, for example, the veil worn by women is at once noticed by the tourist. One may remain for a long time unaware of the fact that a Moslem does not eat pork or that he denies himself daily sexual relations during the month of Ramadan, but the veil worn by the women appears with such constancy that it generally suffices to characterize Arab society. (*Sr* 16–17 / *ADC* 35)

He understood that despite the "patrilineal pattern of Algerian soci-ety," the French colonial powers interpreted the society to have a "mat-rilineal essence." To win Algeria, according to the French, one needed to win its "essence." The battle for Algeria intensified in the Algerian woman. Her veil was thought to be the most significant bastion of resistance. Hence, to vanquish Algeria, the French sought to conquer the veil.

> The officials of the French administration in Algeria, committed to de-stroying the people's originality, and under instructions to bring about the disintegration, at whatever cost, of forms of existence likely to evoke a

national reality directly or indirectly, were to concentrate their efforts on the wearing of the veil, which was looked upon at this juncture as a symbol of the status of the Algerian woman . . . At an initial stage, there was pure and simple adoption of the well-known formula, "Let us win over the women and the rest will follow." (*Sr* 18 / *ADC* 37)

For Fanon, the colonial administration had a distinct policy which could be expressed in the following way: "If we want to destroy the structure of Algerian society, its capacity for resistance, we must first of all conquer the women; we must go and find them behind the veil where they hide themselves and in the houses where the men keep them out sight" (*Sr* 19 / *ADC* 37–8). But this interpretation also speaks to the ambiguity and haste of the French policy. In that policy, the Algerian woman is seen at once independent and oppressed; presuming therefore that she would immediately acquiesce in the oppressor's program was premature. The French interpretation of that relationship was that the Algerian woman chooses to hide herself behind the veil but that even with this independence, she is "kept," restrained. The French liberals aimed to strengthen the independence of the woman. They hoped to do so by wresting her from the grip of Algerian society, a society symbolized, in its oppressive dimension, by Algerian men. They focused on her oppression. Fanon counters the French formulation. He proposes a deeper relationship between the members of Algerian society than was grasped by the French. Fanon asserts:

> The dominant administration solemnly undertook to defend this woman, pictured as humiliated, sequestered, cloistered . . . It described the immense possibilities of woman, unfortunately transformed by the Algerian man into inert, demonized, indeed dehumanized object . . .
>
> In the colonialist program, it was the woman who was given the historic mission of shaking up the Algerian man. Converting the woman, winning her over to the foreign values, wrenching her free from her status, was at the same time achieving a real power over the man and attaining a practical, effective means of destructuring Algerian culture. (*Sr* 19–20 / *ADC* 38–9)

As this program is developed and implemented, the Algerian men are criticized and ridiculed as a psychological battle is also carried on. They are asked to partake in the activities of the colonizers and to submit to the requirements of the colonizer's culture. Fanon tells us of a wonderful example of the extent of the psychological battle waged by European bosses.

> In connection with a holiday – Christmas or New Year, or simply a social occasion with the firm – the boss will invite *the Algerian employee and his*

wife. The invitation is not a collective one. Every Algerian is called in to the director's office and invited by name to come with "his little family." (*Sr* 21 / *ADC* 39–40)

Facing the demand, the Algerian man has two options. He might on the one hand agree to bring his wife along and in effect display her. Or he might on the other hand refuse to bring her along and risk losing his job for insubordination.

Regardless of his decision, the Algerian employee displays to his European boss his oppression of his spouse. For in bringing her to the party he would, being true to the culture, bring her veiled. And of course in this time of "civilization," a veiled woman is synonymous with a kept woman, a restrained woman. By not bringing her, despite the affront to the boss, the Algerian worker would again display that he determines what she does.

This oppression, this hindrance to individual expression, is inconsistent with the fundamental tenets of liberalism. Those tenets suggest that individual liberty is primordial to the healthy society and that governmental interference against an individual is justified to the extent that the individual is prevented from harming others. Certainly the gist of the argument marshalled by the French against the Algerian man is that he is harming and inhibiting the free expression of the Algerian woman's individuality, her genius.

Genius and Fanon's Algeria

According to Macpherson, political philosophies have attempted to balance the necessary powers of government and its instruments with the livelihood and security of the citizenry (1966: 39). In the case of Algeria, it appears that a portion of the citizenry was at risk and her genius was assaulted.[1] The French supposedly sought to free the genius of the Algerian woman. By unveiling the Algerian woman, she would be free to express herself. Unveiling her would also liberate her from the oppression of her husband. Political history tells us that this liberation during the period of French occupation failed.

The attempt to unveil the Algerian woman failed because the French wrongly considered the ramifications of both the attempt and its success. They, according to Fanon, thought that the veil was indeed an element of resistance but that it was simply a form of individual resistance. The veil was thought to be an extension of the resistance of the Algerian male and his reluctance to acquiesce in the avowedly liberating forces of French civilization. And indeed the French thought the veil was a symbol of Algerian men's effort to hold on to a last vestige of waning power – power over Algerian women. Liberating Algerian women from Algerian men's grip would enhance France's progress at secularizing Algeria. Thus, conquering the veil was tantamount to conquest of Algeria.

Fanon's identification of the struggle for the Algerian woman and the land proposes two interpretations. The first of the interpretations addresses the perception that the clash in Algeria is fundamentally a clash between Islam and western culture. The second interpretation, an extension of the first but significantly different from it, refers to our concern in this paper with liberalism. Fanon's assessment of the situation in Algeria in the 1950s reveals that one's expression is as much an expression of one's individuality as it is an expression of one's belonging to a sociocultural environment. Both interpretations contribute to an understanding of the sources of France's failure in Algeria.

> In the large population centers it is altogether commonplace to hear a European confess acidly that he has never seen the wife of an Algerian he has known for twenty years. At a more diffuse, but highly revealing, level of apprehension, we find the bitter observation that "we work in vain" . . . that "Islam holds its prey." . . .
>
> The method of presenting the Algerian as a prey fought over with equal ferocity by Islam and France with its Western culture reveals the whole approach of the occupier, his philosophy and his policy.

In Fanon's eyes, the distinct identity of the Algerian is construed by France as superstitious and insignificant in his or her behavior. The Algerians, facing this assault on their integrity, their culture and their land react in a way believed by Fanon to be reflective of the phenomena of counter-acculturation. He asserts:

> Specialists in basic education . . . for the advancement of backward societies would do well to understand the sterile and harmful character of any endeavor which illuminates preferentially a given element of the colonized society . . . one cannot attack this or that segment of the cultural whole without endangering the work undertaken . . . More precisely, the phenomena of counter-acculturation must be understood as the organic impossibility of a culture to modify any one of its customs without at the same time re-evaluating its deepest values, its most stable models. To speak of counter-acculturation in a colonial situation is an absurdity. The phenomena of resistance observed in the colonized must be related to an attitude of counter-assimilation, of maintenance of a cultural, hence national, originality. (*Sr* 23–4 / *ADC* 41–2)

So for Fanon, to save the Algerian woman is to remove her from her cultural environment and her removal from the cultural environment is achieved when Algerian cultural originality is erased. The person's identity, in Fanon's case the colonized's identity, is linked to her or his national culture. This conception of the integrity of the individual is different from that proposed by liberalism. The individual, in the former view, is not simply encouraged to express his or her peculiar individuality. Rather the individual's expression, despite the obvious understanding of being culturally trained, is wholly an expression of that culture. Her individuality is not divorced from her culture. Her integrity, one might say is founded on that culture.

It seems to me that it is from this background of recognizing cultural integrity that Fanon's contribution to the study of the Algerian struggle becomes significant. But this elucidation also enables one to determine that his criticism of France and of the French in Algeria is one that counters the economic/productive individualism of that country's liberal approach to the emancipation of the veiled woman. So he tells us that "The tenacity of the occupier in his enterprise to unveil the women, to make of them an ally in the work of cultural destruction, had the effect of strengthening the traditional patterns of behavior" (*Sr* 31 / *ADC* 49).

During the period of resistance the Algerian tended to keep herself outside the sphere of combat. The dogged attempts of the French to use her as an ally brought the political leaders of the Algerian struggle to the decision that she be included in the resistance. That decision was crucial, for as the French attacks became more ferocious, the revolutionary leadership decided to enlist the help of women. But Fanon takes care to remind us that despite her co-option in the resistance, she never relinquished her individuality/independence/integrity nor did she relinquish her role in Algerian culture. Her individuality was fully anchored in the culture of that society.

Fanon and Contemporary Algeria

My suggestion thus far is not that individualism is *necessarily* an antagonist of Algerian or any other culture. It is not that liberty and emancipation are not loved, required, or sought by everyone. It is instead that these concepts and their formulation are shaped by the circumstances in which they are thought applicable. Fanon's analysis suggests that the French failed to realize that even if the Algerians were fond of the fundamental principles of liberalism, only they could truly assess the important components of their situation and the components around which the principles might be applied. The French proposal completely dehumanized the oppressed and the attempt to implement that proposal galvanized the struggle for Algerian liberation.

Fanon was aware that it might be said that Algeria would be no better under Algerian rule than it was under French domination, and that at least under French domination it would have had training in French democracy that would have eventually been implemented in Algeria. That continued domination, in short, would have prevented the quagmire that is currently witnessed in Algeria. Furthermore, Algeria has remained immature, supposedly uncivilized, and still unable to govern itself. To this demeaning accusation Fanon would respond that "underdeveloped" people have a "right to govern themselves badly." And admittedly, it did govern itself badly.

In contemporary Algeria, we are witnessing the results of a resurgence to secularize Algeria, to deny it its cultural baggage. Although the struggle taking place in the country currently is one purportedly between the forces of democracy and the forces of dictatorship, or between Islam and western liberalism, one might argue, as I am suggesting here, that fundamentally the struggle in Algeria is a struggle for the cultural integrity of that country. Policies of intervention for purposes of democracy would be as unwise as the attempt to introduce "French liberalism" earlier in the century.

In the above, I hope to have shed light on the difficulties of implementing, unilaterally or not, some interpretations of foreign policies in terms of categorical ideals of human rights, democracy, and individuality. The liberal caution suggested by the principle of non-interference may be the most appropriate of positions, given the complexity of the political situation of the countries where intervention is thought to be a viable policy.

Note

1 The notion of a people or group's genius is a feature of nineteenth-century expressionism that evolved into emancipatory portraits of the self. See Taylor (1979).

14

In/Visibility and Super/Vision Fanon on Race, Veils, and Discourses of Resistance

David Theo Goldberg

For Isidore Goldberg (1916–95)
who taught me about speaking truth to power

Metaphors of visibility and invisibility pervade Fanon's body of work. This perhaps is to be expected. Fanon's corpus is concerned primarily with interrogating the interface of colonialism's various expressions and resistance to them and thus overwhelmingly with the shifting and complex questions of "the color line." The title of Ralph Ellison's justly famous *Invisible Man* indicates that the realities of dominant racial definition, categorization, and experience are all about the modes, significance, and lived implications of visibility and invisibility. Whiteness has long been characterized in terms of light and learning, blackness in terms of darkness and degeneration. Accordingly, visibility carries with it connotations that tend to be appealing – access, opportunity, ability – in short, power; and invisibility has tended to connote absence, lack, incapacity – in short, powerlessness.

Invisibility, Lewis Gordon notes (1995b and 1996c), may manifest itself in one's literally not being seen: a child whose hand is always up in response to the teacher's question is never called upon; people are ignored in moments of distress or emergency in favor of others deemed more important or worthy; some may fail to recognize wrongdoing no matter how extreme because those suffering the wrong do not meet the expectation of those one recognizes (as people, as kin, as important) though one expresses horror when the same condition confronts "one's

I wish to thank Lewis Gordon for his especially helpful suggestions in completing this chapter.

own" (1995b: 76). Invisibility may take the form also of people not being seen because one "knows" them in virtue of some fabricated preconception of group formation. As Ralph Ellison writes, Faulkner's screenplay for *Intruder in the Dust* reveals in exquisite detail the lengths to which a white Southerner would go to reproduce the "Negro" of his imagination when the black man into whom he stumbles one night fails to replicate his preconception (1972: 273–5). In turn, these examples reveal that invisibility is especially enabled by their racialized characterization. Race hides those it is projected to mark as it illuminates those it is supposed not to mark. And it demarcates by the same token all those race marks in black and white.

Fanon's clearly self-conscious use of the conceptual apparatus and ontological experience of the modes of visibility and invisibility are remarkable for their brilliant recognition and articulation of the prevailing meanings these modes embody. His provocative reflections on these various modes are impressive also for the strategic understanding they offer for the contextual utility for resistance of visibility and invisibility. Fanon's comprehension of this deeply contextualized value of visibility *and* invisibility – of the tension between their sometimes affirmative and sometimes negated value – is tied inextricably to his radically anti-essentialist and non-reductionistic metaphysics, ontology, epistemology, and politics. Or so I argue.

Masterminding Supervision of the Visibly Invisible

Fanon's work seems as fresh now as it did at the height of its intellectual and political impact in the 1960s and 1970s. Henry Louis Gates (1991) suggests that the current wave of popularity Fanon's work is enjoying currently has less to do with its clarity and critical incisiveness than its conceptual vagueness. Gates's concern, I think, is overstated. It is true that some contemporary literary theorists have taken license with Fanon's psychoanalytic interrogations, sometimes producing provocative insights but oftentimes obfuscating critical political and philosophical concerns. Fanon's contemporary popularity strikes me rather as following mostly from the growing comprehension recently that the effects of colonialism upon a wide range of countries once colonized have been extended by modified and modernized means. Fanon's incisive analysis facilitates a rich tapestry for understanding why this came to pass, and it does so by uncompromisingly illustrating that politics and epistemology, metaphysics and culture, psychology and technology, ontology and medicine, and the racial and gendered dimensions of social life are deeply intertwined. The depth of insight and the detail in its illustration that Fanon brings to the task are rare indeed.

Underlying Fanon's analysis of visibility and its delimitation lies the Hegelian conception that human beings assume self-consciousness in and through recognizing themselves in those whom they recognize to be their Other. "Man," writes Fanon explicating Hegel, "is human only to the extent to which he wants to impose himself on another in order to be recognized by him" (*Pn* 175–6 / *BS* 216). Recognition both presupposes and reinforces the light of human worth, respect, and esteem. Self-consciousness requires recognition by the Other. Indeed, it is an imposition upon the Other, and thus presupposes the assumption of the Other's existence though not the Other's equality. But one's visibility is predicated also on the assumption of self-determination. Being recognized – whether as self-conscious or as Other, and thus being visible, requires that one be outside of the Other's imposition, free of the Other's complete determination. To establish self-consciousness, then, to be free, one paradoxically has to engage the Other in combative conflict, to risk one's freedom, to place one's very life, one's humanity, in question.

It follows that visibility and invisibility are not simply states or conditions of being. Rather, they characterize, express, reflect, or they are the effects of strategic relations. As such, visibility does not necessarily advance the interests or well-being of those so defined, nor does invisibility necessarily constrain or delimit the satisfaction of such interests. Constitutive or reflective of strategic relations, visibility and invisibility each can serve contextually as weapons, as a defensive or offensive strategy, as a mode of self-determination or denial of it. It is true that invisibility may manifest itself for the most part as powerlessness. The tension between visibility and invisibility is indexed intricately to and mediated by the intersection of multiple subject positions and identity formations, among which the complex mix of ethno-racial, gendered, and class situations, definitions, and expressions mostly dominates. Poor black women, then, are likely the most socially invisible in societies where poverty, blackness, and women historically mark the depths of powerlessness. Under some conditions, nevertheless, invisibility can actually be invoked to advance power, personal or political, or as an expression of power itself. As Fanon observes, "There is among the colonized a considerable effort to keep away from the colonial world and not to expose themselves to any action of the conqueror" (*Sr* 117 / *ADC* 130). Invisible to the colonial conqueror (the phantom of paradise, as Buñuel once put it), the colonized effectively are in a position to delimit the power of the colonizer over their lives; from sites of invisibility, they are thus able to ignore or resist colonial control.

Lewis Gordon astutely characterizes the existential sadist and masochist in terms of their personal control (or lack) thereof over their in/visibility (1996c). The sadist is one who "takes advantage of the invisible dimension of himself as seer to deny the fact of his being seen." The sadist is a subject, before whom all others are objects. *He* defines the terms of engagement, invoking the possibility of his invisibility – a possibility which after all is a function of his capacity to control his self-definition – to order the conditions of relation. Able for so long to determine the terms and conditions of racial definition, whites were able until recently to appear as though racially unmarked. Race marked the other, objectified them as they were racialized. But blackness as a project – a projection of – the white imaginary is a condition of invisibility, a mode of being unseen because unseeable (of not *being*, precisely, at all) (see Gordon 1995a, 1995b, 1995c; 1996c). Ralph Ellison's haunting admonition in *Invisible Man* captures this in short: "I am invisible, understand, simply because people refuse to see me" (p. 3). The black body, as unseen, is reduced to – is the standard for – anonymity (Gordon 1995b; 1996c): "*They* are all alike in their blackness, I'm unable to tell them apart." So *they* can be treated as all alike, theoretically and practically, aesthetically and morally, historically and politically. By contrast, *racially* invisible – the ghosts of modernity, whites could assume power as the norm of humanity, as the naturally given. Unseen racially, that is, unseen as racially marked – or seen precisely as racially unmarked – whites could be everywhere. The evasion of marking, however, becomes by way of a negative dialectic a mode of demarcation. The author of racial law, as law in general, is at once above it but bound by the terms he is committed to establishing. The expression of power is its delimitation. This delimitation marks at the same time the racial condition of the masochist's formation. Seemingly in control of the terms of racial definition, whites necessarily depend for their racial power on being recognized as white by the Other defined in racial terms precisely as black. Thus whites require recognition *qua* white by those whose very human existence they deny. And this is characteristic of the masochistic condition as Gordon defines it: The masochist is one who "throws himself into the gaze of others while denying their otherness" (1996c). Thus whites, set as sadists by way of their invisibly predicated self-determination and definition, reduce themselves to masochistic self-denial in terms of their self-proclaimed invisible otherness.

The colonial condition offers a case of racially encoded sado-masochistic relations. Colonialism renders invisible the lines of power and control both within the colony and especially – through the spatial and administrative technologies of distancing – between absent colonizing power and people and their colonized counterparts. This sadistic invisibility makes possible the partial hiding from view of the source of characteristic control, domination, degradation, and oppression that is the mark of the colonial condition. The fabricated fact of invisibility, worked into the condition of coloniality as it underpins it, renders that condition seemingly natural and so inevitable, a law of racial nature, the natural state of the world. Hidden from view, blind to the world and to themselves, the colonizers transform self-determining subjects into objects, and naturalized objects into colonial subjects, into subjected peoples. Colonialism "succeeds" thus to the extent its social relations of power remain invisible, so long as their presumed naturalism goes unchallenged. Paradoxically, the colonizer strives masochistically for recognition as dominant and powerful; he requires recognition from an Other he fails at once to recognize. Striving for the anonymity of invisibility, the colonizer is desperate at once to be visible. Recognized yet unacknowledged; acknowledged yet unrecognized. Subject but not object; objectified yet not subjected. The colonizer im*pales* himself on the whitened lance of his own projection, driven there by colonial denial and colonized resistance, by the native's invisible presence and the colonized's presented visibility. Caught between supervision and the Super Vision made possible by camouflaged invisibility, the colonized strike back, resorting to the counter gaze made possible by colonial invisibility to derail the colonial surveillance necessarily predicated upon the premise of transparency and the perspicuity of appearance. As Fanon remarks in the context of analyzing what he calls "Medical Supervision" (*Sr* 116 / *ADC* 128), "In the colonial situation, going to see the doctor, the administrator, the constable or the mayor are identical moves" (117 / 130). Such visits help administratively to transform the native into the colonized, self-determining people into colonial subjects. The information licensed by medical, bureaucratic, political, or police visits fuel colonial governmentality just as the information they release is framed – it is ordered and fabricated – by the colonial imperative.

Colonial (Mis)Recognition

Fanon points out that in the colonial situation the primary thrust of the Master in relation to the Slave is not for the sake of recognition but for work. The colonized are dehumanized, their humanity effaced, not simply for the sake of the colonizer's ego satisfaction but for the purpose of the colonized's exploitation (*Pn* 179 / *BS* 220). What colonialism seeks to hide from view, to render invisible about itself, is the grounding fact of its possibility: that colonialism is predicated only on force and fraud. Hobbes, Locke, and Rousseau all exemplify their states of nature in terms of non-European states of being. The fact that force and fraud are the only virtues necessary in the Hobbesian state of nature (the state of "warre') reveals rather that a readier representation of the contractualists' "natural state" is not "the savage peoples of the Americas" and the like (Hobbes: ch. 13) but the colonial condition imposed by Europeans (geographically or racially) upon those deemed non-European.

Colonialism is operationalized at both the material and the representational levels. Materially colonialism seeks to strengthen domination for the sake of human and economic exploitation. Representationally, it seeks to sustain the identity of the ideological or discursive image it has created of the colonized and of the depreciated image the colonized have of themselves. Colonialism thus undertakes at the latter level to extend and maintain a veiling, to effect a strategic invisibility on the part of the colonized: to maintain invisibility socially and politically so as to minimize the costs of economic reproduction and labor enforcement. Through normalization, colonialism is able to hide from view its constitutive forms of domination and exploitation. By making the relations and practices of dominance seem standard, normal, and given, colonialism creates as "acceptable" its central social expressions of degradation and dehumanization, rendering unseen the fact that it makes people what they are not. Colonialism is quite literally untruth, an untruth which to sustain itself must be hidden from view. Fanon speaks of this as "the lie of the colonial situation" (*Sr* 115 / *ADC* 128), a lie that infects the colonized who to survive find that they are "hardly ever truthful before the colonizer" (114 / 127). Thus, like modernity more generally, colonialism is a condition of extreme ambivalence, imposing a structure, an order of things, it inevitably is incapable of sustaining. Drawn to an order, a scheme of classification, it at once cannot sustain because it is both mis- and unrepresentative of a people the very being of whom it negates, the colonial condition faces (off) its impending disorder with differentiation and division, separation and subordination, manipulation and mystification – in short, with fraud and force (see ch. 4 of *Black Skin*; see also Bauman). It is in this sense that Fanon sees himself as engaged analytically, critically, in a form of *un*veiling.

Unmasking the Unveiling

Veiling renders black people invisible by controlling the dominant meanings and representations of blackness. Blackness accordingly is a white construction (*Pn* 11 / *BS* 14). It follows that the process of unveiling involves "humanizing" black people in the face of their being "racialized," accurately re-establishing historical memory in the wake of its deformation, actively insisting on black being in opposition to its overwhelming erasure. "Facing the white," Fanon writes, "the black has a past to make equal, a revenge to take; facing the black, the contemporary white feels the need to recall anthropophagical times."

Thus veiling and unveiling are qualified – indeed, conditioned – by the racialized metaphors of inking and bleaching. Race extends visibility or invisibility to those it categorizes, and it may be used strategically to promote or deny recognition, social elevation, and status. Whites assume visibility in virtue, though often in denial, of their whiteness, and extend visibility to those upon whom whiteness lights (in recognizing the mulatto, for instance; ch. 2 of *Peau noire*). Recognized as black, black people at once are made visible to be rendered invisible, to be "denegrified" (*Pn* 89 / *BS* 100). Fanon insists, rightly it seems to me, that this logic offers only a cruel choice to black people, only a deadly way out and that is into the white world: "Turn white," he writes, "or disappear." The white world controls and dominates, though that domination and control are fragile and tenuous. (Even the variety of black nationalisms and separatist projections are a reaction to the world of white standards and control.) So black people are faced with the dilemma that the principal mode of personal progress and self-elevation open to them is precisely through self-denial, through the effacement, the obliteration, of their blackness. They are predicated, that is, upon the possibility of rendering a significant feature of their self-definition invisible, if not altogether effaced. This invisibility, in turn, is effected through the necessity of recognition by whites which is begrudgingly extended only at the cost of the invisibility of blackness. In other words, this "internalization – epidermalization – of inferiority" (8 / 11) involves at its basis a recognition of a person *as* white. This cognition at once denies whiteness as it extends it, and effaces blackness as it claims to recognize it.

Blackness is transformed into a fabrication of the white imagination: "I discovered my blackness, my ethnic characteristics; I was battered down by tom-toms, cannibalism, intellectual deficiency, fetishism, racial defects, slave ships, and especially, especially: 'Sho' good banana!'" (*Pn* 90 / *BS* 112). The product of all this is – the Negro! Black people, *qua* black, are wiped away, they are replaced by the figure of "the Negro." Invisibility becomes a response to this forced and fabled visibility:

> Already the white looks, the only true looks [*les seuls vrais*], are dissecting me. I am fixed . . . I am disclosed. I feel, I see in those white looks that it is not a new man who enters, but a new type of man, a new genus. Why, a Negro! . . . I slip into corners, I remain silent, I strive for *anonymity*, for *invisibility*. Look, I will accept the lot, as long as no one notices me! (*Pn* 93 / *BS* 116, my emphasis)

There is but a single conceivable response: "Since the other hesitated to recognize me, there remained only one solution: to make myself known." Define oneself visibly to the world, or die.

This self-definition consists broadly in making visible what the invisible hides, and this "magnification" centrally involves, if it does not require, a form of historical excavation, an archaeology. Archaeology turns on not only uncovering the hidden and (purposely) buried, and so not only on making the unseen seen, cognized, and re-cognized; it requires also the extending of a logic of form to the uncovered, a different way of thinking about – quite literally, of *seeing* – it. "The white man was wrong, I was not a primitive, not even a half-man, I belonged to a race that had already been working in gold and silver two thousand years ago" (*Pn* 105 / *BS* 130). This response to the logic of disappearance emphasizes one of the strands in the Du Boisian dilemma of double consciousness: the impossible ideological requirement of the socially dominant that race be denied or ignored and the necessary psychosocial imperative that one is defined in good part by one's race. Fanon furnishes his own formulation of this racial dilemma over color-blindness and color-consciousness:

> In effect what happens is this: as I begin to recognize that the Negro is the symbol of sin, I catch myself hating the Negro. But then I recognize that I am a Negro. There are two ways out of this conflict. Either I ask others to pay no attention to my skin, or else I want them to be aware of it. (*Pn* 159 / *BS* 197)

The dilemma, one America knows only too well because it has been instrumental in shaping it, is an inherent product of racist societies. "*It is the racist who creates the inferiorized*" (*Pn* 75 / *BS* 93, emphasis in original and Fanon's neologism).[1] In this sense, Fanon rightly sees that the underlying sources of racially prompted in/visibility lie in "social structures" (81 / 100). In the face of being confronted with the claim, shouted in his face, that his blackness "was only a term in the dialectic," that it was "Nothingness," Fanon accordingly recognizes the contingent necessity of "standing inside" – of taking on – the "lived-experience of the black," of assuming "negritude" not as "Infinity," but as the required mode of his lived-experience:

> My negritude is neither a tower nor a cathedral,
> it thrusts into the red flesh of the soil,
> it thrusts into the burning flesh of the sky,
> it hollows through the dense dismay of its own pillar
> of patience . . . (*Pn* 111 / *BS* 137–8)

The prevailing logic of whiteness, then – white mythology, as Derrida puts it – is to make invisible the visible and visibly threatening. The logic of negritude, by contrast, is to make visible (necessarily to itself, contingently to the world) what has been rendered invisible by the force of whiteness, by "colonial desire" (Young 1994). Making the invisible visible by its very nature is a *political act*, one that requires symbolic murder (*Pn* 160–1 / *BS* 198–9). In this sense, the political schizophrenia of color consciousness in a society that takes itself to be color-blind calls forth the drive to maintain alterity as a mode of making visible – the "alterity," that is, "of rupture, of conflict, of battle" (180 / 222).

The colonizer's drive to unveil is the desire "to win the battle of the veil at any cost" (*Sr* 29 / *ADC* 47), to unmask and unclothe with the view to dominate, to exploit, to penetrate – in short, to satisfy every whim. Whites, notes Fanon, face the world with an acquisitive stance, from the viewpoint that the world belongs to them. It is this arrogant presumption, one arrogating the world to themselves, that underpins the commodification of human beings, that grounds slavery. This drive in turn prompts local resistance. Thus, "the white man . . . creates the Negro . . . But it is the Negro who creates negritude. To the colonialist offensive against the veil, the colonized opposes the cult of the veil" (29–30 / 47–8). More generally, parameters and paths of resistance and emancipation are initiated by forms oppression assumes. Yet, once initiated, they are not limited by or to oppressive direction or determination. Even when the oppressed assume categories of degradation in the name of resistance, stand inside them as a place of combat, the categories assumed are invested with novel, resistant, redirected and redirecting significance, "a revision of forms of behavior," as Fanon puts it (30 / 48). The veil is assumed – taken on or discarded – as a vehicle of change, its significance not fixed but contextual, responding to instituting the demands of social, political, cultural and economic transformation, as it is symbolically responsible for them.

The veil, in Fanon's analysis, is in part symbol for, in part effect of, the complexity and overdetermined formation that is colonialism. The veil is a cultural artifact, a mark of gender and ethno-racial identity, a site at which race and gender are ordered and mediated. On one hand, the veil represents the distance between colonized and colonizer, the wall between the "European city" and the "native city" (*Sr* 34–5 / *ADC* 51–2), between oppressor and oppressed, rapist and raped, between the obviously powerful and the seemingly powerless, between projections of the modern and the traditional, "the West" and its other. On the other hand, the veil stands for (as it at once enables) a space of self-determination, a possible – because unseen and so undisciplined and literally uncontrollable – realm closed to colonial penetration. Here the veil serves in a complex way to maintain mystery, refuse mastery, and hide history in a double-edged resistant refusal. Seeing but not seen, the veiled woman is suggestive of the forbidden and impenetrable, a forbiddance and impenetrability that "frustrates the colonizer" (26 / 44). "Thus the rape of the Algerian woman in the dream of the European is always preceded by the rending of the veil" – a violent violation and abject humiliation at once of the woman so treated and of the colonized generally (28 / 45).

The western preconception of the veil is that its value is vested in traditional Islamic culture, representative of conservative, male-dominated constraints upon timid, unliberated women.[2] What Fanon shows by contrast is that the value of the veil is deeply contextual, that in the case of Algeria at least the necessity of the veil is linked directly to the spatial colonization of the city (*Sr* 17–18 / *ADC* 36). The European city surrounded the native city, the only opening from which was into the European orbit. The native city and its inhabitants, completely circumscribed, experienced colonial city space as a mode of domination, their movements controlled as their lives were confined, patrolled, and surveiled. The colonial city made the colonized invisible to itself; the native city enabled its people, quite literally at the heart of the colonial city, to be invisible to the colonizer. Within the kasbah, women were protected by the familiar space of the kasbah itself; outside the kasbah, the veil substituted for its protective mantle (34 / 51). While the veil maintained for the colonizer the distance of order and the order of distance, for the colonized the veil hid the threat of resistant disorder as it was able to protect native women from the European gaze and colonial desire (18 / 37). Behind the safety of the veil matters of considerable import got to be conducted. Arms were hidden, transported across enemy territory, false papers delivered by a "woman-arsenal" (37, 41 / 54, 58). The veil, as a form of camouflage, a means of struggle, "protects, reassures, isolates" (44, 42 / 61, 59).

Colonialism accordingly involved an attempt to unveil women and thereby to "save" them (from tradition, from their culture, from native men, from themselves), and thus to master them (*Sr* 25 / *ADC* 43). Women's bodies as objects of desire and media of exchange were fought over and circulated between men, their unveiling pursued to promote penetration: "These test-women, with bare faces and free bodies, henceforth circulated like sound currency in the European society of Algeria . . . With each success, the authorities were strengthened in their conviction that the Algerian women would support western penetration into the native society . . . the flesh of Algeria laid bare" (24 / 42). Transformed via unveiling into desirable commodities, women seemingly found themselves laid bare, objectified, *alienated*. After the initial nakedness of unveiling, however, the unveiled woman assumed the stance, the disposition, of visibility; she took on and charge of the possibilities unveiling made available to advance anticolonial struggle. She became self-assured, determined yet self-controlled (42 / 59), capable of navigating and negotiating the hazardous routes necessary for successful resistance to colonial control. The native woman made a strategic choice to pursue a self-determined undertaking to discard the veil for the sake of advancing a war of position and maneuvre against colonial settlement, domination, and penetration, thereby promoting a transformation in the disposition of the unveiled – a freedom, an unconfinement, a self-possession.

Thus the veil contextually assumes significance in relation to the functions to be performed by veiling/veillessness, especially in relation to the body (*Sr* 45–6 / *ADC* 62). Fanon characterizes this as the "historic dynamism of the veil" (47 / 63): In the case of the Algerian struggle, the veil first served as a mechanism of resistance. By playing on the traditional rigid separation of the sexes, the Algerian woman could work behind the veil, doing things not otherwise possible or permissible precisely "because the occupier was *bent on unveiling Algeria*" (ibid., Fanon's emphasis). Later, once the colonial authorities had worked out the instrumentality of the veil in revolutionary praxis, it was abandoned in favor of a self-confident baring, a diversionary revealing still in service of struggle. After May 1958, as a response to the "modernizing" unveiling of women directed by the demands and forces of *Algérie française*, Algerian women once again – and in the name of self-determination, of stripping the colonizer of his logic – donned the *haik* "but stripped once and for all of its exclusively traditional dimension" (46 / 62).

Similarly, the value and virtue of in/visibility are contextually determined. There are moments, for example, when those working for dramatic social transformation want their struggle to be invisible, unseen though not unfelt; there are other times when its impact is registered fully only when openly conducted and witnessed, where its effects are witnessed, visible, and registered in the media. There is here a question of authenticating what is made visible, and indeed of what is invisible or unseen but known. Obviously the battle over media representation and control is played out around this question. (In chapter 2, Fanon writes at some length of the role played by the "Voice of Algeria" in authentication of the Algerian revolution.) By contrast, those combatting revolutionary or liberatory transformation – the Master, the dominant, the colonialist – want resistance to be squashed, and if not squashed they would prefer it to remain unseen. And then there are moments when they would have it public as a way of instilling fear and counteraction, as a mode of "legitimating" or rationalizing the full force of reaction.

Visibility and Voice, Stereotypes and Supervision

Visibility may assume subtle forms. As with fear or expectation, one may read off a certain psychosocial state of being from people's faces. One can remain informed of social conditions by keeping one's ear to the ground, so to speak, or to the radio, by watching the media or listening carefully to the underground network of information, word of mouth, or the whisper in the street. "The Algerian who detected in the occupier's face the increasing bankruptcy of colonialism felt the compelling and vital need to be informed." To escape the Master's misrepresentations, one needs to "acquire [one's] own source of information" (*Sr* 58 / *ADC* 75).

Radio and television are technologies that can promote invisibility and produce depersonalization: As "the voice of the occupier," "the radio was considered . . . a means used by the enemy to quietly carry on his work of depersonalization of the native" (*Sr* 80–1 / *ADC* 95–6), extending "a daily invitation," as Fanon puts it, "not to go native" (54 / 71). Not unlike the veil, radio and television, technologies of governmentality both, nevertheless can be used to make visible from a place or position of relative invisibility conditions of oppression and liberation. "Buying a radio, getting down on one's knees with one's head against the speaker, is no longer wanting to get the news concerning the formidable experience in progress in the country, it is to *hear* the first words of the nation" (78 / 93). So radio and television make the invisible visible via explication, obviating, reporting, renewing. Like the telephone, though more general and more depersonalized, they could bring together those not only distant but those quite literally unaware of each others' existence or common plight, producing a new (self-)consciousness and a renewed commitment. "The Voice of Algeria, created out of nothing, brought the nation to life and endowed every citizen with a new status, *telling him so explicitly*" (81 / 96). Radio is also a means of revelation, or at least of concealing and revealing. Like the print press, radio, television, and now the computer superhighway can serve as a gauge of the horizon of possibility and probability, even as its parameters are subjected to governmental supervision, or even absolute control. Where these technologies are under direct control of the dominant forces in the country, as they were in apartheid South Africa, for example, they serve not only as instruments of hegemonic oppression but possibly also, and by the same token, as potential sources of information about and insight into the state, the oppressor, the dominant.

Fanon thus recognizes that the links between knowledge, power, and technology make available or hide from view information necessary to the promotion of different interests. Knowledge may be empowering, but power orders knowledge. Technology offers a medium for the dissemination of information but at once mediates the message. To inform is to give form to the empirical, to make visible the hidden, and audible the silent or silenced, just as it makes invisible the seen and inaudible the spoken. "The 'truth' of the oppressor, formerly rejected as an absolute lie, was now countered by another, an acted truth" (*Sr* 59 / *ADC* 76). Colonial governmentality is fueled in part by a rationality of distance and distantiation, and in part by a logic of close constraint. The situational possibility and interface of these modes of domination are made possible by technologies productive of invisibility. Yet this very invisibility can be invoked as a site of resistance, and these same technologies can be mobilized to effect sites of emphatic refusal and spaces of visible and visibly resistant presence, conceived as enacted truths of the oppressed.

Fanon, Freedom and a Discourse of Resistance

Fanon's intricate phenomenology of invisibility invites an open-ended formalization of the modes by which in/visibility may be produced. The modes by which invisibility is effected, Fanon suggests, may be class specific. In the case of a professional class, invisibility will probably be motivated conceptually, stripping people of their ethno-racial belonging or identity, giving rise to intellectual and cultural alienation. In the case of labor, by contrast, invisibility is tied to racially prompted exploitation, and predicated upon racially explicit and contemptuous debasement. This suggests a distinction between invisibility vested in definitional determination, in conceptual considerations, on one hand, and an invisibility necessary to the production of socio-structural architecture, on the other. Beyond this distinction, however, Fanon's detailed analysis reveals that neither form of the invisible is capable of being promoted, let alone sustained, independently of the other. A person's or population's invisibility may emerge in some part or instance as an epiphenomenal effect of socio-structural arrangements, of political economy. Nevertheless, it is likely even then that a discourse of degradation or dismissal, of infantilization or ignorance, has been invoked also to prompt or promote, reify or rationalize the socio-structural disappearance in question. In any case, once invisible, it becomes that much easier in moments of structural transformation, restructuration or socioeconomic rationalization, to take advantage of a more or less invisible group, a "pathetic population," to satisfy structural imperatives like cutting welfare programs or slashing education for those unable to pay their own way, to cover their costs.

As a principal bearer of culture, of His Master's culture in the instance at hand, language purports to serve in a variety of ways to produce invisibility. First, language is claimed to carry the standards not just of *a* civilization, but of civilization as such. "He's a great black poet/writer/ doctor/intellectual" subtly conveys hidden degradation, judgmentally qualifying both intellectual activity and blackness. Beyond this, language (like radio and television) is a technology of governmentality, a means of domesticating the influence of the colonial occupier/master. The occupier's language – in Algeria's case French, in South Africa's English and what became Afrikaans – orders the anarchy, the lack of form, supposedly afoot in the pre-occupied country. So language assists in the domestication of the native people and culture, imposing the order of the *Logos* upon the presumed flux of a society supposedly lacking rationality and the *Geist* of World History. The *Logos* borne by European language is supposed literally to drag primitive society into the modern, the rational, the historical. Against this, the insistent use of native languages and mother tongues becomes not just a simple individualistic means of resistance but the common voice of an emergent nation bent on "unveiling itself."

Fanon exemplifies this contrast in terms of the pull between French and Arabic, between different languages – one foreign and imposed, inserted with outsider imposition, the other local and indigenous; the one European and tied to – as it opened up – European interests and networks, the other inserted into local Arabic concerns, considerations, even constraints. A similar point can be made within the historically contextualized contrasts of a single language in postcolonial settings, for instance, Afrikaans in the case of South Africa. Conceived as the voice of the white marginalized at the turn of this century, Afrikaans assumed at the height of apartheid's power the status of the oppressor's language, an oppressive and oppressing language, silently directing commands to, and diminutions of, the oppressed black masses of that country, most visibly resisted in 1976. For many black South Africans since 1948, however, Afrikaans was learned circumstantially as the medium more necessary than English to negotiate the white world – often the world of work and political engagement, in short, the prospects for survival. It has been transformed into something else in the post-apartheid moment. Afrikaans has been taken up in South Africa's multilingual babel as part of a possibility of producing the new, a hybrid socially and linguistically. In this sense, multilingualism in South Africa serves not so much as an unveiling (which presumes something already there) but a novel creation; not a discovery but an invention, licensing new modes of being and expression, hence new possibilities (see Parker).

As the bearer of culture, language carries and conveys values, and these norms of conception and perception often stereotype, and in stereotyping render invisible, their objects of reference.

> One such family is very well seen [*très bien vue*]: "They're very black but they're all quite nice." . . . With respect to the father, he was given to walking up and down his balcony every evening at sunset; after a certain time of night, it was said, one could no longer *see* him. Of another family, who lived in the country, it was said that on nights when there was a power failure the children had to laugh so that one would be aware of their presence. (*Pn* 132 n / *BS* 164 n, my emphasis)

The invisibility stereotyping effects is produced by virtue of the fact that the person stereotyped emulates the anticipated reaction that the Master's stereotype projects. "In the end, Bigger Thomas acts. To put an end to his tension, he acts, he responds to the world's anticipation" (*Pn* 113 / *BS* 139). Fanon likens the displacement of pre-colonial values by the Master to a conquest:

> it was [quoting René, Ménil] "the consequence of the replacement of the repressed [African] spirit in the consciousness of the slave by an authority symbol representing the Master, a symbol implanted in the subsoil of the collective group and charged with maintaining order in it as a garrison controls a conquered city'. (118 / 145)

This identification of values is produced through education:

> The young black in the Antilles, who in school never ceases to repeat, "our forefathers, the Gauls," identifies his- [or her-] self with the explorer, the civilizer, the white who brings truth to the savages – an all-white truth. There is identification, that is to say that the young black subjectively adopts a white attitude. (*Pn* 120 / *BS* 147)

Claude Steele has offered empirical evidence of such stereotypical reaction in the case of black college students in the US who, though at the top of their class when entering school, replicate and reproduce the prevailing expectation that they will fail and drop out. Cinema, too, is all about the employment of character types, at the extreme, of stereotypes. In striking contrast to Fanon's Tarzan movie experience (124 n / 152 n), Spike Lee interrogates this emulation of the Master's stereotypes in his searingly brilliant film, *Clockers*. Lee has Stripe's brother, Victor, paragon of self-restraint and moral propriety, explode in violent anger and viciously murder the drug dealing store manager of Ahab's, the local take-out joint.[3]

Black people accordingly are made invisible by and through stereotypical whiteness, as a result of "hallucinatory whitening." The mythical Negro is a savage-cannibal (*Pn* 164 / *BS* 203), a penis symbol (127–8, 133, 144 / 157, 165, 177). Like the Jew, blacks stand stereotypically for otherness, defilement, lack. They are conceived as communists, subversives, and radical revolutionaries, in short, as politically driven, evil incarnate, by nature immoral. "In order to achieve morality, it is essential that the black, the dark, the Negro vanish from consciousness" (159 / 194). Where the Jew in addition comes to stand for the figure of the exploitative and lecherous capitalist, the black man comes to represent the image of the criminal. "Both of us stand for Evil. The black man more so, for the good reason that he is black" (145 / 180). The generic invention of black people as inherently inferior at once reduces them to silence, to non-existence, literally and metaphorically to Nothing (113 / 139). Once internalized, stereotypes may manifest incrementally as self-loathing, self-denial, self-effacement. Social science, especially ethnography, has helped significantly to shape these images of the racialized Native, "putting the native in his place," and thus transforming natives into the Native, naïve and needy, hopeless and helpless.

If stereotyping reduces black people to but dull shadows of themselves, then social structure hides them from view, erases them, almost altogether. In the postcolonial period, social structure has served silently to shift behind the veil of ignorance, so to speak, and so largely to silence concern(s) for (though not necessarily about) the racially marginalized. Fanon identifies how this came to pass at the very moment of anti-colonial success. Historically, the French black – steeped in the inessentiality of servitude – was set free by his Master. He did not fight for his freedom (*Pn* 179 / *BS* 221). If anticolonial struggle was the fight for self-determination, for freedom as that most human of values, Fanon suggests that anticolonial (and antiracist) forces allowed the terms of their struggle – the standards and value of freedom – to be defined by the colonial Master (and the racist). "But the Negro knows nothing of the price of freedom, for he has not fought for it. From time to time he has fought for Liberty and Justice, but these were always white liberty and white justice; that is, values secreted by his masters" (179 / 221). The colonial Master, the generically white man, established values and standards others were expected always to (fail to) meet:

> The Negro is a slave who has been permitted to adopt an attitude of master. The white is a master who has permitted his slaves to eat at his table . . . The black has been acted upon. Values that had not been born of his actions, values that had not been the result of the systolic tide of his blood, danced in a hued whirl around him. The upheaval did not make a difference in the Negro. He went from one mode of life to another, but not from one life to another. (*Pn* 178 / *BS* 219)

Given liberty, black people failed in the pursuit of their freedom; extended justice, they were denied the opportunity to fail on their own terms – and so denied the possibility of self-determination and success. The transformation in and of values from those imposed to those driven by and reflecting self-determination and self-definition is a necessary condition of complete visibility. Denied self-determination, denied the freedom to choose one's principles, one is denied self-definition and so the visibility self-definition makes possible and marks.

Conceived in this way, the conditions for visibility suggested by Fanon continue to be eviscerated, eroded, and in some instances they are altogether absent from postcolonial contexts. Constraints upon post-colonial and antiracist struggle set by lack of institutional and structurally defined power extends invisibility of and to the postcolonial dispossessed and oppressed. I close by considering briefly a number of more or less contemporary examples.

In Australia, since at least the 1930s and accelerated from mid-century, governmentality was concerned with the administration of all aspects of Aboriginal life. As Pat O'Malley shows, this governmental administration and control produced, as it presupposed, a form of projected invisibility. Invisible, Aborigines safely could be ignored; visible, they could – they had to – be decimated (see O'Malley: 4). In the late 1950s, the area of central Australia in which relatively large numbers of Aborigines wandered was declared formally by the Australian state to be uninhabited, a "terra incognita" in the center of Australia. Earlier, the state had proscribed intermarriage even between "half" and "full blood" Aborigines, in the attempt to contain by circumscribing them socially and spatially, to set them apart so as to set them aside, to make them visible to – as nothing but objects of – governmentality. Rendered instrumentally and institutionally visible to and through bureaucratic rationality, they were thereby made socially invisible, unseen literally and figuratively in the scheme of Australian social formation and self-identity, nonexistent in the order of the commonwealth of national identity or the "postcolonial" republic of ends. State mandate suggested eugenically breeding out "half-caste" Aborigines through miscegenation with European Australians; "full bloods" in turn would die out naturally in the failure of evolutionary fitness. Assimilation and natural extinction through strictly enforced apartheid would breed the desirable end of Aboriginal invisibility, their "gentle genocide," as O'Malley puts it.

If assimilationism amounts to a policy of promoting the Other's disappearance *qua* Other, their "gentle genocide," then apartheid was the vicious project of making the racially marginalized invisible: socially, politically, economically, spatially. Post-apartheid arrangements – the "new" South Africa – represent the relative emergence of the racially marginalized, their apparent visibility. The process of liberation has made the marginal majority more visible politically, legally, and culturally, even (perhaps especially) in terms of consumptive power. Nevertheless, those who have traditionally dominated in South Africa have resorted to their residual power informally to extend spatial segregation and overall economic dominance. So wealthier whites have not only withdrawn into their self-defined spaces, they have circumscribed and insulated these spaces and the racial nature of their daily experiences. They have walled themselves into their homes, enclosed themselves in some cases literally into their suburban neighborhoods, never venturing outside their suburban borders, policing these spaces with wired fences, alarms, and private armed response units. Thus they continue to set themselves apart from the marginalized whose conditions and lives are draped off, silent and invisible behind the veil of white-washed ignorance.

If globalization has meant anything, it entails that the shifts Fanon suggests in social formation, structure, and culture facing the (former) colonies in the wake of their independence have had deep structural implications also for colonizing and dominant geopolitical powers. Thus Los Angeles, like other cities in the US, has experienced dramatic structural shifts in its mode of structural formation in the postcolonial period since 1945, and especially since the mid-1970s. Indeed, these shifts are linked to postcolonial transformations globally. Nor was the decline and shift in LA's manufacturing base unique to it but represented change in the mode of capital accumulation worldwide (Fordist to flexible, to use David Harvey's terms). Tied to this were a number of related transformations: manufacturing to service jobs (global financial at the high end, social services in both senses at the low), from global power to global partner, from presumptive (indeed presumptuous) homogenous military industrial complex to complex multicultural hybrid, and from a society where work was supposedly work and the rest I suppose a leisurely play, to one where we are increasingly troubled about finding work that pays a living wage and recreation is big business. Los Angeles has witnessed these transformations as visibly as any city in the US, and in its culture (and cultural industry) it has reflected (as it reflects upon) these changes for the rest of the country (and more imperialistically for the rest of the world).

There are further changes attendant to these broader transformations and so more obviously at play there than elsewhere. For one, across roughly the same period the city became identified with new waves of influx, migration, and immigration – and not just from across borders or seas but across the landscape of America (the lure of opportunity, leisure, and play long associated with the image of that city) thus magnifying its already diverse character. The shrinking of traditional and "legitimate" opportunities gave way to the emergence of alternative economies (the creation of new opportunities in the face of their absence); drugs and guns have manifested more visibly, but so also have new cultural forms that opened up in turn other(ed) economic opportunities, as in the case of gangsta rap and hip hop.

At the same time, as Mike Davis, Victor Valle, Rudy Torres, and others have documented in relation to Los Angeles but which is a more general phenomenon (though perhaps especially pressing and visible in Los Angeles), there was a distinct and increasingly self-conscious shift to the privatizing of the public mandate and public services: you get what you can pay for. In this sense, California's Proposition 187 that makes it illegal to provide any social services (including non-emergency medical and educational services) to illegal immigrants and their children is only the latest development in this logic of privatizing the health and educational costs for unskilled labor. The law approved by electoral endorsement of Proposition 187 has no design on ending immigration or the employment of immigrants, only on ensuring that continued source of "waged slavery" by refusing education to immigrants and cheapening the labor supply by privatizing its associated costs.

The effect of all this is to render the population that "occupies" central LA *invisible* politically and economically, to be policed but not seen or heard (from), a population beyond the boundaries of the political imagination save as that unspoken reserve army of labor keeping unskilled wages, and so the minimum wage, in check. Inflation is kept in hand as well on the backs of the unemployed, for the unemployed tend not to vote while consumers stop by at the polls on the way to the mall (or these days at the mall). So the LA implosion in 1992 was neither a riot nor an uprising nor an intifada, not an uprising nor quite a revolt, but the overflowing of anger no longer containable, at once self-defeating as it was other directed. This implosion can be understood as the bitter and pained insistence on visibility – "We are here, deal with us, in every sense of the term" – in the face of the logics and policies of invisibility.

The revolution, as Gil Scott-Heron once suggested, may not be televised but Fanon hints at the fact that it would be deeply linked to technological innovation, though he could not have predicted in the 1950s that the deeper, unseen revolution would turn out to be electronic rather than political. Television and computers are its media, surveillance and supervision its mode, discipline its message, containment its effect. In this context, LA's implosion was about making public the privatizing of marginalization. Related to these deep structural shifts, as should be apparent and has been commented upon by many others, is the transformation in urban space that accompanied them: peripheral suburban spaces de-centering the city and rendering the center marginal. This marginalization is effected by the use of landscape, both natural (for example, rivers as dividing lines) and created (as in the placing of highways to traverse threatening space without having to engage it and also prevent to it expanding, something not altogether successful in 1992). Highways, those quintessentially Los Angeles modes of transportation, thus represent not only communication and speed but also containment and territorialization, something the apartheid state in South Africa employed quite self-consciously for a while with devastating effect. Actually the analogy with South Africa runs deeper. LA is not unlike Johannesburg by the sea, but with its lines of racial demarcation drawn more formally than under apartheid. And white South Africa has been trying now since the beginning of the decade to transform its (sub)urban spaces into a mirror image of LA, emulating the American legacy of privatized apartheid.

There are other features of the social formation of LA 1992 worth emphasizing here. Obviously, the police loom large both in terms of the apparatus of micro-disciplines and as the general form of urban administration and supervision.[4] Helicopters and floodlights ensure the surveiled and supervised visibility of the racially marginalized population within their constructed confines the better to enforce their invisibility from without: beyond the ghetto/barrio, out of sight, out of mind. Prisons will pick up where the population fails to acknowledge its "natural" boundaries. California's commitment to prisons over public schools – "Let's privatize the latter while using public dollars for the former" – is a renewed pledge to the politics of invisibility. This commitment to de-education is almost self-conscious. Statistics show that those with less than an eighth grade education commit significantly fewer crimes than those with an education ranging from eighth grade to a year of college (25 percent of crimes are committed by the former as against over 50 percent by the latter). California is now spending a larger percentage of its state budget on prisons than on higher education. Prisons (and sports stadia) are to the political economy of contemporary US (and particularly Californian) cities what military bases and the defense industry once were. The crisis attendant on economic transformation and its political, legal, and cultural legitimation is being policed by a culture of imprisonment, a newly emphasized if not exactly new technology of invisibility and social disappearance. Prisons in the post-industrial social formation of postmodernity serve two logics. They fuel an extended economy searching for a jump start in the wake of the late military industrial complex, base closings and plant layoffs. And they instantiate the logic of disappearance – the invisibility – of the racially marginalized, the unemployed and "permanently unemployable" population of the city and the state. In a single stroke, governors can assume the rhetoric of Caesar: *veni, vidi.. . .*

In the projection of white superiority and black inferiority, of white visibility and black invisibility, however, the fragility of masterhood is reflected and refracted. In this reflection and refraction there is to be found imprinted, much like a cinematic dissolve, a hint of the insidious invisibility of white people. As the presumptive norm of racial power and elevation, the racial dimension of whiteness could be denied, or at least ignored. If race is Other, whiteness is invisible, the site of racial power and arrogance. While whites could cower for so long behind the presumed invisibility of their whiteness, this paradoxically hides from view the very vulnerability of whiteness and white folk. The presumptive invisibility of whites could be turned against them, their spoiled nature revealing a fragility at the heart of whiteness, its decadence a powerlessness possible to be challenged. Invisible in terms of its whiteness, white power is viciously visible in conception and effect but fragile in application and self-absorption. As such, it can be confronted and condemned, resisted and restricted, diffused and defused.

If the complex state of social Being is reduced now largely to the frame of political economy, then in societies marked exhaustively by commodification and race the poorest of the racially marginalized are reduced virtually to Nothing. Even at these marginal extremes, however, moments exist – fleeting and unexpected though they may be – when this marginal economy may be invoked to stand outside – apart from – the spotlight of state surveillance and supervision, and so beyond its administrative governmentality. It is at these sites that modes of emancipatory resistance are fashioned, making possible moments of radical self-determination, effecting in short what Fanon calls freedom. Invisible at the margins, the marginalized can challenge and sometimes ignore visible power at the very visible and cumbersome center. Or they may appeal to a divided moral economy of the powerful, playing one representative off against another. In a passing reversal, the formerly invisible may become momentarily visible, while the formerly visible are frozen at the margins of their own fabrication. Examples abound: the Zapatistas in Chiapas, those fighting for freedom in South Africa in the dying days of apartheid, the racially marginalized of Los Angeles circa 1992, those carving out cultural hipness in a world where culture and hipness have become paramount.

And so the struggle for visibility so insightfully and incisively interrogated by Fanon continues to be critically significant. It is, after all, the struggle for power, autonomy, self-definition. And it is, perhaps paradoxically, a struggle for which contextually the veil of invisibility can continue to offer strategic value. For invisibility can enable the marginalized even – indeed, especially – at the most depressing moments of degrading dismissal to advance their own sense of themselves, their own ontological commitments, their own frames of knowing and action, a self-defined politics and aesthetics, economy, and culture.

Contexts change, and with them strategies of response. I close, in the spirit of Fanon, with the clarion call of continuing anti- and postcolonial resistance. A closing, and an opening; an ending, and a beginning:

A luta continua . . .

Notes

1 I am tempted to weaken the force of this by reformulating the dilemma as a product of any racially conceived society, not only of fully racist ones. Elaboration of this distinction is beyond my scope here. See my *Racist Culture* (1993: esp. chs 4 and 5).

2 See Helen Watson for discussion of the complex dimensions of the veil for Islamic women.

3 Ahab's itself represents a stereotyped location of exploitative Semitic inner-city commercialism where parasitic capitalism and the illegal drug trade meet. Lee contrasts Ahab's with Victor's night-time, second-job location, a family restaurant run by a Jamaican immigrant who pointedly resists drug transactions on the premises. Significantly, Lee extends the contrast to Rodney's project barbershop, a front for his drug empire. The local hood and don-like father figure to his streetwise clockers, Rodney runs his trade on the exploited backs of late teen labor.

4 It is worth pointing out that Foucault notes that in seventeenth-century France and Germany the term "police" meant the administration of the state, a more general understanding of modes of discipline; see Foucault (1988: 145–62).

Part V

Postcolonial Dreams, Neocolonial Realities

15

Public (Re)Memory, Vindicating Narratives, and Troubling Beginnings: Toward a Critical Postcolonial Psychoanalytical Theory

Maurice Stevens

[What the] history of flashback tells – as psychiatry, psychoanalysis, and neurobiology suggest – is, therefore, a history that literally has no place, neither in the past, in which it was not fully experienced, nor in the present, in which its precise images and enactments are not fully understood. In its repeated imposition as both image and amnesia, the trauma thus seems to evoke the difficult truth of a history that is constituted by the very incomprehensibility of its occurrence.

Cathy Caruth, Psychoanalysis, Culture, Trauma II

Co-performing Nations and the Distaste for Memory

Pursuing George Lipsitz's suggestion that "Time, history, and memory become qualitatively different concepts in a world where electronic mass communication is possible" (1990: 5), we must look to what Paul Virilio has called the "teletopological" space of mediated images to consider the ways in which spatially and temporally located subjectivities have been translated into narratives of self in community, narratives which call out or require the construction and enactment of historic forms (histories) condensed around culturally performed "collective memories" that center questions of identity and privilege identity politics. However, rather than decrying identity politics *writ* large, we must formulate critical questions that will highlight both the delimiting dangers and the political urgency inherent in the articulation of political positions grounded in identities figured in narratives of historical (re)memory. From Alex Haley's *Roots* to Haile Gerima's film *Sankofa*, black/African/ USAmerican practices of historical reconstruction (as forms of historical re-memoration) are usefully understood through the dramatically modified lens of Freud's theory of memory and the psychical functions it facilitates.

While great care must be taken not to pathologize filmic representation of historical reconstructions (including those which posit an unbroken chain of connection to Africa as a point of origin), psychoanalysis can prove quite useful in examining the ways in which some black/ African/USAmerican nationalist narratives are represented, such that they require the selective forgetting of particular historical memories in order to maintain the fantasy of essential sociopolitical identities with fixed positions in what are becoming increasingly overdetermined historical narratives. Examining black nationalist visual representations of "counter memory," and the images employed to represent notions of "authentic" blackness, enables the identification of the specific dangers of nationalist stories that replicate narratives already told, with pre-inscribed plots and patterns of repetition that form a congealed past, itself constituted by the repressed and foreclosed memory-material of history.

Because we must acknowledge (and appreciate) the real changes in social conditions that have come through the mobilization and activism of marginalized groups beneath signs of essentialized "racial" identity, the concerns raised above rest in tension with the important political possibilities generated through and around enactments of identity politics within the USAmerican discursive regime. Nevertheless, in the USAmerican context of racialized social relations, signs of "racial" authenticity have a double function. On one hand, they provide the points of unification and commonality necessary to the efficacy of political advocacy. On the other hand (and simultaneously), political mobilization under the sign of racialized particularity reinscribes commonly held understandings of "racial" fixity that themselves are understood within the context of historically entrenched myths and stereotypes. Consequently, the great USAmerican dilemma gets recast precisely within the tension that exists between "race," "class," "gender," and "sexuality" as discursive formations, on one side, and the moving, touching, desiring bodies upon which these discourses write and about which they remark, on the other. Moreover, these discourses constantly contribute to the sociocultural enactment of dominant or subordinate social relations that themselves call out (and often demand) the production and presentation of vindicating and justifying narratives.

How, then, can we attempt to sharpen the blurred, foregrounded image of USAmerican identity against the sepulchral figure of black/African/USAmerican nationalisms and the functions they effect in the service of the USAmerican psyche without relying upon problematic and essentialist ideas? Psychoanalysis proves particularly useful in this regard because of the significant value it places (at times) on contingency, contradiction, and the elusiveness of "knowability." We cannot, however, employ psychoanalysis uncritically, for the complex and often damaging uses to which psychoanalysis, as a set of discourses, has been put must also be acknowledged. Applied psychoanalysis frequently serves as an authorizing discourse for the proscription and policing of the boundaries between polarized notions of sanity and insanity, pathology and mental health, and perversion and normality. On the other hand, Freud's aim to produce a descriptive model that held few aspirations to prediction and that focused on tracing the development of, and co-constructing the cure for, unpleasurable psychic states, should be commended. Consequently, psychoanalysis is carefully invoked here with a profound ambivalence.[1] Indeed, Fanon's work, which is the focus of this volume, displays a similar sense of ambivalence and permits it to be read as a site of what we shall call *active ambivalence*, a space that describes and performs the sense of alienation, the "massive psychoexistential complex" that Fanon hoped to "destroy" (*Pn* 9 / *BS* 12). We will therefore advance a mode of critical psychoanalysis, ambivalently approaching and retreating from Fanon's pioneering theorizing about the usefulness of psychoanalysis as a means of better understanding the modes and vicissitudes of interpersonal interaction and identity development in the context of colonial domination.

Thoughts on the Black-skin Predicament

In *Black Skin*, Fanon implies the scope of the black-skin predicament as quite clearly located in the tension between the all-encompassing materiality of colonial relations and the often less concrete negotiations of self-imagining in the colonial setting. Fanon insists that:

> There is, in the *Weltanschauung* of a colonized people, an impurity, a defect that forbids any ontological explanation . . . The black among his own in the twentieth century is ignorant of the moment his inferiority comes into being by the other . . . In the white world the man of color

encounters difficulties in the assimilation of his bodily schema. (*Pn* 88–9 /
BS 109–10)

In beginning with the partial analysis of Fanon's psychoanalytic method,
we must ask how an analysis of Fanon's theorization can inform the
construction of a critical psychoanalysis more relevant to reading the
"fact of blackness"[2] in a USAmerican cultural setting. While at one
moment I am drawn to Fanon's methodology because of the ways in
which he centers the "black" body as something both more than and
integrally related to discursive processes and inter-psychic relations, I am
also aware of how this centering requires simultaneously the privileging
of the very complicated process of identification.

Because Fanon saw "Negro pathology" as originating in the process
of assimilation and acculturation perpetuated through institutions of
language and education, he was specifically concerned with the psychical
dynamics associated with the conflict between the "lived-experience of
the black" and the linguistic imposition of an "education to whiteness."
As Fanon explained in relation to Jung's "collective catharsis" and its
essential social function "as a release for collective aggression":

> In the magazines the Wolf, Devil, Evil Spirit, Evil, and Savage are always
> represented by a Negro or Indian; since there are always identifications
> with the victor, the little Negro, quite as easily as the little white boy,
> makes himself an explorer, an adventurer, a missionary . . . who risks being
> eaten by the wicked Negroes . . . There is identification . . . The hero, who
> is white, is invested with all aggression . . . little by little, one can
> observe . . . the formation of a way of thinking and seeing that is essentially
> white. (*Pn* 119–20 / *BS* 146–7)

The black youth learned through histories, folk tales, etc., that the
colonial imaginary held a position of negative value for colonial subjects
and at the same time was taught to identify with the position of positive
value constituted for whites. Only upon actual contact with white society
did the meaning of this self-abrogating identification come to the fore.
Only then would the black-skin subject which Fanon described experience the trauma awaiting him or her. Only then, through the process of
deferred action, could be felt the weighty "crushing objecthood" of
which Fanon spoke.

The interpretive framework available through the concept of identification proved quite useful to Fanon, prompting Diana Fuss, in her essay,
"Interior colonies: Frantz Fanon and the politics of identification," to
posit that one of Fanon's most important contributions came in his
articulation of identification as a product of (and apology for) colonial
relations of domination and subordination. Nevertheless, we will be

critical of identification as a conceptual framework and attend to Fuss's suggestion that "If we are to begin to understand both its political usages and its conceptual limitations, the notion of identification must be placed squarely within its other historical genealogies, including colonial imperialism" (p. 20).

These specific modes of identification imposed upon Fanon's black-skin subject an alienation from both a self-defined subject position and the modes of symbolic production that inform the development and transformation of the position of "other." Thus Diana Fuss can suggest that "Fanon implies that the black man under colonial rule finds himself relegated to a position other than Other" (p. 21). It was the resulting "neurotic orientation" to which Fanon applied his "psychoanalytic classifications," not the least of which was the ego.

Fanon saw the development of the black-skin ego in the context of a collective unconscious. However, he added, "The collective unconscious is not dependent on cerebral inheritance; it is the consequence of what I shall call unreflected cultural imposition" (*Pn* 154 / *BS* 191). The reality that libidinal interest encountered in the colonial setting was a social construction – more directly, a structure of colonial domination. With the kind of ambivalence evident throughout *Black Skin*, Fanon here relied upon a notion of ego development that both depended upon and undermined basic tenets of the Freudian psychoanalytic narrative of "normal" ego development that typically elides cultural differences. Fanon described the "normal" process of the Antillean's ego development as resulting from "an ambiguity that is extraordinarily neurotic" (155 / 192). However, in an environment where libidinal interests encountered a "reality" that already represented one as object, this ambiguity is better understood as a mode of subjectivity (and a position of subject agency) neither accounted for nor counted on within the bounds of psychoanalytic discourse. Moreover, the recognition of the black-skin subject position that Fanon described as the fate of Antilleans encountering white culture was facilitated in relation to whiteness as a self-contained (and self-defined) category.

Indeed, identification, as a psychical mechanism, binds the tension between the "lived-experience of blackness" and the "education to whiteness"; and, as a signifier within psychoanalytic discourse, it defines the ground for the emergent figure of "neurosis" in settings of dominant or subordinate social relations. However, these two functions, while related, are distinct and rely on two countervailing notions of the subject and the location of subject agency. The psychoanalytic subject's agency lies precisely within (and is delimited by) the action of psychic mechanisms, while the social subject's capacity to act and imagine rests in the tension between material experience and discursive production. This

poses a particular set of problems, for even while the space of identification marks the black-skin subject's situatedness within colonial (read:
psychoanalytic) discourse, it is also the location wherein resistant forms
of signification (that is, the performance of mimicry, Bhabha 1994) can
take place. Put another way, the black-skin subject is presented with the
choice that is no choice. Given the Freudian notion of the process of
identification, the colonial subject can only be an object, incapable of
enacting resistance without reinscribing and supporting the psychic relations that determine its "objecthood."

Unfortunately, the field of identification (which both reflects
and rewrites imperialist processes) is also a founding trope in Freudian
psychoanalytic theory. Diana Fuss articulates the dynamics this
way:

> The colonial-imperial register of self-other relations is particularly striking
> in Freud's work, where the psychoanalytic formulation of identification
> can be seen to locate at the very level of the unconscious the imperialist act
> of assimilation that drives Europe's voracious appetite. Identification, in
> other words, is itself an imperial process, a form of violent appropriation in
> which the Other is deposed and assimilated into the lordly domain of the
> self. (pp. 2–3)

Fuss's warning suggests that the process of identification appears as a
product of colonial imposition that is installed at the level of the colonial
subject's unconscious (especially inasmuch as the unconscious can be
considered to represent the repository of libidinal components – some
sadistic and some narcissistic – that exceed the possibilities of identification with external objects). Rather than reading Fuss's text as describing
the colonial subject's status as an object, let us read her as articulating
the way in which the colonial subject, *within a psychoanalytic discourse
that centers identification*, is trapped in a discursive position reserved for
objects. Taking this reading as our point of departure, we can appreciate
it when, in his collection of essays, *The Location of Culture*, Homi Bhabha
reflects on the black-skin predicament as:

> the experience of dispossession and dislocation – psychic and social –
> which speaks to the condition of the marginalized, the alienated, those who
> have to live under the surveillance of a sign of identity and fantasy that
> denies their difference. In shifting the focus of cultural racism from the
> politics of nationalism to the politics of narcissism, Fanon opens up a
> margin of interrogation that causes a subversive slippage of identity and
> authority. (1994: 63)

From the perspective of this "subversive slippage" the black-skin subject
must be understood as a subject with agency that is not confined to the

parameters of psychoanalytic discourse, but instead to the subject position with agency in the space of sociogeny. In this way, we imagine a subject that performs self-imagining in the tension between the lived-experience of blackness and educations to whiteness.

Fanon figured colonization as a process that, while having its sources and structures in the material conditions of the colonial setting, produced effects that extended beyond material conditions to the modes of consciousness they inflect. Consequently, his "sociodiagnostic" emphasized the importance of psychical incorporation as it occurred in the context of social relations. For even while his analysis was psychological, Fanon maintained that "the effective disalienation of the black [entailed] an immediate recognition of social and economic realities" (*Pn* 8 / *BS* 11). Fanon felt that somewhere between the expanse of phylogeny and the specificity of ontogeny resided the cultural particularity of "sociogeny." Indeed, in the space of sociogeny, the ego is decentered, and self-imagining occurs *vis-à-vis* an agency located both within and outside of psychic apparati. In Fanon's understanding of this space, incorporation amounted to the "attempt to acquire – by internalizing them – assets that were originally [and culturally] prohibited" (48 / 59–60). For Fanon's black-skin subject, alienation in the colonial setting was not merely from the product of her or his labor, or even from the modes of production themselves (though, in many cases this too was true). Rather, it was also an alienation from a subject position (even as that subject position was defined as "other" to the colonialist "self"). Fanon sought to undermine the formation of this alienation through the lens of psychoanalysis. According to Fanon:

> The Negro's behavior makes him akin to an obsessive neurotic type, or if one prefers, he puts himself into a complete situational neurosis . . . In the man of color there is a constant effort to run away from his own individuality, to annihilate his being . . . [We] shall see . . . that the Negro, having been made inferior, proceeds from humiliating insecurity through strongly voiced self-accusation to despair. The attitude of the black towards the white, or toward his own race, often duplicates almost completely a constellation of delirium frequently bordering on the region of the pathological. (*Pn* 48 / *BS* 60)

One must remember that this "region of the pathological" is the space of uneven power relations that characterize colonial (and so-called postcolonial) settings. Indeed, as Diana Fuss notes, the predicament of the "other" originates in her or his being "forced to occupy, in a white racial phantasm, the static ontological space of the timeless 'primitive,'" where "the black man is disenfranchised of his very subjectivity." Fanon's intervention worked to undermine this foreclosure and its ontological inexplicability.

In her essay "Mama's baby, Papa's maybe: an American grammar book," Hortense Spillers discusses the origins, effects, and ramifications of the sense of displacement that emerges with the process of "ungendering" common to the political economy of slavery. This sense of displacement resembles the "situational neurosis" that plagues Fanon's black-skin subject (Spillers: 65). In fact, where Spillers tells the story of the captive African female body turned fleshy transcript of historically determined domination, Fanon described the black body bludgeoned flat into the two-dimensional space of the epidermal schema – the black-skin (one word for "I am given no chance, I am over-determined from outside. I am not a slave of the 'idea' that others have of me but of my appearance" (*Pn* 93 / *BS* 116). Spillers sees "US slavery as one of the richest displays of the psychoanalytic dimensions of culture before the science of European psychoanalysis [took] hold" (p. 65). Fanon, in asking "What does a black man want?" (*Pn* 6 / *BS* 8) began with an assumption that psychoanalysis could illuminate (after it had been mapped on to and into the political realities of the colonial setting) "a new family environment capable of reducing, if not eliminating the proportion of waste, in the asocial sense of the word" (39 / 49).

Understanding the danger of alienation – the sense of being enslaved by one's own appearance – in its capacity to result in a unilateral recognition that disabled desire, Fanon posited that "as soon as I desire I am asking to be considered. I am not merely here and now . . . I am" (*Pn* 177 / *BS* 218). Fanon sought to destroy the syntax of the "racial epidermal schema" and demanded "that notice be taken of [his] negating activity insofar as [he pursued] something other than life; insofar as [he] struggle[d] for the birth of a human world – that is say, of a world of reciprocal recognitions" (177 / 218).

Because the mechanisms underpinning Fanon's "world of reciprocal recognitions" centered notions of identification, they required his unevenly critical importation of psychoanalysis. In his critique of the psychoanalytic discourse, as applied in the colonial setting, Fanon questioned the universal applicability of some of its basic contents. In speaking of the notion of neurosis and the Oedipal drama, Fanon reminded his readers "that not even Freud nor Adler nor even the cosmic Jung thought of the blacks in the course of their research" and made the fairly radical assertions that "they were quite right not to have. One often forgets that neurosis is not constitutive of human reality. Like it or not, the Oedipus complex is far from coming into being among Negroes" (*Pn* 123 / *BS* 151–2). Moreover, Fanon complicated the concepts of clearly bounded interiority and exteriority that support the Freudian model of the ego. Fanon even destabilized, at least implicated, traditionally held

ideas regarding the vicissitudes of instinct gratification and ego development by insisting on the socially constructed nature of "reality" and that
"in the Antilles perception [of self] always [occurred] on the level of
the imaginary," and that "it [was] in white terms that one [perceived]
one's fellows" (132, n. 25 / 163, n. 25). Nevertheless, Fanon maintained
the mechanism of identification and the troubling analyses of sexuality
and sexual "perversion" it engenders. Indeed, in his effort to outline
(however tentatively) and describe the space of sociogeny, where identities could be formed through the humanizing process of "reciprocal
recognition," Fanon had to center identification in ways that make his
psychoanalytic method of limited (but not minor) usefulness in our
attempts to transform discursive patterns in the field of the USAmerican
imaginary.[3]

Although it makes little sense to expect Fanon to be critical in ways
that we might be (especially when we have the benefit of his life's work,
as well as those of other important theorists), it is still crucial to the
construction of a useful critical, postcolonial psychoanalysis that we
problematize certain structures basic to Freud's theory in ways that
Fanon was unable. In this way, it becomes clear that at the very moment
that he rejected some of the problematic contents in Freud's story,
Fanon simultaneously made use of aspects of Freud's theory that themselves reinscribed the very patterns of domination and subordination
that he sought to overturn. Sexuality, and the role it plays in Freud's
theory of psychical development, is one of those stories.

Sexuality: Freud's Great Dream

In his introduction to Freud's *Three Essays on the Theory of Sexuality*
(1994), Steven Marcus suggests that "Indeed from the outset, one of the
overt aims of [*The Three Essays*] was to declare the end of a historical
innocence," and to usher in a realistic and modern vision of the "horrors
of the nursery." Freud's *Three Essays* told a story[4] of sexual behavior in
general, and sought to recount the "transformation of the sexual instinct" in particular.

Let us focus on the nexus between Freud's story and the story of
human species evolution, which rested upon the "weak spot" of human
sexual development. Throughout these essays, Freud discusses the normal teleology of sexual development from infantile sexuality through
puberty and into "mature" sexual development. This story's particular
twists and turns have been outlined often and frequently debated. What
will be of interest to us, however, are the forms this story takes and the
ways in which it quietly speaks a myth (a myth that imperialist structures

have been all too ready to hear) while simultaneously demythologizing the innocence of the "folktale" of history.

When Freud maintains that "a disposition to perversions [was] an original and universal disposition of the human sexual instinct and that normal sexual behavior [was] developed out of it as a result of organic changes and the psychical inhibitions occurring in the course of maturation," he implies the point at which his plotting of psychosexual development intersects with notions of societal evolution. The "psychic inhibitions" he mentions are social expectations inscribed and replicated through the punitive judgements of the superego. Moreover, inasmuch as he believes ontogeny to recapitulate phylogeny, his psychical model maps easily into a collective social-psychological representation of an even more teleologically bound evolutionary process. In this way, a particularly European notion of civility could be equated with psychological maturity, and models of "primitive" civilization could be linked to an immature, infantile position in the developmental process. Thus, "inferior races," mentally challenged people, children, and women (of all colors) could be and were identified as driven by primary processes, powerless before sexual impulses, and relatively unpossessed of "higher" character traits like reason, rationality, and control.

Mary Ann Doane illuminates this signifying slippage in her essay "Dark continents: Epistemologies of racial and sexual difference in psychoanalysis and the cinema." Doane traces Freud's use of the term "dark continent" to denote female sexuality. According to Doane, this signifier served as "the historical trace of Freud's link to the nineteenth century colonialist imagination." She argues further that "although Freud did not recapitulate 'an imperialist ideology that urged the abolition of savage customs in the name of civilization,' the binary opposition between the savage and the civilized in their relation to sexuality was a formative element to [sic] his thinking." Doane goes on to discuss the ways in which Freud's theorizing established a metonymic chain of signification that conjoined racial otherness with notions of infantile and female sexuality. According to Doane,

> This is an elaboration of Freud's well known claim that ontogeny recapitulates phylogeny. In the English translation, "race" might seem to be more accurately replaced by "species" since Freud insists, here as well as elsewhere, on mapping the difference between the primitive and the civilized onto a temporal or historical axis rather than a spatial one. The "primitive" is the remote in time, it is the "childhood" of modern man . . . Freud delineates how civilization is born at the expense of sexuality (whose "free reign" is henceforth associated with the "primitive" races, some of whom are undoubtedly located on the dark continent). (pp. 210–11)

Onto-phylogenic recapitulation was not the only melodramatic[5] notion in the psychoanalytic story of sexuality that fits easily into the narratives of social-Darwinism. These narratives have come to outstretch the "psycho-Darwinistic" possibilities of Freud's theory, for Fanon also made use of the Freudian ego as a central psychic structure.

Freud's ego, as an organ of perception and the seat of psychic agency, represented the modification of the id through interaction with perceptions of the external world (reality tests). According to Freud's sequencing, instinctual impulses were generated within the domain of the id and cast into the world seeking objects of their libido, where they encountered reality (specifically the reality of not being satisfied). These impulses then recoiled from this dissatisfaction, withdrawing object cathexis, and sought out a new object. The ego, through a process of identification, introjected an image of the external object and thereby provided an internalized object for the libidinal surges of the id's instinctual impulse. Although Fanon generally agreed with this view of normative ego development, he made use of it ambivalently. On one hand, Fanon felt that the black-skin ego, as the product of "reality tests" constructed through uneven power relations, would "burst apart" when faced with the "unattainable" ontology of "colonized and civilized society." On the other hand, Fanon imagined the fragmented black-skin ego as constantly being "put together again" into a coherent psychic agency functioning at the level of the social. Thus, while Fanon issued a critique of the postulation of "reality" as the a priori universal experience central in ego development, he did not question the notion of the coherent ego as a credible psychic structure, a desired psychic state, or the crucial difference between the ego and the subject in relation to social agency. The way in which Freud's narrative of psycho-sexual development intersected with, for example, other narratives of "civilization" and "progress" at precisely the point of sexuality, made it particularly troubling that, after his discussion of white female sexuality, Fanon was able, perhaps too smoothly, to slip into a discussion of anti-Semitism. This demonstrated exactly how the slippage of signifiers along various narrative trajectories can result in the elision of one form of domination and the privileging of another. Although Fanon's use of psychoanalysis displayed both insight and blindness, his work can suggest how a differently conceptualized psychoanalysis might function.

Envisioning a Critical Postcolonial Psychoanalysis

The "critical psychoanalysis" of which I speak is probing in two important respects. First it seeks to engages critically questions of nationalist desire as represented in the popular cultural production of counter-narratives of history like *Roots* and *Sankofa*. In contextualizing the performance of black nationalisms in the United States, we see the various ways in which the mediation of historical memory has produced "black" subjectivities differently in relation to "whiteness." We must ask: What have been the dominating discursive regimes, what have been their templates of social interaction, through what conceptual structures have they been manifest, and what have been the modes of resistance mobilized against them?

For most European immigrants the image of the United States (and, to some extent, Canada) was historically represented by ruling ideas that have been a part of the American social fabric since its struggle for independence – namely, the essential dignity of the individual human being, the fundamental equality of all people, and the general right to such important things as liberty, freedom, and democracy. Dominant narratives of political, social, and spiritual possibility provided places into which European immigrants could imagine themselves fitting, and it was only upon their arrival – their entrance into actually existing American social relations – that many European immigrants discovered how their unbounded possibility was conditioned by the process of defining themselves as different from or not like those for whom the picture held no foregrounded positions and very little opportunity: Native Americans, Latinos, Asian Americans, African Americans, etc. That is, those "othered" by virtue of "race," nationality, and, at times, religion.

Moreover, the discursive field within the USAmerican context already contained a conceptual framework that facilitated their interpellation as "selves" against dark and savage "others." By accepting roles in, and thereby reinscribing, racialized structures of perception, many European newcomers were afforded the possibility of marking themselves as fully "human" and thereby entitled to the promises of (or the right to co-perform) the freedom, property, democracy, nationhood, etc., that constructed them as "white" and made the United States . . . *America*.

Without sacrificing their private experience of cultural memory, their public identity as "newcomers" could be checked at the door and replaced by an American one that reconfirmed their occupation of "human" subject positions by providing them with a freshly temporalized and newly spatialized identity. They were quite literally *in America now* and could gather in social clubs and community groups to reaffirm ethnic affiliation, while at the same time claiming "whiteness" in the context of public social structures.[6]

African Americans, however, were not "expected" to engage in this slow performance of limited forgetting. Their collective memory was wiped away with forced relocation and the disruption of language and family groups. The process of colonization and the Atlantic slave trade did not merely obscure the black/African/USAmerican historical record, it erased it in quite physically brutal ways. Moreover, there is a complex relationship between the essential role that historic memory plays in the performance of identity, and the pivotal place notions of identity have in the formation of the sense of oneself as human. The complexity of this relationship came to be articulated through and to be constitutive of the patently dehumanizing effects of racialized structures of domination in the United States, resulting in the inscription of discursive images and positions that coded the black/African/USAmericans' lack of "human-ness."

In the face of institutionalized oppression and systematized dehumanization, black/African/USAmericans have engaged in performative practices that, as Lawrence Sullivan suggests in his discussion of performance, entitled *Sound and Senses: Toward Hermeneutic of Performance*,

> [render] perceptible a symbolism of the unity of the senses. The symbolic experience of the unity of the senses enables a culture to entertain itself with the idea of the unity of meaning . . . [I]t is performance that provides a culture the occasion to reflect on the unity of that body of cultural knowledge. (1986: 6)

Thus, whether in the form of musical productions such as *Black Madrid*, filmic representations like *Sankofa*, or even reproduced and represented images of the "Black Power" movement (*Malcolm X, The Panthers*, etc.), these performances have contributed to the constitution of bodies of cultural knowledge that have themselves worked in the service of varied functions. Chief among these functions is the construction of what George Lipsitz has called "counter-memories" (p. 226) and the weaving of vindicating narratives, both of which operate in the service of constituting an essentially *human* black/African/USAmerican subject position, and depend upon the privileging of "originary moments" that function as distant "primal scenes" in the teletopological space of mediated (re)memory.

Positing "essential humanity" in the mode of vindication has necessitated the production of visual "counter-memories" populated by fixed images that, at base, encode ideas of ethnic authenticity. Espousing notions of "blackness" as grounded in phenotypically fixed ideas results in various interpretations of one's external appearance. Such notions signal one's level of connection with Africa, in hetero/sexist ideas of "black" wo/manhood, or in ideas of "race" betrayal as represented through images demonizing "cross-race" sexual interaction and "mixed-race" identification. These images produce two interrelated effects. On one hand, these visual images (while also serving as a kind of trope, constantly locating one in both the text and subtext of dominant historical accounts) act as "figure/ground" images. That is, they function as points of intersection between resistant "counter-memories" and the demeaning and dehumanizing representations of black/African/ USAmericans in dominant historical narratives. As points of metonymic connection, they function similarly to "sexuality" in Freud's theory of psychic development and traditional ideas of human species development. They "fit" into, or allow for the displacement of signifiers, into and between divergent representations of history. Since these multiply signifying images play such an important role in the formation of black/ African/USAmerican identity, the ramifications to identity formation are rather significant. In particular, the multiple signification and the *ambivalent identification* it initiates, require no more and no less than the formation of multiply subjective identities produced in the tension between "counter-memories" and dominant representations of history.

On the other hand, they also function to defend against acts of cultural (re)memory that could relate a history whose representation would necessitate what would be perceived as a "self-negating" identification; that is, what Fanon might have considered the context of an "education to whiteness." In this way, one who identifies as black/ African/USAmerican could view a film like *The Birth of a Nation* and, while recognizing images that assert ideas of phenotypic fixity or demonize "cross-race" sexual acts and "mixed-race" identification, could still manage to defend his or her sense of self by "identifying" with images presented in visual representations of black/African/USAmerican "counter-memory."

Second, the "critical psychoanalysis" I imagine is critical in the sense that it questions the very psychical mechanisms that constitute its foundational repertoire. Consequently, while it will make use of such mechanisms as screen memories, primal scenes, mourning, melancholia, and desire in examining counter-memory of the nationalist type, it will remain suspicious of these categories and the contestable content of their forms. Indeed, through its operation, this critical psychoanalysis will both construct and disavow the rumors of its own demise. In a sense this counter-imagining of memory must operate in the way George Lipsitz has described "counter-memory": as "a way of remembering and forgetting that starts with the local, the immediate, and the personal" (p. 213).

Exploring the process of selection involved in the construction of "counter-memory" from this psychoanalytical point of view involves the notion of the teletopological space. The teletopological space mediates the performance of historical memory. This is accomplished by presenting images on to which are transferred the affect generated through experiences of material conditions such as privation and punishment that are part and parcel of uneven power relations. In this space, images encoding authenticity in relation to "blackness" can also serve as the repositories for notions of self worth and humanity that have been generally underrepresented in the various representational venues of dominant conceptions of history. The teletopological is a space containing culturally produced memory fragments which, as Freud posits,

> show us our earliest years not as they were but as they appeared at the later periods when the memories were aroused. In their periods of arousal . . . memories did not, as people are accustomed to say, *emerge*; they were formed at the time. And a number of motives, with no concern for historical accuracy, had a part in forming them, as well as in the selection of the memories themselves. (1994: 322)

Psychoanalytic theory further suggests that the "accuracy" of these histories/memories proves much less important than the function they serve, and thus might argue that these culturally performed memories act as screen memories that split off, or disavow anxieties inherent in the pre-Oedipal struggle represented in the wish for unbounded connection. In his 1987 essay, Patrick Hutton gives an excellent account of Freud's notion of screen:

> Screen memories are mnemic images that displace deeper, hidden memories. By comparison with the memories they shield, screen memories are of lesser consequence, arouse fewer emotions, and relate to more recent experience. They are projected backward in time to fill the gap created by the repression of the memory of actual experience and thereby to fulfill the conscious mind's need for a coherent sense of life's development . . . the link between the screen memory and the repressed one is an attachment of place rather than of content. The screen memory fits the pattern of the past envisioned in our present fantasies, yet marks the place where the repressed memory of our actual experience may be retrieved. (388)

But what is actually being screened off by these mediated images? Freud's theory might suggest the loss (real or imagined) generated at the point of origin, or the primal moment. Or for Fanon, perhaps, it is the destruction of "black zeal," the immanence of black consciousness, the possibility of experiencing a Negro consciousness (outside of the black-skin subject position) that "does not hold itself out as a lack," or the ontological potential inherent in losing oneself "completely in negritude" (*Pn* 109, 111 / *BS* 135, 137).

Or perhaps, as I suggest, the question is not so much "what" is screened off, but rather "why?" That is, what function is performed by mediated nationalist images that reside in the midst of other images? Precisely because of the nature of the teletopological "image environment" within which we work and live, rather than being of a strict Freudian (or even Fanonian) psychoanalytic nature, critical psychoanalysis must be read through semiotics and postcolonial theory in its application to processes of (re)memory in the USAmerican context. By focusing on the moments of overdetermination consistent across different images of black/African/USAmerican nationalisms and by reading them semiotically as moments of manifest desire, this postcolonial psychoanalysis enters the tension between being "both human and historical," in a way to open new spaces for thought, imaging, and experiencing black/African/USAmerican subject agency, and in a social context where there are indeed desires in images and images of desire.

Notes

1   Ambivalence is advanced here to suggest the psychoanalytic issues Homi Bhabha raises in his essay "The other question," in *The Location of Culture* (1994). He uses it to discuss the ambivalent nature of identification in postcolonial spaces of hybridity. I, however, seek to convey the sense of danger and urgency that accompanies the "multiply-subjective" agent facing discursive systems. Through these systems the agents are consistently determined by images and concepts that deny them of what Judith Butler calls "full recognition." Psychoanalysis is recognized here as one of those systems.

2   What Charles Lam Markmann translates as the "fact of blackness" has also been translated as the "lived-experience of the black." These translations are particularly important because of the way in which they differently locate subject agency (see Judy's and Gordon's essays in this volume, above).

3   Homi Bhabha, in his essay "The other question" and Kobena Mercer in his ICA paper of 1995 "Busy in the ruins of wretched phantasia," have both taken up the notion of "ambivalent identifications" as a powerful perspective from which to examine the "'danger zone' of psychic and social ambivalence as it is lived in the complexity and contradictions of a multicultural body." Mercer suggests that "if the differentiation of self and other depends on repression that splits ego from unconscious, then the ambivalence of identification can be seen to arise from the effects of unconscious phantasy in which the self oscillates between positions of subject, object or spectator to the scene" (1995: 11). For Bhabha, this process can be understood through Freud's theory of the fetish and moments of "multiple belief" that the fetish facilitates. To Bhabha's mind "the role of the fetishistic identification [one mode of ambivalent identification], in the construction of discriminatory knowledges that depend on the 'presence of difference,' is to provide a process of splitting and multiple/contradictory belief at the point of enuncia-

tion and subjectification" (1994: 80). While Bhabha and Mercer's formulations go a long way towards creating room for imagining the postcolonial subject differently, rather than an "oscillation between positions" or "a process of splitting and multiple/contradictory belief," the subject in the space of active ambivalence is located in multiple positions simultaneously. That is, the moments of being multiply subjective represent the simultaneous occupation of subject positions that both support and undermine the humanizing process of "reciprocal recognition."

4   I read Freud's essays on sexuality as describing a "story" in the sense that they represent the displacement of mythic structure into a quasi-literary context. I base my contention on the work of Northrop Frye ("Myth fiction and displacement" from *Fables of Identity*, and Eric Auerbach's discussion of the function of realism as a mode of representation in literature, in his *Mimesis*).

5   I use the term *melodramatic* here in the sense that Mary Ann Doane does in her discussion of inscriptions of racialized and gendered relations in the "representational field" of Hollywood cinema. Doane posits that "melodrama has been consistently defined as the cinematic mode in which social anxieties or conflicts are represented as sexual anxieties or conflicts. From this point of view, it . . . [is] . . . a particularly appropriate arena for the observation of the intersection of race and gender."

6   For further discussion of the complexities involved in the construction of "whiteness," see the work of Ruth Frankenburg, Cheryl Harris, David Roediger, and Ron Takaki (see bibliography).

16

Fanon, African and Afro-Caribbean Philosophy

Paget Henry

For most of its history, the Caribbean intellectual tradition has paid little or no attention to the nature of its philosophical practices. It lacks a clear awareness of its philosophical identity and habits. Indeed, both of these have been eclipsed by the faster rhythms of production in other discourses. This pattern of neglect holds true even for our New World political economists, who have given the tradition its most recent major reformulation. Confronted by the specter of socialist and ex-socialist governments overseeing the International Monetary Fund's structural adjustment programs, this body of thought is now in the throes of a major crisis. As I reflect on our current inability to think our way out of this crisis, I am convinced that this neglect of our philosophical practices is an important part of our paralysis. As heirs to the legacies left by C. L. R. James and Fanon in particular, we have taken their political economy and ignored their philosophy. In what follows, I will examine the impact of Fanon's philosophical practice on our tradition, with the hope that it will help us out of our present impasse.

Like James, Fanon is often treated as a writer who can be understood outside of the Caribbean context in which he spent his formative years. These two are usually situated and evaluated in terms of the European influences on their thinking. Seldom have they been examined in terms of the Caribbean tradition of thought that also influenced them and the significance of their work for this tradition.

My aim will be to bring the Caribbean tradition more into focus. I will examine its peculiar colonial dynamics, what it passed on to Fanon, the degree to which he transcended this heritage, and the extent to which he was able to change it. In short, our focus will be on the impact of the philosophical aspects of the Caribbean tradition of thought on Fanon and the impact of his philosophy on that tradition.

The Caribbean tradition of thought can be viewed as a series of extended dialogues that arose out of European projects of building colonial societies around plantation economies that were based on African slave labor. For example, both the imperial and enslaving aspects of these projects had to be discursively justified. Also, the identity of the colonial state had to be established and its illegitimate claims to power given the appearance of legitimacy. Such issues and indigenous resistance to them constituted some of the foundational concerns of Caribbean intellectual life. The outcomes of these exchanges were not determined by the better argument or the moral rightness of a cause. Rather, they were determined by political criteria as they directly affected the organization of state power and the strength of economic and political elites.

Given the political framework in which the above issues had to be resolved, it is not surprising that many important truths could not be acknowledged in this tradition of thought. The imperatives of economic and political reproduction were such that many falsities had to be dogmatically asserted as true and many truths dogmatically asserted as false. On the basis of these dogmatic assertions, discourse production was largely an exercise in myth-making that inflated European identities while deflating African identities. In short, this was a dogma-ridden tradition, in which questions of identity and culture could be truthfully addressed.

These patterns of necessary misrepresentation are important for understanding the nature and function of philosophy in this tradition. Given the high demand for legitimating and delegitimating arguments, philosophy in this colonial context was largely the handmaiden of ideological production. Hence the social and political nature of philosophy in this region. Answers to cosmogonic, ontological or epistemological questions remained largely unthematized or were imported from abroad. Not only was philosophy confined in this way, it was further restricted by the overvaluations and undervaluations that the tradition found it necessary to impose on the cultures of Europe and Africa. A central item in the tradition's undervaluation of African culture was the dogmatic assertion that it had no philosophy. That African philosophy did exist could not have been acknowledged by the tradition or truthfully discussed. This disenfranchising of African philosophy established philosophy in the tradition as exclusively European. In short, philosophy in the early phases of the Caribbean tradition of thought was exclusively European in identity and sociopolitical in orientation.

Fanon's assault on this tradition was profound, relentless, and explosive. He grew up at a time when the misrepresenting and alienating powers of this tradition were still very strong, in spite of increasing criticism by Afro-Caribbean writers such as Blyden, Garvey, Padmore, and Césaire. Consequently, he was profoundly marked by the ambivalences and misrepresentations of this heritage. On awakening to his deep enmeshment, Fanon's response was that of the anguished individual who must get out of a nightmare. Hence his vision of the Afro-Caribbean as being "rooted at the core of a universe from which he must be extricated" (*Pn* 6 / *BS* 8). The goal of this extrication is not just liberation from the practices and institutions of this tradition, but also "the liberation of the man of color from himself" (ibid.). That is, from the misrepresentations of the tradition that had been internalized.

This emancipatory project struck at the heart of the tradition. It violated the strict prohibitions that had been put on the truthful examination of questions of identity. Breaking this taboo was the major impact that Fanon's work has had on this tradition. It had two important consequences. Although it did not bring an immediate end to colonial misrepresentations, identity problems would never again be resolved in such dogmatic and racist terms. Second, this opening of the debate on identity necessarily challenged some of the dogmas and prohibitions that sustained the distorted evaluations of African and European cultures. The impact of these challenges on the colonial construction of philosophy was not, however, as explosive as its impact on the racist discourses that legitimated the necessary misrepresentation of identity.

From the standpoint of philosophy in the region, Fanon's work was a bold and original departure. It placed questions of ontology squarely on the table and answered them in existential and historicist terms. These were then carefully linked to analyses of the Afro-Caribbean personality and to the Marxist theories of revolutionary transformation. This synthesis of philosophy, psychology, and revolutionary political theory was both stunning and original, and it is still very potent today. However, it was unable to revolutionize basic conceptions of philosophy in the Caribbean tradition and overturn the valuations placed on European and African philosophy. Fanon's synthesis did not trigger an awareness of a local philosophical tradition whose indigenous identity needed thematizing, even though his work changed dramatically the categories, values, and concerns of the tradition. It remained a case of Caribbean philosophy operating without an adequate awareness of its identity and history. Because of this lack, the equating of philosophy with social philosophy was never really overthrown, nor were the evaluations placed on European and African philosophies. Philosophy continued to function primarily as the handmaiden of political struggle, and its master continued to be European in identity.

The emergency of a vibrant and self-conscious Caribbean philosophy will require the breaking of these colonial fetters. Without such an internal decolonization it will not be able to indigenize itself and affirm its unique identity. As postcolonial recovery proceeds, there is usually a progressive indigenizing of discourses. However, it does not occur uniformly across all discourses. Processes of discursive indigenization have occurred more rapidly in Caribbean drama, folklore, religion, music, political economy, and literature than they have in philosophy. The identities of these cultural practices are distinctly more Creole. In these Creole formulations, African as well as European elements are visible. By contrast Afro-Caribbean philosophy is unique in the degree to which it has resisted a similar creolizing of its identity.

As we will see, this greater resistance to creolization points to a number of serious problems confronting Caribbean philosophy that even Fanon's explosive writings were unable to remove. These problems suggest that disenfranchisement was greater in the case of African philosophy than in the cases of music or literature. Even more than James, Fanon followed closely the early attempts to rehabilitate traditional African philosophy, but found them wanting. I will try to show that the constraints, evaluations, and prohibitions that the tradition placed on philosophy were such that they gave Fanon very little but were strong enough to resist his attempt to overthrow them.

The Caribbean Tradition of Thought

As noted earlier the colonial state needed to establish its legitimacy and so made very specific demands on the discursive outputs of our culture. In addition to these limitations the culture of the Caribbean was shaped by the manner in which the colonial state controlled the relations between the African and European traditions. Its primary purpose in doing this was to lessen the undermining effect of the African tradition and increase the legitimacy of European discourses. The former had to be silenced or made to lose authority, while the European had to be established and given more authority. As a result, the institutional framework in which the Caribbean intellectual tradition developed was a very statist one, with opposing patterns of cultural accumulation for its European and African components.

To facilitate these different patterns of cultural accumulation, colonial articulation gave normative priority and state power to European culture, but left African culture without similar political support. This unequal allocation of normative and institutional support created the social conditions for the disintegrating of authority in the African system and the accumulating of authority in the European system. Accumulation in the latter was therefore at the expense of the former. Such a framework for the rapid accumulation of authority (culture capital) was a pressing need if the discourses produced by the European writers of the tradition were to address effectively the legitimacy deficits of the colonial state, and the slave order it had to maintain.

Whether Spanish, British, or French, such statist cultural systems were established in the Caribbean colonies by the middle of the seventeenth century. They were established by the later generations and new arrivals that followed the first set of colonizers. The basic dialogical structure of the Caribbean tradition of thought was evident as early as the sixteenth century in the Spanish colonies. This structure emerged from the debates over Spanish rights to rule over the indigenous population of Caribs, Arawaks and Tainos (Lewis: 43–59). As it developed more fully in the seventeenth century, the dialogical framework of Caribbean tradition was determined by three additional issues: (1) the rise of a sugar planter ideology, which included strong positions on property rights, African slavery, European racial supremacy and white Creole nationalism; (2) an imperial ideology of the political elites that stressed imperial authority in local governance, loyalty to the crown, and white supremacy; (3) the rise of emancipatory counter-claims by enslaved Africans (ibid.: 94–170). Because of the oral nature of native Caribbean and African societies, their members were unable to leave behind written accounts of their positions and responses. Good indications of these can be gained, however, from their resistance and from the texts of colonial writers. Thus the early phases of the tradition are quite unequal in the records they have left behind, though not in substance.

Internal divisions are clear among the writers and leaders of groups in Caribbean societies. For example, among Europeans there were differences between those who were Creole nationalists and those who were loyalists, those who were pro-slavery and those who were anti-slavery. Political elites were divided on how best to govern colonial territories and on the issue of slavery. Enslaved Africans were divided over the best strategies for ending their oppressive condition. In the Spanish colonies, Victoria, Oviedo, Herrera, Las Casas, Jose Antonio Saco, and Bachiller y Morales laid the written foundations of the tradition, taking up the issues of Spanish rights, native Caribbean resistance and African slavery. In the English-speaking Caribbean, the writers of the founding texts were Edward Littleton, Dalby Thomas, Richard Ligon, William Young, Edward Long, Bryan Edwards, James Ramsay, and William Wilberforce. And in the case of the French colonies it was Rochefort, Du Tertre, Père Labat, Moreau de Saint Mercy, Hilliard D'Auberteuil, and the celebrated Victor Schoelcher (Lewis 1987: 129–36).

In the works of these writers, the culture and identity of Africans were examined and positions taken on their enslavement. The nature of European imperialism was examined and for the most part "justified." The merits of white Creole nationalism versus monarchical government, and economic monopoly versus liberalism were all hotly debated in these texts. Most of these early writers were historians or lawyers, many of whom held official positions. Later, we get the creative writers whose novels will also take up such themes as creolization, slavery, and the tragic fate of the native Caribbeans. The positions defended in these texts constituted the European half of the dialogical framework of the Caribbean intellectual tradition.

The other half of this framework was of course shaped by the positions defended by native Caribbeans and Africans. The history of these positions can be divided into two phases: the oral and the written or literate. In the oral phase, the responses of Indians and Africans were most visible in the collective actions they took on behalf of these positions. C. L. R. James has often reminded us that in their collective actions, dominated groups often work out solutions to real life problems that equal in creativity the solutions of individual genii. Consequently, collective actions such as strikes, insurrections, and revolutions can be viewed as the media in which an oral population formulates its answer to a social problem (James 1960). Such actions become the books in which they write and therefore should be read as carefully as the written texts of Labat, Long, or Saco.

On this textual reading of collective action, the slave and ex-slave uprisings that were led by King Court, Cuffy, Cudjoe, Toussaint L'Overture, Fedon, and others, as well as the actions of the slaves that resisted these undertakings, constituted the early African–Afro-Caribbean responses. By the mid-nineteenth century, the individualist and written phase of this response was established without the abandoning of the collective and insurrectionary options. I emphasize the written text in the transition from oral to literate to facilitate Fanon. The founding texts of this literate phase were authored by Robert Love, Edward Blyden, Marcus Garvey, J. J. Thomas, H. Sylvester-Williams. By the second and third decades of the twentieth century, this literate Afro-Caribbean tradition began moving in two distinct directions: the historicist and the poeticist. Among the former were Padmore and James, while Césaire and Firmin fell into the latter category. A little later, Fanon and Arthur Lewis would join the historicist wing, while the ranks of poeticists would see the addition of Glissant, Harris, and Walcott. From James, Lewis, and Fanon, leadership of the historicist wing would pass to Clive Thomas, George Beckford, Norman Girvan, and other members of the New World group. However, it is important to note that the differences between these two approaches were ones of emphasis and priorities regarding historical action and the creative powers of the human imagination. The positions defended by these Afro-Caribbean writers cannot be separated from those taken by their Euro-Caribbean counterparts. Thus J. J. Thomas's book, *Froudacity* (1889) was a direct response to Froude's *The English in the West Indies*.

This in brief is the dialogical structure of the Caribbean intellectual tradition. It arose within a very definite political framework which helped to shape the unequal relations between the European and African participants in its discursive exchanges. These political constraints were such that the writing of books and the making of arguments found themselves subject to patterns of cultural accumulation and disaccumulation that had more to do with sociopolitical stability than truth. As the political wheels of the tradition turned, African culture increasingly lost value and the identity of the Afro-Caribbean moved slowly from being Akan or Yoruba to the pathology of Caliban. At the same time, European culture increased in value and the European identity moved from the adventurous Robinson Crusoe to imperial Prospero.

Philosophy and the Caribbean Intellectual Tradition

In the highly racialized and politicized dialogues of this tradition there was very little room for philosophy. The exchanges were between Caliban and Caliban or Prospero and Prospero. What these exchanges needed were legitimating or deligitimating arguments of an ideological nature. Indeed, among the Euro-Caribbean writers, it is accurate to say that ideological production was the primary output of the earlier phases of this tradition. Ideological machines had the biggest contracts with the political economy of Caribbean societies for producing the images and arguments that would sustain Prospero's dominance. As the dominant discourse, its practitioners were able to mobilize selected aspects of other discourses such as philosophy and history. To these appropriations they added large doses of racist dogma to produce the desired ideological outputs.

In a context of such strong ideological hegemony, there was neither the autonomy or the institutional support for a flourishing philosophy. Consequently, its role in the division of cultural labor was very small. This role was largely auxiliary: supplying the ideological machines with authoritative figures, supporting arguments and philosophical legitimacy – in particular, providing these services for the production of Eurocentric, plantocratic, white supremacist, pro-slavery, anti-slavery, and related kinds of arguments. Hence our earlier characterization of philosophy as the handmaiden of legitimacy enhancing ideological production.

Commandeered into ideological service, philosophy was of political necessity cut off from religion. Particularly in the early centuries, ideological production was separated from religious production. The notion that all men and women were equal before God was too threatening to the social and political relations that had to be maintained between Prospero and Caliban. Hence the early attempts to limit Christianity and notions of basic political rights to Europeans. Thus to the extent that ideology and religion had to be separated, philosophy as the handmaiden of ideology also had to keep its distance from religion. Ideological service for philosophy also meant that Euro-Caribbeans were unable to develop a distinct philosophy of their own. The cultivating of original analogies and concepts that reflected the spacial and temporal dimensions of the region, its geography, its flora and fauna, and its mythopoetics of self-formation was not encouraged. No such original philosophical foundations were laid, and those used in these production processes were largely European imports. Separated from religion and unable to thematize its own organic metaphysical responses to the Caribbean environment, Euro-Caribbean philosophy was reduced to making available selections of European political philosophy that were useful for local ideological production.

The philosophical selections that inform and augment the works of the Euro-Caribbean sector of the tradition were concentrated in areas such as conservative monarchism, liberalism, constitutionalism, rationalism, and eugenics. Thus figures of Burke, Locke, Montesquieu, Rousseau, Diderot, Hume, Hobbes, and Adam Smith loom very large in the tradition. So Bryan Edwards's arguments for more responsible government for Europeans in the colonies are inconceivable without Locke's idea of the consensual bases of government. Similarly, Moreau de Saint-Mercy's critical appraisal of Haitian society draws explicitly on the works Diderot and Rousseau. In the case of Saco, British liberalism was used to criticize Spanish mercantilism and to make the case for plutocratic rule in Cuba. In these and many other cases, the universalist and egalitarian tendencies within these imported philosophies had to be compromised if they were to work in societies with enslaved populations. How these tendencies were contained and adjusted to needs of the local slave order constitutes both the poverty and the distinctness of these ideological productions.

In the case of Edwards, this tension between his liberal and pro-slavery positions were resolved by drawing on two sets of stereotypes: the completely uncivilized nature of life in Africa and the inherent lack of capabilities for modern life among African people. On the latter point, he appeals to the authority of Hume (Lewis: 109–10). The strategy of resorting to similar stereotypes of Caliban can be seen in Arango, Saco, and many others. Writers such as Schoelcher, Ramsay and Bachiller y Morales were the exceptions in that they took the universalist implications of these imported philosophies to their logical conclusions.

This containing of universalist tendencies in order to preserve Calibanized stereotypes of Africans greatly affected Euro-Caribbean views of Africans and their ability to philosophize. As Sylvia Wynter has shown, the rise of the European bourgeoisie was accompanied by the metaphorical appropriation of reason for political purposes. The metaphoric of reason replaced those of blood as criteria for distributing political rights and privileges. The possession or non-possession of reason became a basis for the conferral or denial of political rights (Wynters: 64–7). Thus, in his fight against Carib slavery, Las Casas was at pains to point out, against the opinions of his opponents, that Caribs had the capacity to reason and hence the right to self-rule. Within this global deploying of the metaphoric of reason, Africans fared even worse than native Caribbeans. They occupied the zero point on the scale of human rational capability. Africans were seen as being without the capacity for rational thought and unable to develop it even when educated. Given this exclusion from the rational community, it followed that Africans had no philosophy and could not be philosophers. Euro-Caribbean texts of the tradition repeatedly recognized the dancing, dramatic, oratorical, religious, and musical capabilities of Africans, but never their philosophical capabilities. African philosophy was completely disenfranchised within the tradition. To be precise, it never existed. Thus in terms of the misrepresentation and the general loss of value that African culture suffered within the accumulative dynamics of the tradition, the case of philosophy was particularly severe.

In the Afro-Caribbean layers of this tradition, philosophy also occupies a minor role in the division of cultural labor. Among the insurrectionists and writers who made this half of the tradition, the pressing need was for delegitimating arguments that would counter European claims to political leadership and racial superiority. Also, there was a need for arguments that would legitimate self-rule and de-Calibanize the Afro-Caribbean identity, just as domination had become a crucial problem that Euro-Caribbeans had to legitimate. In this ideologically polarized setting, the discursive space for philosophy was small with tendencies toward contraction and rigidification.

This close relation between philosophy and ideology was a new development. It was a part of the creolization and adaptation of African philosophy to life in Caribbean plantation societies. By contrast, philosophy in traditional African societies existed in a very close relationship with religion. Philosophy functioned as the handmaiden of religion, and to the former as an autonomous practice. African philosophy was visible to the extent that dominant religious world-views were discursively elaborated and collectively acted out in the dramatic discourse of ritual. African religious world-views were cosmocentric as opposed to theocentric. For Africans, the cosmos was primarily spiritual in nature in spite of its material appearance. These two modalities were constructed as a hierarchy of gods, spirits, demons, and souls. Attitudes toward spirituality were ecstatic and participatory, which produced a joyous mysticism that was closely linked to the music of the drums. African religions were world- and life-affirming and not world- and life-rejecting as in the case of some Christian fundamentalists or some East Indian religions. African philosophy developed largely around the defense of this religious world-view, much as positivism developed around the defense of natural science. Thus the idealism of African philosophy can be seen in its defense of the spiritual claims of religion. Its existentialism is in its elaboration of notions of cosmic harmonies, fate, and predestiny to defend its acceptance of world- and life-affirming attitudes. Its ethics are to be found in its defense of religious claims that the gods and ancestors are to be obeyed. Its ontology is in its defense of religious cosmogony, its epistemology in its defense of spiritual knowledge derived from ego-transcending experiences. This was the philosophical heritage that Africans brought to the Caribbean.

However, under the impact of Christianization and the oppressive conditions of plantation slavery, this close relation between philosophy and religion began to dissolve. The demands of ideological production became as strong or stronger than those religions. Consequently, in the genesis of many slave uprisings, large sections of these African religious world-views were philosophically appropriated and made available for ideological purposes. The figures of Macandal and the later leaders of the Haitian revolutions come to mind at this point. In short, even in the oral/insurrectionary phase of the Afro-Caribbean tradition, the nature and role of philosophy are best understood in relation to the dramatic increase in the demand for ideological production.

In the literate phase of the Afro-Caribbean part of the tradition, the transformation of philosophy under the pull of ideology is ever more marked. First, philosophy becomes less African and progressively more European. Second, it moves from being cosmocentric to being Christocentric and then historiocentric. It loses its connections with the gods of African religion and makes its living by appropriating a variety of European philosophies and making them available for local ideological production. In particular, it appropriated European liberalism, constitutionalism, racialism, and socialism. To these were added heavy doses of black or African nationalism to produce the ideological arguments for decolonization and the return of self-rule. Except for the socialist appropriations, the philosophies chosen were very similar to the selections made by Euro-Caribbean writers. However, they were developed very differently by Afro-Caribbean writers such as J. J. Thomas or Garvey. In these writers, the Afro-Caribbean implications of universalist tendencies in the borrowed philosophies were explicitly developed as in the case of anti-slavery ideologues and married to passionate formulations of black nationalism.

This, in brief, was the role of philosophy in the Caribbean intellectual tradition up to the time that Fanon appeared on the scene. This was the conception and approach to philosophy that Fanon inherited from his teachers. Of particular importance for us was the complete disenfranchisement of African philosophy on the grounds that philosophy was not a practice engaged in by "primitive" peoples. One of the strongest taboos that European discourses placed on themselves was that on the open acknowledgment of its tribal or primitive past. These discourses still like to see their origins in classical Greece (stealing Egypt away from Africa along the way) and not in the "primitive" Celts, Britons, Gauls, Saxons, and other tribal groups that populated Europe.

Euro-Caribbeans hid their intense horror of this past with a compelling necessity to present themselves as always having been "civilized." The primitive past of humanity could be viewed through other people, particularly Africans. Consequently, European discourses contain more about the tribal life of Africans than they do about their own. This powerful binary opposition between primitive and civilized is a polarity that the Caribbean tradition inherited from Europe. There is an unbridgeable gap between the two. Thus within the tradition, one cannot say "African and civilized" or "European and primitive." For the same reason, one cannot say "African and philosophical" or "European and non-philosophical." In short, the tradition gave Fanon an ideologically restricted conception of philosophy whose European identity excluded its African counterpart because both occupied the extreme points on the powerful underlying binary, primitive–civilized. The separating of Caribbean philosophy from this binary would clearly be a necessary cultural condition for the decolonization and re-enfranchisement of Afro-Caribbean philosophy.

Fanon, Philosophy, and the Caribbean Tradition

Given these racist features of our intellectual tradition, our next task must be an examination of the impact of Fanon's philosophy on the primitive–civilized binary and related practices that maintained the disenfranchisement of African philosophy. In particular, I will focus on Fanon's existentialism. Many of the same points about the limited role of philosophy in our tradition could be made with James's Hegelianism. The major exception is of course Marxism which has been extensively thematized in regional thought (see Clive Thomas).

Among the historicists, Fanon is unique in the degree to which he explicitly developed a theory of the human self. The more usual pattern among the historicists has been the employing of Cartesian or Marxian notions of the human subject without much question or justification. This holds true for our contemporary political economists, in spite of the very different notion of the subject that Fanon gave us. Among the poeticists, the subject has been constructed primarily in mythopoetic terms.

By the time Fanon arrived on the scene, the patterns of cultural accumulation and disaccumulation within the Caribbean tradition had begun to reverse themselves. Thanks to the cumulative efforts of Garvey, Padmore, Firmin, Janvier, Césaire, and others, Afro-Caribbean cultures were accumulating authority while Afro-Caribbean identities were being de-Calibanized. But in spite of these changes, the binary oppositions, the stereotypes and dogmatic arguments of the tradition, were still strong enough to continue the reproduction of white superiority. It was this continuing ability of the tradition to reproduce black inferiority, in spite of criticism, that engaged Fanon. Thus the primary targets of his attacks were the racist strategies and discourses of the tradition and, only secondarily, its philosophical practices.

Fanon's point of departure was the impact of these racist discourses on the formation of the Afro-Caribbean psyche. The internalizing of their "imago of the Negro," produced what Fanon called "aberrations of affect." At their worst, these aberrations produced in black Caribbeans a desire to be white and European. These aberrations were both psychological and existential in nature, creating a "psycho-existential complex" that dramatically altered the personality of the Afro-Caribbean.

The existential dimensions of this complex are to be found in the "zone of nonbeing" that it opens up within the Afro-Caribbean psyche. Fanon also describes the psychological exposure to this zone as an existential deviation that now becomes a problematic constraint that conditions Afro-Caribbean ego genesis.

By the zone of nonbeing, Fanon is referring to "an extraordinarily sterile and arid region, an utterly naked declivity where an authentic upheaval can be born" (*Pn* 6 / *BS* 8). We encounter this zone of nonbeing in extreme states of ego collapse. Because such states of ego dissolution are terrifying, we normally do everything we can to avoid them. But, as Fanon points out, they can also be the occasions for genuine rebirths. Egos can collapse because they are internally divided, or because they are being recreated or integrated into a larger psychic formation. However, these are not the sources of ego collapse that interest Fanon. Rather, he is concerned with the negative reflections and distorted images of themselves that Afro-Caribbeans saw in the eyes of the colonial other and in the discourses of the intellectual tradition. Fanon assumes that genuine recognition and affirmation from significant others are necessary for healthy ego genesis.

Knowing well the condition of ego collapse and the zone of nonbeing that it opens up, Fanon takes us there several times in *Black Skin, White Masks*. Let us look at two of these instances. The first is clearly an instance of ego collapse brought on by the negative reflections of blackness produced by the tradition.

> "Dirty Nigger!" or simply, "Look, a Negro!"
> I arrived in the world anxious to make sense of things, my spirit filled with desire to be at the origin of the world, and here I discovered myself an object amongst other objects.
> Imprisoned in this overwhelming objectivity, I implored others. Their liberating regard, running over my body that suddenly becomes smooth, returns to me a lightness that I believed lost, and, absenting me from the world, returns me to the world. But there, just at the opposite slope, I stumble, and the other, by gestures, attitudes, looks, fixed me, in the sense that one fixes a chemical preparation with a dye. I was furious. I demanded an explanation. Nothing happened. I exploded. Now the tiny pieces are collected by another self. (*Pn* 88 / *BS* 109)

Here Fanon is moving painfully back and forth between projecting his ego out into the world and its collapse into the zone of nonbeing. The description reveals the fragility of the ego in this state, and its dependence on the movements, attitudes, and glances of the other. It also reveals an ego that is unable to launch and stabilize itself. Each time it attempts to constitute itself, the effort ends in a collapse which is followed by another attempt. In Fanon's language, this is an ego that has no ontological resistance to the look and evaluation of the white.

Our second visit to the zone of nonbeing reveals more of the creative possibilities of this region and the expanses beyond it.

> I feel in myself a soul as immense as the world, truly a soul as deep as the deepest rivers, my chest has the power to expand without limit. I am a master and I am advised to adopt the humility of a cripple. Yesterday, awakening to the world, I saw the sky turn upon itself utterly and wholly. I wanted to rise, but the disemboweled silence fell back upon me, its wings paralyzed. Without responsibility, straddling Nothingness and Infinity, I began to weep. (*Pn* 114 / *BS* 140)

This instance of ego collapse gives Fanon more than just exposure to nonbeing with its paralyzing silence. It also gives him a glimpse of the infinity that includes but extends beyond the zone of nonbeing. This infinite oceanic consciousness can genuinely transform any complex-ridden ego, if only it can conquer its fear and creatively negotiate its way in the zone of nonbeing.

By exploring these zones beyond the borders of the ego, Fanon had taken the analyses of the Afro-Caribbean psyche to new philosophical depths. His uniqueness within the historicist school is largely determined by the extent to which he fearlessly explored these regions. His explorations exposed for us the ground out of which the Afro-Caribbean ego emerges and against which it must secure its everyday existence. This ground conditions the normal process of ego genesis, which requires the support of positive interpersonal relations for it to have a stable existence above the ground. Without such cultural and interpersonal support, egos tend to collapse into their ground under the pressure of its "gravitational" pull. This vulnerability is the existential deviation that Calibanized images and evaluations of the tradition produced in the Afro-Caribbean psyche.

The complex associated with this deviation was psycho-existential in nature. Consequently, Fanon's theory of the self was not exclusively existential. In fact, the existential was only one of its dimensions. Ego formation for Fanon was also conditioned by the many defense mechanisms and neurotic strategies identified by Freud. Hence the strong Freudian elements in Fanon's theory. Third and most important, ego genesis is also conditioned by the system of binary oppositions, values, discourses, and practices that a culture or tradition imposes on its members. Fanon conceptualizes this layer as the logical equivalent of Jung's collective unconscious. But, unlike Jung's collective unconscious, Fanon's is not the result of "cerebral inheritance." On the contrary, it becomes a part of an individual through "the unreflected cultural imposition" (*Pn* 156 / *BS* 191).

In addition to the more scholarly works that constituted a part of this layer, Fanon also emphasized images and values internalized from movies, magazines, jokes, and other forms of popular expression.

This emphasis on the sociocultural layer over the existential and the psychological points to Fanon's historicism. This layer is for Fanon thoroughly historicized. Traditional as well as colonial orders of discourse rise and decline as the historical process moves ever onward. Consequently, personality structures and the psycho-existential complexes that shape them are necessarily historicized by this changing of cultural orders. This penetration of the existential by history and culture explains Fanon's provocative claim that "ontology . . . does not permit us to explain the being of the black." This requires culture and history. "For the black no longer has to be black; he is it in front of the white" (*Pn* 88 / *BS* 110). This is Fanon's historicism asserting itself at the heart of his existentialism.

To complete our analyses of Fanon's existentialism, we must return to the zone of nonbeing. We have already noted Fanon's suggestions that it could be the locus of a "genuine upheaval," of a rebirth. But he also added without explanation the following caution: "In most cases, the black lacks the advantage of being able to accomplish this descent into a real hell" (*Pn* 6 / *BS* 8). Fanon is here suggesting that the discourses of the Afro-Caribbean tradition were not able to navigate the individual across the difficult waters of this zone. Hence Fanon's turn to European existentialism for the language and concepts with which to explore the existential depths of the Afro-Caribbean psyche.

From European existentialism, Fanon inherited the basic concept of nonbeing that he used to describe the conditions of aridity and paralysis that often follow ego collapse. This is an abstract philosophical representation of these states that could have been described differently in the languages of myth, religion, or ritual.

From this tradition, Fanon also inherited the distinction between the in-itself and the for-itself. Logically, the former was the equivalent of Fanon's infinity and the latter of the existential aspects of his model of the self. For Sartre, the for-itself represented the basic emergence and growth that are conditioned by the zone of nonbeing. The "gravitational" pull of the latter establishes a basic lack in the existence of the for-itself. It attempts to overcome this lack through a compensatory project of being. The goal of this project is to establish the for-itself (consciousness) as a full positivity by restoring the being negated by the zone of nonbeing. In other words, it is to be a for-itself with all the powers of consciousness, and at the same time possess the full positivity of the in-itself. For Sartre, this project of being an in-itself-for-itself is a necessary but impossible one. Hence the anguish of the for-itself. Nonetheless, this dialectic between being and nothingness and the projects it necessitates are inescapable. It conditions ego formation by imposing upon it the structure and dynamics of its problematic projects (Sartre 1956a).

This language and its related concepts find their way into Fanon's analysis of the zone of nonbeing in the Afro-Caribbean psyche. He also borrows from Hegel, Kierkegaard, and Jaspers. The following passage shows us the way in which Fanon used this language and redeployed some of its concepts:

> Thus human reality as in-itself-for-itself can be achieved only through conflict and through the risk that conflict implies. This risk means that I go

beyond life toward a supreme good that is the transformation of subjective certainty of my own worth into a universally objective truth. (*Pn* 177 / *BS* 218)

Here the influences of Hegel and Sartre are unmistakable. However, Fanon is here employing the language and concepts of this tradition to articulate a possibility for the Afro-Caribbean that neither had imagined. In other words, the language is that of European existentialism, but the experience is Afro-Caribbean.

Fanonian, African, and European Existentialism

By incorporating these existential dimensions, Fanon revolutionized the treatment of black identity within our intellectual tradition. He opened up questions of ontology that hitherto had gone unaddressed. Compared to the dogmatic and stereotypical treatment of Afro-Caribbean identity in the European layer of our tradition, this was a revolutionary counter-statement that de-Calibanized blackness. Like the counter-discourses of J. J. Thomas, Garvey, Padmore, and Césaire, Fanon's work was a major contribution to reversing the patterns of cultural accumulation and disaccumulation within the tradition.

In addition to its impact on patterns of accumulation, Fanon's revolutionary approach to the self had two important consequences for philosophy in the region. First, it provided Caribbean philosophy with a new model of the self. This was not the rational, solitary, and enclosed model of the subject that the tradition had inherited from Hume or Adam Smith. Fanon's model was less closed and less securely centered. It opened the self to possibilities of collapse, to its rootedness in a collective unconscious, and beyond that to its grounding in infinity. This remains an unsurpassed achievement in Caribbean philosophy.

The second important consequence of Fanon's approach to the self was that it established a solid link between the zone of nonbeing in the Afro-Caribbean psyche and the existential tradition of European philosophy. It was a new move within the tradition. This existential coding liberated the zone from its invisibility and non-recognition in dominant discourses of the tradition. It supplemented the emancipatory appropriations of European liberalism, socialism, constitutionalism, and surrealism that was evident in the works of Garvey, James, Césaire, and other Afro-Caribbean writers. At the same time, it was in sharp contrast with the repressive use to which many of these same philosophical appropriations were put by Euro-Caribbean writers.

In spite of these important contributions to Afro-Caribbean philosophy, Fanon's analysis of black identity did not revolutionize the basic position or the overall functioning of philosophy in the Caribbean intellectual tradition. This was so for two reasons. First, it did not change the intertextual location of Caribbean philosophy. Fanon's work linked it primarily to the production of an emancipatory political theory. Thus it remained very much the handmaiden of ideology. In the polarized colonial context it was difficult for it to be otherwise. Separated from art, religion, and its own original vision, the intertextual location of philosophy remained the same.

The second reason why Fanon's contribution did not revolutionize regional philosophy was that his existentialism left the identity of Caribbean philosophy as European and as white as it found it. At the same time that it was helping to destroy racist discourses, the linguistic coding of Fanon's existentialism reinforced Caribbean philosophy's over-identification with Europe and its under-identification with Africa. This is the underlying pattern that needs to be changed. Fanon's decision to appropriate the language and concepts of European existentialism while excluding African ones presented no major challenge to this pattern. This choice left African existentialism and African philosophy as a whole still unrecognized and still under the spell of that powerful binary opposition, primitive–civilized. Consequently the European identity of Caribbean philosophy remained essentially unchanged.

This is not to suggest that Fanon was unaware of the above problem of overidentification, or that he did not make original contributions with his appropriation of the language and concepts of European existentialism. As indicated above, it was an Afro-Caribbean experience that he analyzed with this language. Although I am of the view that Caliban can say something new and original in the language of Prospero (Henry and Buhle 1992b: 111–42), my point is that Fanon's specific philosophical formulations did not have the weight or critical mass to break the underlying binary that disenfranchised African philosophy and inhibited the emergence of a distinct regional philosophy. This failure says nothing about the quality or originality of Fanon's philosophy, but it says a lot about the discursive authority that it had to overcome.

Fanon did not turn to European existentialism because there was no African or Afro-Caribbean existentialist discourse. Rather, it was because he was unable to break the spell of Calibanization that the tradition had cast over it. If African and Afro-Caribbean cultures have supported viable egos, then they must have found discursive solutions to the "gravitational" pulls of nonbeing. Fanon's failure to recognize and appropriate these discourses was indicative of the power of the tradition.

Earlier, we noted that Fanon's existentialism was grounded in experiences of ego collapse that were brought on by the negative reflections of blackness that pervade our tradition. The existentialism of traditional Africa also derived from experiences of ego collapse or displacement. However, these experiences were of a spiritual and not a racial origin. Conscious and controlled exercises in ego dissolution or suspension are spiritual practices that many societies cultivate. In Africa techniques of ego transcendence center on the rhythms of the drums and getting into trance states. In the East, these techniques center on the practice of meditation. In traditional Africa, the vision of reality that anchored cultural life was in large part derived from states in which the ego had been silenced. In other words, Africans were experienced explorers of the realms beyond the borders of the ego. More important, they had developed the discursive ability to code those supreme existential moments in which the human self is confronted with the conditions of its possibility or non-possibility.

The realities discovered by African explorers were not coded in the impersonal language of being and nonbeing, in-itself and for-itself. On the contrary, they were coded in the more personal language of gods and spirits who were in charge of various aspects of creation, including the process of ego genesis and hence ego performance. In the crucial notions of fate and destiny, we had the hidden instruments through which human self-formation was subjected to the control of the gods. The individual's relation to his or her destiny was made problematic by two factors: the relative autonomy of the human will and the fact that we could be in the dark about our real destiny.

These factors set the stage for the African to be at odds or in harmony with his or her destiny, that is, with the forces beyond the borders of the ego. To the extent that the individual is not in accord with the gods, he or she will experience the "gravitational" pull of nonbeing or the anger of the gods, both of which can result in personal failure or ego collapse. To the extent that the individual is in harmony with the gods, he or she will experience confirmation, guidance, and help in personal projects. The individual will experience the upward, "heliotropic" pull of the power of being or the blessings of the gods. Both of these will lead to ego affirmation and personal success. The pushes and pulls of these "gravitational" and "heliotropic" forces on the individual are very reminiscent of Kierkegaard's descriptions of being "educated by anxiety" (see pp. 155–62).

This discourse of fate is the foundation of African existentialism.[1] It is beautifully portrayed in Achebe's *Things Fall Apart*, and ethnographically reproduced in the works of scholars such as Fortes (1959) and Rattray (1923) on the Tellensi and the Ashanti. It contains the language and concepts that Africans have used to describe the relationship between the ego's self-formation and its expansive ground.

Africans brought this discourse, with its gods and practices of ego transcendence, with them to the Caribbean. In the colonial context of Caribbean societies, this discourse was forced to historicize and Christianize itself. In making these adaptations, it incorporated secular ideologies of liberation and syncretized itself with the more ritualized and ego transcending aspects of European Christianity. Thus with the passage of time, personal fate came to be understood either in Afro-Christian, primarily Christian, terms or through secular ideologies of historicism.

Since this discourse existed, why didn't Fanon include it in his existential explorations? It was certainly not because he was unaware of it. He was too close to Césaire and other poeticists for him not to know about it. Even more than James, Fanon followed closely the developments that were taking place in African ethnophilosophy. References to them can be found throughout *Black Skin*. Given these facts, it must be that in spite of being there, Fanon did not find them capable of meeting the challenge he was confronting.

This challenge was to break the power of European discourses to negate or neutralize the counter-discourses of colonized Afro-Caribbeans. Fanon was in search of a philosophy that could repel the discursive bullets, even the physical bullets, of European colonialism. "What use are reflections on Bantu ontology," asks Fanon, "when striking black miners in South Africa are being shot down? (*Pn* 149 / *BS* 184). Or, "When a bachelor of philosophy from the Antilles refuses to apply for certification as a teacher because of his color, I say that philosophy has never saved anyone" (22 / 28–9). Fanon is clearly in search of a philosophy that can counter "the lived-experience of the black" as it had been constructed in the tradition.

Like the other discourses of the poeticists, Fanon did not find the discourse of fate really capable of restoring an African meaning to "the lived-experience of the black." It could not neutralize the "primitive" images with which blackness was associated, or counter the existential deviations and ego collapses that these images produced in the Afro-Caribbean psyche. It couldn't because the discourse of fate carried the same markings of blackness. These markings Calibanized it, robbed it of objective value and its capacity to counter-punch. Consequently, for Fanon, to use it in an argument against Europeans was to lose the argument before it began. This loss would have nothing to do with logic, evidence, or truth, but with the authority European philosophical discourses had accumulated at the expense of African ones. The power differential between the two was still so wide that Fanon experienced the latter as having little or no ontological resistance in the face of the former.

This becomes clear as Fanon matches various black counter-arguments against white stereotypes and devaluations, using his own ego-genesis to test the ontological strengths of both. Here is Fanon testing the ability of a negritude argument to support his ego.

> I rummaged frenetically through all of black antiquity. What I found there took my breath away. In his book, *L'Abolition de l'esclavage* Schoelcher presented us with compelling arguments. Since then, Frobenius, Westermann, Delafosse – all of them white had joined the chorus: Segou, Djennne, cities of more than a hundred thousand people; accounts of learned blacks (doctors of theology who went to Mecca to interpret the Koran). All of that, exhumed from the past, spread with its insides out, made it possible for me to find a valid historic place. (*Pn* 105 / *BS* 130)

Feeling as if he had "put the white man back into his place," Fanon experiences a moment of contentment and ego stability. But then the white man responds:

> Lay aside your history and your research on the past, and try to put yourself into our rhythm. In a society such as ours, industrialized to the extreme, scientized, there is no longer any place for your sensitivity. It is necessary to be strong to be allowed to live. What matters now is no longer playing the game of the world but subjugating it with integrals and atoms . . . When we are tired of our lives in our buildings, we will turn to you as we do to our children – to the innocent, the ingenuous, the spontaneous. (*Pn* 106 / *BS* 132)

The negritude argument did not hold up against this response. Fanon experiences ego collapse; his reasons were countered by "real reasons," his arguments by "real" arguments. The fact that Fanon did not explicitly mention the discourse of fate is not really important. It would have failed his ontological test just like the others, leaving Fanon with another experience of ego dissolution. Like the negritude argument, it would have been countered by "real" reasons and "real" arguments – real because of the authority European existentialist discourses had accumulated in relation to this discourse of fate.

Fanon, Creolization, and Afro-Caribbean Philosophy

Fanon's failure to change the European identity of Caribbean philosophy was clearly the result of his inability to liberate it from its enmeshment in values and markings of the tradition. This failure to liberate Caribbean philosophy from its colonial complex is all the more striking, as such emancipations were taking place in literature, dance, music, and other media of expression. This points to the special situation of Afro-Caribbean philosophy: the extreme degree to which it was disenfranchised from the community of discourses.

Given this persistence of the European identity, it is not surprising that Fanon's philosophy did not lead to a creolizing of Caribbean philosophy in the way that the works of Lamming, Reid, Harris, Selvon, and others led to the creolizing of Caribbean literature. Caribbean philosophy is yet to undergo a similar change. Given the increases in authority that Afro-Caribbean discourses have accumulated since Fanon, the key question for us is whether or not such a change is now possible. That is, with the corresponding loss of authority by Euro-Caribbean discourses, will Afro-Caribbean philosophy now be able to claim its rightful place in the community of discourses? I think this is not only possible, but highly desirable.

Creolization is an active project that would indigenize Caribbean philosophy and end its state of Calibanization and limited activation. The existence of more advanced states of creolization in other discourses points to the uneven rates at which recovery has been taking place in the various dimensions of the Caribbean imagination. These differential rates also indicate the problem areas in our capacity for symbolically representing local realities. The limited capabilities of areas such as philosophy must affect our performances in stronger areas such as literature.

Glissant has suggested that these differential rates of recovery have left our postcolonial imagination with limited vision and an inability to see the whole. In areas such as myth and philosophy, Glissant sees a continuing failure of mythopoetic and discursive processes to root themselves in local experiences of time and space, flora and fauna, work and play (Glissant 1992: 17–26). These areas of symbolic immobilization have created fissures, blanks and nonfunctioning spots on the Caribbean imagination as a whole. Because of these cleavages, it is unable to produce comprehensive pictures of itself, or adequately reflect its natural and social environments.

This absence of comprehensive pictures of ourselves points to our limited capacity to philosophically represent ourselves. By its nature, philosophical discourse tends toward the systematically integrated view. Glissant suggests that the prevalence of the folktale as a medium of collective self-representation is indicative of this reluctance to form comprehensive pictures of ourselves. Folktales deal with particular events and therefore generate stories that cannot be generalized (Glissant: 94). I think the use of the novel as our primary medium of self-exploration sends a similar message. If we are to have comprehensive pictures of ourselves, we must remove the blocks on the philosophical and other dimensions of the Caribbean imagination. Philosophy is an indispensable practice in our division of cultural labor. Without the full functioning of its African and European dimensions, our vision will be narrowed, and our capacity to understand ourselves limited.

To free the philosophical and other underperforming spots on the Caribbean imagination, Glissant suggests a project of creolization, one in which intellectual workers would re-enter the long-concealed areas of our imagination and undo the binary oppositions and negative evaluations that block African and European elements from creatively coming together. These subterranean voyagers should strive to open blocked arteries and channels so that rates of creolization would synchronize and capacities for discursive representation would increase more uniformly. Such changes would make more operational the underlying unity of our imagination and reconnect philosophy, folktales, literature, etc., to the unconscious patterns, rhythms, and images that make this unity possible. In short, creolization is a process of semio-semantic hybridization that can occur between the arguments, vocabularies, phonologies, or grammars of discourses within a culture or across cultures. This is the context in which we can envision the re-enfranchising of African and Afro-Caribbean philosophies, the re-establishing of their ability to accumulate authority and their capacity for ontological resistance.

Such a creolizing of Caribbean philosophy must begin with subterranean plunges of the type suggested by Glissant. At these depths, African and Afro-Caribbean philosophies must be freed from the legacy of invisibility and entrapment in the binaries of colonial discourses. With their visibility and legitimacy restored, this philosophical heritage must be allowed to find its own equilibrium in the processes of semio-semantic hybridization that have creolized other discourses. In this Creole framework, the African discourse of fate should find a place in any discussion of Afro-Caribbean existentialism. However, this inclusion would be related to its ability to reflect the existential realities of Caribbean people. In other words, its inclusion would not be the result of the repressive authority it had accumulated over other discourses.

Such a Creole philosophy means going beyond the philosophical models we inherited from James and Fanon. In their models, Caribbean philosophy recovered a knowledge of itself and its society by drawing on the discourses of the western tradition. Given the nature of the colonial situation, such a period of philosophical dependence is probably a necessary phase. If reconstruction proceeds, this pattern of dependent borrowing must give way to processes of philosophical indigenization. The levels of philosophical dependence inherited from James and Fanon are not consistent with our modern aspirations and national self-projections. Paradoxically, to move closer to its own modernity, Caribbean philosophy must creolize itself by breaking its mis-identifications with European and African philosophies and allowing them to remix within the framework of more organic relations with local realities.

Conclusion

I have attempted to examine the impact of our intellectual tradition on Fanon and his impact on the practice of philosophy within the tradition. The results suggest that while Fanon's work rocked the foundations of racial and identity discourses, its impact on the practice of philosophy was less earthshaking. It left largely intact the European identity of Caribbean philosophy, as well as its intertextual position as the handmaiden of ideology. To meet the challenges confronting us, we desperately need the contributions of our philosophical imagination. To decolonize and activate this imagination, we must do more than just absorb Fanon's philosophical contributions; we must also include and supersede them in a project of creolization.

Unfortunately, much of Fanon's philosophy has not yet been fully absorbed. His bold and innovative linking of existentialism and political economy has been largely ignored by our New World political economists. Before we can take on the bigger task of creolizing Caribbean philosophy, we must complete the smaller ones of carefully analyzing and absorbing the philosophical contributions of major figures like James and Fanon. As our current political economy continues to lose authority in relation to the International Monetary Fund's structural adjustment programs, the need for the missing philosophical vision grows ever more acute. Like Fanon's philosophy, this vision must include and go beyond political economy. It must also break with the ideologically restricted models of philosophy that have been dominant in the region by changing its intertextual relations and expanding its interests to include the nature of Caribbean subjectivity. The founding categories and world transforming powers of political economy must be linked to problems of Caribbean subjectivity in new and more profound ways. This should be the new intertextual location of Caribbean philosophy as (like Fanon) it attempts to establish the hidden threads between Caribbean discourses of art and political economy. Given the changes in postcolonial patterns of cultural accumulation, this new intertextual address should be a lot more hospitable than when Fanon tried to live there. These mediatory challenges would not only provide Caribbean philosophy with a unique kind of writing, but also set it on the path of discovering its own Creole identity.

Notes

1   For a more detailed treatment of this discourse, see my "African and Afro-Caribbean Existentialism" in Lewis Gordon (1996a).

17

Fanon and the Contemporary Discourse of African Philosophy

Tsenay Serequeberhan

To my knowledge, the intrinsic affinity between Fanon's reflections on the African liberation struggle and the central issues that animate the hermeneutical orientation in contemporary African philosophy have never been explored. As I will argue in this paper, such a bond does exist, grounded as it is on the historico-political and existential fact that the discourse of contemporary African philosophy, as a whole – in its thematic elaboration and concrete actuality – presupposes both the historico-political success and failure, or limitation, of the African liberation struggle.

To this extent contemporary African philosophy is an intellectual offshoot and an integral part, on the plane of reflective thought, of the presently truncated struggle for African self-emancipation.[1] As is well known, Fanon was a leading protagonist of this struggle. And more than most, he shaped the theoretical and practical self-understanding of this emancipatory project.[2]

In view of the above I will show, in what follows, how some of the central concerns of contemporary African philosophy are, in interesting ways, prefigured by Fanon's theoretical concerns. In remembering Fanon in this way, as a progenitor, my aim is to turn to a figure of our past in order to explore the *concerns* of our present in view of the possibilities of our future.[3]

I

Within the contemporary discourse of African philosophy these *concerns* are what Okonda Okolo aptly describes as a "problematic that oscillates between a naive ethnophilosophy and an unproductive criticism" (Okolo: 201). Paulin Hountondji's position, which Okolo describes as "an unproductive criticism" and which has come to be known as the "geographic" conception of African philosophy is, for Marcien Towa: "The current of thought [that] . . . does not occlude African thought, it openly excludes it" (1971: 201).

In rejecting the ethnophilosophic *occlusive* assumption of the singular unanimity of traditional African thought, what needs doing for Towa, contra Hountondji's *exclusion*, is to explore the multiple variety of traditional African views and conceptions, not only "out of a concern for knowing ourselves," but also because "there is nothing that says we could not find anything precious in [these] conceptions" (p. 196). Towa has in mind, then, an African philosophy that explores the indigenous cultural and historico-political heritage of Africa in the context of the present situation of the diverse peoples of the continent and aimed at the critical and politically radical self-transformation of Africa (1971).

As Towa himself has noted, it is the "revolutionary *négritude*" of Aimé Césaire, the theoretical efforts of Nkruma's *Consciencism*, and the factually and concretely oriented problematic of Fanon that inspire his work in African philosophy.[4] In the same vein Theophilus Okere and Lucius Outlaw, in rejecting Hountondji's position and in being critical of the ahistorical antiquarian project of ethnophilosophy, aim to engage and philosophically explore the concrete and lived problems of contemporary Africa.[5] It is then this strand, in the contemporary discourse of African philosophy, that is positively envisioned by Fanon's work.

In exploring the anticipatory nexus of Fanon's work I will thus engage, in a critical manner, the contemporary concerns of African philosophy, concerns that thus far have oscillated, as noted above, between ethnophilosophy and its sterile foes. I will begin by presenting a sketch of the various strands that constitute the contemporary discourse of African philosophy. I will then engage some of Fanon's relevant texts. My limited aim is to gauge the manner in which Fanon envisions and thus serves as a forebear of the hermeneutical orientation in contemporary African philosophy.

II

As presently constituted African philosophy has a rather equivocal orientation. The texts that compose it focus on either documenting the worldviews of ethnic Africans or philosophically engaging African problems and concerns.[6] The hesitation embodied in this equivocation has been the enigmatic focus around which the debate has thus far unfolded.

In the words of Kwasi Wiredu, we have, on the one hand, a "semianthropological paraphrase of African traditional beliefs" (1991: 88). In stark distinction to this documentary antiquarianism – that is, ethnophilosophy – we have, on the other hand, the views of Wiredu, Paulin Hountondji, Peter Bodunrin, and Henry Odera Oruka – that is, the school of professional philosophy – which in so many words, poses a false and stark dichotomy between a supposedly "true universalistic" philosophy and the "culturally particularistic" indigenous thought of traditional Africa.[7] In this perspective Africa has been, thus far, either pre-philosophical or non-philosophical, and the authors listed above (minus Oruka), view themselves as among the early pioneers of African philosophical thought. For these authors, African philosophy is merely a "geographic designation"[8] which, properly speaking, is constituted by their work and the naïve documentary efforts of their ethnophilosophical colleagues.

It is in contradistinction to the enigma of this duplicity that the hermeneutical perspective in contemporary African philosophy constitutes itself. This perspective counters itself both to the *particularistic antiquarianism* of ethnophilosophy and to the *abstract universalism* of professional philosophy. It does so in an effort to think through the historicity of postcolonial "independent" Africa. It is thus fully cognizant of the fact that its own "efforts at theorizing . . . are inscribed interior to the ways and means" that tradition itself – that is, our modern-day African inheritance – "utilizes for its own preservation, renewal, and perpetuation" (Okolo: 209).

The hermeneutical orientation in contemporary African philosophy sees itself, on the level of theory, as the appropriation and continuation of African emancipatory hopes and aspirations.[9] For, as Fanon observed in 1955, in the context of his native Martinique, the concrete process of anticolonial confrontation and emancipation is a "metaphysical experience" (*Pra* 27 / *TAR* 23). It is the lived historicity of this "metaphysical experience" that the hermeneutical orientation in contemporary African philosophy makes the object of its reflections. For Fanon, as for the hermeneutical orientation in contemporary African philosophy, this metaphysical experience is that which needs to be properly queried and explored in order to actualize the possibility of self-emancipation.

Reflective thought, in this context, is aimed at the possibilities of self-emancipation dialectically mediated by the negativity of the present. In contrast to the above, what is unacceptable in both of the previous positions is that, in a strange sort of way, the seemingly contrary perspectives of ethnophilosophy and professional philosophy, implicitly share the "prejudice that views Africa as primitive and with a purely mythical mentality" (Towa 1991: 192). Ethnophilosophy does so by inadvertently valorizing the essentialist stereotypical notions of Africa and Africans. The best example of this is Senghor's oft-quoted remark – a standard of ethnophilosophy – that "reason is hellenic and emotion is negro."[10] Professional philosophy, on the other hand, is implicated in the "prejudice that views Africa as primitive" by universalizing, as ontologically normative, the specific metaphysical singularity of modern European existence.

Regarding both of these seemingly "contrary" and equally unpalatable positions Towa writes:

> The danger to which African philosophy is currently exposed is that of a real blockage. The ethnophilosophers strive to occlude and replace it with their concealed credo. [On the other hand] . . . scientists [that is, scientistically oriented philosophers] and epistemologists dismiss it overtly in the name of science or the commentary on science. (p. 193)

He further notes that "The current of thought represented by P. Hountondji [professional philosophy] does not occlude African thought, it openly excludes it, in the name of scientificity, as not in the least pertinent" (1991: 191). Beyond this double "blockage" by occlusion (ethnophilosophy) and exclusion (professional philosophy) contemporary African philosophy is concretely oriented toward thinking the lived problems and concerns that arise from the actuality of postcolonial Africa. As Towa correctly points out, philosophy is

> the thought of the essential, the methodical and critical examination of that which, in the theoretical order or in the practical order, has or should have for humanity a supreme importance. Such is philosophy in its abstract and entirely general essence. (p. 194)

The generality of this essence is specified by the differentiated particularity – cultural, historical, and political – within which a philosophical discourse is articulated. It is determined by the historico-cultural and political actuality it is emersed in and secures the concerns of its problematic by systematically articulating and appropriating the lived-life issues and problems of its concrete context. In other words, philosophical reflection – African or otherwise – in this view, is a grasping and exploring of real life issues aimed at the enhancement, the perpetuation, or critique of the lived-context out of which reflection originates. For, as Towa affirms,

> One has to see that any particular philosophy is always elaborated by philosophers who are not themselves abstractions, but are beings of flesh and bones who belong to a continent, to a particular culture, and to a

specific period. And for a particular philosopher to really philosophize is necessarily to examine in a critical and methodic manner the essential problems of his milieu and of his period. He will thus elaborate a philosophy that is in an explicit or implicit relation with his times and his milieu. (pp. 194–5)

For *us*, the "time" and the "milieu" within which the discourse of contemporary African philosophy is elaborated are the enigmatic presence and actuality of our postcolonial present. To think the historicity of this present means to query concretely the contradictions of African "independence," that is, to constitute out of our "essential problems" the central and guiding questions for African philosophical thought. This then is the defining aspect of the African hermeneutical orientation: it is the theoretically interpretative effort aimed at grasping and exploring the "essential" problems of our lived present.

Thus in *our* specific politico-historical and cultural context and beyond the rather sterile dispute between ethnophilosophy and its scientistic critics, it is important to note that the concerns of African philosophy are focused on the possibility of overcoming the misery and political impotence of *our* postcolonial present. The veracity of this situation is grounded on the fact that, for Africa today, the question against which life is staked is that of the political, economic, and cultural-existential survival of the continent. For ultimately, as Antonio Gramsci puts it, "The philosophy of an historical epoch is . . . nothing other than the 'history' of that epoch itself . . . History and philosophy are in this sense indivisible: they form a bloc" (p. 345).

Hence, given the above, in its impotent actuality, postcolonial Africa poses the challenge of self-transformation and the concrete actualization of its present chimerical "independence." On the level of thought this puts into question the inherited and taken-for-granted conception of African "independence," as the guise and mask of neocolonialism. It does so, furthermore, in view of the suffering millions that have been victimized by the lived *actuality* as opposed to the hoped-for *ideality* of an "independent" Africa.

In terms of all that has been said thus far, the challenge of our postcolonial situation is grounded, then, in the failed actuality of the present. It is the concrete manifestation of our failure to overcome the structural and historico-cultural vestiges of colonialism. It is in and out of the agonies suffered in these three decades of "independence" that the future possibilities of the diverse people of Africa have to be reflected on and engaged. This, then – beyond the glories and suffering of our precolonial and colonial past – is what evokes thought in the context of the present.

In the chapter of *Les Damnés* entitled "The misadventures of national consciousness," Fanon had accurately anticipated these decades of misery and political impotence. The remedy he suggested, appropriate now as then, was that we "grow a new skin" and "develop a new thinking" and in so doing invent the concrete actuality of our existence. For Fanon, this "new thinking" is itself the moment of a self-reflective and self-reflexive thought, which is internal to and arises out of the struggle to overcome colonial and neocolonial subjugation.

In thinking the historicity out of which it is being secreted, the hermeneutical orientation of contemporary African philosophy is presently engaged in "developing a new thinking." To this extent, this orientation is the critical and reflective appropriation of Fanon's politico-philosophical perspective, and of all those who struggled to actualize the possibility of African freedom. Thus, if Fanon anticipates our concerns, this is so precisely because we have actively inherited and made our own the questions that he, among others, inaugurated.

III

It is a bland truism to say that the thirty years succeeding the publication of *Les Damnés* have been, for Africa, years of rampant and violent neocolonialism. Given this historical and political context, what we need to do next is to characterize properly the thematic actuality of the hermeneutical orientation in African philosophy in its relation to Fanon. As already indicated, the efforts of this orientation are focused on thinking the possibility of an autochthonous and self-standing Africa. In other words, African philosophical thought, as Towa puts it, is committed to an

> auto-centric Africa which is the center of its own conceptions, of its decisions and the actualization of the totality of its spheres of essential activity: political, economic and spiritual; a fraternal Africa, which will respect this same auto-centric principle as it applies to itself and as it applies to other peoples.[11]

Indeed, as is well known, the political aspiration of thinking through the possibility of a genuinely "auto-centric" and independent Africa was, for Fanon, the center of all his theoretic and practical concerns.

In fact, his work and life as a whole were dedicated to actualizing and consummating this "auto-centric" possibility, starting from the lived-phenomenal actuality of the "various attitudes that the [colonized African] adopts in contact with white civilization" (*Pn* 9 / *BS* 12). For

Fanon, the labor of thought and hence of philosophy, in this context, has to be focused on these factual-existential and alienated "various attitudes" with the aim of radically altering the pent-up residual and "reactional" endurance of the colonized into a free *actional* (*Pn* 180 / *BS* 222) orientation to life as a process of self-creation.

For him, the singular purpose or aim of reflective thought is to assist in the process of the colonized's own concrete self-actualization. To the very end, Fanon saw himself as an advocate of the colonized in the process of bringing about their own emancipation. On this point, Fanon's letter to his friend Roger Tayeb, four weeks before his death, is very revealing. Fanon writes:

> Roger, what I wanted to tell you is that death is always with us and that what matters is not to know whether we can escape it but whether we have achieved the maximum for the ideas we have made our own. What shocked me here in my bed when I felt my strength ebbing away along with my blood was not the fact of dying as such, but to die of leukemia, in Washington, when three months ago I could have died facing the enemy since I was already aware that I had this disease. We are nothing on earth if we are not in the first place the slaves of a cause, the cause of the peoples, the cause of justice and liberty. I want you to know that even when the doctors had given me up, in the gathering dusk I was still thinking of the Algerian people, of the peoples of the Third World, and when I have persevered it was for their sake. (Zahar 1974: xx)

In this sense Fanon was a phenomenologist of decolonization and his thinking is a critical and situated hermeneutics, interior to and arising from, the struggle of those whose existence was *damned* by the actuality of colonialism and neocolonialism.[12]

The character of our Otherness or alterity – in contact or contrast to a despotic Europe – is thus a basic focus of this thought. In the concluding section of the penultimate chapter of *Black Skin, White Masks*, Fanon, strongly invoking Nietzsche, sharply draws the contrast between "action" and "reaction" and observes that the latter is grounded on resentment (*Pn* 180 / *BS* 222). To the extent then that postcolonial "independent" Africa continues to ape and mimic the historicity of Europe it is still grounded on resentment. It is "reactional" and is defined by that which it claims it has overcome. In this context to become "auto-centric" would be for Africa to achieve an "actional" orientation toward its contemporary situation and effectively confront its present neocolonial – that is, "reactional" – actuality. In other words, it would go beyond its truncated present.

Thus, as far back as 1952 Fanon was already exploring the theoretical promise of an "auto-centric" Africa, out of the limits and possibilities marked out by the African colonial experience. But how did Fanon view the experience of colonialism? In the first chapter of *Les Damnés*, Fanon tells us that the "thing" which has been colonized becomes human "during the same process by which it frees itself" (*Dt* 67 / *WE* 37). For Fanon, the anticolonial struggle is the process of self-overcoming the status of "thing-hood" forcefully imposed on the colonized. Colonialism is the thingification of the colonized, that is, their expulsion from history.

In view of the above, and beyond the initial and necessary counter-violence engendered by colonialism, the colonized need to reclaim the historicity of their own lived existence. For ultimately,

> The concrete problem we find ourselves up against is not that of a choice, cost what it may, between socialism and capitalism as they have been defined by men of other continents and of other ages. (*Dt* 133 / *WE* 99)

To go beyond this predetermined "choice," the formerly colonized need to overcome their non-historicity by inaugurating "invention into existence" (*Pn* 186 / *BS* 229). In this perspective, liberation and political independence, beyond the Cold War, become a process of historico-cultural self-creation. This is the concrete process by which humanity is reintroduced "into the world" (*Dt* 144 / *WE* 106) and history is opened up to the formerly colonized.

Properly speaking postcolonial society is grounded not only on the "disappearance of colonialism but also" and more importantly on "the disappearance of the colonized" (*Dt* 294 / *WE* 246). For this to be possible colonial emancipation has to terminate the history of *imperious* Europe in Africa – the only Europe *we* have known thus far – and invent the existence/historicity of the formerly colonized out of the actuality and the needs of the present. The extent to which this has been achieved is, for Fanon, the standard by which the demise of colonialism is gauged. If, on the other hand, this does not happen in whatever form (given the historical particularities of different countries and regions) then all we are left with is "a few reforms at the top, a flag waving: and down there [that is, in the bush, beyond the Europeanized centers of *évolué* Africa] an undivided mass . . . endlessly marking time" (*Dt* 186 / *WE* 147).

The prophetic accuracy of Fanon's insights on the failures and short-comings of African independence is today beyond dispute. This same prophetic insight is echoed in Towa's observation:

> To enslave [that is, colonize] a people means to contain [or restrict] them to activities which do not serve their own needs, but someone else's, for an end [or purpose] which is not theirs, but someone else's. The enslaved people is thus inserted, as a mere instrument, into a practical process whose movement and goals remain alien and unknown to it. Hence, the

culture produced is not their own, but someone else's. The enslavement of
a people dries up its culture at its source. (1979: 84–5)

Independent Africa, thus far – the hopes and aspirations of Fanon and
others of his generation notwithstanding – has not been able to resusci-
tate and tap into its own historical and cultural resources, that is,
overcome its internalized enslavement. Taking the negativity of this
situation as its immediate background and point of departure, the
hermeneutical orientation in African philosophy aims at reviving and
appropriating the cultural and historical resources of the continent out of
the needs and in the context of the present. It is, in other words, an
attempt to overcome, on the level of theory, the enslavement that still
negatively and decisively marks from within our contemporary African
existence.[13]

Taking its starting point from the situation of the formerly enslaved,
the hermeneutical orientation in African philosophy positions itself and
finds its concerns in the felt need to overcome – on all levels and
concretely – this enslavement. It is in this regard a call to conscience to
the generation which, having inherited the theoretical and lived legacy of
African liberation – with all its contradictions – must in turn enhance and
transmit this legacy to the future. In so doing, in Fanon's words, this
generation "ought to use the past with the intention of opening the
future" (*Dt* 280 / *WE* 232).

Thus, this claiming of a "famous" forefather should not be understood as a vain, narcissistic and idle pastime, undertaken to placate the
vanity of one's theoretical ancestry. Rather, within the contemporary
discourse of African philosophy, the claim to such a theoretic lineage is
the affirmation of a determined and radical anti-neocolonialism. For
ultimately, "[e]ach generation must out of relative obscurity discover its
mission, fulfill it, or betray it" (*Dt* 251 / *WE* 206).

To claim Fanon as a progenitor in the practice of his thought is to
articulate a specific position aimed at thinking the demise of neocolonial
domination in all of its forms. Since, in the context of the present, to
think is to "fulfill" or "betray" the unrealized hopes and aspirations of
our heritage. This then is the explicit intent of African philosophy in its
hermeneutical incarnation.

To invoke Fanon in this context is to "discover" the "mission" of
redressing the disappointments of past generations and engage in the
struggle, on the level of theory, to actualize – out of the needs of the
present – the promise of the future. This is an effort aimed at appropriating the as-yet unrealized possibilities of the past in the historicity of
one's generation. It is the recognition of this theoretic and existential

situation that constitutes and structures the hermeneutical orientation in the contemporary discourse of African philosophy.

As Okolo puts it, properly speaking, the hermeneutical situation of contemporary African philosophy is that of the

> formerly colonized, the oppressed, that of the underdeveloped, struggling for more justice and equality. From this point of view, the validity of an interpretation [or of a philosophic orientation] is tied to the validity of a struggle – of its justice and of its justness. (p. 208)

In all of this, Fanon and the originative impetus of his work occupy a central paradigmatic place. This is so precisely because like him, we too, in the words of Theophilus Okere, are engaged with "Africa in metamorphoses" (p. 121). This process of transfiguration is, on the level of thought, the phenomenological exploration and explication of how the colonial situation can unfold and does unfold towards the possibility of African self-emancipation. This process, on the level of existence, is its own self-actualization. For Fanon, through and out of this historical process, which is necessarily violent, the colonized "thing" reclaims its humanity. Borrowing a phrase from Hegel one can say that, for Fanon, self-emancipation, properly speaking, is "the process of its own becoming . . . and only by being worked out to its [very] end is it actual" (Hegel 1977: 20, par. 18).

As Fanon points out in *Les Damnés*, the coming to consciousness of colonized westernized intellectuals goes through several self-negating phases. Initially we have the moment of assimilation and the appropriation of the dominant culture of the colonizer. This phase is sublated by the moment of return to self that the colonized intellectual inaugurates in rejecting assimilation. The apex of this dialectical movement is the realization by the westernized intellectual that, his or her intellectual labors, properly speaking, can bear fruit only as *acts of service* in the struggle of the colonized and the neocolonized. This is what Fanon refers to as "the fighting phase" in the concrete self-formative and self-emancipatory odyssey of the colonized intellectual (*Dt* 268 / *WE* 222).

Within the discourse of contemporary African philosophy this is the place occupied by the hermeneutical orientation. Beyond the documentary naïveté of ethnophilosophy and the "critical" refutations of professional philosophy, the hermeneutical orientation is concerned solely with critically supplementing, on the level of theory, Africa's own concrete efforts at a radical self-emancipation. In this regard it appropriates, for itself, as a theoretic program, the calling and vocation that Fanon so admirably fulfilled in the span of his short life.

Notes

1 In this regard see Theophilus Okere (1983: vii). See also Lucius Outlaw (1987: *passim*).

2 See Pietro Clemente (1971) and International Tribute to Frantz Fanon, Record of the Special Meeting of the United Nations Special Committee Against Apartheid (1978).

3 Homi Bhabha's forward to the British edition of *Black Skin, White Masks* (Cf. Bhaba 1986: xxiii).

4 Towa (1971: 36–37) for Césaire, and p. 54 for the reference to Nkrumah and Fanon.

5 See Okere (1983), Outlaw (1987), and Serequeberhan (1994).

6 Some of the texts in this debate are collected in my *African Philosophy* (1991). This equivocation holds true also for Francophone Africa. In this regard see, V. Y. Mudimbe (1983). For a recent anthology organized around this same divide see Albert G. Mosley (1995).

7 The following are the main texts of this orientation: Paulin J. Hountondji, *African Philosophy: Myth and Reality* (1983); Kwasi Wiredu, *Philosophy and an African Culture* (1980); H. Odera Oruka, *Sage Philosophy* (1990); Peter O. Bodunrin, "Which kind of philosophy for Africa?" (1981).

8 In this regard see Hountondji's original formulation of this view (1992: 66).

9 In this regard, see Okere (1983). The contents of this work were first produced in 1971 as a doctoral dissertation at the Institut Supérieur de Philosophie of the Catholic University of Louvain. As V. Y. Mudimbe points out, this study has the merit of having inaugurated the hermeneutical orientation in the contemporary discourse of African philosophy (1985: 210–11).

10 For Senghor's own defensive remarks regarding this rather controversial if not outrageous statement, see his "The spirit of civilization or the laws of African Negro culture" (1956: 52). For a more recent and very sympathetic reading of Senghor's perspective, see Gbadegesin (1991).

11 Towa (1979: 87). The English version of this text is my own slightly altered rendering of a private translation by Dr Victor Manfredi. It should be emphasized that Towa's conception of an "auto-centric" Africa has nothing to do with Molefi Kete Asante's notion of "Afrocentrism." Towa's notion is a formulation aimed at grasping the concrete historico-political process of African self-emancipation. In this regard it is analogous to the EPLF's (Eritrean People's Liberation Front) notion of "self-reliance." Regarding this last point, see James Firebrace and Stuart Holland (1985: 127–40).

12 On this point, see my book (1994: 151, n. 41 and related discussions in chapters 3 and 4) and Gordon (1995b).

13 In this regard Hountondji's recent critical remarks regarding the extroversion of our technical and scientific activities is very insightful. See Hountondji 1990 and 1992. Interestingly enough, the position that Hountondji articulates in these papers is not fully congruent with the views of his main work (1983).

18

On the Misadventures of National Consciousness: A Retrospect on Frantz Fanon's Gift of Prophecy

Olufemi Taiwo

According to Alan Barth, "judicial dissent . . . is, at its best, a form of prophecy in the Biblical sense of that term. It reflects, at least on occasion, not only a protest against what the dissenter deems error or injustice, but an Isaiahlike warning of unhappy consequences. Like a seer, the dissenter sometimes peers into the future. He will be accounted wise or foolish as the unfolding of events proves him right or wrong" (1974: 3). This description captures the salient features of prophecy that are relevant to this essay. The views with which we are concerned, when they first articulated, ran counter to and were condemnations of alternative views that were then dominant. Those alternative views were deemed erroneous by Frantz Fanon. To that extent, Fanon was a dissenter from received wisdom. He also warned of the dire consequences that would result if the conditions he highlighted were not radically altered. Of course, Fanon did peer into the future and, given how much the unfolding of events has proven him right, I wish to celebrate his wisdom, and offer him as a shining example of how useful good social science can be.

It is unusual for the biblical idea of prophecy to be put in the same proposition with social science. But, as will be shown presently, there are solid grounds for proceeding in this manner. A good social science must explain social phenomena. This is not enough; it is equally important that its explanation of past phenomena help us to anticipate and prepare

This chapter is dedicated to the students in my Advanced Political Philosophy classes at the Obafemi Awolowo University, Ile-Ife, Nigeria, from 1986 to 1989.

for future ones. This last requirement is the interface between prophecy and good social science and it deserves some analysis. There are three attributes shared by a social scientific model and a jeremiad: description, explanation, and prediction. In ways that mirror social scientific models, there is a description, in a jeremiad, of what is wrong in the community. For example, biblical prophets gave stark descriptions of the many sins and transgressions prevalent in their community, the corruption and debaucheries of the rulers, the absence of righteousness and upstandingness among their fellows. Secondly, the explanation of the misfortunes of the community was that the people had strayed from the path of righteousness laid out for them by the divine authority. Finally, in the prophecy, there was a warning that unless the divine word was heeded, dire consequences would follow. But there is at least one clear difference between biblical prophecy and good social science: in social scientific models, the "Thus saith the Lord" of a prophecy is replaced with the authority of analysis, theoretical paradigms, and empirical investigations. Nonetheless, in the same way that failure to heed the word of the Lord will mean perdition, so will failure to heed the warning in social scientific prophecy lead to social dislocation and crisis in the community.

I have elected to focus on the prophetic character of social science because of one other similarity between the jeremiad and social scientific prediction. Both, especially when they come in the form of a dissent, are motivated by a commitment, a moral vision that the situation that has provoked the "Isaiahlike warning of unhappy consequences" is wrong, and that the consequences foretold are undesirable. Fanon's prophecy, too, was part of a dissent. For he dared to diverge from what then was received opinion about the prognosis for newly independent African countries. Kwame Nkrumah's exhortation sums up this wisdom about what independence held in store for the African peoples: "Seek ye first the political kingdom." The idea was that as soon as colonized Africans inherited political power, all their other heart's desires – good government, social services, "life more abundant" – would be added. Fanon diverged from this optimism about the promise of the political kingdom and this is where his seer-status comes into focus.[1] The prophet-as-seer has its counterpart in the social-scientist-as-savant. In this role, the social scientist establishes connections among myriad social phenomena, interprets them, identifies trends and tendencies and, in the best of times, anticipates possible new developments and directs our attention to them. The dissenting judge assumes the prophetic role in retrospect when in later times his or her dissenting judgment turns out to have been well ahead of its time and becomes the new wisdom in changed circumstances. The name we give to such people resonates with seer-like allusions: we often call them "visionaries." So understood, it is easy to see how and why Fanon's anticipations make a good fit with the idea of prophecy. Like a seer, Fanon peered into the future of the newly independent countries. As a savant, he was able to decipher the hieroglyphics of social processes in such a way that, with hindsight, we may now adjudge him wise since the unfolding of events has proven him right, for the most part.

Les Damnés de la terre was originally published in 1961, the same year that Fanon died. By itself, little significance is attached to that year, or to the fact that his book was issued then. But this year takes on added significance when juxtaposed with the historical importance of the preceding year, 1960, for 1960 was the year in which many erstwhile colonial countries won independence from colonial rule. This independence provided the background for Harold Macmillan's euphoric declaration that a wind of change was blowing over Africa. His statement was symptomatic of the enthusiasm and near universal optimism that marked the advent of independent states in Africa. The optimism was not without grounds. Given the violence of colonialism and its direct role in retarding the growth and development of colonial territories, it was no surprise that all and sundry thought that independence would usher in a period of development in self-governing nation-states. With hindsight informed by an over three-decade-long history of failures, big and small, in most African countries, many social scientists and other scholars are now busy offering *post-hoc* analyses of what is generally called "the African predicament." However, unlike most of his contemporaries, especially those who had secured for themselves a lien on the fruits of independence, Fanon had been a dissenting voice in the chorus of enthusiasm that greeted the advent of flag independence (nominal independence) and was one of the earliest to posit the limits of the phenomenon. Like a seer, Fanon the dissenter had peered into the future and left us a legacy of forebodings about how precarious that future – our present – might be.

Well before 1960, in a series of essays, articles, and speeches, now published as *Toward the African Revolution*, and more importantly, in *Les Damnés*, Fanon had raised severe questions about the process of decolonization and about the fitness to rule of the classes that were poised to occupy the ruling institutions in the new states. On the basis of these analyses, Fanon the prophet was able to issue his Isaiah-like warning of future unhappy consequences. In what follows, I present in juxtaposition Fanon's predictions, and evidence of their accuracy, about several African countries, but in the main, Nigeria. Nigeria has been the object of my research for almost a decade and will be the main focus of attention now. The chapter entitled "The misadventures of national consciousness" (from *les Damnés*) is the inspiration for this paper, and provides most of the examples of Fanon's predictions. I argue, first, that Fanon's predictions have been accurate. Then, I suggest that their accuracy must be traced, in part, to his profound understanding of the nature of colonialism and its enabling philosophies.

Fanon's prophecy covered all aspects of life in the new states, ranging from their economic prospects, or lack thereof, to the fortunes of their youths, and their attitudes to culture. I do not propose to consider all of these aspects. Rather, as in the chapter that inspired this essay, my focus is on what Fanon called "the misadventures of national consciousness." There are two different but related distinctions that are central to Fanon's discussion but remain unarticulated by him. The first is that between what he called "pseudo-independence" and what is to be understood by "real independence," which is assimilated to *liberation*. "Flag independence" or "pseudo-independence" is the result of negotiations between the nationalist leaders of the colonies and their colonial overlords. It is independence that leaves the colonized with the many outward manifestations of independence – their own flag, national anthem, law-making bodies made up mostly of their own kind – but without any real control over the destinies of their lands and people. They lack control because they ignore a salient feature of the colonial encounter: its Manichaeanism, which created two starkly opposed worlds in the colonial universe. Fanon argued that this division, in which the colonized is typified as the embodiment of evil and, accordingly, divested of the minimal elements of humanity, was a product of violence and, throughout the colonial period, was sustained by violence. Violence was at the root of the contradictions, paradoxes, and incomprehensibility of colonialism. For the colonized to break free from the colonial straitjacket to gain genuine independence, "the total destruction of the colonial system" is called for. Fanon writes,

> True liberation is not that pseudo-independence in which ministers having a limited responsibility hobnob with an economy dominated by the colonial pact.
> Liberation is the total destruction of the colonial system, from the preeminence of the language of the oppressor and "departmentalization," to the customs union that in reality maintains the former colonized in the meshes of the culture, of the fashion, and of the images of the colonialist. (*Pra* 109 / *TAR* 105)

The second distinction that remains latent in Fanon's discussion is that between "national consciousness" and "social and political consciousness." The idea of national consciousness hides a tension in his discussion that needs to be recognized, even if it cannot be resolved here. On one hand, he suggests that national consciousness is required to prosecute the anticolonial struggle. Let us recall the basic division of colonial society between the colonizer and the colonized. Colonialism also did its best to divide the colonized and frustrate the emergence of a common consciousness among them. An authentic anticolonial struggle required the creation of a common identity, a national identity, that would enable the colonized to reject all the efforts of the colonizer to deracinate them. On the other hand, national consciousness, when it refuses or fails to advance to the level of liberation, to complete decolonization, is easily perverted into parochialism and provincialism. It is easy to see why this is the case. If the idea of national consciousness does not progress beyond what is necessary to drive out the colonialists, once the colonial presence is removed, the danger always exists that the independence coalition might crumble and dissolve into factions identified, not by ideologies, but by ethnic, religious, and other particularistic traditions. There would be enough office-seekers as well as other political kinds willing to exploit various differences – ethnic, religious, etc. – to vault themselves into positions they do not otherwise deserve. Fanon could see from the few examples of independent states whose short lives he was privileged to witness that the requirements of decolonization could be perverted by their successor ruling classes into a narrow concern with "national consciousness." However, for decolonization to be complete, the new states must quickly move from the narrow concern with national consciousness to the more inclusive and presumably more progressive terrain of social and political consciousness. If this doesn't take place, unhappy consequences are bound to follow. The struggle against colonialism was fought on the platform of nationalism. Nevertheless, true decolonization is less about creating new nations than it is about creating new modes of being human. The danger is that those who lead the anticolonial struggle, unless they are acutely aware of the difference between the two possibilities just mentioned, might rest content with national consciousness. When this happens,

> national consciousness, instead of being the all-embracing crystallization of the innermost hopes of the people, instead of being the immediate and most obvious result of the mobilization of the people, will be in any case only an empty shell, a crude and fragile travesty of what might have been. (*Dt* 189 / *WE* 148)

Fanon warned that the total destruction of the colonial system, which he deemed a desideratum of liberation or true decolonization, was not about to take place. The principal reason for his pessimism concerned the character of the class that was set to take over in the new states.

> The national middle class which takes over power at the end of the colonial regime is an underdeveloped middle class. It has practically no economic power, and in any case it is in no way commensurate with the bourgeoisie

of the mother country which it hopes to replace. In its narcissism, the
national middle class is easily convinced that it can advantageously replace
the middle class of the mother country. But that same independence which
literally drives it into a corner will give rise within its ranks to catastrophic
reactions, and will oblige it to send out frenzied appeals for help to the
former mother country. The university and merchant classes which make
up the most enlightened section of the new state are in fact characterized
by the smallness of their number and their being concentrated in the
capital, and the type of activities in which they are engaged: business,
agriculture, and the liberal professions. Neither financiers nor industrial
magnates are to be found within this national middle class. The national
bourgeoisie of underdeveloped countries is not engaged in production, nor
in invention, nor building, nor labor; it is completely canalized into activities of the intermediary type. Its innermost vocation seems to be to keep in
the running and to be part of the racket. The psychology of the national
bourgeoisie is that of the businessman, not that of the captain of industry.
(*Dt* 190–1 / *WE* 149–50)

The preceding excerpt is part of the descriptive moment in Fanon's
jeremiad. There are other scattered throughout his writings, which we
shall cite as they become necessary. He specifies what the successor
ruling class ought to do in each case. He identifies what he calls "the
calling fate has marked out for it" and demands that the class "betray"
that calling. His prognostication on the consequences that will follow
should the class fail to betray its calling (completely sever ties with the
mother country, and seek to reinvent humans on new foundations, a
"new humanism" he calls it) represents the prophetic moment in his
jeremiad.

In an underdeveloped country an authentic national middle class ought to
consider as its bounden duty to betray the calling fate has marked out for
it, and to put itself to school with the people: in other words to put at the
people's disposal the intellectual and technical capital that it has snatched
when going through the colonial universities. But unhappily we shall see
that very often the national middle class does not follow this heroic,
positive, fruitful, and just path; rather, it disappears with its soul set at
peace into the shocking ways – shocking because anti-national – of a
traditional bourgeoisie, of a bourgeoisie which is stupidly, contemptibly,
cynically bourgeois. (*Dt* 191 / *WE* 150)

What then does this bourgeoisie do? How has it managed to fulfill the
worst elements prophesied by Fanon? Let us take the economy first. Our
example is drawn from Nigeria. The geopolitical entity now called
Nigeria was a creation of British colonialism. It is the product of the
amalgamation, in 1914, of the erstwhile colony of Lagos and the Protec-
torates of Northern and Southern Nigeria. This was done to facilitate

smoother and less expensive administration of the then British possession. Colonialism was no benevolent extension of civilization into some picturesque but obscure corners of the globe ravaged by savagery although some of its apologists would like us to believe that it was. It was a response to the rapacious demands for raw materials by the markets of emergent capitalism in the eighteenth and nineteenth centuries. The end-result of the imperialist domination of Nigeria (an area then characterized by different types of pre-capitalist economies), was the opening of the way for capitalist penetration, which was guided by the need to increase the output of manufacturing industry in the mother countries. However, imperialism could not encourage competition from the development of indigenous capitalisms. Fanon points out that "under the colonial system, a middle class which accumulates capital is an impossible phenomenon" (*Dt* 191 / *WE* 150). Capitalist development did just about enough in Nigeria to ensure a profitable extraction of mineral wealth and other raw materials. Fanon knew that. He correctly identifies this as one of the principal contradictions in the colonial enterprise. For colonialism to have been a truly epochal movement that brought various African societies to "the modern age," it would have had to introduce authentic capitalist social relations and foster a capitalist-type development of the means of production in those societies. To do so, capitalism had to contend with the possibility that home industries in mother countries would have to compete with colonial industries and risk losing out. Additionally, given the Manichaean division of the colonial world into the two diametrically opposed spheres of the human and civilized (colonizer's), and the non-human and uncivilized (colonized's), it would have been surprising had the colonial state decided that Africans could be "capitalists." The convergence of a racialized capitalism and the need to preserve the upper hand held by the metropolitan industries meant that the colonial regime, in almost every case in Africa, could only permit the emergence of a compradoral class and not a genuine bourgeoisie. That was what happened in Nigeria and it had serious implications for the subsequent evolution of classes in the country.

During the colonial era, Nigeria was incorporated into the world capitalist economy. As a consequence of the situation just described, it was not admitted as an equal partner. On the contrary, Nigerian production was subordinated to the needs of international capitalism, especially of the British variety. "In order to secure their own profits, colonial interests blocked the development of indigenous capitalism and limited the development of peasant production" (Williams 1976: 12). In the nationalist ferment that followed 1945, the indigenous elite that had been created or adapted to subserve the administrative and political interests of the colonial ruling classes felt short-changed. The glaring inequalities of colonial society frustrated their highest aspirations. The agitation for decolonization soon began in earnest. In a classic case of what Antonio Gramsci might have called a "passive revolution," the British, "through their control of the political process of decolonization, promoted class and power relations which would ensure the continued domination of Nigeria by international capitalism" (Williams: 28). It is what Nigeria's pre-eminent social historian, Segun Osoba, has called a "programmed transition to neocolonial dependence." The British transferred the colonial state (in the restricted sense of the governmental apparatus) to an elite they had created in colonial society and whose fidelity to their compradoral role within capitalism they (the British) had no cause to doubt.

A ruling class emerged from the womb of colonial society which did not have its roots in its dominance in the sphere of production, but rather owed its being to its willingness to play agent, trading post, to international capitalism. Osoba puts its succinctly:

> The power distribution between the Nigerian national bourgeoisie and the international bourgeoisie of the Western imperialist metropolises, is akin to that subsisting between an *agent* and *a principal* in a capitalist market system. The Nigerian bourgeoisie and through it, the national economy, are dependent on the international capitalist bourgeoisie and the global imperialist economic order in precisely the same way as a business agent is dependent on his principal with all the implications of unequal exchange and exploitative relations appertaining to an agent–principal or client–patron system. (Osoba 1979: 63)

Sentiments like those expressed by Osoba[2] were quite central to the problematic that dominated social science in Africa and Latin America in the 1970s under the rubric of "dependency theory." Whatever the rights and wrongs of this problematic, some of its plausibility is drawn from the vantage point of witnessing African bourgeoisie breakdown for close to two decades of the post-independence era. But Fanon did not have twenty years or, as we have at the present time, over thirty years of watching things go awry. This is what he wrote in *Les Damnés*:

> Since the middle class has neither sufficient material nor intellectual resources (by intellectual resources we mean engineers and technicians), it limits its claim to the taking over of business offices and commercial houses formerly occupied by the settlers. The national bourgeoisie steps into the shoes of the former European settlement: doctors, barristers, traders, commercial travelers, general agents, and transport agents . . . From now on it will insist that all the big foreign companies should pass through its hands, whether these companies wish to keep on their connections with the country, or to open it up. *The national bourgeoisie discovers its historic mission: that of intermediary.*

Seen through its eyes, its mission has nothing to do with transforming the nation; it consists, prosaically, of being the transmission line between the nation and a capitalism, rampant though camouflaged, which today puts on the mask of neocolonialism. The national bourgeoisie will be quite content with the role of the Western bourgeoisie's business agent, and it will play its part without any complexes in a most dignified manner. But this same lucrative role, this cheap-Jack's function, this meanness of out-look and this absence of all ambition symbolize the incapability of the national middle class to fulfill its historic role of bourgeoisie. (*Dt* 193–4 / *WE* 152–3, my emphasis)

Nigeria is a particularly instructive instance of the uncanniness of Fanon's prophecy. Of all African countries, Nigeria was, and still is, best positioned to challenge the dominance of international capitalism. The country is extremely rich in natural resources, including significantly, a land area most of which is cultivable, and some of the biggest bodies of water in the continent. It bucks the trend that Fanon identified: there is no paucity of intellectual resources. Quite the contrary, the country has probably the biggest contingent of qualified human power in the conti-nent. It has potentially the largest market: more than 80 million inhab-itants. It was one of the few countries that were not monocultural economies at independence: the country was a leading producer of cocoa, groundnuts, and palm oil, in addition to its substantial reserves of crude petroleum and even more substantial natural gas reserves. Yet it was only in 1995, that cocoa production began to rise again, thirty-five years after independence, and about twenty years after a disastrous collapse in the 1970s; it no longer produces groundnuts, and now imports palm oil from Malaysia, a country to which it not only used to export the same product, but one which was a direct beneficiary of Nigeria's technical superiority in the sixties! This was a country that came into money in a big way in the seventies, thanks to the primacy of oil in the world market. That was a historic opportunity to build a new country and put an infrastructure in place for a self-sustaining economy. What happened instead would scandalize even the most optimistic among us. Nigeria first exported crude oil in 1958. "Between 1970 and the collapse of world oil-prices in the early 1980s, $100 billion of oil money flowed into Nigeria's government coffers" (Pedder: 4). Yet, by the end of 1983, the country had nothing to show for these stupendous earnings; but it had accumulated internal debts the value of which is yet to be determined and $36 billion in foreign debts! This is why the country is such a good example of the fulfillment of Fanon's prophecy.

At independence, the path of revolution was not one that was even considered by the Nigerian national bourgeoisie. It was not part of its

agenda to set the national economy "on a new footing." Nor was capitalism on the agenda. This might come as a surprise to those who are
familiar with the social science literature on African political economy.
For it is part of the received wisdom in radical and non-radical social
science alike that the British set Nigeria on the capitalist path of development at independence. However, as we have pointed out, the British
colonizers stifled the emergence of capitalist social relations in colonial
Nigeria. The consequences predicted by Fanon followed inexorably in
the Nigerian case. The following is his general description of the bourgeoisie of the ex-colonies:

> From the beginning the national bourgeoisie directs its efforts toward
> activities of the intermediary type. The basis of its strength is found in its
> aptitude for trade and small business enterprises, and in securing commis-
> sions. It is not its money that works, but its business acumen. It does not
> go in for investments and it cannot achieve that accumulation of capital
> necessary to the birth and blossoming of an authentic bourgeoisie. At that
> rate it would take centuries to set on foot an embryonic industrial revolu-
> tion, and in any case it would find the way barred by the relentless
> opposition of the former mother country, which will have taken all precau-
> tions when setting up neo-colonialist trade conventions. (*Dt* 221 / *WE*
> 179)

We cite some instances. The ruling classes in Nigeria have remained
mired in their compradoral roles. Schemes of nationalization and
indigenization have come and gone. For example, in 1972, the Nigerian
government promulgated a law[3] that sought to reserve certain sectors
of the Nigerian economy exclusively for nationals and severely restrict
foreign participation in others. The deadline for implementation was set
for 1974.[4] The law was further strengthened in 1976. By 1994, though,
the law had been abrogated owing largely to pressures from the International Monetary Fund, the pressures coming mainly as a part of the
Structural Adjustment Programme that had been in force in the country
for close to ten years. Even when the Indigenization Law, as it was
called, was in effect, very few Nigerian businessmen bothered to move
into large-scale production. Quite the contrary, many of them went to
great lengths to subvert the letter and spirit of the law by acquiescing in,
or actively conniving at, sundry subterfuges concocted by many foreign
principals: many acted as fronts while others agreed to become token
indigenous representatives so that foreign owners could meet the required indigenous content in their operations. They did most of these
things for what were at best very meager returns compared to what the
country routinely lost to profit repatriation or wholesale export of capital.
Thus, even when the country had oil money in the seventies, it never

witnessed the emergence of captains of industry, only the persistence of "traders" puffed up by their seeming affluence whose scope is often exaggerated by the vast seas of poverty within which they did and still do operate. The ultimate in Nigerian business achievement used to be and still is to become a "commission agent," or a "manufacturer's representative" for an overseas, preferably "western," principal. It is not unusual to find many rich men in Nigeria who have no other means of production beside their political connections or their business cards. Their entire operation consists of facilitating contacts between manufacturers and local importers, or between government and overseas suppliers. Many have become rich making "introductions."

To underscore the dominance of compradoral activities we might refer to Nigeria's upside-down approach to industrialization. Power supply remains erratic in all parts of the country, with deleterious consequences on industrial activities. Furthermore, the country first exported crude oil in 1958, but it did not establish a petrochemical plant until 1987. The steel mill it started building in the seventies has eaten up at least $10 billion, and is yet to be completed. Meanwhile, in a classic manifestation of its penchant for short-term thinking and quick profits, small steel mills that were contracted out and executed as turnkey projects have been built and they depend for their technology and other inputs on the metropolitan countries. These were mills built in part in response to the contention by western experts that the steel-city-model of a steel mill was no longer necessary. But even these are teetering on the verge of collapse in Nigeria's bleak economic landscape. It does not matter in the least that they are collapsing: they already yielded a profit, long before they were commissioned, for the facilitators who handled the "introductions" and the procurement of supplies.

In the interim, awash in oil money, but totally devoid of good sense about how to spend it, the country in the late seventies built, in joint ventures with Volkswagen, Peugeot, Steyr, and Leyland, assembly plants for the different vehicles made by these transnational corporations from "completely-knocked-down" components.[5] All of them depended on the country's capacity to earn foreign exchange from oil sales. So when oil prices collapsed, and as soon as the foreign reserves were depleted, the supply of completely knocked down components dried up, and the plants collapsed. But did the Nigerian ruling classes miss their favorite brand vehicles? Of course not. For none of the brands assembled in Nigeria were considered luxurious enough to sate the appetite of the rulers for pomp and circumstance in their preferred modes of transportation: Mercedes Benz, Volvo, and lately, Lexus limousines! Anticipating these developments by at least two decades, Fanon had written:

This bourgeoisie which turns its back more and more on the people as a whole does not even succeed in extracting spectacular concessions from the West, such as investments which would be of value for the country's economy or the setting up of certain industries. On the contrary, assembly plants spring up and consecrate the type of neo-colonialist industrialization in which the country's economy flounders. (*Dt* 218 / *WE* 176)

What becomes of the huge commissions that the leading members of the ruling classes accumulate from their compradoral activities? And of the proceeds from the sale of the country's resources, kickback from contract awards, and other corrupt activities? It is normal for critics and analysts alike to bemoan the prevalence of corruption in countries like Nigeria. As much as one ought to condemn corruption, I am inclined to believe that the issue is sometimes overdrawn. After all, we ought to remember that in other countries too, for example, the United States, corruption was and still is a fact of life in business and government dealings. Nor could we hold up too many instances of capital accumulation as shining examples of ethical behavior. The critical differences are that in other countries (1) the most egregious instances of corruption attract serious sanctions, and (2) the proceeds from corrupt practices are effectively "laundered" through reinvestment in legitimate ventures, a process that practically ensures respectability for their inheritors. Therein lies the critical difference with the national bourgeoisies of the ex-colonies in Africa. According to Fanon:

> With its wave lengths tuned in to Europe,[6] it continues firmly and resolutely to make the most of the situation. The enormous profits which it derives from the exploitation of the people are exported to foreign countries. The young national bourgeoisie is often more suspicious of the regime it has set up than are the foreign companies. The national bourgeoisie refuses to invest in its own country and behaves toward the state that protects and nurtures it with, it must be remarked, astonishing ingratitude. It acquires foreign securities in the European markets, and goes off to spend the weekend in Paris or Hamburg. The behavior of the national bourgeoisie of certain underdeveloped countries is reminiscent of the members of a gang, who after every holdup hide their share in the loot from the other members who are their accomplices and prudently start thinking about their retirement. Such behavior shows that more or less consciously the national bourgeoisie is playing to lose if the game goes on too long. They guess that the present situation will not last indefinitely but they intend to make the most of it. (*Dt* 215 / *WE* 173–4)

Thus every time things go awry with the governments that they set up, they always find their way into cozy exiles in the mother countries where they go to enjoy their loot. They have no confidence in the future of their countries and it is a sign of their confidence in the survival of the mother countries that they'd much rather invest there than in their "home" countries. At the same time as Zaire is bankrupt, its President Mobutu Sese Seko is regularly cited as one of the world's richest men. No one has ever mentioned the capitalist enterprises founded and nurtured by Mobutu, and "captain of industry" he definitely is not. Like him, many African heads of state, government functionaries, rich men, and their ilk, past and present, own choice pieces of real estate in various western countries and boast of vast deposits in their bank accounts, both secret and open. They manage to amass these amounts of wealth at the same time as their local currencies have become worthless, and their countries' economies are reeling under the weight of repayments of loans, most of which never benefited the country in the first place![7]

Whatever is not stored away is frittered away in amazing examples of conspicuous consumption: wild parties at which sterling and dollar are the preferred currencies of *arriviste* transactions! Wealthy Nigerians are notorious for their profligacy. They think nothing of sending their new girlfriends to London or Paris for weekend shopping sprees, just to impress the lucky women. In the name of a spurious piety, some of them go to Jeddah, Saudi Arabia, for weekly Friday observances. They never tire of accumulating the latest in electronic gadgets from the world's supermarkets even when they do not know how to use them or, as is often the case, never use them. In order to hide the stagnation, decline even, that results from its profligacy and incompetence, "to mark this regression, to reassure itself and to give itself something to boast about, the bourgeoisie can find nothing better to do than to erect grandiose buildings in the capital and to lay out money on what are called prestige expenses" (*Dt* 207 / *WE* 165). So now there is a Basilica in Yamoussoukro, Côte d'Ivoire that outdoes the splendors of St Peter's; Nigeria built a 32-story NECOM building in Lagos that was gutted in one fire incident because the fire service lacked appropriate equipment to reach above the fourth floor. In 1977, Nigeria hosted FESTAC in a National Theatre built by Bulgarians, modeled after a sports complex in Sofia! Nigeria built a new capital whose blueprint was made by a Japanese architect; and shortly before its overthrow in 1983, the Shehu Shagari regime toyed with the idea of building a rival to the CN Tower in Toronto, Canada, reputed to be the tallest free-standing structure in the world! These things have happened in a country that has lost many university professors on the death-traps that it calls roads, on journeys undertaken because they either didn't have access to telephones or couldn't get their own telephones to work!

I should not complete this litany of prophecy and fulfillment without a word about the impact on youth. This has added significance for me because of the remote origins of this paper. Some biographical information is in order. Fanon served me and my generation of youth activists in Nigeria as an inspiration in our practice and our theoretical reflection on the situation in the 1970s. But it was not until I had returned from graduate school and started teaching in Nigeria that I had my first opportunity to teach Fanon's texts as political philosophy. Of course, I knew how solid Fanon's social scientific credentials were. But it was not until an incident in my Advanced Political Philosophy class in Ile-Ife sometime in 1987 that I came to an awareness of the prophetic character of Fanon's work. We were discussing "The misadventures of national consciousness." Somewhere in the discussion, some of my students called my attention to the fact that what is contained in that chapter was in the main uncannily true of the Nigerian experience and that no violence would be done to the text if we substituted "Nigeria" for all occurences of "country" or "national". I have not read the text the same way ever since! What he had to say about young people was so true in their experiences that, as they said then, he could have been talking about their generation, twenty-seven years after flag independence.

> The large proportion of young people in the underdeveloped countries raises specific problems for the government, which must be tackled with lucidity. The young people of the towns, idle and often illiterate, are a prey to all sorts of disintegrating influences. It is to the youth of an underdeveloped country that the industrialized countries most often offer their pastimes. Normally, there is a certain homogeneity between the mental and material level of the members of any given society and the pleasure which that society creates for itself. But in underdeveloped countries, young people have at their disposition leisure occupations designed for the youth of capitalist countries: detective novels, penny-in-the-slot machines, sexy photographs, pornographic literature, films banned to those under sixteen, and above all alcohol . . .
>
> In this domain, the government's duty is to act as a filter and a stabilizer. But the youth commissioners in underdeveloped countries often make the mistake of imagining their role to be that of youth commissioners in fully developed countries. They speak of strengthening the soul, of developing the body, and of facilitating the growth of sportsmanlike qualities. It is our opinion that they should beware of these conceptions. The young people of an underdeveloped country are above all idle: occupations must be found for them. (*Dt* 237–8 / *WE* 195–6)

The young are as idle as ever. Playgrounds are almost nonexistent. There were library services when I was growing up in the sixties. The library, which had a precarious existence at the best of times, has become extinct. Even those bad movies that used to dominate our leisure time are no longer available. For many young people sex is now the most readily available recreational outlet! The situation has become worse with the virtual collapse of the education system. The streets of the country's cities teem with teenagers who either are dropouts, or unemployed, or underemployed graduates of the education system. They have made veritable bazaars of major thoroughfares in the cities hawking things or, in the case of females, their bodies. Many have become bit players in Nigeria's burgeoning involvement in the international drug trade. Dare one hope for the future in light of this awareness?

I have tried to show in the discussion thus far that Fanon had a gift of prophecy and that it is time to acknowledge what a superior prophet he was. Recall Barth's suggestion that a prophet "will be accounted wise or foolish as the unfolding of events proves him right or wrong." I hope to have shown in the preceding pages that events, at least in Nigeria, have proved him an extremely wise prophet. By way of conclusion, it is appropriate to suggest an explanation for Fanon's gift of clairvoyance concerning the fortunes of Africa's then newly independent states. A good explanation must include some reference to his aptitude as a student of western philosophy and its intellectual history. His analysis of the philosophical underpinnings of colonialism in Africa was incomparable. He correctly apprehended the contradictions that were at the centre of the colonial enterprise and how these subverted whatever good intentions might have had any role in colonialism. Liberty, equality, and fraternity could not underpin the relationship of colonizer and colonized. Nor could colonialism extend formal bourgeois equality without undermining its legitimacy to tell others how they ought to live. Violence was the guarantor and principle of colonial rule. Hence, at a time when so many thought that championing the cause of independence was a harbinger of a bright new day dawning, Fanon discerned something about the nature of the colonial situation that persuaded him that, without more than that, independence would not do the trick of restoring unity to the fractured reality of the colonized. In other words, colonialism was no school from which accomplished statesmen and women could have emerged.

Notes

1 It should be pointed out that the danger always exists that our seer in either situation might be easily assimilated to the charlatan of popular experience. While this danger is unavoidable, it should not deter us from exploring the fecund possibilities inherent in the notion of the prophet-as-seer.
2 See also Bade Onimode 1983, especially Part 2, and 1985: 39–42.

3 *Nigerian Enterprises Promotion Decree 1972.* See Sayre P. Schatz (1977: ch. 3), also Claude Ake (1978: ch. 2).

4 Here is what a government panel had to say in 1976 about the implementation of the law: "Confirmed cases of compliance after proper inspection numbered only 314 as at 30th of June, 1975, that is only about 33 per cent. The enterprises exempted from the Decree, many of them on questionable grounds, numbered 81. Defaulters have, up to the time of the Report (1976) not been brought to book – two years after the original appointed day of 31st March, 1974" (*Federal Military Government's Views on the Report of the Industrial Enterprises Panel,* Lagos: Federal Ministry of Information: 4). Cited in Onimode 1985: 50.

5 "CKD (completely knocked-down) components" is the production and manufacturing term which refers to the basic components or parts of an automobile. In this case, CKD components were shipped to Nigeria.

6 The following story may be apocryphal but it is instructive. It is said that in Nigeria's misguided monument to opulence, the Nicon Noga Hilton Hotel, in the capital city of Abuja, for some time after its commissioning had its radio receivers in the guest suites permanently tuned in to the BBC and the VOA. One could not tune in to *any* local radio station!

7 The latest example is Nigeria's "missing" $12 billion windfall from the increased oil sales the country enjoyed while the Gulf War of 1991 lasted.

Part VI

Resistance and Revolutionary Violence

19

Jammin' the Airwaves and Tuning into the Revolution: The Dialectics of the Radio in *L'An V de la révolution algeriénne*

Nigel Gibson

We have seen the rapid and dialectical progression of the new national requirements . . . Algerian society made an autonomous decision to embrace the new technique and tune itself in on the new signalling systems brought into being by the Revolution.

Frantz Fanon

I

Colonial society presents itself as a Manichaean one. The colonizer is represented as everything good, human, and living; the colonized as bad, brutish, and inert. It is a society of total separation, not one in the service of a higher synthesis. In this situation, the colonized inhabits "a zone of non-being," as Fanon puts it in *Black Skin, White Masks*, out of which no new activity can be generated. In his essay, "This is the voice of Algeria," in *L'An V de la révolution algeriénne* (*Sociologie d'une révolution*), he argues that

> Before the rebellion, there was the life, the movement, the existence of the settler, and on the other side the continued agony of the colonized. Before the rebellion there was the truth of the colonizer and the nothingness of the colonized. (*Sr* 61 / *ADC* 78)[1]

Before the rebellion, "being" and "nothingness" operated along color lines. This was not an ontological absolute but a definite social and psychological reality which characterized two "species" of men and women: the colonizer and the colonized.[2] In this situation, the colonizer is the "unceasing cause" and "absolute beginning" and the colonized is nothing, literally nihilated.[3] Colonialism represented the cessation of history for the colonized and, in short, the veritable death of the dialectic.

It has appeared to some that Fanon is a Manichaean philosopher; I want to suggest in contradistinction that Fanon is a dialectical thinker (I can do no more than intimate my larger claim, which is that his dialectic has far more in common with Hegel's concept of negativity than is generally thought).

The distinction between the time *before* the rebellion and the time *of* the rebellion constitutes an important division in Fanon's thought. It is in the context of the incipient revolution, in which a shift occurs in the colonized's consciousness. However, one can see how this initial negation of colonialism is filled out only if one begins to think of Fanon in a non-reductive way.

Through the experience of the revolution, the colonized's Manichaean consciousness breaks down and is sublated by what Fanon calls a "radical mutation" in consciousness. One example of this process is the changing attitudes to the radio – the subject of this paper. In terms of the dialectic, we can see how the radio, which was totally rejected by the colonized during the colonial period, is taken over by them and used as a weapon in the struggle for liberation. In short, it undergoes a "dialectical development" (*Sr* 68 / *ADC* 84) and becomes the mediation in the development of a national consciousness.

There are two phases of anticolonial resistance. The first is elemental rather than organized. In this context, it is the actions of the occupier that, Fanon argues, "determine the centers around which a people's *will to survive* becomes organized" (*Sr* 29 / *ADC* 47, my emphasis). Around these particular aspects of culture a "whole universe of resistances" is developed. For example, if people use religious arguments to justify their resistance, Fanon maintains, they are arbitrarily advanced "to justify the rejection of the occupier's presence" (*Sr* 78 / *ADC* 93).[4] These arguments are negative protests, a kind of obstinacy that puts a value on tradition, not on tradition itself, but on tradition as a refuge from what colonial Algeria was intent on doing. Fanon calls this negativity a "defense mechanism." For example, the performance of certain rituals manifested faithful observance of tradition and, more importantly, resistance to the colonizer who was bent on destroying those traditions.

In the colonial context even the doctor is perceived as part of the system functioning similarly to a policeman and is very often associated with the army. In this atmosphere, there is a real difficulty, Fanon adds, in being "objective." There is no objective truth. There is no neutral standpoint; everything is touched by the colonial system. In the colonial set-up the whole idea of what is truth is Manichaean. For the native, saying "no" to the French "yes" can be the only truth. It is an absolutely intransigent attitude that provides no room for any qualification. The absolute here is one of two extreme Manichaean possibilities. Indeed, any qualification is judged as a slip-up, an opening to accept the colonial world: "[E]very qualification is perceived by the occupier as an invitation to perpetuate the oppression, as a confession of congenital impotence" (*Sr* 108 / *ADC* 122). In other words, any agreement with the colonizing society is an acceptance, a sign of a willingness to integrate. It is an either/or world where the native must react in a "undifferentiated, categorical way" (*Sr* 108 / *ADC* 122).

These two phases of resistance, or negativity, are central to the development of a fighting culture, defined simply by "the thesis that men change at the same time that they change the world" (*Sr* 12 / *ADC* 30). Whereas the first stage expresses the contradictory interrelation of tradition and resistance, the second stage expresses the *necessary* breaking up of this interrelation. A radical mutation in consciousness occurs in connection with the revolution and through it the native becomes a historical protagonist. This "fighting phase" of anticolonial resistance

> does not give back to the national culture its former values and shapes; this struggle which aims at a fundamentally different set of relations between men cannot leave intact either the form or content of the people's culture. (*Dt* 294 / *WE* 245–6)

It is the fight for liberation, Fanon argues, "which sets culture moving and opens to it the doors of creation" and aims at totally new relations between people. In short, the liberation struggle is dialectical.

With regard to the issue of medicine, Fanon notes that new techniques shunned by the Algerian people were adopted during the "course of the fight." What happens is that the "mechanical sense of detachment and mistrust" of anything associated with the colonial regime begins to fall away. The revolution that imbues all aspects of life and culture with a new dynamism fosters the creation of a new sense of self-identity which is critical of the previous intransigence. It is a dialectical development where something that was viewed as part of the colonial system of oppression is taken over by the colonized and used by them in the struggle.

One illuminating example of this dialectical and radical mutation is found in his essay "This is the voice of Algeria" about the change in attitudes to the radio. Before turning to that essay in *Sociologie d'une révolution* I want to mention parenthetically that this radical mutation operates within a revolution and is quite different from the mutation he speaks of in *Black Skin*.

II

> Having a radio meant seriously going to war . . . It was hearing the first words of the nation . . . (*Sr* 78 / *ADC* 93)
>   The identification of the voice of the Revolution with the fundamental truth of the nation has opened up limitless horizons. (*Sr* 82 / *ADC* 97)

During the war of independence, the radio became an essential part of the liberation struggle because it could reach everybody. Through listening to radio broadcasts, those not directly involved in the armed struggle came to identify with the liberation movement, and the nation's "coming to be" (and any non-reductive engagement with Fanon's concept of violence should take this into account).[5] Yet how did attitudes to such a western technological import, alien to the indigenous culture, and one that had been resisted by the Algeria masses, undergo such a change and become an important medium in the revolutionary struggle?

In its first guise, the radio manifested a link to "civilization" and "culture" for the settler. As a colonial import, the radio at first helped invent a sense of community for the settler, an invention, Fanon argues, that "strengthen[ed] his certainty in the historic continuity of the conquest." The radio up to 1945 represented the French in Algeria; the news was of France, the music of Paris; it was part of the reality of colonial power. Before 1945, the radio, as a technical instrument of the dominant society, was essentially a means of cultural resistance and protection for the isolated Europeans against "Arabization," but it also represented an actual coercive force over certain sections of the dominated society.

The radio was a "technique in the hands of the occupier . . . [and] a symbol of French presence" (*Sr* 55 / *ADC* 72–3). Additionally, as a "bearer of language" the radio existed in colonial society in "accordance with a well-defined statute."

> Before 1954, the receiving instrument, the radiophonic technique of long-distance communication of thought, was not a neutral object . . . switching on the radio meant giving asylum to the occupier's words; it meant allowing the colonizer's language to filter into the heart of the house . . . Having a radio meant accepting being besieged from *within* by the colonizer. (*Sr* 77 / *ADC* 92)

Fanon notes that, from the colonialist's point of view, a view mirrored in positivist sociology, the native's resistance to the radio was a reactionary one based on feudal traditions, and religious and patriarchal hierarchies. Radios were resisted because they threatened the stability, the "traditional types of sociability," and the traditional views of the family (*Sr* 52 / *ADC* 70). Fanon discounts such views as artificial. He argues instead that it is *only from the standpoint of that initial resistance* that one can comprehend the "radical transformation" that had taken place among the colonized as well as the change in the significance of tradition in connection to the national war.

The rejection of the radio is an expression of the resistance among the colonized to the extension of the colonialists' "sensory powers." Put simply, there was no reason for the colonized to listen to the French broadcasts because under colonialism Algerian society "never participate[d] in this world of signs" (*Sr* 56 / *ADC* 73). The fact that Radio Alger was "Frenchmen speaking to Frenchmen" about things French underscored the native's reaction to the radio.

The interesting thing is that the radio became transformed into an object that could advance the notion of a new revolutionary consciousness by involving the masses in the day-to-day events of the liberation struggle. How Fanon accounts for this change touches on the dialectical character of the "radical mutation" in consciousness among those who were not directly involved in the fighting.

Because the masses couldn't read the press they had been "relatively uninvolved in the struggle"[6] and consequently there was a tendency during the early period of the anticolonial war to overestimate the movement's successes (akin to the weakness in spontaneity in chapter 2 *Les Damnés*). Rumors, which spread quickly by word of mouth, replaced any sense of objectivity and tended to reinforce the native's assurance that some battle had been won or an area of land liberated. Additionally, Fanon points to the "pathological nature" of the individual who thinks he can just go out and blow up the local police station and declare victory. He calls them "hysterical cases" (*Sr* 61–2 / *ADC* 79).

It was the radio that provided the vehicle for a radical change. By 1956, as the masses became aware of a "Voice of Free Algeria" a "real shift occurred," he writes; "in less than twenty days the entire stock of radio sets was bought up" (*Sr* 66 / *ADC* 82–3). There were battery sets for those living in rural areas without electricity.

Since 1956 the purchase of a radio in Algeria has meant, not the adoption of a modern technique for getting news, but the obtaining of access to the only means of *entering into communication with the Revolution, of living with it.* (*Sr* 67 / *ADC* 83)

This living with the revolution or undergoing its domestication was a sign of negativity that Fanon argued was both historical and dialectical (*Sr* 68 / *ADC* 84). A technology that had been considered a totally alien object, was no longer part of the "occupier's arsenal" but became the "primary means of resisting" the psychological and military pressures of the colonialists. More than a technological convenience, it provided a means of communicating with the revolution. The power of the radio to speak across a whole nation acted to unify that nation. It brought together all the "fragments and splinters." It fit together the "scattered acts" of rebellion "into a vast epic." The radio helped organize the resistance into a "national and political idea." In short, it helped create the nation:

> We have seen the rapid and dialectical progression of the new national requirements . . . Algerian society made an autonomous decision to embrace the new technique and tune itself in on the new signalling systems *brought into being by the Revolution*. (*Sr* 68 / *ADC* 84)

The power of the radio thus became seditious and the importance of "establishing contact with the official voice of the revolution became *as important* for the people as acquiring weapons or munitions for the National Army" (69n / 85n). Listening to *The Voice* was put on the same level as helping the armed militants and gave one a privileged "right of entry into the struggle":

> The Algerian who wanted to live up to the Revolution, had at last the possibility of hearing an official voice, the voice of the combatants explain the combat to him, tell him the story of the Liberation on the march, and incorporate it into the nation's new life. (*Sr* 69 / *ADC* 85)

Listening to the radio not only had results similar to partaking in violence but, Fanon claims, it actually involved the native in an almost physical struggle akin to the armed struggle.

The French reaction to *The Voice* was to jam it and make it inaudible. *The Voice* responded by re-broadcasting from a second station. A new form of struggle, the battle of the air waves, began: "The listener involved in the battle of the waves, had to figure out the tactics of the enemy, and in an almost *physical way* circumvent the strategy of the enemy" (*Sr* 69 / *ADC* 85). More than a merely internal experience, this intense effort drew the listeners into a collective battle that brought the native closer to the real fight of the revolution and the feeling that he or she was part of it.

Fanon describes a room full of people with one person glued to the radio listening for any news. At the end of the broadcast the audience would ask about a specific battle that had been mentioned in the French press which the "interpreter" had not heard *The Voice* mention:

> But by common consent, after an exchange of views, it would be decided that the Voice had in fact spoken of these events . . . A real task of reconstruction would then begin. Everyone would participate, and the real battles of yesterday and the day before would be re-fought in accordance with the deep aspirations and unshakable faith of the group. The listener would compensate for the fragmentary nature of the news by an *autonomous creation of information. (Sr* 70 / *ADC* 86)

Here we have a further development of a "radical mutation" in the consciousness of the oppressed, who has now entered history and become an author in its invention. How is this different from the earlier "inventions of the mind" by the "hysteric," where the native, deprived of news, would assume a victory won, or even the war of liberation successfully completed?

With the radio jammed by the French authorities, the people would listen to the "fuzz" all day waiting for some announcement. At the end of the day they would insist, after some debate, that they had heard *The Voice* speak of certain engagements that they had been following. The idea of truth now took on a different character as it was developed in a social and revolutionary democratic context. Fanon called it the "practice of freedom" which took place in "the structure of the people." In this context it was not the actual sounds of *The Voice* but people's collective interpretation that represented the creative moment. The meanings attached to the fuzz and to the voices the "hysteric" heard about victory were both interpretations. But what the "hysteric" heard was more akin to the wish for freedom found in the native's dreams described in *Les Damnés*. It was the work of the unconscious rather than the conscious mind. The difference between the "hysteric's" inventions or the native's rituals, dances, and dreams, on one hand and on the other, the groups in which the news was interpreted and created, was that the latter form allowed for a dialogue that aided both the working out of the fragments of information and the new national consciousness.[7] The very act of listening to the radio represented a new relationship between organization, epitomized by the "choppy, broken voice," and the masses mediated by the militant. The militants' authority shifted from one of telling the listeners what had happened to one of listening to them and accepting, "by common consent [and] . . . after an exchange of views" the "reconstruction" of events by those in the room (*Sr* 70 / *ADC* 86). Because of its directly democratic form, this organizational context did not stifle the creative energies of the native but encouraged them. It encouraged, whether consciously or not, the "imagining" of concrete battles and an "inner perception" of the nation which became "materialized in an irrefutable way." Thus the importance of listening to the often uninterpretable sounds from the radio lay not merely in receiving information but in [being] at one with the struggle." The shift from the hysteric's "hearing voices" to the revolutionary subject's hearing *The Voice* represented part of the real, not hallucinated, disintegration of colonialism.[8] Fanon recognizes that under these conditions "claiming to have heard the Voice of Algeria was, in a certain sense, distorting the truth." But it meant making a choice between two lies, the "enemy's congenital lie and the people's own lie, which suddenly acquired a dimension of truth" (*Sr* 71 / *ADC* 87). Moreover, it represented the transcendence of the radio *qua* receiver. The interpretation of the fuzz indicated the importance of the group's "own working existence," as Marx put it when speaking of the Paris Commune. It was an indication of the people taking the creation of the nation into their own hands; of realizing that the future lay with them, and not some other telling them what to think. This is a constant theme of the later chapters of *Les Damnés*. Through listening to the crackling, and "the excruciating din of the jamming, the Algerian would imagine not only words, but concrete battles" (*Sr* 71 / *ADC* 88). In other words, the French jamming and resulting inaudible character of much of the broadcast did not effect, Fanon maintains, the "reality and [the] power" of *The Voice*. In fact, as the fuzz became louder, and more pervasive, the broadcast came to represent news of an important battle which the French wanted to conceal. Indeed it represented at the same time a dialectical progression which helped liberate the people from *The Voice* as a "directive," giving it the role of mediation in the revolutionary process and the sense that they were the authors of the new nation.

Additionally, the search for *The Voice* across the wavelengths introduced the native to other voices and "other prospects." In other words, in place of the old monologue of the colonial situation, where the voice of colonialism was the only one, there now appeared a whole range of views. The colonial word was devalued and, in its place, *The Voice* had helped create a "fundamental change in the people," a change that "out of nothing [had] brought the nation to life and endowed every citizen with a new status" (*Sr* 81 / *ADC* 96).

The "radical mutation" of the native's consciousness that had brought about a complete change in attitude toward the radio was, Fanon argued, "not a back and forth" or "an ambivalence but rather . . . a dialectical progression" (*Sr* 75n / *ADC* 90n). This dialectical progression was not a synthesis but a "radical change in valence." One example of this transformation into its opposite was the native's attitude to the French language which underwent such significant change that it became "an instrument of liberation." (One should take note that Fanon's insistence is antithetical to Homi Bhabha's privileging of ambivalence. Fanon is clear that the mimicry of the black-skin white-mask, while maybe transgressing boundaries, is at most that of an enfranchised slave.)

Astonishingly, Fanon argued that it was the radio broadcasts in French that "liberate[d] the enemy language from its historic meanings" (*Sr* 74 / *ADC* 89).⁹ The language of order, threat, and insult was transformed into its "antithesis" and "lost its accursed character, revealing itself to be capable also of transmitting, for the benefit of the nation, the messages of truth that the latter awaited." Ironically, Fanon added it was the revolution, or more precisely the use of French in revolutionary radio broadcasts, that was encouraging the spread of the heretofore resisted French language. Before 1954, French was a sign of the influence of the occupier with "ontological implications within Algerian society" (*Sr* 76 / *ADC* 91). French was "refused" as a language of oppression and Arabic was the language of choice in the nationalist movement. But the revolution "stripped the Arabic language of its sacred character," just as it stripped away the negative connotations of the French language. Listening to radio aided a vast mutation in the people's consciousness because it reflected and assisted their desire to be involved in a dialogue:

> Every Algerian felt himself to be called upon and wanted to become a reverberating element of the vast network of meanings born of the liberating combat. (*Sr* 80 / *ADC* 94)

The existence of *The Voice*, Fanon argued, became part of the positive in the negative that helped liberate the masses from the Manichaean viewpoint and opened up a vast array of libertory meanings and possibilities.

Notes

The epigraph is from Fanon *Sr* 68 / *ADC* 84.

1   The last sentence is inexplicably left out of the English edition and can be found on p. 62 of *L'An V de la révolution algeriénne.*

2   Fanon claims in *Black Skin, White Masks* that the application of Sartre's speculations on the existence of the Other "to a black consciousness proves fallacious. That is because the white man is not only The Other but also the master, whether real or imaginary" (*Pn* 112 n. 22 / *BS* 138n).

3   "In the man of color," he writes, "there is a constant effort to run away from his own individuality and to annihilate his own presence" (*Pn* 48 / *BS* 60).

4   He notes that there is no "rational" basis for this position.

5   Fanon decided to write about the importance of the radio and not about his
    experience as a journal editor. The radio could reach a vast section of the
    population. It was not geographically or socially limited and brought the
    "message of the revolution" to all. The bulletins and newsletters which did
    speak of immediate events were frequently seized and destroyed and could
    never match the radio's audience, its geographic reach, or the speed of its
    reaction to events.
6   Here the subject is not the urban elite.
7   The language here alludes to Freud's interpretation of dreams. And the fuzz
    appears like a dream "fragment" found in waking life, but the emphasis here
    is conscious, deliberated decision-making with eyes on the future rather than
    on the past. That is why Fanon also thinks that the radio will have "an
    exceptional importance in the country's building phase" (*Sr* 82 / *ADC* 97).
8   He adds that the difference between the hysteria of the dominant group and
    that of the colonized was that "the colonizer always translated his subjective
    states into acts, real and multiple murders" (*Sr* 62 / *ADC* 79).
9   But we cannot assume that the majority of listeners, especially those who had
    little contact with the French, would understand the language of the radio
    broadcast. Fanon does not address this, but we can only assume that the
    "interpreter" who had made sense of the fuzz also translated the message of
    The Voice. For the peasant, perhaps, whether he has heard "fuzz" or French
    is beside the point; it has come from the authority of *The Voice*.

20

Fanon on the Role of Violence in Liberation: A Comparison with Gandhi and Mandela

Gail M. Presbey

In his book on Fanon, Richard Onwuanibe insists that we understand Fanon as a humanist above all, regardless of the fact that he is often popularized as an advocate of violence. Does this assertion entail a moral contradiction? Can one who wishes death to his enemies be ultimately regarded as a humanist? Onwuanibe makes his case by arguing that Fanon's constant goal was to foster the full development of humanity, extending human dignity, freedom, love, care, and justice to all the exploited. Fanon strictly saw violence as only legitimate in the cause of self-defense of the oppressed. Colonialism had to be ended to provide the new context in which the majority of people could thrive and regain their health and dignity (Onwuanibe: xiii, 2). Yet others, like Mohandas Gandhi, whose goals were similar to Fanon's, reject violence as a means because it goes against humanistic values of preserving life.

  Both Gandhi and Fanon stressed the importance of upholding one's culture in the face of western attempts at hegemony. Cultural differences between India and Algeria, Hinduism and Islam, affected how each interpreted the struggle for liberation in their own context. Understanding these differences will help us to see why they came to different conclusions about the methods appropriate for pursuing a similar goal. For example, both saw their colonized countries as sick and in need of health; but they had radically different ideas of medicine. Both agreed that the oppressed had to win their independence in a way that would free them from neocolonial continuations of domination, but their approaches to winning their independence were different. In each case the cultural background provided the larger context for the understanding of these issues. Mandela walks a line between these two thinkers, stressing the importance of nonviolence while eventually turning to limited use of violence.

Metaphors of Health

Fanon concentrates on the rejuvenating and restorative effect that participating in the struggle against oppression has for the oppressed person. This does not necessitate doing a violent deed with one's own hands; the most important aspect is changing one's own self-identity once one becomes committed to opposing the colonizer. For example, even trying to listen to the revolutionary *Voice of Algeria* radio broadcast can be a transformative act. Nevertheless Fanon asserts on several occasions that the struggle must be violent.

A likely source for Fanon's description of violence as rehabilitative and healing is his overall concern with health, both mental and physical. Perinbam states that Fanon deliberately chose the word "detoxify" to describe one of the results of violence (particularly the resistance of the colonized); a colonized person would be "poisoned" by the "toxins" of the colonial syndrome, such as low self-esteem. As a psychiatrist, he was sensitive to the fact that the social environment can be a hindrance to mental health and, if it is, so one should escape the situation by violence if necessary (Perinbam: 22, 80). The goal was not just to save the individual but to make the society once again into a healthy place for all to thrive mentally and physically. In an *El Moudjahid* article in 1957, Fanon stated that "The independence of Algeria is not only the end of colonialism, but the disappearance, in this part of the world, of a gangrene germ and the source of an epidemic" (*Pra* 60 / *TAR* 64).

Fanon studied in France with Tosquelles, who believed that the psychiatrist's role was to help the patient reintegrate into society, and not to isolate and categorize the patient. When studying the source of the patient's problems, rather than searching through the patient's childhood, the recent interactions between the patient and family members and friends are studied. It is in this sense that Fanon was concerned with the organic, meaning related, health of individuals in society. In the context of war-torn Algeria, Fanon treated the war weary and traumatized with unfailing energy and compassion (Perinbam: 56–7). Fanon's emphasis on reintegration was in marked contrast to the practices he first found in use at the hospital in Blida-Joinville. When he first got there he was shocked to see a room full of sixty-nine mental patients, all in straitjackets and tied to their beds. Fanon's first action was to order that they all be released from their bonds (Hansen 1977: 41; see also Onwuanibe: ix).

As a practitioner of modern medicine, Fanon was familiar with procedures of medicine and surgery, both of which can be seen as a violent attack upon whatever enemy in the body is bent on destroying healthy tissue. Antibiotics kill foreign germs which have invaded; surgery cuts out parts of the body that have become corrupted through cancer and tumors.

We can find this same use of metaphors of health in Gandhi's work. Although Gandhi was not a medical doctor like Fanon, he saw nursing as having an important role in his life; no matter what was happening at the time he would drop everything to attend to a sick family member or friend (Erikson: 109–11). A firm believer in healing through prayer, Gandhi would not take his own son to the medical doctor even when he was deathly ill. Instead, his method of nursing was to sit patiently by the bedside of the sick person, for days if necessary, and pray constantly. Regarding self-treatment for his own ills, Gandhi was a firm believer that "the cure lay not in taking medicine internally but in dietetic changes assisted by external remedies" (Gandhi 1940: 270). He was prone to blame his sicknesses on some lack of moral discipline in himself. For example, his account of the reason for his catching dysentery was that he had allowed his wife to tempt him; refusing all medicine, Gandhi was finally cured by having ice packs applied all over his body (pp. 341–3).

Gandhi recounted the story of a serious outbreak of the black plague in South Africa among gold miners. Medical doctors were not available, and a nurse assigned to the patients succumbed herself. He and several volunteers went there and prayed, and three plague victims accepted "earth treatment" in which wet earth bandages were applied to their heads and chests. Two of these three survived, and all the others died (pp. 217–18).

In his biography of Gandhi, Louis Fischer points out that Gandhi once submitted to surgery (an appendectomy) while serving a sentence in Yeravda Central Prison. Nevertheless his usual stance was to reject professional medical advice. Even while recuperating from the surgery after his release from jail at a beach near Bombay, he "converted the seaside villa into a temporary hospital where ailing associates, summoned from near and far, gave Gandhi pleasure by submitting to his mud packs, water baths, food fads and massage" (Fischer: 237–8). Today in India one can find health spas run by Gandhi followers that base their cures on hot baths, mud, and magnets, rejecting all modern medicine and surgery. With this as a background, no wonder metaphors of "restoring health" mean something very different in the Gandhian context.

This reluctance to cut open the body, as in surgery, or even to attack viruses through medicine, could be seen metaphorically as another example of his commitment to nonviolence. To be a physician of society, then, would not involve violence or coercion. Gandhi's methods of external remedies encourage the body to respond but don't compel an outcome. This fits with his overall philosophy that meaningful changes in behavior can't be forced. As he explained, "We may not replace the slavery of the governments by that of the non-cooperationists. We must concede to our opponents the freedom we claim for ourselves and for which we are fighting" (Terchek: 206). His repeated message was that he would patiently wait for the oppressor to have a change of heart and therefore change behavior. Such faith in the human ability to change meant Gandhi was often crushed when someone, such as General Smuts of South Africa, went back on his word. Gandhi had been convinced that Smuts had sincerely had a change of heart (Gandhi 1950: 190–1). But this same kind of faith was needed to believe that Gandhi's health cures would work; it is not hard to imagine that not all could have as much faith in such cures as he did.

In defense of his own model of surgery, Fanon could accuse Gandhi of being out of touch with the dire circumstances of colonialism. For Fanon and the "native" viewpoint which he represented, nothing less than the "surgery" of violence could root out the evil powers from the colonized country. As Fanon explained in 1958, "French colonialism is a war force; it has to be beaten down by force. No diplomacy, no political genius, no skill can cope with it" (*Pra* 101 / *TAR* 97). He saw close at hand the disastrous effects of the war on the patients he served, and so was desperate in his eagerness to see the war finished and the Algerian people triumphant.

However, if we are to hold Fanon to a "surgery" or "medical" model, he himself must admit that there are limits to violence in successful surgery. The patient must at all times be viable; if too much is removed, particularly of necessary organs, the patient dies. And there are times when surgery is so dangerous that medical solutions are proposed as safer for the patient. For example, a cancerous tumor too close to the brain will not be operated upon, but instead chemotherapy will be used. On the level of politics, this metaphor would point to the need for caution at certain moments. For example, there may be circumstances in which violent attack of enemies would result in too high a death toll, whereas in some other strategies of resistance the resulting government backlash would be easier to absorb, although still painful.

Independence

Samir Amin has helpfully outlined the several ways in which colonists milked the resources of the colonies, by mining its minerals, by using its "labor reserves," and by appropriating for itself agricultural produce (Amin, in Appiah: 163). There is also the damage done to the indigenous culture, its value systems, and political structures, as Fanon outlines in *Sociologie d'une révolution* and elsewhere. Renate Zahar, in her account of Fanon, summarizes the history of abuse that Africa had been subjected to, and shows how emancipation is therefore necessary (Zahar 1974: 74–5). Certainly, therefore, this parasitical and destructive colonial relationship must be halted, if not by exterminating the "whites" then either by banishing them or by getting them to give up their unjust privilege and to accept a position in politics and economics as equals. Such a conclusion is put forward by Fanon and, with it, Fanon justifies killing the enemy.

For the victim of violence, it is hard to say that there is any healing taking place. Fanon's own works catalog the damage to physical and mental well-being that violence brings to a person (*Dt* 301–2 / *WE* 251–2; Perinbam: 11). In fact, it is at the point of violence that an aggressor is saying that he or she is giving up on being able to reform, change, or heal the victim in any way, but merely wants them to submit or die. This is of course why Gandhi refuses violence, even against the former oppressors of India, whether they be the British themselves, or the wealthy Indian landowners. He does not want to give up on a single individual.

Gandhi argued that since the oppressors had skills that would be needed by a free India in the future, it would be much better to convert the rich to the cause; if they were killed, the movement for change would be diminished. Gandhi suggests that one does not want to kill the goose that laid the golden egg (Gandhi 1958: 205). This suggests that the rich became so because they had skills, knowledge, and industry. Gandhi would therefore like to see them continue to exercise those attributes, but for the benefit of the wider community rather than just for themselves. The feasibility of this transfer of skills is problematic. For one thing, it may not be easy to change the desires of the rich from motivation for self-gain to the benefit of society. Secondly, the amassing of wealth may have had more to do with ownership of wealth and resources; if the distribution of such resources were to be changed, we may find that the former rich are no longer capable of continuing to make themselves rich. For example, if land were gained by depriving others, and then employing others at low wages to work the land, what aspect of this economic enterprise would produce transferable skills? Insofar as successful and ecologically sound agricultural practices are put into use, these skills would indeed continue to be useful.

Gandhi continually saw independence as something to be gained through self-control. He suggested that it was laziness that led to the Indians relying upon the British to do things for them, such as governing them, running their schools, etc., which they should have been doing themselves. Therefore he imagined independence being won through self-discipline. Instead of going to the police or courts to settle disputes, they should settle them by going to village elders or *panchyrats*. Instead of buying cloth from the British, they should weave their own. Make the British superfluous, then they'll have to leave. The world-view which spawned this strategy was one of Hindu asceticism, where self-control was a spiritual virtue and the way to happiness. Gandhi blamed his own community's weakness for their present position as imperial subjects. He wanted them to regain their strength, not through violence, but through an inner resolve or discipline.

What does Fanon think about the option of nonviolent methods? In the Algerian context, those ideas are all suggested by the native bourgeoisie, who suggested it because their interests were actually the same as the colonizers. The elites denounced violence and wanted compromise, so that the colonizers would hand the rule over to them (*Dt* 93 / *WE* 62). Also, the native elite used moral arguments, but didn't help those in slavery. They tried to shame the slave-drivers and put forth humanitarian goals for the government, but when the crucial time came they spoke out against mass mobilization, the only thing that would end that slavery (*Dt* 98 / *WE* 67). It could however be argued that the native bourgeoisie as Fanon describes them were not so much advocating "nonviolent action" as they were advocating accommodation and compromise.

Gandhi's hopes to convert the oppressor have unsure results, and in any case take time. Fanon wants the oppression to stop as soon as possible, and so however sensitive he may be to the traumas of the colonizers, and however dedicated he may be to bringing them to health (it should be remembered that half the patients at Blida-Joinville were white settlers), Fanon's overriding concern was the reinstatement of an independent Algeria so that the majority of the population could regain their health. He was therefore willing to risk the death of his opponents in this war of liberation (Perinbam: 56).

The Question of Heavy Casualties

Barbra Deming in her essay "On revolution and equilibrium" challenges Fanon on what she sees as his overdependence on violence. She suggests that nonviolent methods result in fewer casualties being suffered in the long run, since it makes the oppressor think twice about retaliating with counter-violence. She explains carefully, however, that this does not mean that there will be no casualties, only fewer than if violence were used (Deming: 102–3). We could imagine that she would point to the high death toll in Algeria to illustrate her point. Likewise, Jan Zielonka explains that it was fear of high casualties that encouraged Solidarnosc to choose nonviolent non-cooperation in their struggle against the Soviet-backed PZPR government in power in Poland (Barton-Kriese: 53).

The early strategy of the African National Congress (ANC) in South Africa was directly influenced by Gandhi's nonviolent action. Albert Luthuli, a Zulu chief who was elected president of the ANC in 1952, led campaigns of massive disobedience against unjust laws in a Defiance Campaign. He insisted as late as 1962 that nonviolence as a method must be strictly adhered to, because "as long as our patience can be made to hold out, we shall not jeopardize the South Africa of tomorrow by precipitating violence today" (Barton-Kriese: 80).

Nelson Mandela and members of the ANC in South Africa also assumed and feared that retaliatory violence would escalate when they decided to form Umkonto we Sizwe and consequently used limited violence for their cause. Yet Mandela explains that the ANC nevertheless embarked upon violent resistance because they wearied of the fruitlessness of their efforts. Even if Deming was right and the 39 people killed from 1957 to 1960 in nonviolent protests in South Africa did not rearly match the thousands upon thousands killed and tortured in Algeria during these same years, the feeling, nonetheless, of the lack of progress, and the continued hardships of living under apartheid, made the resistance movement in South Africa decide to make the stakes higher (Mandela: 324–5, 329–30).

However, Mandela describes a careful selection process for a method of violence that would take the least lives. Carefully chosen sites for sabotage would cripple the economy and make a point; but lives would not be taken because of special concern for the healing process, since avoiding direct loss of lives "offered the best hope for future race relations" (Mandela: 327). Throughout his testimony, Mandela explains that his long-term goal was a unified and harmonious interracial South Africa, and so methods that would drive the races further apart were always avoided. To extend our metaphor, Mandela's choice of sabotage was a sort of "laser surgery," which hopes to accomplish its goal with as little human suffering as possible so that healing can take place quickly.

Listening to the People

Mandela noted that part of the ANC decision to depart from their long history of nonviolent struggle was the fact that the people were no longer satisfied with nonviolence and yearned for violent expression of their anger. Mandela was afraid that if the ANC did not make itself relevant to the needs of the people by giving them the guidance and structure required for a limited and calculated use of force against apartheid, the people themselves would find their own, and perhaps more destructive, ways to express the violence they desired. Mandela was particularly concerned that their aggressiveness would turn inward, and that they would hurt each other and put their own communities under stress (Mandela: 324).

Interestingly enough, Gandhi describes a similar scenario as the impetus for his nonviolent protests. As he explains, there was a need to channel the violent impulses of the Indians who felt impatient to do something; he hoped that action of a nonviolent kind would meet their need to do something, in a helpful and non-destructive mode. He thought that most Indians did not want to act violently, and that participation in the resistance would be much more widespread if only nonviolent methods were used. As he said,

> It is certain that India cannot rival Britain or Europe in the force of arms. The British worship the war-god and they can all of them become, as they are becoming, bearers of arms. The hundreds of millions in India can never carry arms. They have made the religion of non-violence their own. It is impossible for the varnashrama system to disappear from India . . . The highest place in India is assigned to the brahmana dharma – which is the soul force. Even the armed warrior does obescience to the Brahmin. So long as this custom prevails, it is vain for us to aspire for equality with the West in force of arms. (Gandhi 1990: 52–3)

Likewise, Fanon's reasons for preferring violence as a method lay in his listening to the desires of the native Algerians. He did not want to thwart their desires, but rather to channel them in a positive direction. Since the native Algerians had no desire to "love" their colonizers, as Gandhi would have insisted they did, Fanon rejected the nonviolent method; to do otherwise would have been to impose a plan upon them.

Perinbam explains that the tradition of Islam is the background against which violent struggle in Algeria can be understood and legitimated. Islam divides the world into dar-al-Islam (the domain of Islam) and dar-al-harb (the domain of war), a division which parallels the description of the Manichaean world in *Les Damnés*. The "jihad" tradition helped participants in revolution see the French as enemies of God as well as of themselves, and so gave them the courage to risk their lives while fighting for a cause greater than themselves (Perinbam: 103). Although there are some Muslims who are dedicated to nonviolence and insist that "jihad" should not be understood as physical war but rather a spiritual battle, such views are in the minority (see Hassan: 417, 423).

Remember that Fanon's account of the native's longing for violence is first descriptive, and later evaluative. First he begins by his psychological study of violence as the native sees it; Fanon here is anthropologist and psychologist. Afterwards, he switches to his strategic revolutionary mode and decides whether this urge for violence can be put to use. Fanon does not think the violent urges of the natives from the countryside can be ignored. He thinks that they must be given expression, although the natives must be politically educated and the stage of indiscriminate violence must be brief. Although Fanon often seems to take the natives' point of view, he is not one of the natives himself. Rather, just like the native bourgeoisie who want to use the masses' threat of violence to catapult themselves into power, Fanon wants to use their brief display of spontaneous, indiscriminate violence to catapult a better government into power. Although in the first chapter of *Les Damnés* he gives an almost phenomenological description of colonization from the native's point of view, in the rest of the book Fanon goes on to say that the colonized person's vision must be modified by education and political organization. The main problems Fanon sees with violence, as the colonized want to practice it, has to do with its motivation and its target. Its motivation is revenge, and its target is indiscriminate.

Fanon predicts that the "unmixed and total brutality" of the colonized, "if not immediately combated, invariably leads to the defeat of the movement within a few weeks" (*Dt* 185 / *WE* 147). By itself violence motivated by revenge is not enough. More is needed for a revolution to be successful than just killing the leaders. The system has to be changed.

Fanon condemns this indiscriminate killing. He describes how the revolutionary, who has indiscriminately slaughtered all who seemed to be oppressors, reaches gradual states of realization in the course of combat. Violence teaches its people, Fanon states (*Dt* 186 / *WE* 147). The revolutionaries notice that while they are breaking up the colonial oppression they are setting up another system of exploitation. This sickens them. They see that they had a too-simple conception of the overlords. It is the example of some of the white settlers who go over to the other side, fighting with the Arabs, accepting suffering and death, that disarms the general hatred that the natives feel towards the foreign settlement (183–4 / 145). Then it is time to move into the later, more discriminating stages of the fight.

Contrary to the opinion of some who think that these "shades of meaning" will only blur what was once a very clear situation – with the good guys on one side and the bad on another – Fanon insists that this heightened awareness is good and important (*Dt* 184 / *WE* 146). Hatred and resentment cannot sustain a war of liberation (177 / 139). The immediacy of "muscles" is a mirage; knowledge is needed. If violent rebels are not educated, the colonists will infiltrate, try to divide the groups, and redirect the violence (176 / 137–8).

Just as successful surgery is brief, and not a "way of life," so Fanon hopes that revolutionary violence will be brief. As one would recover from surgery best by practicing healthy eating and exercise, so also a newly won freedom and a newly founded government demands care and attention from well-meaning and reflective individuals for it to recover from the trauma of violence. Fanon therefore argues that there may be some cases in which brief surgery is the quickest and surest way to health.

Violence as Creating Self-respect and Hope

Fanon explains that the "native", with his traits of laziness, crime, etc, was created by the settler; when the settler, during decolonization, is thrown out, the "new humanity" can come to be. "Decolonization is the veritable creation of new men. But this creation owes nothing of its legitimacy to any supernatural power; the 'thing' which has been colonized becomes man during the same process by which it frees itself" (*WE*: 36–7).

Gandhi himself often asserted that fighting was better than cowardice or acquiescence. The satyagrahi, a name coined by Gandhi to signify the one who challenged unjust structures, maintained a psychology akin to the soldier and was willing to die for a just cause. Step one was to realize one's own dignity, that one does not deserve the treatment one receives from the colonizer. Having that insight, one should join with others to confront the opponent. Although a nonviolent action may not always be as successful strategically as a violent action, it could serve the same psychological function (Gandhi: 53–4).

Gandhi's analysis of the source of problems of self-identity and self-esteem are quite similar to Fanon's. Gandhi noticed that the imposed system of colonialism sowed the seeds of fear, hatred, envy and helplessness. Colonialism uprooted old values, without fully accepting the supposedly assimilated as "British" (Terchek: 203–4). Gandhi insisted that people needed to feel self-respect, and that the cause of helplessness could be attributed to social conditions. He noted that many in India were crippled by colonialism, industrialism, and a corrupted notion of caste. Owing to these influences, most responded in varied ways by either hugging their chains, or striking out against any vulnerable target, or by passively withdrawing from the world. Gandhi admits that "most people who attempted to break away from submissiveness did so violently." Nevertheless he considered the nonviolent response a case of active courage superior to that of the warrior (Terchek: 198–9).

It must be remembered that although Fanon often speaks of violence as the means of humanity recreating itself, he speaks more of the role of action and education as creating this new humanity. Against the idea that what is needed most is a strong, central revolutionary party (which only masks domination), Fanon insists that what is needed most is to educate the people politically (*Dt* 222 / *WE* 180). To develop the brains of a people, you need a trustworthy political party (227 / 185). It is also important to organize and enlighten those who live in the countryside. If peasants do not understand reforms, even if they're objectively good, they will not comply (*Dt* 155 / *WE* 117). However the new leaders should not replace the initiative of the people; rather, they should nurture it.

An episode that Fanon recounts in order to prove violence's indispensability could also be used to argue for the necessity of struggle, whether violent or nonviolent. In Fanon's account of France's granting of "independence" to Martinique, recounted in his earlier book *Black Skin, White Masks*, Fanon expressed the frustration of the Martinican who, because France has "willingly" given independence without a fight, is reduced to saying "thank you" to the French government for a freedom not fought for or "won." In fact, Martinicans sponsored the erection of "thank you" statues in France (*Pn* 179 / *BS* 220–2). Here Fanon wishes that the struggle was violent. Why? Who wishes that events were more violent than they were, and are we not usually relieved when violence is averted? Let me try to voice what I think Fanon's explanation would be.

The consciousness of the Martinican would have been changed after violence. They would have seen France as its true enemy instead of its smiling, deceiving friend. Therefore, they would have had a sounder self-identity in relation to the French. Secondly, although "independence" was achieved, the independence after an armed struggle would have had a different character. It could more radically diverge from the colonial model, by disrupting the easy transition between the colonial government and the native elite. So the effects of violence would have been both psychological and practical.

However, it is possible for a nonviolent movement to have the same consciousness-raising ability. In Gandhi's terms, the Martinicans acquiesced. They did not have the experience of fighting, whether violently or nonviolently, for their freedom; and so they were not transformed by their struggle.

Fighting nonviolently for independence does not necessarily entail continuing a relationship of economic dependence with the former colonizer. Gandhi insisted on *hind swaraj*, or independence for India, even to the point of reverting to handwoven cloth rather than relying on Britain for imported machine-woven cloth. Even though Gandhi's influence on the newly independent government of India was limited, India did indeed pursue a path of nonalignment and a policy of making in India all of the goods to be bought there.

Many colonizing countries tried to convince the newly independent nations that it was in the new nation's own self-interest to continue colonial economic relations. Fanon aptly describes this as a moment when the native bourgeoisie see their opportunity take the place of the former colonizers in the power structure. But the key to avoiding this too-easy transition involves either, or both, a native bourgeoisie committed to the cause of the people, and an informed and active people who understand that economic independence is in their best self-interest. These radical perspectives can be forged in the process of nonviolent political action, as in the case of India; not all nonviolent transitions, therefore, will end in a Martinican style of neocolonialism.

Parallels between Violent and Nonviolent Strategy

Fanon, in his analysis of the Arab cause in French-dominated Algeria, does not think that the Arab forces can overpower the French forces in a straightforward military sense. Rather, he thinks that they can only "pick at" the French forces, so that they become bogged down in protecting themselves against the terrorist acts, to such an extent that it becomes unprofitable to continue the police repression. In this way Fanon expresses his confidence that the colonizers are rationally self-interested, and have no desire to kill all the natives, for that would damage their profits (*Dt* 95–6 / *WE* 73–4). As Fanon explains:

By what aberration of the spirit do these men, without technique, starving and enfeebled, without experience with methods of organization, confronted with the military and economic might of the occupation, come to believe that only violence will free them? How can they hope to triumph? ... The truth is that there is no colonial power today which is capable of adopting the only form of contest which has a chance of succeeding: the prolonged establishment of large forces of occupation. (*Dt* 105 / *WE* 73–4)

The same convictions regarding strategy are expressed by C. L. R. James:

The plain truth is that a colonial people gets self-government when the cost of withholding it from them is too much for His Majesty's Government – usually because the people are determined to have it and show, even if they have to be shot down in thousands, that they will not be denied. (James 1971: 109)

In this way Fanon's strategy parallels the nonviolent strategies of Gandhi, Thoreau, and others. They hope, through nonviolent rather than violent means, to cause a general insubordination that would be very costly to control. The rulers in such a context would have a vested interest in saving themselves money, and in ensuring the existence of workers who could be exploited in the future. It was just such a context that was missing for the Jews in Europe during the Nazi expansionism. Hitler was repeatedly willing to go against his own convenience and profit to exterminate the Jewish population.

Both Fanon's methods, and the nonviolent methods, have much in common, despite the fact that they're often conceived of as opposite strategies. Both strategies count on the colonizer's forces giving up the battle, even though they have the weapons and power to obliterate the entire colonized population. However, success is not guaranteed. Fanon's forces can heighten their acts of terror; Gandhi's followers can become more extreme in their non-cooperation. Neither can force the hand of an opponent equipped with superior technological weaponry; but the people's actions can make the colonizers' actions seem more and more ridiculous to themselves. But there is no guarantee that the latter will happen; who can explain, for example, why the Portuguese clung more tenaciously to their colonies than the other European nations, at a loss to Portugal as well as at a loss to the African people?

Conclusion

As Erik Erikson states regarding both Fanon and Gandhi,

An implicit therapeutic intent, then, seems to be a common denominator in theories and ideologies of action which, on the level of deeds, seem to exclude each other totally. What they nevertheless have in common is the intuition that violence against the adversary and violence against the self are inseparable; what divides them is the program of dealing with either. (Erikson: 437)

This chapter has shown that there is much in common between the ideas of violent and nonviolent theorists of liberation, such as Fanon, Mandela, and Gandhi, regarding strategy; and scholars and activists would do well to learn lessons from these thinkers. All three see the importance of analyzing society to search for the source of social ills that affect individual physical and psychological well-being. But although their diagnoses are similar, their prescriptions are quite different: just how the ills of colonial government should be addressed and dealt with differs greatly between the three. This paper has shown how the background and religious beliefs of the different populations in India and Algeria influenced the ways in which their struggles for independence were understood, leading them to embrace different means of accomplishing their similar goals.

Just which of these approaches is the most humanistic: the quick and total violence described by Fanon, which claims to be humanistic because it quickly creates the social climate in which health can be gained; the limited violence directed toward material resources advocated by Mandela, which hopes to force the enemy to give in while preserving as much as possible the future hope of healing the community; or the nonviolent challenge advocated by Gandhi, which preserves the life of the opponent in hopes of winning them to the right cause, but requires more patience and self-control than the other methods? All three put limits on violence and injustice that are often ignored in both the daily workings of an oppressive system and the specific acts of violence used to enforce the system. Any of the three, when compared to the unhindered continuance of domination, emerge as humanistic. Which of the three strategies is best may have to be left up to the concrete circumstances of each situation, where history and culture play a role in shaping the consciousness of the people.

21

Fanon's Tragic Revolutionary Violence

Lewis R. Gordon

The objects the imitator represents are actions, with agents who are necessarily either good men or bad – the diversities of human character being nearly always derivative from this primary distinction, since the line between virtue and vice is one dividing the whole of mankind.

Aristotle

We know that tragedy usually involved a "change from prosperity to adversity," as Aristotle put it, though for Aristotle the only reason for having a king as the protagonist was the fact that he had fortune and prosperity to lose. And yet we know that the welfare of a king involved the welfare of his people, so his misfortune or misconduct would appear to explain the misfortune of his people.

Eva Figes

He only can understand the deep satisfaction which I experienced, who has himself repelled by force the bloody arm of slavery. I felt as I never felt before. It was a glorious resurrection, from the tomb of slavery, to the heaven of freedom. My long-crushed spirit rose, cowardice departed, bold defiance took its place; and I now resolved that, however long I might remain a slave in form, the day had passed forever when I could be a slave in fact. I did not hesitate to let it be known of me, that the white man who expected to succeed in whipping, must also succeed in killing me.

Frederick Douglass

Les Damnés de la terre, Fanon's classic work in liberation theory, is more than a rich presentation and virulent critique of both colonialism and, as William Jones (1995) observes, its neocolonial mutation. It is also a powerful statement of the problem that Fredric Jameson calls the problem of *mediation*: "How do we pass, in other words, from one level of social life to another, from the psychological to the social, indeed, from the social to the economic?" (p. xiv). In Jameson's dialectic, if we were to place freedom after each adjective, we would find that we move from psychological freedom to political-economic freedom. But can the mediation involved in a transition from colonialism to postcolonialism ever be nonviolent? Fanon's response is both famous and infamous.

Fanon's response has suffered from much misunderstanding primarily because of a failure to understand the role of two particular phenomena in his thought. The first aspect is his existential-phenomenological humanism. The second one is the role of tragedy as a dramatic resource and human signifier.

Colonialism is a tragic situation. The opening passage of Fanon's discussion of violence in *Les Damnés* is practically prescient of Eva Figes's observations on tragedy in our epigraph:

> At whatever level one studies it – encounters between individuals, new names for sports clubs, networks [*composition humaine*] at cocktail parties, of the police, of directing boards of national or private banks – decolonization is quite simply the replacing of one "species" of men [and women] by another "species" of men [and women]. Without transition, there is a total, complete, absolute substitution . . . Its unusual importance is that it constitutes, from the first day, the minimum demand of the colonized. To tell the truth, the proof of success resides in a changed social panorama from the bottom up . . . But the eventuality of this change is equally lived in the form of a terrifying future in the consciousness of another "species" of men and women: the colonizers. (*Dt* 65–6 / *WE* 35–6)

Here, the tragic stage is set. Aristotle defines tragedy as "the representation of an action that is serious and also, as having magnitude, complete in itself . . . with incidents arousing *pathos* and fear, wherewith to accomplish its *catharsis* of such emotions" (149b24–28, emphasis added).[1] In pathos, one suffers from and with another's suffering; and in identifying the achievement of catharsis, which in ancient times referred to the medicinal activity of purgation and cleansing, we arrive at the following observation. Tragedy presents actions to the community that elicit communal suffering. The tragic lesson is that setting things "right," and thereby setting the community right, calls for violent intervention – horrible interventions. Tragedy addresses the terror of mediation. So does Fanon.

A dimension of Fanon's discussion of violence that has received much attention is the cathartic elements or cleansing force of violence in his two-stage theory of liberatory mediation. The oppressed, he claims, achieve psychological liberation, or cleansing, by violating the oppressor.[2] They are then free to go on with the more organized forms of violence (praxis), that are necessary for the building of a new, liberated society. It should be noted, however, that although Fanon advances this thesis, to see this aspect of his discussion as its crux would be a case of seeing trees without seeing the forest. The objection that is most often raised against Fanon's argument, for instance, is that psychological release through violence on another human being does not necessarily create a psychological state that is conducive to a political one.

On the question of the relation of the psychological to the political, Figes observes a similar error in Freud's psychoanalytic treatment of tragedy.[3] She argues that, interesting as Freud's ruminations on tragedy as aesthetic expression of libidinous desire may be, they ultimately betray a limitation of classical psychoanalysis: its failure to account for the *audience's* role in tragic presentation and the irrelevance of the characters' apperception, whether conscious or subconscious, of their actions. On the other hand, we may take recourse to earlier theories of tragedy, like Hegel's, Schopenhauer's, and Nietzsche's. From the standpoint of our focus on actions, Hegel's thesis of conflicting Right is on target, since it focuses on *action*. In Sophocles' *Antigone*, for instance, tragedy emerges as King Creon's rightful condemnation of a traitor and his niece Antigone's rightful efforts to provide a proper burial for her brother, who, in spite of his act of treason remains her brother in body and subsequently in spirit. A problem with Hegel's focus, however, is that it, too, fails fully to appreciate the point of audience, because for the Greek (and Elizabethan) audiences, there was a definite *right* that was to be exemplified by the characters in the drama.[4] Schopenhauer, on the other hand, presents tragedy as an indirect bringing to consciousness of that which we attempt dearly to avoid – the crime of existence itself and the irretrievable fall of the just and the innocent. In the first volume of *The World as Will and Idea*, he writes that in tragedy

> The unspeakable pain, the wail of humanity, the triumph of evil, the scornful mastery of chance, and the irretrievable fall of the just and innocent, is here presented to us; and in this lies a significant hint of the nature of the world and of existence. It is the strife of will with itself, which here, completely unfolded at the highest grade of its objectivity, comes into fearful prominence. (p. 326)

An effect of "fearful prominence" is the suspension of egoistic attachments:

> The egoism which rests on [the phenomenal world] perishes with it, so that now the *motives* that were so powerful before have lost their might, and instead of them the complete knowledge of the nature of the world,

which has a *quieting* effect on the will, produces resignation, the surrender
not merely of life, but of the very will to live. (p. 327)

The conclusion of resentment re-emerges with great emphasis in the
third volume:

What gives to all tragedy, in whatever form it may appear, the peculiar
tendency towards the sublime is the awakening of the knowledge that the
world, life, can afford us no true pleasure, and consequently is not worthy
of our attachment. In this consists the tragic spirit: it therefore leads to
resignation. (p. 213)

In Schopenhauer we find, albeit through an analysis whose point of
departure is the question of motives, a direct assessment of tragedy's
impact on the audience. But his conclusion of quietude, resentment, and
pessimism destroys the dynamism of tragedy as *human* and *political*
presentations. Schopenhauer ultimately makes life itself tragic, which
makes even the notion of a "fall" incoherent and the specific content
of setting things right before the *community* problematic. Nihilism and
pessimism are hardly tragedy's message, unless Schopenhauer's Will
becomes a naturalized, and therefore ideological, proverbial "system" or
life-world that no one can change. Our criticism of Hegel applies here in
an ironic way, given Schopenhauer's well-known hatred of Hegel. The
Greek audience would not have recognized Schopenhauer's conclusion
of resentment as a *goal* of tragedy, but a condition for which tragedy is a
remedy.

Nietzsche, on the other hand, deals both with what the audience
recognizes and forgets, but in his case it is the *audiences*, at particular
historical moments, who are rendered problematic. He focuses on communal elements of song and dance and the role of the chorus in the
evolution of tragedy, and he adds a twist on the Aristotelian theme of
catharsis by opening up the question of the community's releasing vital
energies in the tragic event (1956: esp. 46–69). But again, there are
questions of right that need to be addressed beyond the scope of decadence (the Apollonian triumph of Socrates) and roles of song and dance
(the celebration of Dionysus). Why do kings and queens fall? Nietzsche
has explored answers to this question in works such as *Will to Power* and
Beyond Good and Evil. A conclusion that can be drawn from those works
is that Nietzsche's conception of tragedy comes from the standpoint of
the powerful, where, being boundless, it becomes difficult to see why
they should be bound at all. They *are* the tragic rulers. The audience is
therefore left with a false sense of right. In Nietzsche's account, the
matter of right,

which sounds so grandly edifying to certain politicians (as though the democratic Athenians had represented in the popular chorus the invariable moral law, always right in face of the passionate misdeeds and extravagances of kings) may have been suggested by a phrase in Aristotle, but this lofty notion can have had no influence whatever on the original formation of tragedy, whose purely religious origins would exclude not only the opposition between the people and their rulers but any kind of political or social context. (1956: 47)

Thus, at a certain stage in the history of Greek tragedy, the people are offered "right," and therein lies tragedy's death "by suicide" through Euripidean/Socratic rationalism instead of Dionysian ecstacy (p. 69). In Nietzsche's favor, it is worth noting that Dionysus is, among other manifestations, the god of tragedy. Like Schopenhauer, however, Nietzsche's ancient audiences at first face resentment on the one hand, and what tragedy ultimately offers them is a moment's glimpse beyond their egoism – a glimpse that, in its physical manifestation, is exemplified by the ecstasy of the crowd in celebration.[5] The problem is that Nietzsche's celebrated call for a transvaluation of values rids tragic audiences of their historic role in the drama, which they never transcended nor transvalued, for again the question of seeing things set right re-emerges with full force. Even if ecstatic, musical, and religious expression and experience were among the audiences' goals, they also stood as cathartic moments of specific political content; for example, the actions of an individual of high stature, by virtue of his or her political place in the community, affected the entire community. This conclusion holds whether the individual is a king, a high priest, or a god.

Our reference to bearing rightness alludes to the etymological source of tragedy itself. From the Greek words *tragos* (meaning goat) and *ôidê* (meaning song), tragedy carries the burden of the proverbial burden-carrier itself: the scapegoat. As Figes notes,

> The origin of the word "tragedy" is thought to lie in the Greek word for a goat, and though the ritual associations are obscure one inevitably thinks of the Israelite scapegoat, which Aron was required to send into the wilderness with the sins of the community on its back. The rituals of cleansing and atonement did in fact require two goats, the second one being sacrificed for a sin-offering. We know that animal sacrifices were made at the start of drama festivals in Athens, as at other important public gatherings, such as the political assembly. (p. 11)

The appeal to "ritual" is not without its critics. In *Greek Tragedy in Action*, Richard Taplin, for instance, has criticized this view for being motivated by what he regards as an effort to barbarize the Greeks for contemporary, multicultural political aims (pp. 161–2). Tragedy, he argues, is a fundamentally aesthetic affair. His argument does not entail, however, that the *content* of tragedy is not political and that the values presented are not those of the society in which the tragic text is composed. We therefore need not worry about Figes's appeal to rituals, since the basic point is that aesthetic affairs are often rich with political content. Figes's discussions of the what emerges in tragic texts is illuminating in this regard:

> Tragedy in the theatre is the sad story of a central protagonist who, either deliberately or by accident, offends against the most fundamental laws of his society, those laws which are so basic as to be considered divine . . . In tragedy a community can see [how] . . . the central protagonist who has polluted his environment, *bringing disruption on himself and the community within which he lives*, is eliminated, whereupon peace and order are restored. Whether that protagonist intended to break the divine social laws or not is beside the point. (pp. 11–12, emphasis added)

Returning to *Antigone*, Creon is, for the Greek audience, a *flawed* king. But Antigone is also *flawed* by dint of origin. Like her brothers, she is progeny of the unholy marriage of a flawed king to a flawed queen: Oedipus (whose name for ancient Greek audiences is recognizable as both knowing-foot and swollen-foot) and his mother Jocasta.[6] All of these characters are oddly "set up" for suffering, for it is in fulfilling who they are, by virtue of their publicly recognized roles of power and communal responsibility, in fine, their characters, their strengths and their flaws, that they encounter what they must do. All of them bring calamity upon their community. For the community's demands to emerge, the kind of rightful action that must emerge is the reconstitution of justice. In other words, regardless of the characters' points of view, the world must be placed back into a certain order. The tragedy in tragedies is therefore that the "innocence" of the characters who occupy a wrongful place in the drama is ultimately irrelevant. Thus, the tragic protagonist finds himself guilty by virtue of deed and circumstance, not intent, and finds himself suffering, ironically, for the sake of justice. The tragic drama cleanses the community of its own evasions. Justice is tragically restored.

But what about the modern scapegoats: aboriginal peoples, people of color (particularly "blacks"), Jews, Muslims, women, gays, the working and "under" classes, and so on?[7] The immediate response is that, in such cases, there is not tragedy but blatant injustice, for the burden of bearing the community's evils is placed upon the *powerless* instead of the powerful. In effect, the tragic stage has been turned upside down. The revolutionary possibility of tragedy is thus that its object of degradation, if you will, is always the powerful. But the irony of tragedy is that it promises a form of restoration that can never truly be "as things were before." Tragedy is, fundamentally, in Sartrean language, progressive-regressive.

For Fanon, the oppressed confront the oppressor on multiple levels. On the situational level, an oppressed individual confronts the oppressor as an objective limitation of humanity. It is irrelevant what the colonized or oppressed individual may think of himself in relation to members of the colonizing or oppressing group. Everyday he confronts the objective reality of his life's inequality to theirs. His death will never rip through the overdetermined anonymity of nature-like existence. He looks around him at the slaughterhouse that constitutes, say, colored life in the modern and contemporary ages and he finds it difficult to distinguish colored life from that of the array of other animals that sink each day into the belly of consumption, death, and irrelevance. At times of trouble, it is the whites who are scurried off to safety; in the midst of thousands of colored deaths, it is the loss of an occasional white life that rips into the consciousness of the world – the world, in this case, usually coded as "free" or "civilized," which means, ultimately, European, Western, white. In the prisons, the colonized see colored captives, especially in cases where colonizers are victims of violent crimes, but rarely see colonizers, and nearly never colonizers in cases where the colonized, which often means people of color, are victims of colonizers' violent crimes. Eventually, it becomes important to equalize matters. If the colonized cannot make a colonized or colored life as good as that of a colonizer or white one, they can at least make a white one no more valuable than a colonized or colored one; they can, that is, bring the white god down to humanity.

Here we see the stages of a tragic story. For in its symbolic form, violence always takes the path of someone's being dragged "downward." In revolution or violence the human being tragically emerges out of a violent situation of "gods" and the "damned."

At this point, it is necessary for us to explore some features of violence. We shall not spell out the many ways in which Fanon has used the word "violence," since there is ample literature on that elsewhere.[8] Instead, we shall focus on a construction of violence that emerges from Fanon's focus on lived-experience.

Violence is fundamentally subjective apprehension of objective reality; where there is no subjectivity, there is no violence – although there can be violation. A person can, for instance, be violated while asleep. In violence and violation, however, there is a crossing of a threshold, there is the squeezing of options from the realm of choice. In this regard, violence is a relative intentional or situational phenomenon. What mediates the relativity of violent phenomena are both intentional apprehension of the phenomena and contextual norms of justice and injustice that constitute the meanings of such phenomena. On the question of the normative assessment of violence, it is when violence is linked to the innocent that there is victimization; and when linked to the guilty, retribution.

But guilt and innocence are often blurred by the interests that dominate violent situations. Muggers who physically harm their victims often complain, for instance, that their victims "deserved" what happened to them because of their stupidity or their slow responses. Rapists often describe their victims as controlling the circumstances; in fact, they may even try to construct *themselves* as victims of female "enticements." Or consider cases of racism. The cry of white victimization from the "progress" of "minority" groups in Europe and North America has reached the point of becoming shrill. As long as the justice of the status quo is presumed, *any* response that portends real change will take the *form* of violence.

For Fanon, colonialism is fundamentally a violent situation since the stage is set in motion between two kinds of interest: the interest of the colonizer and the interest of the colonized. From the standpoint of the colonizer, his place in the colony is not an unjust one. To replace him is to replace the innocent. For the colonized, his previous place in his society was not an unjust one. Thus, the fact that he has been replaced reflects an injustice. The former faces the threat of violence; the latter is already living it. The situation begins to take on tragic dimensions when the discourse on method – mediation – emerges with teleological import: "The last shall be first."

There are uncomfortable dimensions of the problem which those in power will be unwilling to address – unwilling, ultimately, because they are used to having others' cake and eating it too: the very conditions that they may place upon the praxis of oppressed people may ultimately be conditions that will make no difference (see Robinson 1983: especially p. 243). If the oppressor or the colonizer perceives the very notion of a postcolonial society as a violent condition – violent because it displaces him – then his very call for a nonviolent solution amounts to the preservation of colonialism, or at least a transformation of colonialism into a condition that he will prefer, which amounts to a form of *neo*colonialism.

It can be said, then, that in this regard, Fanon is right. Nonviolent transformation of power boils down to no transformation of power. Violence is broader than bullets, knives, and stones. Violence, fundamentally, is a form of taking that which has been or will be refused. Regardless of the perceived justice or injustice of the matter, regardless of the place of power in the matter, as long as someone is losing something that he currently has and wants to keep, there is violence.

Moreover, since oppression is ultimately an objectified reality supported by the precarious edifice of human reality, both actors, the oppressed and the oppressor, face a Catch 22 in the period of liberation. For just like the oppressed, when all is said and done, the oppressors are, in reality, human beings. The tragic scapegoat who bears the burden of the sins of colonialism, then, is human being itself. In this regard, the oppressed and the oppressor converge as sufferers during the period of liberation. If the postcolonial, postracist world is to emerge, the problem of its emerging through the resistance and eventual submission of colonizers and racists is faced by the colonizers. The tragedy of the colonial and racist situation, then, is the price that has to be paid for the emergence of such a society. If the master's dirty values are accepted as a source of liberation, then no slave can be free without being tarnished with dirty hands. But why must the colonized be "clean"?

In *Peau noire*, Fanon portended this dimension through Jean-Jacques Rousseau's adage, which he cites by way of Nietzsche, that the tragedy of the man is that he was once a child. The adult world carries the burden of godless freedom. It is a freedom without a mother or a father. In the midst of this freedom, humanity becomes the source of value. But the violence that emerges, first in the period of conquering one sector of humanity and then in the period of that sector's efforts toward its emancipation, challenges the very core of human potential and self-recognition. By the penultimate chapter of *Les Damnés*, Fanon draws out this dialectic through an examination of case-studies of torturers and resistance-terrorists. The torturer's violence pushes him directly into the face of human misery; the resistance-terrorist's actions push him into the world of an irremediable fact. Even oppressors suffer. Both face an existential reality in the midst of which trembles the possibility of a human being. For despite the chains of command, despite the various decision-makers at play, what eventually confronts both the torturer and the resistance-terrorist is the sheer anonymity of the Enemy. The enemy whom he has learned to hate is peculiarly absent from the shrieking flesh-and-blood reality in the torture chamber. The enemy who dominated Algeria seemed peculiarly absent from the flesh-and-blood realities sipping coffee outside a café at the moment before the bomb's explosion shattered them to pieces (see *Dt* 303 / *WE* 253). Perhaps the most disturbing example in this section of *Les Damnés* is the case of the two Arabic boys who killed their best white friend (323–4 / 270–2). After asking the 14-year-old why he had killed his white friend, Fanon reports that

[The boy] did not answer the question but asked me had I ever seen a European in prison. Had there ever been a European arrested and sent to prison after the murder of an Algerian? I told him that in fact I had not seen any Europeans in prison. (*Dt* 324 / *WE* 271)

The tragedy faced by any one seriously engaged in struggle against the institutional encouragement of dehumanization is that institutionalized dehumanization is fundamentally a state of war. In such a state, the ordinary anonymity of which we spoke earlier (pp. 79–80, above) is saturated with a pathological consciousness that makes any feature of human beings beyond their typifications fall to the wayside. To see colonialism and racism clearly is to see that where such conceptions of reality reign, there is a shift in the presuppositions of justice and fairness that may have operated within traditional mores and folkways. In the tragic struggle between the cause of liberation and the cause of colonial preservation, there is the painful rationality of an adult philosophical anthropology. We say adult here because of our previous allusion to the tragic adult in every child. In a child's world, there is no room for tragedy because values in such a world are so serious that they pretend that they are what they are not. In the adult world, values take on an ironic veneer. In the adult world, there are places in which justice and fairness are no longer relevant concerns. Even if it is argued that it is *wrong* for certain violations to occur, in the adult world such an argument is irrelevant, ultimately, if there is no will to change the fact that they continue to occur. The colonized people's struggle for liberation should not, then, be treated as the same as the colonizers' violence (which is a maintenance of colonialism). For in the accomplishment of the former's struggle is the possibility, fragile though it may be, of a world that is not by dint of its very structure violent. We find a historical version of this dimension of emancipatory violence in C. L. R. James's classic study, *The Black Jacobins*, from which I offer the following passage for consideration:

The slaves destroyed tirelessly . . . They knew that as long as these planta-tions stood their lot would be to labour on them until they dropped. The only thing was to destroy them. From their masters they had known rape, torture, degradation, and, at the slightest provocation, death. They re-turned in kind. "Vengeance! Vengeance!" was their war-cry, and one of them carried a white child on a pike as a standard. And yet they were surprisingly moderate, then and afterwards, far more humane than their masters had been or would ever be to them. They did not maintain this revengeful spirit for long. The cruelties of property and privilege are always more ferocious than the revenges of poverty and oppression. For the one aims at perpetuating resented injustice, the other is merely a momentary passion soon appeased. As the revolution gained territory they spared

many of the men, women, and children whom they surprised on planta-
tions. To prisoners of war alone they remained merciless. They tore out
their flesh with red-hot pincers, they roasted them on slow fires, they
sawed a carpenter between two of his boards. Yet in all the records of that
time there is no single instance of such fiendish tortures as burying white
men up to the neck and smearing the holes in their faces to attract insects,
or blowing them up with gun-powder [from the anus], or any of the
thousand and one bestialities to which they had been [routinely] subjected.
Compared with what their masters had done to them in cold blood, what
they did was negligible, and they were spurred on by the ferocity with
which the whites in Le Cap treated all slave prisoners who fell into their
hands. (pp. 88–9)

In a note after the phrase, "they were surprisingly moderate," James
writes, "This statement has been criticised. I stand by it." One wonders
who these critics were in terms of the audience they signified. When
writers such as James and Fanon write on revolution, the cathartic effect
sought is from the audience for whom these texts are ultimately de-
signed. Although the powerful is "seen," made apparent through being
laid bare by texts such as *The Black Jacobins* and *Les Damnés de la terre*,
there is a form of violence that is played out to cleanse the readers just
as ancient drama cleansed its audiences through the pathos of the
powerful. But there is an ironic twist to the stage that is set by the
revolutionary writer. Unlike the theater in which an audience sits for
dramatic edification through communal suffering, there is no exit awaiting revolutionary subjects beyond their resolute awareness, reflection,
and decision to create one. *Les Damnés de la terre* thus stands to the
oppressed reader as a tragic text about a tragic world.

Thus, as an addendum to the formulation of violence in *Les Damnés*
stands the ironic place of tragedy in the drama. For it is only human
beings who are capable of tragedy, and in the unfolding of a tragic
version of a particular, institutionalized version of human reality is
the accountability of human beings who maintain structures that
militate against human being. In effect, then, Fanon's theory of violence,
in both its cathartic and organizing forms, is connected to his critical anthropology in a provocative way: it reveals the implications of a
humanity that attempts to evade the challenge and responsibility of
growing up.

Notes

1   This is my revision of Ingram Bywater's translation of the *Poetics* in Richard
    McKeon (ed.) *The Basic Works of Aristotle*.

2 For discussion, see Hansen's *Frantz Fanon* (1977: ch. 5), and Jinadu's *Fanon* (ch. 4).

3 For his sustained discussions on society with the use of characters in myths and classic tragedies, see Freud's *Civilization and its Discontents* (1961), and *Character and Culture* (1963). See also his *An Outline of Psycho-Analysis* (1969).

4 For Hegel's discussion of tragedy, see *The Introduction to Hegel's Philosophy of Fine Art* (1886) as well as *The Philosophy of Fine Art* (1920) and *The Phenomenology of Spirit* (1977).

5 For developed discussion on crowds, see Elias Canetti's *Crowds and Power* (1984).

6 For the entire story, Sophocles (1954).

7 Blacks hold a special place in the people of color designation because of the mythology that emerged around blackness and sin, wherein black people have been historically synonymous with "cursed" people. For discussion, see Eulalio Baltazar (1973), and Gordon (1995a: Parts III and IV).

8 For a summary of Fanon's usage and citation of the literature on violence, see especially Hansen (1977: 116–21 and 168 n. 1) and Jinadu (pp. 14 and 44–52).

Afterword

"Bread and Land": Frantz Fanon's "Native Intellectual"

Joy Ann James

> The people . . . take their stand from the start on the broad and inclusive position of bread and land: how can we obtain the land, and bread to eat? And this obstinate point of view of the masses, which may seem shrunken and limited, is in the end the most worthwhile and the most efficient mode of procedure.
>
> *Frantz Fanon*

The essays that comprise *Fanon: A Critical Reader* testify to Fanon's significance for contemporary thought and contribute to the continuing debates on Fanon the liberation theorist. Fanon in turn offers his own assessment of the writers and readers of this volume. In *Les Damnés de la terre*, he distinguishes between the "civil servant" or state intellectual and the "native intellectual" or revolutionary thinker. Reminding intellectuals that radical liberatory theory serves those lacking sufficient land and bread, Fanon presents the native intellectual, the thinker committed to justice, as a mirror for our reflections. In placing the mirror squarely before us, Fanon warns us not only of intellectual concealment, but against an intellectualism that distances itself from the specificity of justice struggles in order to offer truncated concepts of liberation and a myopic view of repression.

For Fanon, the issue of the intellectual's rejection or welcome by "the people" is inconsequential. What matters to those struggling against material, cultural, and spiritual oppression is that "all resources should be pooled." For Fanon, "pooling" our intellectual, spiritual, and material resources enhances the development of the privileged intellectual.

The pooling of the resource of intellectuals for a liberation effort is often problematized by the limitations of their training which inhibit their ability to communicate with non-elites. The people, Fanon writes, are not hostile to the analyses of intellectuals; rather, they oppose technical speech alien to their lives. The specialist, preoccupied with details, is liable to downplay the importance of instrumental politics and speech in organizing, and thereby, Fanon observes, "forget the real object of the struggle."

Noting that intellectuals who use inaccessible language "can easily prove that the masses have to be managed from above," he maintains: "Everything can be explained to the people, on the single condition that you really want them to understand." Whereas a language of conceal-ment excludes the disenfranchised, self-criticism – which Fanon defines as a "communal process" and an "African institution" that supports critical thought, rather than individualistic introspection – expands democratic politics. In fact, he argues, "the village understands with disconcerting rapidity" what isolated or alienated individuals struggle to comprehend. Consequently, self-criticism among peoples working for their rights can transform elites by breaking through their aloof stances and dissimulation.

Unlike today's fashionable popular cultural intellectual, Fanon's na-tive intellectual is disciplined by the daily revolutionary struggle for independence, freedom, bread, and land. Perhaps the affinity that progressives, blacks, or Third World peoples feel toward Fanon is that he neither argued for sophisticated critiques as a surrogate for activism nor romanticized black or mass culture as inherently revolutionary. Instead, Fanon set high standards reflecting the even higher stakes for the native intellectual engaged in social change. Measuring the useful-ness of theory and the efficacy of intellectuals by their ability to deliver, he writes with conviction: "Truth is that which hurries on the break-up of the colonialist regime." For making such declarations in favor of liberation theory, Fanon has been criticized and dismissed by intellectu-als on both the native and dominant-cultural divide. Sometimes, as Lewis Gordon notes, he is dismissed without serious consideration for his political thought by intellectuals who write "as though there is nothing to be liberated from but liberation discourse itself" (1995b: 146).

Our time of heightened racism and repression, manifesting itself in punitive policies toward the poor and incarcerated, has spurred some intellectuals to grapple with the challenges of Fanon's revolutionary theory. In our critical readings of Fanon, we may consider what Fanon's dissection of the polarized existence of colonizing master and colonized servant suggests for the polarities of our time: the social stratification in wealth and poverty, racial castes, and sexual abuse. In this postcolonial or neocolonial era, Fanon's legacy remains influential for intellectuals confronting the neocolonial, globalized economy, the debt crisis, and the genocidal policies of so-called postcolonial governments.

Since the political life and work of Frantz Fanon advocate the decolonization of not only language and imagination but also the materiality upon which language and the mind reflect, we might also, in reconsidering our relationship to Fanon's legacy, reassess our relationships with radical intellectuals incarcerated for their revolutionary intent. In the US, Mumia Abu Jamal, Geronimo Pratt, Susan Rosenberg, Marilyn Buck, Leonard Peltier, and Carmen Valentin all followed the "obstinate view of the masses" for bread and land as well as the Fanonian dictum that "the minimum demands of the colonized" and a successful revolutionary struggle mandate "a whole social structure being changed from the bottom up." Fanon's native intellectual strategically responds to human oppression as if the life of the mind experiences political ethics and revolutionary politics as more than tropes.

Viewing the political agency of intellectuals through the framework of Fanon's "revolutionary intent," we invariably find ourselves connected to those most vulnerable to exploitation and oppression. Since the prey of the police, the military, the prisons, state executions, and wars are foremost in Fanon's reflections, he sees the relevance of engaged intellectuals as tied to their proximity to political struggle. Fanon writes that the Algerian revolution benefited Algerian intellectuals by allowing them to encounter "the extreme, ineffable poverty of the people" as well as "to watch the awakening of the people's intelligence and the onward progress of their consciousness."

In the US the civil rights, human rights, and poor people's movements of the late 1950s and 1960s, and the American Indian Movement of the early 1970s, similarly enabled critical thinking and democratic politics among US intellectuals by placing them in a contact with America's "colonized." Today, the struggles of the people – red, brown, black, yellow, white, in reservations, barrios, ghettos, sweatshops, labor camps, and penal institutions – will provide new meanings for understanding the significance of Frantz Fanon and his native intellectual for the next century.

Bibliography

Works by Fanon

1948.   *Tam Tam*. February 21 issue, edited by Fanon.
1949–50.   "Les mains parallèles"; "L'oeil se noye"; and "La conspiration" (three plays).
1951/2.   "Troubles mentaux et syndromes psychiatriques dans Hérédo-Dégénération-Spino-Cérébelleuse. Un cas de Maladie de Friedreich avec délire de possession." University of Lyon: dissertation.
1951a.   "L'Expérience nord-africaine." *Esprit* (February), Paris.
1952.   *Peau noire, masques blancs*. Paris: Éditions de Seuil.
1953a.   "Sur quelques cas traités par la méthode de Blini," with F. Tosquelles and Saint Alban. Congrès des médecins aliénistes et neurologues de France et des pays de langue française, 51st session, Pau, July 20–6.
1953b.   "Note sur les techniques de cures de sommeil avec conditionnement et contrôle électroensépholographique." Congrès des médecins aliénistes et neurologues de France et des pays de langue française, 51st session, Pau, July 20–6.
1953c.   "A propos d'un cas de syndrome de Cotard avec balancement psychosomatique," with M. Despinoy *Les Annales Médico-Psycholoques* 2.
1953d.   "Indication de thérapeutique de Bini dans le cadre des thérapeutiques institutionelles," with F. Tosquelles. Congrès des médecins aliénistes et neurologues de France et des pays de langue française, 51st session, Pau, July 20–6.
1953e.   "Sur un essai de réadaptation chez une malade avec épilepsie morphéique et troubles de caractère grave," with F. Tosquelles.

Congrès des médecins aliénistes et neurologues de France et des pays de langue française, 51st session, Pau, July 20–6.

1953f. "Note sur les techniques des cures de sommeil avec conditionnement et contrôle électro-encéphalographique," with M. Despinoy and W. Zenner. Congrès des médecins aliénistes et neurologues de France et des pays de langue française, 51st session, Pau, July 20–6.

1954. "La socialthéraphie dans un service d'hommes musulmans: difficultés méthodologiques," with J. Azoulay. *L'Information Psychiatrique* 4, no. 9.

1954/5. "Introduction aux troubles de la sexualité chez les Nord-Africains," with J. Azoulay and F. Sanchez. Unpublished manuscript.

1955a. "Antillais et Africains." *Esprit*, Paris. (Appears also in *Pra* and *TAR*.)

1955b. "Réflexions sur l'ethnopsychiatrie." *Conscience Maghrebeine* 3.

1955c. "Conférence sur les catégories de l'humanisme moderne." Unpublished lecture presented at Blida.

1955d. "Aspects actuels de l'assisance mental en Algérie," with J. Dequeker, R. Lacaton, M. Micucci, and F. Rame. *L'Information Psychiatrique* 31, no. 11.

1955d. "Conduites d'aveu en Afrique du Nord," with R. Lacaton. Congrès des médecins aliénistes et neurologues de France et des pays de langue française, 53rd session, Nice, September 5–11.

1956a. "Attitude du musulman maghrebin devant la folie," with F. Sanchez. *Revue pratique de Psychologie de la Vie Sociale et d'Hygiène Mentale* 1.

1956b. "Lettre à Français." (Also appears in *Pra* and *TAR*.)

1956c. "Lettre ou Ministre-Résident." (Also appears in *Pra* and *TAR*.)

19556. "Le T.A.T. chez la femme musulmane: sociologie de la perception et de l'imagination," with C. Geromini. Congrès des médecines aliénistes et neurologues de France et des pays de langue française, 54th session, Bordeaux, August 30.

1956d. "Racisme et culture." Presented at the First Congress of Black Writers and Artists, Paris, September.

1957a. "Le phénomène de l'agitation en milieu psychiatrique: Considérations générales – signification psychopathologique," with S. Asselah. *Maroc Médical* (January).

1957b. Report of a press conference given in his capacity as speaker of the FLN in Tunis, *Le Monde*, Paris, June 5.

1957c. "Déceptions et illusions du colonialisme français." *El Moudjahid* 10 (September).

1957d. "L'Algérie face aux tortionnaires français." *El Moudjahid* 10 (September).

1957e. "A propos d'un plaidoyer." *El Moudjahid* 12 (November).

1957f. "Les intellectuels et des démocrates français devant la révolution algérienne." *El Moudjahid* 15 (December).

1958a. "Aux Antilles, naissance d'une nation?" *El Moudjahid* 21 (January).

1958b. "A propos d'un cas de spasme de torsion," with L. Levy. *Tunisie Médicale* 36, no. 9.

1958c.   "La farce qui change de camp." *El Moudjahid* 21 (April).

1958d.   "Décolonisation et indépendance." *El Moudjahid* 23 (May).

1958e.   "Une crise continuée." *El Moudjahid* 24 (May).

1958f.   "Vérités orenuères à propos du problème colonial." *El Moudjahid* 24 (July).

1958g.   "La leçon de Cotonou." *El Moudjahid* 28 (August).

1958h.   "Appel aux Africains." *El Moudjahid* 28 (August).

1958i.   "Lendemains d'un plébisite en Afrique." *El Moudjahid* 30 (October).

1958j.   "La guerre d'Algérie et la libération des hommes." *El Moudjahid* 31 (November).

1958k.   "L'Algérie et Accra." *El Moudjahid* 34 (December).

1958l.   "Accra: l'Afrique affirme son unité et définit sa stratégie." *El Moudjahid* 34 (December).

1959a.   *L'An V de la révolution algérienne.* Paris: Français Maspero. See 1968, when later published as *Sociologie d'une révolution.*

1959b.   "Fureur raciste en France." *El Moudjahid* 42 (May).

1959c.   "Premiers essais de méprobamate injectable dans les états hypocondriaques," with L. Levy. *La Tunisie Médicale* 37, no. 10.

1959d.   "L'hospitalisation de jour en psychiatrie: Valeurs et limites," with C. Geronimi. *La Tunisie Médicale* 38, no. 10.

1959–60.   *Recontres de la société et de la psychiatrie. Notes de cours donnés par Frantz Fanon.* Tunis: Université d'Oran, études et reserches sur la psychologie en Algérie.

1960a.   "La sang coule aux Antilles sous domination française." *El Moudjahid* 58 (January).

1960b.   "Unité et solidarité effective sont les conditions de la libération africaine." *El Moudjahid* 58 (January).

1960c.   "Cette Afrique à venir." Conference for Peace and Security in Africa, Accra, April. Abridged version in *El Moudjahid* 63 (April).

1960d.   Address to the Afro-Asian Conference in Conakry, April. Abridged version in *El Moudjahid* 63 (April).

1960e.   "The stages of imperialism." *Provisional Government of the Algerian Republic: Mission in Ghana* 1, no. 6 (December).

1961a.   *Les Damnés de la terre.* Préface de Jean-Paul Sartre. Paris: François Maspero SARL (Cahiers Libres Nos. 27/28); repr. 1970 and 1982 (Petite Collection Maspero 20).

1961b.   "La mort de Lumumba: Pouvions-nous faire autrement?" *Afrique Action* 19 (February). (Included in *Pra* and *TAR.*)

1963.   *The Wretched of the Earth.* Preface by Jean-Paul Sartre. Translated by Constance Farrington, New York: Grove Press.

1964.   *Pour la révolution africaine: Écrits politiques,* repr. 1979. Paris: François Maspero (Cahiers Libres Nos. 53/54).

1965a.   *A Dying Colonialism.* Trans lated by Haakon Chevalier with an introduction by Adolfo Gilly, repr. 1970. New York: Monthly Review Press; Grove Press.

1965b.   *The Wretched of the Earth.* London: MacGibbon & Kee.

1967.   *Black Skin, White Masks.* Translated by Charles Lam Markmann.

New York: Grove Press (Originally published 1965 by Grove Press).

1967/8.   *Toward the African Revolution*. Translated by Haakon Chevalier. New York: Monthly Review Press, Grove Press.

1968.   *Sociologie d'une révolution*. Paris: François Maspero.

1970a.   *The Wretched of the Earth*. London: Penguin.

1970b.   *Toward the African Revolution*. Translated by Haakon Chevalier. London: Penguin.

1970c.   *Black Skin, White Masks*. Translated by Charles Lam Markmann. London: Paladin.

1979.   *Pour la Révolution Africaine: Écrits politiques*. Paris: François Maspero.

1986.   *Black Skin White Masks*. Translated by Charles Lam Markmann with a foreword by Homi Bhabha. London: Pluto Press.

1991.   *Les Damnés de la terre*. Préface de Jean-Paul Sartre. Paris: Éditions Gallimard.

Works by Other Authors

(Asterisks mark works on Fanon and works with extensive or influential discussion of his work.)

*Adams, P., 1970. "The social psychiatry of Frantz Fanon." *American Journal of Psychiatry* 127: 109–14.

Ahmad, A., 1992. *In Theory: Classes, Nations, Literatures*. London: Verso.

Ake, C., 1978. *Revolutionary Pressures in Africa*. London: Zed Press.

Appiah, A., 1992. *In My Father's House: Africa in the Philosophy of Culture*. New York: Oxford University Press.

*Arendt, H., 1969. *On Violence*. New York: Harcourt Brace & Jovanovich.

Aristotle, 1932. Peri Poiêtikês. In *Aristotle: "The Poetics"; Longinus: "On the Sublime"; Demetrius: "On Style,"* ed. and trans. W. Hamilton Fyfe. London: William Heinemann.

——1941. *The Basic Works of Aristotle*, ed. with intro. by R. McKeon. New York: Random House.

Aronson, R., 1992. "Sartre on progress." In *The Cambridge Companion to Sartre*, ed. C. Howells. Cambridge: Cambridge University Press.

*Asante, M. K., 1988. *Afrocentricity*. Trenton, NJ: Africa World Press.

——1993. "Racism, consciousness, and Afrocentricity." In *Lure and Loathing*, ed. G. Early. New York: Allen Lane.

Aubin, H., 1939. "Introduction à l'étude de la psychiatrie chez les Noirs," *Annales Médico-psychologiques* 1.

Auerbach, E., 1953. *Mimesis*, Princeton, NJ: Princeton University Press.

Azoulay, J., 1954. "Essai de sociothérapie dans un service d'aliénés musulmans." Medical thesis. University of Algiers.

——with F. Fanon, 1954. "La socialthérapie dans un service d'homnes musulmans: difficultés méthodologiques." *L'Information Psychiatrique* 4, no. 9.

——with F. Fanon and F. Sanchez, 1954/5. "Introduction aux troubles de la sexualité chez us Nord-Africains." Unpublished manuscript.

Baldwin, J., 1993. *The Fire Next Time*. New York: Vintage Books.

Baltazar, E., 1973. *The Dark Center: A Process Theology of Blackness*. New York: Paulist Press.

Barth, A., 1974. *Prophets with Honor: Great Dissents and Great Dissenters in the Supreme Court*. New York: Vintage.

Barton-Kriese, P., 1995. *Nonviolent Revolution*. Nairobi: Shirikon Publishers. ·

Bauman, Z., 1991. *Modernity and Ambivalence*. Ithaca, NY: Cornell University Press.

Beauvoir, S. de, 1965. *The Force of Circumstances*. Trans. R. Howard. New York: G. P. Putnam's Sons.

——1992. *The Prime of Life*. Trans. Peter Green. New York: Paragon House.

Beck, E. A., 1993. "On phenomenology and medicine." *Study Project in Phenomenology of the Body Newsletter* 6, no. 2: 9–10.

Bell, D., 1992. *Faces at the Bottom of the Well: The Permanence of Racism*. New York: Basic Books.

*Bennoune, M., 1988. *The Making of Contemporary Algeria, 1830–1987*. Cambridge: Cambridge University Press.

*Bergner, G., 1995. "Who is that masked Woman? or, The role of gender in Fanon's *Black Skin, White Masks*." *Publications of the Modern Language Association* 110, no. 1: 75–88.

*Bernasconi, R., 1995. "Sartre's gaze returned: The transforming of the phenomenology of racism." *Graduate Faculty Philosophy Journal* 18, no. 2: 201–21.

Berthelier, R., 1994. *L'Homme magreebin dans la littérature psychiatrique*. Paris: Éditions l'Harmattan.

*Bhabha, H., 1983. "Difference, discrimination, and the discourse of colonialism." In *The Politics of Theory*, ed. F. Barker. London: Colchester.

——1986a. "Signs taken for wonders: Questions of ambivalence and authority under a tree outside Delhi, May 1817." In *"Race," Writing, and Difference*, ed. H. L. Gates Jr., Chicago: University of Chicago Press.

*——1986b. "Remembering Fanon: Self, psyche and the colonial condition." Foreword to *Black Skin, White Masks*. London: Pluto Press.

*——1990. "Interrogating identity: the postcolonial prerogative." In *Anatomy of Racism*, ed. D. T. Goldberg. Minneapolis, Minn.: University of Minnesota Press.

*——1994. "The other question." In *The Location of Culture*. New York: Routledge.

*Blackey, R., 1974. "Fanon and Cabral: A contrast in theories of revolution for Africa." *Journal of Modern African Studies* 12 (June).

Blassingame, J., 1972. *The Slave Community: Plantation Life in the Ante-Bellum South*. New York: Oxford University Press.

*Bodunrin, P. O., 1981. "Which kind of philosophy for Africa?" In *Philosophy in the Present Situation of Africa*, ed. A. Diemer. Wiesbaden: Franz Steiner Verlag GmbH.

*Boucebci, M., 1990. "Aspects actuels de la psychiatrie en Algérie," *L'Information Psychiatrique* 10, no. 66 (December).

*Bouillon, A., 1981. *Madagascar, le colonisé et son âme: Essai sur le discours psychologique colonial*. Paris: Éditions l'Harmattan.

Bourdieu, P. and Passeron, J.-C., 1977. *Reproduction in Education, Society, and Culture*. Beverly Hills, Calif.: Sage.

*Bouvier, P., 1971. *Fanon*. Paris: Éditions Universitaires.

Bragg, R., 1995. "Emotional march gains a repentant Wallace." *New York Times*: A-1.

Brown, R., 1965. *Social Psychology*. New York: Free Press (2nd edn 1986).

*Bulhan, H. A., 1979. "Black psyches in captivity and crises." *Race and Class* 20, no. 3.

*——1980a. "Frantz Fanon: The revolutionary psychiatrist." *Race and Class* 21, no. 3.

*——1980b. "The revolutionary psychology of Frantz Fanon and notes on his theory of violence." *Fanon Center Journal* 1, no. 1.

*——1980c. "Dynamics of cultural in-betweenity: An empirical study." *International Journal of Psychology* 15.

*——1981. "Psychological research in Africa: Genesis and function." *Race and Class* 23, no. 1, and in *Présence Africaine* 23, no. 1.

*——1985. *Frantz Fanon and the Psychology of Oppression*. New York: Plenum Press.

Butler, J., 1992. "Critically queer." *GLQ* 1.

Cabral, A., 1969. *Revolution in Guinea: Selected Texts*. Ed. and trans. Richard Handyside. New York: Monthly Review Press.

——1970. *National Liberation and Culture*. Occasional Paper No. 57. Syracuse, NY: Maxwell Graduate School, Syracuse University.

Camus, A., 1991. *The Rebel: An Essay on Man in Revolt*. Trans. A. Bower, with Foreword by Sir H. Read. New York: Vintage Books.

Canetti, E., 1984. *Crowds and Power*. Trans. C. Stewart. New York: Farrar Straus Giroux.

Capécia, M., 1948. *Je suis martiniquaise*. Paris: Corréa.

——1950. *La Négresse blanche*. Paris: Corréa.

Carmichael, S. and Hamilton, C., 1967. *Black Power*. New York: Vintage Books.

Cassinelli, C. W., 1976. *Total Revolution: A Comparative Study of Germany under Hitler, the Soviet Union under Stalin, and China under Mao*. Santa Barbara, Calif.: Clio Books.

*Caute, D., 1970. *Frantz Fanon*. New York: Viking Press.

Césaire, A., 1972. *Discourse on Colonialism*. Trans. Joan Pinkham. New York: Monthly Review Press.

*Cherif, M., 1966. "Frantz Fanon: La science au service de la révolution." *Jeune Afrique* 295 (4 September).

*Chidi, A., 1981. "Ayi Kewi Armah and the mythopoesis of mental decolonization," *Ufahamu: Journal of the African Activist Association* 10, no. 3 (spring).

*Clemente, P., 1971. *Frantz Fanon, tra esistenzialism e rivoluzione*. Bari: Casa Editrice Guis.

Cohen-Solal, A., 1987. *Sartre: A Life*. London: Heinemann.

Coiplet, R., 1950. "La Négresse blanche (revue)." *Le Monde*: 7a (22 Avril).

Cose, E., 1993. *The Rage of a Privileged Class*. New York: Harper Collins.

Crouch, S., 1993. "Who are we? Where did we come from? Where are we going?" In *Lure and Loathing*, ed. G. Early. New York: Allen Lane.

Cruse, H., 1967. *The Crisis of the Negro Intellectual*. New York: Quill.

Darity, Jr., W. A., 1983. "The managerial class and surplus population." *Society* 22 (November/December): 54–62.

——1991. "Underclass and overclass: Race, class, and economic inequality in the managerial age." In *Essays on the Economics of Discrimination*, ed. E. P. Hoffman. Kalamazoo, Mich.: W. E. Upjohn Institute for Employment Research.

——with Cotton, J. P. and Hill, H., 1994. "Race and inequality in the managerial age." In *African-Americans: Essential Perspectives*, ed. W. L. Reed. Westport, Conn.: Auburn House.

Davis, A. Y., 1983. *Women, Race, and Class*. New York: Vintage Books.

*Davis, H., 1978. *Toward a Marxist Theory of Nationalism*. New York: Monthly Review Press.

Debray, R., 1967. *Revolution in the Revolution?* New York: Grove Press.

Deming, B., 1990. "On revolution and equilibrium." In *Nonviolence: Theory and Practice*, ed. R. L. Holmes. Belmont, Calif.: Wadsworth Publishing.

*Depestre, R., 1986. "Critique of negritude." In *Frantz Fanon, Soweto, and American Black Thought*, ed. L. Turner and J. Alan. Chicago: News and Lecters.

Derrida, J., 1994. *Specters of Marx*. New York and London: Routledge.

*Doane, M. A., 1991. "Dark continents: Epistemologies of racial and sexual difference in psychoanalysis and the cinema." In *Femmes Fatales: Feminism, Film Theory, Psychoanalysis*. New York: Routledge.

Dostoyevsky, F., 1968. *Great Short Works of Fyodor Dostoyevsky*. Ed. with intro. by R. Hingley. New York: Perennial Classic, Harper & Row.

Douglass, F., 1968. *Narrative of the Life of Frederick Douglass, an American Slave, Written by Himself*. New York: New American Library.

Drake, S. C., 1993. "Diaspora studies and Pan-Africanism." In *African Dimensions of the African Diaspora*, 2nd edn, ed. J. E. Harris. Washington, DC: Howard University Press.

Du Bois, W. E. B., 1965. *The World and Africa*. New York: International Publishers (first published 1947).

——1966. *The Souls of Black Folk*. Intro. by S. Redding. New York: Dodd, Mead & Co. (first published 1903).

——1968. *The Autobiography of W. E. B. Du Bois: A Soliloquy on Viewing My Life from the Last Decade of its First Century*. Ed. H. Aptheker. New York: International Publishers.

——1969. *The Souls of Black Folk*. Introductions by Dr N. Hare and A. F. Poussaint, MD. New York: Signet Classic.

——1986. *Writings*. New York: Library of America.

Dunn, F., 1993. "The educational philosophies of Washington, Du Bois, and Houston: Laying the foundations for Afrocentrism and multiculturalism." *Journal of Negro Education* 62.

Durkheim, E., 1964. *The Division of Labor in Society*. New York: Free Press.

Dworkin, R., 1984. "Liberalism." In *Liberalism and its Critics*, ed. M. Sandel. Oxford: Blackwell Publishers.

Early, G. (ed.), 1993. "Introduction." In *Lure and Loathing: Essays on Race, Identity, and the Ambivalence of Assimilation*. New York: Allen Lane.

Edelman, M., 1988. *Constructing the Political Spectacle*. Chicago: University of Chicago Press.

Ellison, R., 1972. *Shadow and Act*. New York: Vintage Books.

——1975. *Invisible Man*. New York: Vintage Books (first published 1948).

Erikson, E., 1969. *Gandhi's Truth: On the Origins of Militant Nonviolence*. New York: W. W. Norton.

*Esebe, P. O., 1994. *Pan-Africanism: The Idea and Movement, 1776–1991*, 2nd edn. Washington, DC: Howard University Press.

Estell, K., 1994. *African America: Portrait of a People*. Detroit, Mich.: Visible Ink.

Evans, F., 1993. *An Introduction to Theories of Personality*, 4th edn. Hillsdale, NJ: Erlbaum.

*Eze, E. (ed.) Forthcoming. *African Philosophy in American Terrain*. Oxford: Blackwell Publishers.

*Fairchild, H. H., 1994. "Frantz Fanon's *The Wretched of the Earth* in contemporary perspective." *Journal of Black Studies* 25.

*Fanon, J., 1982. "Pour Frantz, pour notre mère," *Sans Frontière* (February).

Figes, E., 1976. *Tragedy and Social Evolution*. New York: Persea Books.

Firebrace, J. and Holland, S., 1985. *Eritrea: Never Kneel Down*. Trenton, NJ: Red Sea Press.

Fischer, L., 1951. *The Life of Mahatma Gandhi*. London: Jonathan Cape.

Fortes, M., 1959. *Oedipus and Job in West African Religion*. New York: Cambridge Univerity Press.

Foucault, M., 1973. *The Birth of the Clinic*. Trans. A. M. Sheidan Smith. New York: Vintage Books.

——1988. "The political technology of Individuals." In *Technologies of the Self*, ed. L. Martin, H. Gutman, and P. Hutton. Amherst, Mass.: University of Massachusetts Press.

Frankenberg, R., 1993. *White Women, Race Matters: The Social Construction of Whiteness*. Minneapolis, Minn.: University of Minnesota Press.

Franklin, J. H., 1993. *The Color Line: Legacy for the Twenty-First Century*. Columbia, Mo.: University of Missouri Press.

Freire, P., 1990. *Pedagogy of the Oppressed*. Trans. Myra Bergman Ramos. New York: Continuum.

Freud, S., 1961. *Civilization and its Discontents*, standard edn. Trans. J. Strachey. New York: W. W. Norton.

——1963. *Character and Culture*. Ed. P. Rieff. New York: Collier Books.

——1969. *An Outline of Psycho-Analysis*, revised edn. Trans. J. Strachey. New York: W. W. Norton.

——1994. *Three Essays on the Theory of Sexuality*. Trans. and ed. J. Strachey, intro. by S. Marcus. New York: Basic Books. ["Screen Memories," 1899 S.E. IV.]

Frye, N., 1990. *Myth and Metaphar: Selected Essays, 1974–88*. Ed. R. D. Denham. Charlottesville, Va.: University of Virginia Press.

*Fuss, D., 1974. "Interior colonies: Frantz Fanon and the politics of identification." *Diacritics* 24, nos. 2–3.

Gaines, Jr., S. O. and Reed. E. S., 1994. "Two social psychologies of prejudice: G. W. Allport, W. E. B. Du Bois, and the legacy of Booker T. Washington." *Journal of Black Psychology* 20.

——1995. "Prejudice: From Allport to Du Bois." *American Psychologist* 50.

Gandhi, M. K., 1940. *An Autobiography or the Story of My Experiments with Truth.* Trans. M. Desai. Ahmedabad: Navajivan Publishing House.

——1948. *Nonviolence in Peace and War,* vol. 1, 3rd edn. Ahmedabad: Navajivan Publishing House.

——1950. *Satyagraha in South Africa.* Trans. V. G. Desai. Ahmedabad: Navajivan Publishing House.

——1958. *All Men are Brothers.* New York: UNESCO/Columbia University Press.

——1990. "On Satyagraha." In *Nonviolence: Theory and Practice,* ed. R. L. Holmes. Belmont, Calif.: Wadsworth Publishing.

Garrabé, J. (ed.), 1994. *Philippe Pinel.* Le Plessis-Robinson, France: Les empêcheurs de penser en rond.

*Gates, Jr., H. L. (ed.), 1986. *"Race," Writing and Difference.* Chicago: University of Chicago Press.

*——1991. "Critical Fanonism." *Critical Inquiry* 17.

Ghadegesin, S., 1991. *African Philosophy: Traditional Yoruba Philosophy and Contemporary African Realities.* New York: Peter Lang.

*Geismar, P., 1969. "A biographical sketch." *Monthly Review* 21 (May).

*——1971. *Frantz Fanon.* New York: Dial Press.

Geertz, C., 1980. *The Theatre State in Nineteenth-Century Bali.* Princeton, NJ: Princeton University Press.

✓ *Gendzier, I., 1973. *Frantz Fanon: A Critical Study.* New York: Pantheon Books.

Gentis, R., 1995. "François Tosquelles, 1912–1994." *Esquisses Psychanalytiques* 22 (May).

*Gibson, N., Forthcoming. "Beyond manicheanism: a critical study of Frantz Fanon's dialectic of liberation." Dissertation, Columbia University, New York, Political Science Dept.

Giddings, A., 1984. *The Constitution of Society.* Berkeley, Calif.: University of California Press.

Gilligan, C., 1982. *In a Different Voice.* Cambridge, Mass.: Harvard University Press.

Gilman, S., 1993. *Freud, Race, and Gender.* Princeton, NJ: Princeton University Press.

Giovanni, N., 1993. "Black is the noun." In *Lure and Loathing,* ed. G. Early. New York: Allen Lane.

Glazer, N., 1975. *Affirmative Discrimination: Ethnic Inequality and Public Policy.* New York: Basic Books.

Glissant, E., 1992. *Caribbean Discourse.* Charlottesville Va.: University of Virginia Press.

*Gooding-Williams, R. (ed.), 1993. *Reading Rodney King, Reading Urban Uprising.* New York: Routledge.

*Goldberg, D.T. (ed.), 1990. *Anatomy of Racism*. Minneapolis, Minn.: University of Minnesota Press.

——1993. *Racist Culture: Philosophy and the Politics of Meaning*. Oxford: Blackwell, Publishers.

Goldstein, J., 1987. *Console and Classify*. New York: Cambridge University Press.

*Gordon, L. R., 1995a. *Bad Faith and Antiblack Racism*. Atlantic Highlands, NJ: Humanities Press.

✓*——1995b. *Fanon and the Crisis of European Man: An Essay on Philosophy and the Human Sciences*. New York and London: Routledge.

*——1995c. "Sartrean bad faith and antiblack racism." In *The Prism of the Self: Essays in Honor of Maurice Natanson*, ed. S. G. Crowell. Dordrecht, Netherlands: Kluwer Academic Publishers.

*——1995d. "'Critical' mixed-race?" *Social Identities* 1, no. 2 (summer).

*——(ed.), 1996a. *Existence in Black: An Anthology of Black Existential Philosophy*. New York and London: Routledge.

*——1996b. "Black existential philosophy." In *Existence in Black*.

*——1996c. "Existential dynamics of theorizing black invisibility." In *Existence in Black*.

*——1996d. "A tragic dimension of our neocolonial postcolonial world." In *African Philosophy in American Terrain*, ed. E. Eze. Oxford: Blackwell Publishers.

*——(ed.), with R. White. Forthcoming. *Black Texts and Black Textuality: Constructing and De-constructing Blackness*. Lanham, Md.: Rowman & Littlefield.

Gouldner, A., 1982. *The Dialectics of Ideology and Technology*. New York: Oxford University Press.

Gramsci, A., 1975. *Selections from "The Prison Notebooks."* Trans. and ed. Q. Hoare and G. N. Smith. New York: International Publishers.

Gutman, Herbert G., 1976. *The Black Family in Slavery and Freedom 1750–1925*. New York: Vintage Books.

Gwaltney, J. L., 1980. *Drylongso: A Self-Portrait of Black America*. New York: Random House.

Hall, R. E., 1992. "Bias among African-Americans regarding skin color: Implications for social work practice." *Research on Social Work Practice* 2.

*Hansen, E., 1972. "Frantz Fanon: A bibliographical essay." *Pan-African Journal* 5 (winter): 387–405.

*——1974. "Frantz Fanon: Portrait of a revolutionary intellectual." *Transition* 46: 25–36 (October–December).

*——1977. *Frantz Fanon: Social and Political Thought*. Columbus, Oh.: Ohio State University Press.

Harbi, M., 1954. *La Guerre commence en Algérie*. Paris: Histoire Julliard.

*——1980. *Le FLN: mirage et réalité*. Paris: Éditions Jeune Afrique.

Hardy, G., 1925. *Histoire coloniale et psychologie ethnique*. Paris: Revue de l'Histoire des Colonies Françaises.

——1929. *Psychologie et colonization*. Paris: Le Monde Nouveau.

——1934. *Psychologie avant-tout*. Paris: Outre-Mer.

—— 1936. *Pour une étude de la mimique*. Alger: Revue Africaine.

—— 1939. *La Géographie psychologique*. Paris: Gallimard.

—— 1947. "La psychologie des populations coloniales," *Revues de Psychologie des Peuples* 3.

Harris, C., 1993. "Whiteness as property." *Harvard Law Review* 106, no. 8.

Harris, L. (ed.), 1983. *Philosophy Born of Struggle: Afro-American Philosophy since 1917*. Dubuque, Ia.: Kendall/Hunt.

Hassan, R., 1995. "Islamic view of human rights." In *The Philosophical Quest: A Cross-Cultural Reader*, ed. G. M. Presbey *et al.* New York: McGraw-Hill.

Hegel, G. W. F., 1886. *The Introduction to Hegel's Philosophy of Fine Art*. Trans. B. Bosanquet. London: K. Paul, Trench & Co.

—— 1920. *The Philosophy of Fine Art*, vols I-IV. Trans. F. P. B. Somaston. London: G. Bell & Sons.

—— 1931. *The Phenomenology of Mind*. Trans. J. B. Ballie. London: Allen & Unwin.

—— 1956. *The Philosophy of History*. Trans. with a preface by J. Sebree, a preface by C. Hegel, and a new introduction by C. J. Friedrich. New York: Dover Publications.

—— 1967. *The Philosophy of Right*. Trans. with notes by T. M. Knox. London: Oxford University Press.

—— 1970. *Phänomenologie des Geistes*. Frankfurt: Suhrkamp Verlag.

—— 1977. *The Phenomenology of Spirit*. Trans. A. V. Miller, with analysis of the text and foreword by J. N. Findlay. Oxford: Oxford University Press.

—— 1989. *Science of Logic*. Trans. A. V. Miller. Atlantic Highlands, NJ: Humanities Press.

Heidegger, M., 1977a. *Basic Writings*. Ed. D. F. Krell. New York: Harper & Row.

—— 1977b. *The Question Concerning Technology and Other Essays*. Trans. and intro. by W. Lovitt. New York: Harper & Row.

—— 1988. *Hegel's "Phenomenology of Spirit."* Trans. P. Emad and K. Maly. Bloomington, Ind.: Indiana University Press.

*Henry, P., 1993. "C. L. R. James, African and Afro-Caribbean philosophy," *C. L. R. James Journal* (winter): 17–36.

*—— 1996. "African and Afro-Caribbean existentialism." In *Existence in Black*, ed. L. R. Gordon. New York and London: Routledge.

—— and Buhle, P. (eds), 1992a. *C. L. R. James' Caribbean*. Durham, NC: Duke University Press.

*—— and —— 1992b. "Caliban as deconstructionist: C. L. R. James and Post Colonial Discourse." In *C. L. R. James' Caribbean*.

Hobbes, T., 1975. *Leviathan*. London: Penguin (first published 1651).

hooks, bell, 1992. *Black Looks: Race and Representation*. Boston, Mass.: South End Press.

*Hountondji, P., 1983. *African Philosophy: Myth and Reality*. Bloomington, Ind.: Indiana University Press.

—— 1990. "Scientific dependence in Africa today," *Research in African Literatures* 21, no. 3 (fall).

—— 1992. "Daily life in Black Africa: Elements for a critique." In *The Surreptitious Speech: "Présence Africaine" and the Politics of Otherness 1947–1987*, ed.

and intro. by V. Y. Mudimbe. Chicago and London: University of Chicago Press.

Howitt, D. and Owusu-Bempah, J., 1994. *The Racism of Psychology: Time for Change*. New York: Harvester/Wheatsheaf.

Huntington, P., 1996. "Gender, fragmentation, and solidarity," in *Existence in Black*, ed. L. R. Gordon. New York and London: Routledge.

Husserl, E., 1910–11. "Philosophie als strenge Wissenschaft." *Logos* I: 289–341.

—— 1931. *Ideas: General Introduction to Pure Phenomenology*. Trans. W. R. Boyce Gibson. London: George Allen & Unwin; New York: Macmillan.

—— 1960. *Cartesian Meditations: An Introduction to Phenomenology*. Trans. D. Cairns. Dordrecht: Nijhoff.

—— 1965. *Phenomenology and the Crisis of Philosophy: "Philosophy as a Rigorous Science" and "Philosophy and the Crisis of European Man."* Trans. with an intro. by Q. Lauer. New York: Harper Torchbooks.

—— 1969. *Formal and Transcendental Logic*. Trans. D. Cairns. The Hague: Nijhoff.

—— 1970. *The Crisis of European Sciences and Transcendental Phenomenology: An Introduction to Phenomenological Philosophy*. Trans. with an intro. by D. Carr. Evanston, Ill.: Northwestern University Press.

—— 1982. *Ideas Pertaining to a Pure Phenomenology and to a Phenomenological Philosophy*. Trans. F. Kersten. The Hague: Nijhoff.

Hutton, P. H., 1987. "The art of memory reconceived: From rhetoric to psychoanalaysis." *Journal of the History of Ideas* 47, no. 3 (July–September).

*Irele, A., 1969. "Literature and ideology in Martinique: Reé Maran, Aimé Césaire, Frantz Fanon." *Research Review* 5, no. 3, Trinity Term (Ghana University Institute of African Studies): 1–32.

—— 1981. *The African Experience in Literature and Ideology*. London: Heinemann.

Jackson, J. G., 1970. *Introduction to African Civilizations*. New York: Citadel Press.

James, C. L. R., 1960. *Modern Politics*. Port of Spain: PNM Publishing Company.

—— 1971. "Colonialism and national liberation in Africa: the Gold Coast revolution." In *National Liberation: Revolution in the Third World*, ed. N. Miller and R. Aya. New York: Fress Press/Collier-Macmillan.

—— 1989. *The Black Jacobins: Toussaint L'Ouverture and the San Domingo Revolution*, 2nd rev. edn. New York: Vintage.

—— 1993. *The C. L. R. James Reader*. Ed. with intro. by A. Grimshaw. Oxford: Blackwell Publishers.

James, J. A., 1996a. *Resisting State Violence in US Culture*. Minneapolis, Minn.: University of Minnesota Press.

—— 1996b. *Transcending the Talented Tenth: Race Leaders and American Intellectualism*. Foreword by L. R. Gordon. New York and London: Routledge.

Jameson, F., 1971. *Marxism and Form: Twentieth-Century Dialectical Theories of Literature*. Princeton, NJ: Princeton University Press.

Jewell, K. S., 1993. *From Mammy to Miss America and Beyond: Cultural Images and the Shaping of US Social Policy*. New York: Routledge.

Bibliography

*Jinadu, L. A., 1986. *Fanon: In Search of the African Revolution*. London: KPI/ Routledge & Kegan Paul.

Jones, J. M., 1987. "Racism in black and white: A bicultural model of reaction and evolution." In *Eliminating Racism: Profiles in Controversy*, ed. P. A. Katz and D. A. Taylor. New York: Plenum.

Jones, W. R., 1983. "Liberation strategies in black theology: Mao, Martin, or Malcolm?" In *Philosophy Born of Struggle: Anthology of Afro-American Philosophy from 1917*, ed. L. Harris. Dubuque, Ia.: Kendall/Hunt.

*—— 1995. "Fanon and Oppression." Fanon Today: Rereadings, Confrontations, Engagements. Eleventh Annual Symposium on African-American Philosophy and Culture, West Lafayette: African-American Studies and Research Center, Purdue University.

Kaufman, W., 1974. *Nietzsche: Philosopher, Psychologist, Antichrist*, 4th edn. Princeton, NJ: Princeton University Press.

Kayode, M. O. and Usman, Y. B. (eds), 1986. *The Economic and Social Development of Nigeria*. Zaria: Panel on Nigeria since Independence Project.

Kierkegaard, S., 1980. *The Concept of Anxiety: A Simple Psychologically Orienting Deliberation on the Dogmatic Issue of Hereditary Sin*. Trans. and ed. and notes by R. Thomte in collaboration with Albert B. Anderson. Princeton, NJ: Princeton University Press.

King, L. M., Moody, S., Thompson, O., and Bennett, M., 1983. "Black psychology reconsidered: Notes toward curriculum development." In *Mental Health and People of Color: Curriculum Development and Change*, ed. J. C. Chunn, II, P. J. Dunston, and F. Ross-Sheriff.

King, Jr., M. L., 1964. *Why We Can't Wait*. New York: Mentor.

Koundoura, M., 1989. "Naming Gayatyri Spivak." *Stanford Humanities Review*.

Lacan, J., 1966. *Écrits 1*. Paris: Éditions du Seuil.

Lauriol, L., 1938. "Quelques remarques sur les maladies mentales aux colonies." Medical thesis, Paris.

*Lazreg, M., 1990. "Feminism and difference: The perils of writing as a woman on women in Algeria." In *Conflicts in Feminism*, ed. M. Hiersch and E. F. Keller. New York and London: Routledge.

Le Bon, G., 1894. *Les Lois psychologiques de l'évolution des peuples*. Paris: Félix Alcan.

*Lemelle, S. J., 1993. "The politics of cultural existence: Pan-Africanism, historical materialism, and Afrocentricity." *Race and Class* 35.

Lewis, G., 1987. *Main Currents in Caribbean Thought*. Baltimore, Md.: Johns Hopkins University Press.

Lipsitz, G., 1990. *Time Passages: Collective Memory and American Popular Culture*. Minneapolis, Minn.: University of Minnesota Press.

Locke, A., 1989. *The Philosophy of Alain Locke: Harlem Renaissance and Beyond*. Ed. L. Harris. Philadelphia, Pa.: Temple University Press.

Lorde, A., 1993. "The master's tools will never dismantle the master's house." In *Feminist Frontiers*, ed. L. Richardson and V. Taylor. New York: McGraw-Hill.

Lowenthal, D., 1967. "Race and color in the West Indies." *Daedalus* (spring).

*Lucas, P., 1971. *Sociologie de Frantz Fanon.* Algiers: SNED (Societé Nationale d'édition et de diffusion).

Lyotard, J.-F., 1984. *The Postmodern Condition: A Report on Knowledge.* Trans. G. Bennington and B. Massumi. Minneapolis, Minn.: University of Minnesota Press.

McBride, W. L., 1991. *Sartre's Political Theory.* Bloomington, Ind.: Indiana University Press.

*McCulloch, J., 1983. *Black Soul, White Artifact: Fanon's Clinical Psychology and Social Theory.* Cambridge: Cambridge University Press.

McKnight, R., 1993. "Confessions of a Wannabe Negro." In *Lure and Loathing,* ed. G. Early. New York: Allen Lane.

Macpherson, C. B., 1966. *The Real World of Democracy.* Oxford: Oxford University Press.

McPherson, J., 1993. "Junior and John Doe." In *Lure and Loathing,* ed. G. Early. New York: Allen Lane.

Mandela, N., 1970. "The case for a violent resistance movement." In *The Africa Reader: Independent Africa,* ed. W. Cartey and M. Kilson. New York: Random House.

Mannoni, O., 1950. *Psychologie de la colonisation.* Paris: Éditions du Seuil.

——1993. *Prospero and Caliban.* Trans. P. Powesland. Ann Arbor, Mich.: University of Michigan Press.

Manning, K. R., 1993. "Race, science, and identity." In *Lure and Loathing,* ed. G. Early. New York: Allen Lane.

Marable, M., 1993. "Beyond racial identity politics: Towards a liberation theory for multicultural democracy." *Race and Class* 35.

*Martin, G., 1974. "Fanon's relevance to contemporary African political thought." *Ufahamu* 4 (winter): 11–34.

*Martin, T., 1970. "Rescuing Fanon from the critics." *African Studies Review* 13 (December).

Marx, K., 1963. *Early Writings.* Trans, and ed. by T. B. Bottomore, with foreword by E. Fromm. New York, Toronto, London: McGraw-Hill.

——and Engels, F., 1978. *The Marx–Engels Reader,* 2nd edn. Ed. R. C. Tucker. New York: W. W. Norton.

Masilela, N., 1994. "Pan-Africanism or classical African Marxism?" In *Imagining Home: Class, Culture and Nationalism in the African Diaspora,* ed. S. Lemelle and R. D. G. Kelley. London: Verso.

Matuštík, M., 1993. *Postnational Identity: Critical Theory and Existential Philosophy in Habermas, Kierkegaard, and Havel.* New York: Guilford Press.

M'Bodj, M., 1978. "Aspects de la psychiatrie dans le monde." *Psychopathologie Africaine* 14.

Mead, L., 1986. *Beyond Entitlement: The Social Obligations of Citizenship.* New York: Free Press.

——1992. *The New Politics of Poverty: The Nonworking Poor in America.* New York: Basic Books.

*Memmi, A., 1957. *Portrait du colonisé précédé du portrait du colonisateur.* Paris: Éditions Buchet-Chastel.

——1965. *The Colonizer and the Colonized.* New York: Orion Press.

——1968. *Dominated Man*. New York: Orion Press.

*——1971a. "Frozen by death in the image of Third World prophet." *New York Times Book Review*, May 14; 5, 20.

*——1971b. "La vie impossible de Frantz Fanon." *Esprit* (September): 248–73.

Mercer, K., 1995. "Busy in the ruins of wretched phantasia." Unpublished text from Institute for Contemporary Arts exhibition, May, from the conference: Working with Fanon: Contemporary Politics and Cultural Reflection.

Merleau-Ponty, M., 1961. *Phenomenology of Perception*. Trans. C. Smith. Atlantic Highlands, NJ: Humanities Press.

——1964. *"The Primacy of Perception" and Other Essays on Phenomenological Psychology, the Philosophy of Art, History and Politics*. Ed. with an intro. by J. M. Edie. Evanston, Ill.: Northwestern University Press.

——1968. *The Visible and the Invisible: Followed by Working Notes*. Ed. C. Lefort and trans. Alphonso Lingis. Evanston, Ill.: Northwestern University Press.

Mill, J. S., 1975. *On Liberty*. Ed. David Spitz. New York: W. W. Norton.

Mitchell, E. P., 1993. "Du Bois's dilemma and African American adaptiveness." In *Lure and Loathing*, ed. G. Early. New York: Allen Lane.

Mitchell, K., 1993. "MTV: Real Racist." *People's Weekly World*.

Mook, D. G., 1983. "In defense of external invalidity." *American Psychologists* 38.

Morel, B. A., 1857. *Traité des dégénérescences physiques, intelletuelles et morales de l'espèce humaine*. Paris: J. B. Baillière.

Moses, W. J., 1993. "Ambivalent maybe." In *Lure and Loathing*, ed. G. Early. New York: Allen Lane.

Mosley, A. G., 1995. *African Philosophy*. Engelwood Cliffs, NJ: Prentice-Hall.

Mudimbe, V.Y., 1983. "African philosophy as an ideological practice: The case of French-speaking Africa." *African Studies Review* 26, nos. 3/4 (September/ December).

——1985. "African gnosis: Philosophy and the order of knowledge." *African Studies Review* 29, nos. 2/3 (June/September).

Murray, C., 1984. *Losing Ground: American Social Policy, 1950–1980*. New York: Basic Books.

Myers, L. J., 1993. *Understanding an Afrocentric World View: Introduction to an Optimal Psychology*, 2nd edn. Dubuque, Ia.: Kendall/Hunt.

Natanson, M., 1986. *Anonymity: A Study in the Philosophy of Alfred Schutz*. Bloomington, Ind.: Indiana University Press.

*Neill, M., 1982. "Guerrillas and gangs: Frantz Fanon and V. S. Naipaul," *Ariel: A Review of International English Literature* 13, no. 4 (October).

*Nghe, N., 1963. "Frantz Fanon et le problème de l'indépendance." *La Pensée* 107 (February): 23–36.

Nietzsche, F., 1956. *"The Birth of Tragedy" and "The Genealogy of Morals."* Trans. F. Golffing. Garden City, NY: Doubleday.

——1966. *Beyond Good and Evil: Prelude to a Philosophy of the Future*. Trans. and with a commentary by W. F. Kaufmann. New York: Vintage Books.

——1968. *The Will to Power*. Trans. W. F. Kaufmann and R. J. Hollingdale, NY: Vintage Books.

——1969a. *On the Genealogy of Morals*. Trans. W. F. Kaufmann and R. J. Hollingdale. NY: Vintage Books.

——1969b. *Thus Spoke Zarathustra: A Book for Everyone and No One*. Trans. and intro. by R. J. Hollingdale. Baltimore, Md.: Penguin Books.

——1974. *The Gay Science*. Trans. W. F. Kaufmann. New York: Vintage Books.

Nigerian Enterprises Promotion Decree 1972, 1977. In *Nigerian Capitalism*, ed. S. P. Schatz. Berkeley, Calif.: University of California Press.

*Nisbet, R., 1973. *The Social Philosophers: Community and Conflict in Western Thought*. New York: Washington Square Press.

Nisbet, R. E. and Ross, L., 1980. *Human Inference: Strategies and Shortcomings of Social Judgment*. Englewood Cliffs, NJ: Erlbaum.

*Nobles, W. W., 1986. *African Psychology: Toward Its Reclamation, Reascension, and Revitalization*. Oakland, Calif.: Black Family Institute.

Nye, R., 1984. *Crime, Madness, and Politics in Modern France: The Medical Concept of National Decline*. Princeton, NJ: Princeton University Press.

Okere, T., 1983. *African Philosophy: A Historico-Hermeneutical Investigation of the Conditions of its Possibility*. Lanham, Md.: University Press of America.

Okolo, O., 1991. "Tradition and destiny: Horizons of an African philosophical hermeneutics." In *African Philosophy*, ed. T. Serequeberhan. New York: Paragon House.

O'Malley, P., 1995. "Gentle genocide: State policies and the government of desert Aboriginal peoples in Central Australia." *Social Justice* 21.

Onimode, B., 1982. *Imperialism and Underdevelopment in Nigeria: The Dialectics of Mass Poverty*. London: Zed Press.

——1983. "Nigeria: The dynamics of the challenge of underdevelopment." In *The Economics and Social Development of Nigeria*, ed. M. O. Kayode and Y. B. Usman. Proceedings of the National Conference on Nigeria since Independence. Zaria Panel on Nigeria since Independence Project (March), Zaria, Nigeria.

*Onwuanibe, R. C., 1983. *A Critique of Revolutionary Humanism: Frantz Fanon*. St Louis, Mo.: Green.

*Oruka, H., Odera, 1990. *Sage Philosophy*. New York: E. J. Brill.

Osoba, S., 1979. "The deepening crisis of the Nigerian National Bourgeoisie." *Review of African Political Economy* 14.

Outlaw, L., 1987. "African 'Philosophy': Deconstructive and reconstructive challenges." In *Contemporary Philosophy: A New Survey*, vol. 5, *African Philosophy*, ed. G. Floistad. Dordrecht: Nijhoff.

Parker, K., 1996. "Gendering a language, liberating a nation: women writing in Afrikaans and the 'New' South Africa," *Social Identities* 2, no. 2 (spring).

*Parry, B., 1987. "Problems in current theories of colonial discourse." *Oxford Literary Review* 9.

Patterson, O., 1982. *Slavery and Social Death: A Comparative Study*. Cambridge, Mass.: Harvard University Press.

Pedder, S., 1993. "Let down again." *The Economist*, August 21.

*Perez, A., 1989. "Sartre, Memmi et Fanon." *Présence Francophone: Revue Internationale de Langue et de Litterature* 35.

*Perinbam, B. M., 1982. *Holy Violence: The Revolutionary Thought of Frantz Fanon*. Washington, DC: Three Continents Press.

Perrot, M., (ed.), 1980. *L'Impossible Prison: recherches sur le système pénitentiaire au XIXe siècle*. Paris: Éditions du Seuil.

Pick, D., 1989. *Faces of Degeneration: A European Disorder (c.1848–c.1918)*. New York: Cambridge University Press.

Pierterse, J. N., 1992. *White on Black: Images of Africa and Blacks in Western Popular Culture*. New Haven, Conn.: Yale University Press.

Pollard, A. B., III., 1993. "The last great battle of the West: W. E. B. Du Bois and the Struggle for African America's soul." In *Lure and Loathing*, ed. G. Early. New York: Allen Lane.

Porot, A., 1918. "Notes de psychiatrie musulmane." *Annales Médico psychologiques* 1.

——1922. "Quelques aspects de l'âme indigène," Conférence à la langue de l'enseignement à Oran, March.

*Postel, J. and Quetel, C. (eds), 1994. *Nouvelle Histoire de la psychiatrie*. Paris: Dunod.

*Prasad, M., 1992. "The 'other' worldliness of postcolonial discourse: A critique." *Critical Quarterly* 34, no. 3.

Ramirez, M., III, 1983. *Psychology of the Americas: Mestizo Perspectives on Personality and Mental Health*. New York: Pergamon.

Rattray, R. S., 1923. *Ashanti*. London: Oxford University Press.

Rawls, J., 1971. *A Theory of Justice*. Cambridge, Mass.: Harvard University Press.

Raymond, J., 1986. *A Passion for Friends: Towards a Philosophy of Feminine Affection*. Boston: Beacon Press.

*Robinson, C., 1983. *Black Marxism: The Making of the Black Radical Tradition*. London: Zed Press.

✓ ——1993. "The appropriation of Frantz Fanon." *Race & Class* 35, no. 1: 79–91.

Roediger, D., 1991. *The Wages of Whiteness: Race and the Making of the American Working Class*. London: Verso.

Ronnell, A., 1994. *Finitudes Score: Essays for the End of the Millennium*. Lincoln and London: University of Nebraska Press.

Rothman, B. K. and Caschetta, M. B., 1995. "Treating health: Women and medicine." In *Women: A Feminist Perspective*, 5th edn, ed. J. Freeman. Mountain View, Calif.: Mayfield.

Rousseau, J.-J., 1971. *"Discours sur les sciences et les arts" et "Discours sur l'origine et les fondements de l'inégalité parmi les hommes*. Chronology and intro. by J. Roger. Paris: Flammarion.

——1986. *The First and Second Discourses together with the Replies to Critics and "Essay on the Origin of Languages."* Trans. and ed. by V. Gourevitch. New York: Harper Torchbooks.

*Sabbagh, S., 1983. "Going against the West from within: The emergence of the West as an Other in Frantz Fanon's work." Dissertation, University of Michigan, Ann Arbor.

*Said, E., 1989. "Representing the colonized: Anthropology's Interlocutors." *Critical Inquiry* 15 (winter).

Sartre, J.-P., 1943. *L'Être et le néant: essai d'ontologie phénoménologique*. Paris: Gallimard.

——1948. "Orphé Noir." In *L'Anthologie de la poésie nègre et malgache*, ed. L. Senghor. Paris: Presses Universitaires de France.

——1955. *The Respectful Prostitute*. In *"No Exit" and Three Other Plays*. New York: Vintage.

——1956a. *Being and Nothingness: A Phenomenological Essay on Ontology*. Trans. with an intro. by H. Barnes. New York: Philosophical Library. ·

——1956b. *Being and Nothingness: A Phenomenological Essay on Ontology*. Trans. with an intro. by H. Barnes. New York: Washington Square Press.

*——1961. "Préface" to *Les Damnés de la terre*. Paris: François Maspero. Also published 1964 in *Situations V*. Paris: Gallimard.

*——1963. "Preface" to *The Wretched of the Earth*. Trans. C. Farrington. New York: Grove Press.

——1964a, unpublished. 1964 Rome Lecture Notes. Paris: Bibliothèque Nationale.

——1964b. *The Words: The Autobiography of Jean-Paul Sartre*. Trans. B. Frechtman. New York: George Braziller.

——1968a. *Search for a Method*. Translated with an introduction by H. Barnes. New York: Vintage Books.

——1968b. *Existentialism is a Humanism*. London: Methuen.

——1968c. *Communists and the Peace*. Trans. M. H. Fletcher. New York: George Braziller.

——1974. *Between Existentialism and Marxism: Sartre on Philosophy, Politics, Psychology, and the Arts*. Trans. J. Mathews. New York: Pantheon Books.

——1976a. *Anti-Semite and Jew*. Trans. G. Becker. New York: Schocken Books (Originally published in 1946).

——1976b. *Black Orpheus*. Trans. S. W. Allen. Paris: Présence Africaine.

——1981. *The Idiot of the Family*, vol. I. Trans. C. Cosman. Chicago: University of Chicago Press.

——1987. *The Idiot of the Family*, vol. II. Trans. C. Cosman. Chicago: University of Chicago Press.

——1988. "Black Orpheus." Trans. J. MacCombie. In *"What Is Literature?" and Other Essays*, ed. with an intro. by S. Ungar. Cambridge, Mass.: Harvard University Press.

——1991a. *Critique of Dialectical Reason*, vol. I, *Theory of Practical Ensembles*. Trans. A. Sheridan-Smith and ed. J. Rée. London: Verso. (London New Left Books version was published in 1976.)

——1991b. *Critique of Dialectical Reason*, vol. II (unfinished), *The Intelligibility of History*. Ed. A. Elkaïm-Sartre and trans. Q. Hoare. London: Verso.

——1992. *Notebooks for an Ethics*. Trans. by D. Pellauer with a foreword by A. Elkaïm-Sartre. Chicago: University of Chicago Press.

Saussure, L. de., 1899. *La Psychologie de la colonisation française dans ses rapports avec les sociétés indigènes*. Paris: F. Alcan.

Schatz, S. P., 1977. *Nigerian Capitalism*. Berkeley, Calif.: University of California Press.

Scheler, M., 1994. *Ressentiment*. Trans. L. B. Coser and William W. Holdheim. Intro. M. S. Frings. Milwaukee, Oreg.: Marquette University Press.

Schellenberg, J. A., 1978. *Masters of Social Psychology: Freud, Mead, Lewis, and Skinner*. Oxford: Oxford University Press.

Schmitt, R., 1995. *Beyond Separateness: The Social Nature of Human Beings, Their Autonomy, Knowledge and Power*. Boulder, Colo.: Westview.

Schopenhauer, A., 1883. *The World as Will and Idea*, vols I–III, 7th edn. Trans. R. B. Haldane and J. Kemp. London: Kegan Paul, Trench, Trubner & Co.

Schrag, C. O., 1980. *Radical Reflection and the Origin of the Human Sciences*. West Lafayette, Ind.: Purdue University Press.

Schutz, A., 1962. *Collected Papers*, vol. I, *The Problem of Social Reality*. Ed. with an intro. by M. Natanson, with a preface by H. L. Van Breda. The Hague: Nijhoff.

—— 1964. *Collected Papers*, vol. II, *Studies in Social Theory*. Ed. with an intro. by A. Brodersen. The Hague: Nijhoff.

—— 1966. *Collected Papers*, vol. III, *Studies in Social Phenomenological Philosophy*. Ed. I. Schutz. The Hague: Nijhoff.

—— 1967. *Phenomenology of the Social World*. Trans. G. Walsh and F. Lehnhert, with an intro. by G. Walsh. Evanston, Ill.: Northwestern University Press.

—— 1970. *Reflections on the Problem of Relevance*. Ed. R. M. Zaner. New Haven, Conn.: Yale University Press.

—— 1978. *The Theory of Social Action: The Correspondence of Alfred Schutz and Talcott Parsons*. Ed. Richard Grathoff. Bloomington, Ind.: Indiana University Press.

—— 1987. *The Family Idiot*, vol. 2. Trans. Carol Cosman. Chicago: University of Chicago Press.

—— and Luckmann, T., 1973. *The Structures of the Life-World*. Trans. Richard M. Zaner and H. Tristram Engelhardt, Jr. Evanston, Ill.: Northwestern University Press.

—— and —— 1989. *The Structures of the Life-World*, vol. II. Trans. R. M. Zaner and David J. Parent. Evanston, Ill.: Northwestern University Press.

*Sekyi-Otu, A. Forthcoming. *Fanon's Dialectic of Experience*. Cambridge, Mass.: Harvard University Press.

Senghor, L. S., 1956. "The spirit of civilization or the laws of African Negro culture." *Présence Africaine* 8–10 (June–November).

—— 1964. *Liberté I: Négritude et humanisme*. Paris: Éditions de Seuil.

*Serequeberhan, T. (ed.), 1991. *African Philosophy: The Essential Writings*. New York: Paragon House.

—— 1994. *The Hermeneutics of African Philosophy*. New York: Routledge.

*Sharpley-Whiting, T. D., forthcoming (a). *Black Female Bodies, White Male Imaginations: Images of Black Women in Nineteenth-Century French Narratives on Black Femininity*.

—— forthcoming (b). *Frantz Fanon and Feminism*. Lanham, Md.: Rowman & Littlefield.

—— and R. White (eds), forthcoming. *Spoils of War: Women, Revolutions, Culture*.

Solomon, R. C., 1990. "Nietzsche, postmodernism, and resentment: A genealogical hypothesis." In *Nietzsche as Postmodernist: Essays Pro and Con*, ed. C. Koelb. Albany, NY: State University of New York Press.

——1994. "One hundred years of *Ressentiment*: Nietzsche's *Genealogy of Morals*." In *Nietzsche, Genealogy, and Morality: Essays on Nietzsche's Genealogy of Morals*, ed. R. Schacht. Berkeley, Calif.: University of California Press.

Sophocles, 1954. *Sophocles I: Oedipus the King* (Trans. D. Grene), *Oedipus at Colonus* (Trans. R. Fitzgerald), *Antigone*, (Trans. E. Wyckoff). Ed. with Intro. by D. Grene. Chicago: University of Chicago Press.

*Spillers, H., 1987. "Mama's baby, Papa's maybe: An American grammar book." *Diacritics* 17, no. 2 (summer).

Stampp, K., 1956. *The Peculiar Institution: Slavery in the Ante-Bellum South*. New York: Vintage Books.

Staples, R., 1993. "The illusion of racial equality: The black American dilemma." In *Lure and Loathing*, ed. G. Early. New York: Allen Lane.

Sullivan, L., 1986. *Sound and Senses: Toward a Hermeneutics of Performance*. Chicago: University of Chicago Press.

Swain, G., 1977. *Le Sujet de la folie*. Toulouse: Rhadamante.

Szasz, T. S., 1970. *The Manufacture of Madness: A Comparative Study of the Inquisition and the Mental Health Movement*. New York: Harper & Row.

——1971a. "The Negro in psychiatry: An historical note on psychiatric rhetoric," *American Journal of Psychotherapy* 25, no. 2.

——1971b. "The sane slave: An historical note on the use of medical diagnosis as justificatory rhetoric," *American Journal of Psychotherapy* 25, no. 2.

——1974. *The Myth of Mental Illness: Foundations of a Theory of Personal Conduit*. New York: Harper & Row.

Taft, R., 1973. "Migration: Problems of adjustment and assimilation in immigrants." In *Psychology and Race*, ed. P. Watson. Chicago: Aldine.

Takaki, R. T., 1990. *Iron Capes: Race and Culture in 19th-Century America*. New York: Oxford University Press.

Taplin, R., 1978. *Greek Tragedy in Action*. London: Routledge.

Taylor, C., 1979. *Hegel and Modern Society*. New York: Cambridge University Press.

——1991. *The Ethics of Authenticity*. Cambridge, Mass.: Harvard University Press.

Terchek, R., 1983. "The psychoanalytic basis of Gandhi's politics." In *Studies on Ghandi*, ed. V. T. Patil. New Delhi: Sterling Publishers.

Thomas, A. and Sillen, S., 1972. *Racism and Psychiatry*. New York: Brunner/Mazel.

Thomas, C., 1974. *Dependence and Transformation*. New York: Monthly Review Press.

Tosquelles, F., 1984. *Éducation et psychothérapie institutionnelle*. Mantes-la-Ville: Hiatus Édition.

Todorov, T., 1989. *Nous et les autres*. Paris: Éditions du Seuil.

——1993. *On Human Diversity, Nationalism, Racism, and Exoticism in French Thought*. Trans. C. Porter. Cambridge, Mass.: Harvard University Press.

Towa, M., 1971. *Essai sur la problématique philosophique dans l'Afrique actuelle*. Cameroun, Yaounde: Éditions Cle.

——1979. "Proposition sur l'identité culturelle." *Présence Africaine* 109 (First Quarterly).

—— 1991. "Conditions for the affirmation of a modern African philosophical thought." In *African Philosophy*, ed. T. Serequeberhan. New York: Paragon House.

Tronto, J. C., 1989. "Women and caring: What can Feminists learn about morality from caring?" In *Gender/Body/Knowledge: Feminist Reconstructions of Being and Knowing*, ed. A. M. Jagger and S. K. Bordo. New Brunswick, NJ: Rutgers University Press.

Truth, S., 1993. "Address to the Ohio Women's Rights Convention (1851)." In *Crossing the Danger Water: Three Hundred Years of African-American Writing*. Ed. with an intro. by D. Mullane. New York: Anchor Doubleday.

Ture, K. and Hamilton, C. V., 1992. *Black Power: The Politics of Liberation*. New York: Vintage Books.

*Turner L., 1989. "Frantz Fanon's journey into Hegel's 'Night of the Absolute,'" *Quarterly Journal of Ideology* 13, no. 4.

*—— 1991. "The Marxist humanist legacy of Frantz Fanon," *News & Letters* 38, no. 10 (December).

*—— and Alan, J. (eds), 1986. *Frantz Fanon, Soweto, and American Black Thought*. Chicago: News and Letters.

Valentine, C. A., 1968. *Culture and Poverty: Critique and Counter-Proposals*. Chicago: University of Chicago Press.

Valery, P., 1957. "La Cruise de l'esprit," in *Oeuvres*, vol. 1. Paris: Gallimard, Bibliothèque de la Pleiade.

van Dijk, T. A., 1993. *Elite Discourse and Racism*. Newbury Park, Calif.: Sage.

Walker, M., 1988. *Richard Wright, Daemonic Genius: A Portrait of the Man, a Critical Look at his Work*. New York: Warner Books.

*Walters, R. W., 1993. *Pan-Africanism in the African Diaspora: An Analysis of Modern Afrocentric Political Movements*. Detroit, Mich.: Wayne State University Press.

Warren, M., 1988. *Nietzsche and Political Thought*. Cambridge, Mass.: MIT Press.

Watson, H., 1994. "Personal responses to global process." In *Islam, Globalization and Postmodernity*, ed. A. Ahmed and H. Donnan. London: Routledge.

Weber, E., 1976. *Peasants into Frenchmen: The Modernization of Rural France, 1870–1914*. Stanford, Calif.: Stanford University Press.

Weber, M., 1922. *Wirtschaft und Gesellschaft*. Tübingen: Mohr.

Weed, P. L., 1973. *The White Ethnic Movement and Ethnic Politics*. New York: Praeger.

West, C.. 1993a. *Prophetic Reflections: Notes on Race and Power*. Monroe, Me.: Common Courage Press.

—— 1993b. *Prophetic Thought in Postmodern Times*. Monroe, Me.: Common Courage Press.

—— 1993c. *Race Matters*. Boston, Mass.: Beacon Press.

—— 1994. *Keeping Faith: Philosophy and Race in America*. New York: Routledge.

*White, J. S. and Parham, T. A., 1990. *The Psychology of Blacks: An African-American Perspective*, 2nd edn. Englewood Cliffs, NJ: Prentice-Hall (First published in 1984).

Williams, G. (ed.), 1976. *Nigeria: Economy and Society*. London: Rex Callings.

Wilson, R. McL., 1967. "Mani and Manichaeism." In *The Encyclopedia of Philosophy*, vol. 5, editor-in-chief, P. Edwards. New York: Macmillan Publishing Company and the Free Press.

Wiredu, K., 1980. *Philosophy and an African Culture*. Cambridge: Cambridge University Press.

——1991. "On defining African philosophy." In *African Philosophy*, ed. T. Serequeberhan. New York: Paragon House.

*Woddis, J., 1972. *New Theories of Revolution: A Commentary on the Views of Frantz Fanon, Régis Debray and Herbert Marcuse*. New York: International Publishers.

*Worsley, P., 1972. "Frantz Fanon and the 'Lumpenproletariat.'" *Socialist Register*. New York: Monthly Review Press.

Wright, R., 1940. *Native Son*. New York: Harper & Brothers.

Wynters, S., 1992. "Beyond the categories of the master conception: The counterdoctrine of the Jamesian poiesis." In *C. L. R. James' Caribbean*, ed. P. Henry and P. Buhle. Durham, NC: Duke University Press.

X, Malcolm. 1965a. *Malcolm X Speaks*. Ed. George Breitman. New York: Grove Press.

——1965b. *The Autobiography of Malcolm X*. New York: Ballantine.

Young, R., 1990. *White Mythologies*. London: Routledge.

——1994. *Colonial Desire*. London: Routledge.

*Zack, N., 1993. *Race and Mixed-Race*. Philadelphia, Pa.: Temple University Press.

——(ed.), 1995. *American Mixed-Race*. Boston, Mass.: Rowman & Littlefield.

*Zahar, R. 1959. *Kolonialismus und Entfremdung: Zur Politischen Theorie Frantz Fanons*. Frankfurt: Europäische Verlagsanstalt.

*——1970. *L'Oeuvre de Frantz Fanon*. Paris: François Maspero.

*——1974. *Frantz Fanon: Colonialism and Alienation, Concerning Frantz Fanon's Political Theory*. Trans. W. F. Feuser. New York: Monthly Review Press.

Zizek, S., 1993. "Caught in another's dream of Bosnia." In *Why Bosnia: Writings on the Balkan War*, ed. R. Ali and L. Lifschultz. Stony Creek, Conn.: Pamphleteer's Press.

*Zolberg, A. and Zolberg, V., 1966. "The Americanization of Frantz Fanon." *Public Interest* 9.

Index